Grademaker Study Guide

for use with

Third Canadian Edition

Marketing

Lamb Hair McDaniel Faria Wellington

Prepared by
DIANE SERAFINI
Dawson College

THOMSON
NELSON

Australia   Canada   Mexico   Singapore   Spain   United Kingdom   United States

Contents

Introduction

The *Grademaker Study Guide* was specifically written to accompany *Marketing, Third Canadian Edition*, by Charles W. Lamb, Jr., Joseph F. Hair, Jr., Carl McDaniel, Faria, and Wellington. The purpose of *Grademaker* is to help you review the material in the text, practice using the material, and check your understanding. The *Grademaker* is designed to help you get more out of reading and studying your text and to help you prepare for exams.

For each chapter in your text, this *Study Guide* provides the following materials:

1. **Responses to beginning-of-chapter learning objectives.** This section provides an overall perspective on the focus and goals of the text chapter.

2. **A one-page pretest.** This short test provides you a chance to test how much you understand the chapter material so that you can focus your study efforts on material that you have not yet grasped.

3. **An outline of the chapter materials.** The extensive outline sets forth the chapter structure, summarizes the major topics, and defines key terms.

4. **Fill-in-the-blank vocabulary exercises.** This section provides an alphabetized list of key terms for your reference and allows you to test your recognition of key terms and to master important definitions.

5. **True/False questions.** These questions are designed to test your recall of key terms, marketing terminology, and marketing concepts.

6. **Agree/disagree questions.** These questions are designed to provide more in-depth critical thinking about topics covered in the chapter.

7. **Multiple-choice questions.** These questions are designed to test your ability to apply chapter concepts to marketing situations.

8. **Scenario questions.** Each chapter contains a scenario of a real or fictional business and follow-up questions that help you test your knowledge and understanding of key chapter concepts.

9. **Essay questions and problems.** Essay questions test your ability to integrate chapter information and to apply knowledge to broad concepts and relationships between marketing concepts. Problems that appear in selected chapters test your ability to apply analytical tools and technical marketing methods.

10. **Application problems.** One or two problems will require you to put marketing concepts to work. These solutions may not necessarily have a pat answer but will make you think about chapter concepts.

11. **Solutions to all exercises, questions, and problems.** These solutions are presented at the end of the *Study Guide*. Rationales are provided for false questions and all multiple-choice questions, and complete answers are provided for all pretest questions, essay and problem questions. Text page numbers are also provided for answer reference. The solutions are provided to help you evaluate your understanding of the material in the text chapter. You should refer to these answers only after you have completed the questions.

The outlines and all exercises are tied to the text through the learning objectives. Numbered learning objectives identify the material that covers each objective. If you are having trouble with a concept, review the material in the text identified by the same learning objective number.

Always read the text before using the *Grademaker*. *Grademaker* is not a substitute for the text, but rather a tool that will enhance your understanding of text material. The material in the *Grademaker* is presented in the order that the topics are covered in each text chapter. This allows you to refer to the text for any sections that may pose difficulties. After reading your text, review the text material by reading through the learning objectives and chapter outline in *Grademaker*. Then carefully work through each set of exercises and questions, making sure that you understand why the correct answers are correct. Answers to the essay questions are suggestions only and may not precisely match your responses.

Grademaker can help you learn and evaluate your knowledge only to the extent that you use it correctly and regularly. Good luck with your course and the text. Marketing is an exciting field of study, and the intention of *Grademaker* is to help you capture that excitement.

CHAPTER 1: AN OVERVIEW OF MARKETING

LEARNING OBJECTIVES

1   Define the term "marketing"

Marketing is the process of planning and executing the conception, pricing, promotion, and distribution of ideas, goods, and services to create exchanges that satisfy individual and organizational objectives.

2   Describe four marketing management philosophies

Four competing philosophies strongly influence the role of marketing and marketing activities within an organization. These philosophies are commonly referred to as production, sales, marketing, and societal marketing orientations.

    The production orientation focuses on internal efficiency to achieve lower prices for consumers. It assumes that price is the critical variable in the purchase decision.

    A sales orientation assumes that buyers resist purchasing items that are not essential and that consumers must be persuaded to buy.

    The marketing orientation is based on an understanding that a sale predominantly depends on the customer's decision to purchase a product and on the customer's perception of the value of that product. Responsiveness to customer wants is the central focus of the marketing orientation.

    The societal marketing orientation holds that the firm should strive to satisfy customer needs and wants while meeting organizational objectives and preserving or enhancing both the individual's and society's long-term best interests.

3   Discuss the differences between sales and market orientations

Selling Orientation	*Marketing Orientation*
Organization's focus is inward on the firm's needs	Focus is outward on the wants and preferences of customers
Business is defined by its goods and services offered	Business is defined by benefits sought by customers
Product is directed to everybody	Product is directed to specific groups (target markets)
Primary goal is profit through maximum sales volume	Primary goal is profit through customer satisfaction
Goals are achieved through intensive promotion	Goals are achieved through coordinated marketing

4   Describe the marketing process

Marketing managers are responsible for a variety of activities that together represent the marketing process. These include: matching the role of marketing with the firm's vision and mission, setting objectives, analyzing internal and external information, developing strategy, planning a marketing mix, implementing strategy, designing performance measures, and evaluating and adjusting strategy.

5   Describe several reasons for studying marketing

Marketing provides a delivery system for a standard of living, which is a monumental task in a society such as Canada, where a typical family consumes 2.5 tons of food per year. No matter what an individual's area of concentration in business, the terminology and fundamentals of marketing are important for communicating with others in the firm.

    Between one-fourth and one-third of the entire civilian work force in Canada performs marketing activities. Marketing offers career opportunities in areas such as professional selling, marketing research, advertising, retail buying, distribution management, product management, product development, and wholesaling.

    As a consumer of goods and services, everyone participates in the marketing process every day. By understanding marketing, one can become a more sophisticated consumer.

Answer the following questions to see how well you understand the material. Re-take it after you review to check yourself.

1. Marketing is defined as:

2. What five conditions must be satisfied for any kind of exchange to take place?

3. The four variables of the marketing mix are:

4. Four marketing management philosophies are:

5. List five ways in which a marketing orientation is different from a sales orientation.

6. List seven steps in the marketing process:

7. Name four reasons for studying marketing:

1   Define the term "marketing"

I.   What Is Marketing?

   A.   Marketing is a philosophy or a management orientation that stresses the importance of customer satisfaction, as well as a set of activities used to implement this philosophy.

   B.   The Canadian Marketing Association definition of marketing:

   Marketing is the process of planning and executing the conception, pricing, promotion, and distribution of ideas, goods, and services to create exchanges that satisfy individual and organizational goals.

   C.   The Concept of Exchange

   The concept of **exchange** means that people give up something in order to receive something that they would rather have.

   1.   The usual medium of exchange is money. Exchange can also be through barter or trade of items or services.

   2.   Five conditions must be satisfied for an exchange to take place:

   a.   There must be at least two parties.
   b.   Each party has something that might be of value to the other party.
   c.   Each party is capable of communication and delivery.
   d.   Each party is free to accept or reject the exchange offer.
   e.   Each party believes it is appropriate or desirable to deal with the other party.

   3.   Exchange may not take place even if all of these conditions exist, but these conditions are necessary for exchange to be possible.

2   Describe four marketing management philosophies

II.   Marketing Management Philosophies

   Four competing philosophies strongly influence an organization's marketing activities. These philosophies are commonly referred to as production, sales, marketing, and societal orientations.

   A.   Production Orientation

   The **production orientation** focuses on internal capabilities of the firm rather than on the desires and needs of the marketplace. The firm is concerned with what it does best, based on its resources and experience, rather than with what consumers want.

   B.   Sales Orientation

   A **sales orientation** assumes that more goods and services will be purchased if aggressive sales techniques are used and that high sales result in high profits.

C.   Market Orientation

    1.   The **marketing concept** states that the social and economic justification for an organization's existence is the satisfaction of customer wants and needs while meeting organizational objectives.

    2.   The marketing concept involves:

        a.   Focusing on customer wants and needs so the organization can differentiate its product(s) from competitors' offerings
        b.   Integrating all the organization's activities, including production, to satisfy these wants and needs
        c.   Achieving long-term goals for the organization by satisfying customer wants and needs legally and responsibly.

    3.   A **market orientation** involves obtaining information about customers, competitors, and markets; examining the information from a total business perspective; determining how to deliver superior customer value; and implementing actions to provide value to customers.

    4.   Understanding your competitive arena and competitor's strengths and weaknesses is a critical component of market orientation.

    5.   Market-oriented companies are successful in getting all business functions together to deliver customer value.

D.   Societal Marketing Orientation

    1.   The philosophy called a **societal marketing orientation** states that an organization exists not only to satisfy customer wants and needs and to meet organizational goals, but also to preserve or enhance individual's and society's long-term best interests.

    2.   This orientation extends the marketing concept to serve three bodies rather than two: customers, the organization itself, and society as a whole

3   Discuss the differences between sales and market orientations

III.   Differences Between Sales and Market Orientations

A.   The Organization's Focus

    1.   Sales-oriented firms tend to be " inward looking", as they focus on satisfying their own needs rather than those of customers.

    2.   Market-oriented firms derive their competitive advantage from an external focus. Departments in these firms coordinate their activities and focus on satisfying customers.

B.   Customer Value

    1.   **Customer value** is the ratio of benefits to the sacrifice necessary to obtain those benefits.

    2.   Creating customer value is a core business strategy of many successful firms.

3. Marketers interested in customer value

    a. Offer products that perform
    b. Give consumers more than they expect
    c. Avoid unrealistic pricing
    d. Give the buyer facts
    e. Offer organization-wide commitment in service and after-sales support

C. Customer Satisfaction

Customer satisfaction is the feeling that a product has met or exceeded the customer's expectations. The organizational culture focuses on delighting customers rather than on selling products.

D. Building Relationships

Relationship marketing is a strategy that entails forging long-term partnerships with customers and contributing to their success.

1. The Internet is an effective tool for generating relationships with customers.
2. Customers benefit from stable relationships with suppliers.
3. A sense of well-being occurs when one establishes an ongoing relationship with provider.

E. The Firm's Business

1. A sales-oriented firm defines its business in terms of the goods and services it offers, like an encyclopedia publisher defining itself simply as a book publisher/seller.

2. A market-oriented firm defines its business based on the *benefits* customers seek.

3. Why is this customer benefit definition so important?

    a. It ensures the firm keeps focusing on customers
    b. It encourages innovation and creativity by reminding people that there are many ways to satisfy customer wants.
    c. It stimulates an awareness of changes in customer desires and preferences.

4. Focusing on customer wants does not mean that customers will always receive the specific goods and services they want.

F. Those To Whom the Product Is Directed

1. A sales-oriented organization targets its products at "everybody" or "the average customer." However, few "average" customers exist.

2. The market-oriented firm

    a. Recognizes that different customer groups have different wants
    b. Targets specific subgroups of customers
    c. Designs special products and marketing programs for these groups

G. The Firm's Primary Goal

1. The goal of a sales-oriented firm is profitability through sales volume. The focus is on making the sale rather than developing a long-term relationship with a customer.

---

2. The ultimate goal of most market-oriented organizations is to make a profit from satisfying customers. Superior customer service enables a firm to have large amounts of repeat business, customer loyalty, and higher profit margins.

H. Tools the Organization Uses to Achieve Its Goals

1. Sales-oriented firms seek to generate sales volume through intensive promotional activities, mainly personal selling and advertising.

2. Market-oriented organizations recognize that promotion is only one of the four basic tools that comprise the marketing mix.

   The tools are the marketing mix elements (the four P's): product, place (distribution), promotion, and price.

3. The important distinction is that market-oriented firms recognize that each of the four components of the marketing mix is of equal importance: sales-oriented organizations view promotion as the primary means of achieving their goals.

4   Describe the marketing process

IV. The Marketing Process

Marketing managers are responsible for a variety of activities in the marketing process:

A. Understanding the organization's mission and vision, and the role marketing plays.

B. Setting marketing objectives

C. Gathering, analyzing, and interpreting information about the organization's situation, including its strengths and weaknesses, as well as opportunities and threats in the environment.

D. Developing marketing strategy by deciding exactly which wants and whose wants the organization will try to satisfy, and by developing appropriate marketing activities to satisfy the desires of selected target markets.

E. Implementing the marketing strategy

F. Designing performance measures

G. Periodically evaluating marketing efforts and making changes if needed.

5   Describe several reasons for studying marketing

V. Why Study Marketing?

A. Marketing Plays an Important Role in Society

   Marketing provides a delivery system for a complex standard of living. The number of transactions needed everyday in order to feed, clothe, and shelter a population the size of the one in Canada is enormous and requires a sophisticated exchange mechanism.

B. Marketing Is Important to Businesses

The fundamental objectives of most businesses are survival, profits, and growth. Marketing contributes directly to achieving these objectives.

Marketing provides the following vital business activities:
1. Assessing the wants and satisfactions of present and potential customers
2. Designing and managing product offerings
3. Determining prices and pricing policies
4. Developing distribution strategies
5. Communicating with present and potential customers

C. Marketing Offers Outstanding Career Opportunities

1. Between one-fourth and one-third of the entire civilian work force in Canada performs marketing activities.

2. Marketing offers career opportunities in areas such as professional selling, marketing research, advertising, retail buying, distribution management, product management, product development, and wholesaling.

3. Increasing importance of the global marketplace.

D. Marketing Affects Your Life Every Day

1. As consumers of goods and services, we participate in the marketing process every day.

2. Almost 50 cents of every dollar consumers spend goes to pay marketing costs such as market research, product research and development, packaging, transportation, storage, advertising, and sales-force expenses.

VOCABULARY PRACTICE

Fill in the blank(s) with the appropriate term or phrase from the alphabetized list of chapter key terms.

customer satisfaction	marketing orientation
customer value	production orientation
empowerment	relationship marketing
exchange	sales orientation
marketing	societal marketing orientation
marketing concept	teamwork

1 Define the term "marketing"

1. The process of planning and executing the conception, pricing, promotion, and distribution of ideas, goods, and services to create exchanges that satisfy individual and organizational objectives defines

    _____.

2. When consumers give up something (such as money) to receive something they would rather have (such as a product), this is known as a(n) _____.

---

2 Describe four marketing management philosophies

3. There are four alternative marketing management philosophies. The first focuses on the firm's internal capabilities rather than the needs and desires of the marketplace; this is the _____. The second philosophy is the _____, which assumes that buyers resist purchasing nonessential items, so aggressive sales techniques should be used to sell more products. The third philosophy, which focuses on customer needs and wants, is the _____. Finally, a firm that decides to preserve long-term best interests of its customers and society has adopted the _____.

4. When a firm focuses on customer wants, integrates all firm activities to satisfy these wants, and achieves long-term goals by satisfying these wants legally and responsibly, the firm is using the _____.

3 Discuss the differences between sales and market orientations

5. The ratio of the benefits to the sacrifice necessary to obtain those benefits is termed

    _____.

6. When a marketer feels that a product meets or exceeds customers' expectations, then _____ has been created.

7. A strategy of forging long-term partnerships with customers is called _____. It means that firms can become part of their customer's organization and contribute to its success.

8. When people combine their efforts to accomplish common objectives, they are practicing

    _____.

9. Marketing-oriented firms may give their employees expanded authority to solve customer problems immediately. This is known as _____.

Check your answers to these questions before proceeding to the next section.

TRUE/FALSE QUESTIONS

Mark the statement **T** if it is true and **F** if it is false.

1 Define the term "marketing"

_____ 1. A marketing exchange cannot take place unless each party in the exchange has something that the other party values.

2 Describe four marketing management philosophies

_____ 2. The owners of the Plane Rubber and Tire Company are pleased with their low unit costs and high production volumes. Salespeople are unnecessary because buyers are always waiting for new tires to come off the assembly line. Plane currently has a production orientation.

_____ 3. The president of Hoppity Flea Collars does not find it necessary to conduct much marketing research because the telephone selling campaign has been such a successful marketing strategy. Hoppity has a marketing orientation.

_____ 4. Having a sales orientation is the same as having a market orientation since both have the ultimate goal of satisfying customer needs.

3 Discuss the differences between sales and marketing orientations

_____ 5. You are about to start manufacturing and selling ferret food. You have met with your board of directors and you all discussed the benefits and sacrifices regarding the purchase of your food. Knowing the ratio of benefits to sacrifices allows you to specify how much customer value you will achieve.

4 Describe the marketing process

_____ 6. The marketing mix variables are product, place, promotion, and price.

_____ 7. The marketing process includes the development of strategies for the marketing mix but does NOT include an analysis of the organization's situation.

5 Describe several reasons for studying marketing

_____ 8. The objectives of most marketing activities include survival, profits, and growth.

_____ 9. Only about one-tenth of the nation's workforce is engaged in marketing activities.

Check your answers to these questions before proceeding to the next section.

AGREE/DISAGREE QUESTIONS

For the following statements, indicate reasons why you may agree and disagree with the statement.

1. The marketing concept actually encompasses both the sales concept and the production concept.

   Reason(s) to agree:

   Reason(s) to disagree:

2. Marketing is the job of everyone in a business organization, not just the marketing department.

   Reason(s) to agree:

   Reason(s) to disagree:

3. Only students who are majoring in marketing should be required to take marketing courses.

Reason(s) to agree:

Reason(s) to disagree:

MULTIPLE CHOICE QUESTIONS

Select the response that best answers the question, and write the corresponding letter in the space provided.

1 Define the term "marketing"

_____ 1. Which of the following is NOT true about marketing?
   a. Marketing is a philosophy that stresses customer satisfaction.
   b. Marketing is a process.
   c. Marketing can involve any number of parties.
   d. Marketing can be used for ideas, goods, or services.
   e. Marketing involves products, pricing, promotion, and distribution.

_____ 2. In order for exchange to occur:
   a. a complex societal system must be involved
   b. each party must have something of value to the other party
   c. a profit-oriented organization must be involved
   d. money or other legal tender is required
   e. organized marketing activities must also occur

_____ 3. If you were in the marketing consulting business which of the following clients could you not serve?
   a. The Montreal Museum of Fine Arts which needs to determine what exhibits should it offer visitors
   b. The Province of Ontario, which needs to attract tourists
   c. Dr. Susan Scott, an orthopedic surgeon wishing to open a practice in your home town
   d. The World Gym, which needs to determine where to locate its next outlet for customers
   e. All of these could be served by a marketing consultant.

_____ 4. You are concerned with managing the exchange between the Red Cross and its blood donors. Which of the following costs would you have to be concerned about to create the ideal exchange?
   a. The travel costs incurred by donors visiting the Red Cross blood donation sites.
   b. The personal energy and time expended by the donator
   c. The opportunity costs lost by not engaging in some other activity
   d. All of these are marketing costs that would be of concern to someone managing the exchange situation
   e. None of these are costs of exchange situations

2 Describe four marketing management philosophies

_____ 5. Fred Stone, the owner of Neanderthal Products, Inc. is production-oriented. If you were in charge of his marketing operations, which of the following statements might you use as a guiding principle if you wished to meet Mr. Stone's demand?
   a. "I'm a customer and everyone is like me. I buy on price, therefore everyone does, as well."
   b. "We need to buy the fastest production equipment as possible to raise productivity and keep prices at the lowest possible level."
   c. "We produce the best widgits in the market place."
   d. All of these would be consistent with Mr. Stone's demands.
   e. None of these would be consistent, because all reflect a sales orientation.

_____ 6. Peter's company does an excellent and efficient job of churning thousands of Nit-Pickers off the assembly line every day. One problem with this _____ approach to marketing is the failure to consider whether Nit-Pickers also meet the needs of the marketplace.
   a. customer orientation
   b. sales orientation
   c. discount orientation
   d. marketing orientation
   e. production orientation

_____ 7. Jack Niven's company markets golf club polish. Jack knows that buyers may consider the product nonessential, and he assumes that if he hires a team of aggressive, persuasive salespeople, buyers will buy more of the polish. Jack has a:
   a. sales orientation
   b. production orientation
   c. promotion orientation
   d. marketing orientation
   e. customer orientation

_____ 8. Beth has noticed the lack of specialty recycling centres in her community, although local neighbourhood clubs have repeatedly asked the city to provide such centres. Beth has decided to become certified in waste disposal and hopes to open a battery and motor oil recycling centre next year. She hopes to include the innovative service of home pickup and delivery of recyclables. This business philosophy supports a(n) _____ orientation.
   a. production
   b. sales
   c. retail
   d. marketing
   e. enterprise

_____ 9. The Ajax Insurance Company tells its salespeople to try to sell life insurance to everyone they meet or contact. In contrast, the Family Shelter Insurance Company concentrates on special insurance plans designed for single parents. Family Shelter is:
   a. missing out by not concentrating on the average customer
   b. a company that would state that they are in the business of selling insurance
   c. a selling-oriented company
   d. recognizing that different customer groups have different needs and wants
   e. aiming at a goal of profit through maximum sales volume

_____ 10. Bob & Gary's is a contemporary ice cream manufacturer that donates 10 percent of its earnings to the restoration of the Amazon rain forest. Bob & Gary's has which type of orientation?
   a. production
   b. sales
   c. promotion
   d. marketing
   e. societal marketing

3 Discuss the differences between sales and market orientations

_____ 11. A sales orientation _____; while a marketing orientation _____
   a. achieves profit through customer satisfaction; achieves profit through maximum sales volume
   b. targets specific groups of people; targets everybody
   c. delivers superior customer value; focuses on selling goods and services
   d. has an "outward" focus; has an "inward" focus
   e. uses intensive promotion to maximize profits; uses coordinated interfunctional activities

4 Describe the marketing process

_____ 12. Which of the following is NOT a part of the marketing process?
   a. understanding the organization's mission
   b. developing performance appraisals for marketing personnel
   c. designing performance measures
   d. setting objectives
   e. determining target markets

_____ 13. The marketing manager for Oil of Olan, a skin care product, is working with an advertising agency to develop a new TV commercial that targets teen-agers. Which of the following marketing mix variables best describes this activity?
   a. product
   b. price
   c. target market
   d. distribution
   e. promotion

5 Describe several reasons for studying marketing

_____ 14. Jackie is a food science major at a state university and hopes to operate the family restaurant after graduation. Jackie has been advised to take a marketing course in the school of business as an elective, but she thinks this would be a waste of time. You are her friend and a marketing major. You advise that:
   a. marketing is not relevant for a business like a family restaurant
   b. Jackie declare a business minor because she needs a backup career
   c. more nutrition and gourmet cooking classes will be most useful for Jackie
   d. the main reason to take marketing is to teach Jackie how to advertise the restaurant
   e. marketing knowledge will help Jackie to understand how she can satisfy consumers' needs and wants

_____ 15. Jon owns a small laboratory that makes bifocal contact lenses. His company is growing fast, and there are many things he does not understand about his customers. Should Jon take a marketing course?
   a. Yes, because marketing is synonymous with selling, and Jon will want to learn aggressive sales techniques to continue the company's growth
   b. No, because he can hire an advertising firm and will not need further knowledge of marketing
   c. No, because marketing is a minor function in business
   d. Yes, because the concept of marketing will help Jon to better serve and satisfy his customers
   e. Yes, because marketing teaches businesses how to sell products that people don't need

Check your answers to these questions before proceeding to the next section.

SCENARIO

After you read the marketing scenario, answer the questions that follow.

The fictitious Freedom Mutual Insurance Company is a leading provider of life, medical, property, and casualty insurance to consumers. Before 2002, sales agents of Freedom Mutual were trained to aggressively take business away from their competitors by offering lower prices on similar insurance coverage or by creating packages with more features. Sales agents had strict quotas to maintain, and bonuses were granted on the number of new accounts and the amount of revenue the agents brought into the company.

In 2002, the company began to change its way of conducting business. Sales agents were still trained to bring in new accounts, but they were also given incentives to keep existing business. Sales assistants input many types of data about their policyholders into a new database, thus creating a rich profile of each customer. Current policyholders are sent messages about additional coverage they may need as changes in the family (birth of a new child, new car, etc.) occur. In addition, customers are asked fill out a survey twice a year about the service that they have received from their insurance agent and any suggestions for improvement.

_____ 1. Before 2002, Freedom Mutual Insurance Company followed a marketing orientation.

_____ 2. In 2002, Freedom Mutual changed from a sales orientation to a marketing orientation.

_____ 3. Because of its new focus on existing policyholders, Freedom Mutual will likely lose revenue in the short-run because agents will be too busy to focus on new business.

Multiple Choice:

_____ 4. After 2002, Freedom Mutual paid more attention to its existing customers by keeping updated customer profiles and tracking major "life changes" that may require new coverage. This is an example of:
  a.   a production orientation.
  b.   customer satisfaction.
  c.   relationship marketing.
  d.   a societal marketing orientation.
  e.   a database orientation.

_____ 5. Before 2002, Freedom Mutual's target market can be described as
  a.   everybody.
  b.   current policyholders.
  c.   people who already have insurance.
  d.   people with high incomes.
  e.   people with insurance from competing firms

_____ 6. In order to adopt a true marketing orientation, Freedom Mutual should:
  a.   train all personnel – not just sales agents –to focus on customer satisfaction.
  b.   change its mission statement to be more customer-oriented.
  c.   target certain market segments who would most benefit from the company's offerings.
  d.   do all these.
  e.   do none of these.

Short Answer:

7. If you were the national marketing director for Freedom Mutual, what kinds of activities would you most likely be involved with? (Name at least seven activities.)

ESSAY QUESTIONS

1. The concept of exchange is crucial to the definition of marketing. What are the five conditions that must be satisfied for an exchange to take place? Can marketing occur even if an exchange does not take place?

2. Assume you are a marketing manager. Describe the marketing strategy for each of the four orientations of marketing management philosophy.

3. Name and describe five key areas in which a market orientation differs from a sales orientation.

4. Name and briefly define the marketing process activities.

The objective of this assignment is to understand the differences between the marketing concept – a fundamental objective for the entire course – and other business philosophies.

Look up the following Web sites of marketing organizations or products:

- McDonald's Restaurants: **http://www.mcdonalds.com**
- Pepsi-Cola: **http://www.pepsi.com**
- Procter & Gamble: **http://www.pg.com**
- Intel: **http://www.intel.com**

For each Web site:

1. Review the Web sites thoroughly and click on several different links.
2. List the elements on the Web site that you believe are marketing-oriented.

3. Describe why you believe these elements are marketing-oriented.

4. List the elements on the site that you believe are NOT marketing-oriented (i.e., they are sales-oriented or production-oriented.).

5. Describe why you believe these elements are NOT marketing oriented.

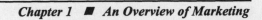

CHAPTER 2: STRATEGIC PLANNING FOR COMPETITIVE ADVANTAGE

1 Understand the importance of strategic marketing and know a basic outline for a marketing plan

Strategic marketing planning is the basis for all marketing strategies and decisions. The marketing plan is a written document that acts as a guidebook of marketing activities for the marketing manager. By specifying objectives and defining the actions required to attain them, a marketing plan provides the basis on which actual and expected performance can be compared. Creating a complete marketing plan is not a simple or quick effort. And the plan is only as good as the information it contains and the effort, creativity, and thought that went into its creation. Many of the elements in the plan are decided upon simultaneously and in conjunction with one another. Every marketing plan is unique to the firm for which is created.

Basic factors that should be covered include business mission, setting objectives, performing a situation analysis, selecting target markets, delineating a marketing mix, and establishing ways to implement, evaluate, and control the plan.

2 Develop an appropriate business mission statement

The mission statement is based on a careful analysis of benefits sought by present and potential customers and analysis of existing and anticipated environmental conditions. The firm's long-term vision, embodied in the mission statement, establishes boundaries for all subsequent decisions, objectives, and strategies. A mission statement should focus on the market or markets the organization is attempting to serve rather than on the good or service offered.

3 Describe the criteria for stating good marketing objectives

Objectives should be realistic, measurable, and time specific. Objectives must also be consistent, and indicate the priorities of the organization.

4 Explain the components of a situation analysis

In the situation or SWOT analysis, the firm should identify its internal strengths (S) and weaknesses (W) and also examine external opportunities (O) and threats (T). When examining external opportunities and threats, marketing managers must analyze aspects of the marketing environment n a process called environmental scanning. The six most often studied macro-environmental forces are social, demographic, economic, technological, political and legal, and competitive. During the situation analysis, the marketer should try to identify any strategic windows. Additionally, it is crucial that marketing identify a differential advantage and establish that it is a sustainable competitive advantage.

5 Identify sources of competitive advantage

Competitive advantage is a set of unique features of a company and its products that are perceived by the target market as superior to the competition. The three types of competitive advantage are cost (being the low cost competitor in an industry), differentiation (providing something unique that is valuable to buyers), and niche (effectively serving a single segment of the market) strategies.

6 Identify strategic alternatives and describe tools used to help select alternatives

Firms can use the strategic opportunity matrix to allow firms to explore four options: market penetration, market development, product development, and diversification. Firms select the alternative that best helps them reach their overall strategic goal: market share or profit. Corporate culture plays a large role in the selection process.

There are several major techniques for selecting alternatives. The portfolio matrix is a method of determining the profit potential and investment requirements of a firm's SBUs by classifying each as a star, cash cow, dog, or problem child and then determining appropriate resource allocations for each.

7 Discuss target market strategies

The target market strategy identifies which market segment or segments to focus on. The process begins with a market opportunity analysis, or MOA, which describes and estimates the size and sales potential of market segments that are of interest to the firm. In addition, an assessment of key competitors in these market segments is performed. After the market segments are described, the firm may target one or more segments.

The three strategies for selecting target markets are appealing to the entire market with one marketing mix, concentrating on one segment, or appealing to multiple market segments using multiple marketing mixes.

8 Describe the elements of the marketing mix

The term **marketing mix** refers to a unique blend of product, distribution, promotion, and pricing strategies designed to produce mutually satisfying exchanges with a target market. Distribution is often referred to as place, thus giving the "four P's" of marketing: product, place, promotion, and price. Products can be tangible goods, ideas, or services. Distribution strategies are concerned with making products available when and where customers want them. Promotion includes personal selling, advertising, sales promotion, and public relations. Price is what the buyer must give up to obtain a product.

9 Explain why implementation, evaluation, and control of the marketing plan is necessary

After selecting strategic alternatives, plans should be implemented, that is, put into action. The plan should be evaluated to see if it has achieved its objectives. The final step in the strategic planning process, control, is the alteration of plans, if necessary. A marketing control system ensures that marketing goals are achieved within guidelines.

10 Identify several techniques that help make strategic planning effective

Effective strategic planning should be treated as an ongoing process, not an annual exercise. Effective planning requires creativity and should challenge existing assumptions about the firm and the environment. Perhaps the most critical element is the support and participation of top management. Their involvement in planning must be sincere and ongoing.

Answer the following questions to see how well you understand the material. Re-take it after you review to check yourself.

1. List and briefly describe six major elements of a marketing plan.

2. Name and briefly describe four strategic alternatives that can be used by a firm.

3. List and briefly describe a tool that can be used to select a strategic alternative.

4. What is a marketing strategy?

5. List and briefly describe the four Ps ("marketing mix").

1 Understand the importance of strategic marketing and know a basic outline for a marketing plan

I. The Nature of Strategic Planning

A. Marketing managers must plan, organize, and control marketing activities. They must develop both long-range (strategic) and short-range (tactical) plans.

1. **Strategic planning** is the managerial process of creating and maintaining a fit between the organization's objectives and resources and evolving market opportunities.

2. Strategic decisions require long-term resource commitments with major financial consequences. A good strategic plan can help to protect a firm's resources against competitive onslaughts.

3. Strategic marketing management addresses two questions: What is the organization's main activity at a particular time? And how will it reach its goals?

B. What is a Marketing Plan?

3. **Planning** is the process of anticipating future events and determining strategies to achieve organizational objectives in the future.

4. **Marketing planning** involves designing activities relating to marketing objectives and the changing marketing environment.

5. Issues such as product lines, distribution channels, marketing communications, and pricing are all delineated in the **marketing plan.**

C. Why Write a Marketing Plan?

1. The **marketing plan** is a written document that acts as a guidebook of marketing activities for the marketing manager.

2. The marketing plan allows you to examine the external marketing environment in conjunction with the inner workings of the business, allowing the firm to enter the marketplace with an awareness of possibilities and problems.

D. Marketing Plan Elements

There are elements common to all marketing plans, such as defining the business mission and objectives, performing a situation analysis, delineating a target market, and establishing components of the marketing mix.

E. Writing the Marketing Plan

Creating a complete marketing plan is not a simple or quick effort. And the plan is only as good as the information it contains and the effort, creativity, and thought that went into its creation.

1. Many of the elements in the plan are decided upon simultaneously and in conjunction with one another.

2. Every marketing plan is unique to the firm for which it was created.

3. Basic factors that should be covered include business mission, setting objectives, performing a situation analysis, selecting target markets, delineating a marketing mix, and establishing ways to implement, evaluate, and control the plan.

2   Develop an appropriate business mission statement

II. Defining the Business Mission

A. The firm's **mission statement** is the long-term vision based on a careful analysis of benefits sought by present and potential customers and analysis of existing and anticipated environmental conditions.

B. Defining the business in terms of goods and services rather than in terms of the benefits customers seek is sometimes called **marketing myopia**. In this context, the term *myopia* means narrow, short-term thinking, which can threaten an organization's survival.

C. The organization may need to define a mission statement and objectives for a **strategic business unit (SBU),** which is a subgroup of a single business, or collection of related businesses within the larger organization.

Strategic business units will have the following characteristics:

1. A distinct mission and a specific target market
2. Control over their resources
3. Their own competitors
4. Plans independent of the other businesses in the organization

3   Describe the criteria for stating good marketing objectives

III. Set Marketing Plan Objectives

A **marketing objective** is a statement of what is to be accomplished through marketing activities.

A. Marketing objectives should be realistic, measurable, and time specific.

B. Objectives communicate marketing management philosophies, provide direction, serve as motivators, are a basis for control, and force executives to clarify their thinking.

4   Explain the components of a situation analysis

IV. Conducting a Situation Analysis

A. A situation analysis is sometimes referred to as a **SWOT analysis**. That is, the firm should identify its internal strengths (S) and weaknesses (W) and also examine external opportunities (O) and threats (T).

B. **Environmental scanning** is the collection and interpretation of information about forces, events, and relationships in the external environments that may affect the future of the organization.

C. The six most often studied macroenvironmental forces are social, demographic, economic, technological, political/legal, and competitive.

5   Identify the sources of competitive advantage

V.   Competitive Advantage

    A.   **Competitive advantage** consists of a set of unique features of a company and its products that are perceived by the target market as significant and superior to the competition.

    B.   Factor or factors that cause customers to patronize a firm and not the competition.

    C.   There are three types of competitive advantages.

        1.   A **cost-competitive advantage** results from being the low cost competitor in an industry while maintaining satisfactory profits. Sources of cost-competitive advantages include:

            a.   **Experience curves** tell us that costs decline at a predictable rate as experience with a product increases.
            b.   Efficient labour resulting from pools of cheap labour.
            c.   Removing frills and options from a product or service.
            d.   Designing products for ease of production or using reverse engineering to cut research and design costs.
            e.   Reengineering through downsizing, deleting unprofitable product lines, closing obsolete factories, or renegotiating supplier contracts.
            f.   Use of production innovations such as new technology and simplified production techniques.
            g.   Developing new, more efficient, methods of service delivery.

        2.   **Product/service differentiation** exists when a firm provides something unique that is valuable to buyers beyond simply a lower price. Sources of differential advantage include:

            a.   Brand names offer enduring competitive advantage
            b.   Recognized product reliability
            c.   Unmatched customer service.

        3.   A **niche competitive advantage** seeks to target and effectively serve a single segment of the market. This is a viable option/ strategy for:

            a.   Small companies having limited resources
            b.   Segments with good growth potential not crucial to the success of large companies

    D.   Building Tomorrow's Competitive Advantage

        1.   The sources of future competitive advantages are the skills and assets of the organization.

        2.   A **sustainable competitive advantage** is a function of the speed with which competitors can imitate a leading company's strategy plans.

6   Identify strategic alternatives and describe tools used to help select alternatives

VI.   Strategic Directions

    A.   To discover a marketing opportunity or strategic window, management must know how to identify the strategic alternatives. One method is the strategic opportunity matrix.

---

1. A firm following a **market penetration** alternative would try to increase market share among existing customers.

2. **Market development** is a strategic alternative that attracts new customers to existing products, perhaps by expanding the target market or expanding geographically.

    The ideal solution is finding new uses for old products that will stimulate additional sales among existing customers while also bringing in new buyers.

3. A **product development strategy** entails the creation of new products for present markets. Advantages of this strategy are current knowledge of the target market and established distribution channels.

4. **Diversification** refers to a strategy of increasing sales by introducing new products into new markets. This strategy can be very risky when a firm is entering unfamiliar markets.

B. Selecting a Strategic Alternative

Several tools aid corporate decision makers in selecting a strategic alternative. **A portfolio matrix** is a tool for allocating resources between products or strategic business units on the basis of relative market share and market growth rate.

It is also important to recognize several factors that affect the selection, including corporate philosophy and culture:

1. Most companies have a philosophical stance on the issue of immediate profit versus market share. In the long run these are compatible goals, but in the short run there may be a conflict.

2. The portfolio matrix from the Boston Consulting Group specifies four share/growth categories for SBUs:

    a. **Stars** are market leaders and growing fast. Stars have large reported profits but require a lot of cash to finance the rapid growth.
    b. **Cash cows** usually generate more cash than is required to maintain its market share. They are in a low-growth market but have dominant market share.
    c. **Problem children**, also called **question marks**, exhibit rapid growth but poor profit margins. They have a low market share in a high-growth industry. Problem children require a tremendous amount of cash to obtain better market share.
    d. **Dogs** have low growth potential and small market share. Most dogs eventually leave the marketplace. The firm often harvests them by cutting all support costs to a bare minimum.

3. After classifying the various SBUs into the matrix, the next step is to allocate future resources for each.

7 Discuss target market strategies

VII. Describing the Marketing Strategy

Marketing strategy involves selecting and describing one or more target markets, and developing and maintaining a marketing mix that will produce mutually satisfying exchanges with target markets.

A. Target Market Strategy

1.   A market segment is a group of individuals or organizations that share one or more characteristics. **Market opportunity analysis** is the description and estimation of the size and sales potential of market segments that are of interest to the firm.

2.   Target market(s) can be selected by appealing to the entire market with one marketing mix, concentrating on one segment, or appealing to multiple market segments using multiple marketing mixes.

8   Describe the elements of the marketing mix

VIII. The Marketing Mix

The term **marketing mix** refers to a unique blend of product, distribution, promotion, and pricing strategies designed to produce mutually satisfying exchanges with a target market.

Distribution is sometimes referred to as place, thus giving us the **"four P's"** of the marketing mix: product, place, promotion, and price.

A.   Product Strategies

The heart of the marketing mix, the starting point, is the product offering and product strategy. The product includes its package, warranty, after-sale service, brand name, company image, and many other factors.

B.   Distribution Strategies

Distribution strategies, which usually involve wholesalers and retailers, are concerned with making products available when and where customers want them. Physical distribution also involves all the business activities that are concerned with storing and transporting raw materials or finished products.

C.   Promotion Strategies

Promotion includes personal selling, advertising, sales promotion, and public relations. Promotion's role in the marketing mix is to inform, educate, persuade, and remind target markets about the benefits of an organization or a product.

D.   Pricing Strategies

Price is what a buyer must give up to obtain a product. Price is often the most flexible of the four marketing mix elements, the quickest element to change. Price is a very important competitive weapon and very important to the organization, because price multiplied by the number of units sold equals total revenue for the firm.

9   Explain why implementation, evaluation, and control of the marketing plan are necessary

IX.   Following Up The Marketing Plan

A.   **Implementation** is the process of gaining the organizational compliance required to put marketing strategies into action. Brilliant marketing strategies are doomed to fail if they are not properly implemented.

Chapter 2 ■ Strategic Planning for Competitive Advantage

B. **Evaluation** entails gauging the extent to which marketing objectives have been achieved during a specified time period.

C. **Control** provides the mechanisms for evaluating marketing results in light of the strategic plan and for correcting actions that do not help the organization reach those goals within budget guidelines.

    1.   A **marketing audit** is a thorough, systematic, periodic evaluation of the goals, strategies, structure, and performance of the marketing organization.

    2.   The marketing audit has four characteristics

    Comprehensive - The marketing audit covers all the major marketing issues facing an organization and not just trouble spots.

    Systematic - The marketing audit takes place in an orderly sequence and covers the organization's marketing environment, internal marketing system, and specific marketing activities. The diagnosis is followed by an action plan with both short-run and long run proposals for improving overall marketing effectiveness.

    Independent - The marketing audit is normally conducted by an inside or outside party who is independent enough to have top management's confidence and to be objective.

    Periodic - The marketing audit should be carried out on a regular schedule instead of only in a crisis.

10 Identify several techniques that help make strategic planning effective

X.   Effective Strategic Planning

Effective strategic planning requires continual attention, creativity, and management commitment.

A.   It is not an annual but an ongoing process.
B.   Sound planning is based on creativity. The firm needs to challenge existing assumptions.
C.   Perhaps the most critical element is the support and participation of top management

---

VOCABULARY PRACTICE

Fill in the blank(s) with the appropriate term or phrase from the alphabetized list of chapter key terms.

cash cow	marketing plan
competitive advantage	marketing planning
control	marketing strategy
cost competitive advantage	market opportunity analysis
diversification	market penetration
dog	mission statement
environmental scanning	niche competitive advantage
evaluation	planning
experience curves	portfolio matrix
four P's	problem child (question mark)
implementation	product development
market development	product/service differentiation
market opportunity analysis (MOA)	star
marketing audit	strategic business unit (SBU)
marketing mix	strategic planning
marketing myopia	sustainable competitive advantage
marketing objective	SWOT analysis

---

1   Understand the importance of strategic marketing and know a basic outline for a marketing plan

1.   The managerial process of creating and maintaining a fit between the organization's objectives and resources and evolving market opportunities is _____.

2.   The process of anticipating events and determining strategies to achieve organizational objectives is _____, while designing activities relating to marketing objectives and the changing marketing environment is _____.

3.   The written document that acts, as a guidebook of activities in the areas of product, place, promotion, and price is known as the _____.

2   Develop an appropriate business mission statement

4.   The foundation of any marketing plan is the answer to the question, "What business are we in and where are we going?" The answer is the firm's _____.

5.   Defining a business in terms of goods and services rather than in terms of the benefits customers seek is called _____, meaning narrow, short-term thinking.

6.   After defining its mission, an organization may need to divide its firm into subgroups that have their own planning and operations. One of these sections would be called a (n) _____.

3   Describe the criteria for stating good marketing objectives

7.   A statement of what is to be accomplished with marketing activities is a (n) _____.

4   Explain the components of a situation analysis

8.   A situation analysis that allows the company to determine its present status, its current capabilities, and its future expectations is the _____.

9.   The identification of market opportunities and threats to provide guidelines for the design of marketing strategy is known as _____. Forces identified with this process include social, demographic, economic, technological, political/legal, and competitive forces.

5   Identify sources of competitive advantage

10.   When a firm or its products have a set of unique features that are perceived by the target market as significant and superior to the competition, the firm is said to have a (n) _____.

11. WestJet is a good example of a company with a (n) _____ since it represents the low-cost competitor in the airline industry and maintains good profit margins. WestJet is able to achieve this through _____, which show costs declining at a predictable rate as experience with a product increases.

12. Some companies compete using _____, an advantage that is achieved when a firm provides something that is unique and valuable to buyers beyond simply offering a lower price. Other companies may compete using a (n) _____which occurs when a company targets and effectively services a single, usually small, segment of the market.

6 Identify strategic alternatives and describe tools used to help select alternatives

13. Firms can conceptualize strategic alternatives with the strategic opportunity matrix, which describes four possible growth opportunities. If a firm tries to increase market share through present products marketed to existing customers, it is following the _____ alternative. If the firm is attracting new customers to its existing products, _____ is taking place. If the firm creates new products for present markets, it is engaging in _____. Finally, if the firm increases sales by introducing new products into new markets, the firm is opting for _____.

14. To determine SBU cash contributions and requirements, managers can use a framework that classifies each SBU by growth and market share. This is the _____, which describes four categories according to growth and market share dominance. The category that describes a fast-growing market leader is a (n) _____. The category that would describe high market share SBUs that are in low-growth markets is the _____. SBUs that exhibit rapid growth but poor profit margins are _____. Finally, an SBU with a low-growth potential and a small market share would be called a (n) _____.

15. To be successful in the long run, companies should have a (n) _____, a competitive advantage that cannot be copied by the competition.

7 Discuss target market strategies

16. The activities of selecting and describing one or more target markets and developing and maintaining a marketing mix to satisfy these markets is known as a (n) _____.

17. When marketers want to estimate the size and sales potential of market segments, as well as assess key competitors in these market segments, they conduct a (n) _____.

8 Describe the elements of the marketing mix

18. The unique blend of product, distribution, promotion, and pricing strategies designed to produce mutually satisfying exchanges with a target market is the _____. These elements are also known as the _____.

9 Understand why implementation, evaluation, and control of the marketing plan is necessary

19. The phase of the marketing process in which marketers gain the organizational compliance required to put marketing strategies into action is termed _____. The phase in which marketers gauge the extent to which objectives have been achieved during a specified time period is the process of _____. Finally, providing mechanisms for correcting actions is called _____.

20. A thorough, systematic, periodic evaluation of the goals, strategies, structure, and performance of the marketing organization is a (n) _____.

Check your answers to these questions before proceeding to the next section.

TRUE/FALSE QUESTIONS

Mark the statement **T** if it is true and **F** if it is false.

1 Understand the importance of strategic marketing and know a basic outline for a marketing plan

_____ 1. The owner of the Ace Auto Store is considering the permanent price reduction of all inventories to position the store as the lowest-priced auto parts store in town. This is an example of strategic decision-making.

_____ 2. The first step in developing a marketing plan is the creating a SWOT analysis.

2 Develop an appropriate business mission statement

_____ 3. Mike's Motos manufactures and sells mopeds, scooters, and other small motorcycles. Management does not define the business in terms of offered products; instead, the business is defined as "serving transportation needs for students." Mike's Motos suffers from marketing myopia because it has ignored the fact that students can get transportation from cars, buses, and bicycles.

3 Describe the criteria for stating good marketing objectives

_____ 4. Pets Market has the marketing objective of being the best retailer of pet food and supplies in the country. This would be considered a useful objective.

4 Explain the components of a situation analysis

_____ 5. An example of a "threat" which a tobacco manufacturer could use in its SWOT analysis could include impending legislation that lessens the amount of advertising tobacco companies can do.

_____ 6. You have been hired to collect and analyze information about factors that may affect your new company. You are also responsible for identifying market opportunities and threats. Your job can be summarized as "environmental scanning."

_____ 7. AirJet has an aging fleet of aircraft, which may convey an image of danger. This represents a threat.

6 **Identify strategic alternatives and describe tools used to help select alternatives**

_____ 8. Twinky Tins has been producing the same assortment of cookie tins for the life of the company. The company has decided that its products, targeted at bakeries, would also fulfill the needs of household consumers. Pursuing this new market would be an example of market development.

_____ 9. Finkle's Fishing Rods has just developed a new line of tackle boxes that further meet the needs of Finkle's fishing customers. This is an example of product development.

7 **Discuss target market strategies**

_____ 10. Your school of business is engaged in describing and estimating the size and sales potential of market segments (such as traditional students, executives, and the local community). In addition, the school is assessing major competitors (such as other colleges and educational programs). Your school is conducting a market opportunity analysis.

8 **Describe the elements of the marketing mix**

_____ 11. A small, independent motion picture studio decides to use theatres to advertise a new artistic movie release. This is an example of using "place" in the marketing mix.

9 **Understand why implementation, evaluation, and control of the marketing plan is necessary**

_____ 12. The control process actually begins while planning is taking place.

_____ 13. A marketing audit is a control device used primarily by large corporations to study past performance.

Check your answers to these questions before proceeding to the next section.

AGREE/DISAGREE QUESTIONS

For the following statements, indicate reasons why you may agree and disagree with the statement.

1. Every organization—profit or non-profit—can use the same basic outline for a marketing plan.

    Reason(s) to agree:

    Reason(s) to disagree:

2. Since the business environment is ever changing, it is a waste of time to do a situation analysis.

    Reason(s) to agree:

Reason(s) to disagree:

3. The tools used to help select strategic alternatives—such as the portfolio matrix—are only meant for large firms.

   Reason(s) to agree:

   Reason(s) to disagree:

4. Implementation is secondary; strategy is more important.

   Reason(s) to agree:

   Reason(s) to disagree:

MULTIPLE CHOICE QUESTIONS

Select the response that best answers the question, and write the corresponding letter in the space provided.

1 Understand the importance of strategic marketing and know a basic outline for a marketing plan

_____ 1. If Plan-O-Co is proceeding through the decision-making phases involved in the strategic planning process, which of the following activities is NOT being performed?
a. defining the business mission
b. conducting a situation analysis
c. developing strategic alternatives
d. designing a marketing information system to solve specific problems
e. establishing strategic business units

_____ 2. Production Aid Consultants, Inc., has recently been engaged in several special meetings where issues such as business mission, situation analysis, market and growth alternatives, and implementation approaches have been discussed. Production Aid is apparently engaged in:
a. target market planning
b. writing the mission statement
c. the strategic planning processes
d. business analysis
e. strategic contingency planning

2 Develop an appropriate business mission statement

___ 3. Frito-Lay defines its business as "snack-food" rather than just "corn chips." This is an example of:
   a. a marketing mix strategy
   b. a mission statement
   c. quantifiable goals
   d. a financial statement
   e. organizational accomplishment

___ 4. Sharon Mauser, the senior vice president of Progressive Products, Ltd. is in the process of developing Progressive's organizational mission statement. Which of the following factors should she consider when developing such a mission statement?
   a. What benefits do present customers need and want
   b. What benefits will potential customers need and want
   c. What existing environmental conditions will influence the choices made in the future by Progressive Products, Inc.
   d. What anticipated environmental conditions will influence the choices made in the future by Progressive Products, Inc.
   e. All of these should be considered by Ms. Mauser

___ 5. By defining its business as "running department stores" instead of "providing a range of products and services that deliver value to Canadian families," Sears is engaging in:
   a. market segmentation
   b. marketing myopia
   c. market development
   d. strategic planning
   e. product differentiation

___ 6. A high tech company has the business mission of "providing high quality products at a fair price to customers." This mission statement
   a. is an example of marketing myopia.
   b. is too broad of a statement to be of use in serving customers.
   c. could stifle creativity in discovering opportunities to serve customers.
   d. is not sincere enough.
   e. does not meet customer needs.

___ 7. AT&T sells many products and services in addition to telephones. Some of these include computers, modems, fax machines, and a variety of business and home long-distance telephone services. How would this be best justified in the strategic planning process?
   a. New business units are needed to continue growth.
   b. Local delivery has high market attractiveness.
   c. Diversification is needed to survive.
   d. This mission statement recognizes the firm as a communications company, not just a telephone manufacturer.
   e. It is more efficient to produce a wide variety of products.

___ 8. Pepsico is a large conglomerate that has separate subsidiaries called Pepsi-Cola (soft drinks), Tropicana (juices), Pepsi Bottling, and Frito-Lay (snack foods). Each of these subsidiaries has its own functional departments, its own planning, its own financial goals, and its own target markets. These subsidiaries may also be called
   a. product market niches
   b. diversified divisions
   c. strategic business units
   d. strategic alliances
   e. heterogeneous elements

3 Describe the criteria for stating good marketing objectives

____ 9. As the marketing director for a new pharmaceutical that prevents baldness, you have been asked by the CEO to provide marketing objectives for the next year. Your product is the second one of its type in the market. Which of the following is the most appropriate objective?
   a. To generate sales of $20 million during the first year of the launch.
   b. To attain a market share of 100 percent in the first year.
   c. To significantly increase the company's sales.
   d. To be number one in the market for baldness-prevention products.
   e. To be known as the best product in the baldness-prevention market.

4 Explain the components of a situation analysis

____ 10. Gabble's Granola has set up a committee to formally study its current status and capabilities and its future expectations. Gabble's Granola is conducting a(n):
   a. marketing audit
   b. profit and loss statement
   c. environmental scan
   d. situation analysis
   e. strategic window search

____ 11. When Sam joined the Dale Corporation, he noticed some interesting characteristics about the company. Instead of being encouraged to take risks, employees were chastised for making mistakes. The marketing department was not used to taking the leadership in pricing; it simply reacted to what competition was doing. The corporate culture of the company is a (n):
   a. internal strength
   b. external threat
   c. internal threat
   d. internal weakness
   e. external weakness

____ 12. In a SWOT analysis, strengths and weaknesses represent the _____ environment and opportunities and threats represent the _____ environment.
   a. cultural, economic
   b. economic, cultural
   c. internal, external
   d. external, internal
   e. political, competitive

6 Identify strategic alternatives and describe tools used to help select alternatives

____ 13. When Disney started targeting its theme parks toward adults rather than just children, it was selecting which strategic alternative?
   a. product development
   b. market development
   c. market penetration
   d. product penetration
   e. diversification

____ 14. Starbucks, the giant gourmet coffee retailer, started selling its own branded ice cream to its current coffee customers. This is an example of a strategy called:
   a. market development
   b. market penetration
   c. product penetration
   d. product development
   e. diversification

15. Licoh, a manufacturer of printing equipment, recently bought a local baseball team to increase its overall sales. Licoh is following the strategy of:
    a. market penetration
    b. product development
    c. product penetration
    d. market development
    e. diversification

16. The Formula Foods Corporation has used a system to classify its various subsidiaries or divisions to determine the future expected cash contributions and the future requirements for each division. The divisions have been designated as cash cows, dogs, stars, and problem children. Formula Foods is using:
    a. the portfolio matrix
    b. market share analysis
    c. response functions
    d. the market attractiveness matrix
    e. the company strength matrix

17. The baking products division of Basic Foods, Inc., is the market leader in a mature and low-growth market. The baking products division generates more dollars than is required in order to maintain market share, and in portfolio matrix terms it is known as Basic Food's:
    a. green light
    b. cash cow
    c. star
    d. dog
    e. spotlight

18. In its portfolio of business subsidiaries, Tupple Toys has three units that are showing rapid growth but poor profit margins. Apparently, everything about these units demands more and more additional cash. In the Boston Consulting Group's portfolio matrix, these units would be classified as:
    a. dogs
    b. cash cows
    c. problem children
    d. stars
    e. leeches

19. A local private college has been offering an accounting program for several years. The program has a large but declining enrolment, and the program represents the largest income earner for the business division. The recommended strategic option is to:
    a. cultivate
    b. divest
    c. hold
    d. harvest
    e. build

20. Which of the following strategies is normally used for a "star?"
    a. build
    b. hold
    c. eliminate
    d. harvest
    e. divest

21. Which of the following strategies is normally used for a "cash cow?"
    a. build
    b. hold
    c. eliminate
    d. harvest
    e. divest

7 Discuss target market strategies

_____ 22. A power tool company has done consumer research and describes its customers as being male, 28-55 years of age, married, 62 percent high school graduates, and earners of below-average income. This is the group of consumers most likely to buy the tools and is referred to as the:
a. social responsibility group
b. exchangers
c. target market
d. advertisees
e. scanned environment members

8 Describe the elements of the marketing mix

_____ 23. John Porter is the new vice president of marketing and is designing the marketing mix for his company. The starting point of Mr. Porter's marketing mix will be the:
a. analysis of what production equipment is available and owned by the company
b. design of the promotion campaign to be used for the product
c. selection of the places through which the good or service will be sold
d. development of the good or service to be sold
e. determination of the price to be charged for the good or service, enabling future revenues and budgets to be estimated

_____ 24. Barak Austin is thinking about opening a new hardware and home improvement store in a community that research has shown needs more outlets. On which area of the marketing mix should he focus his attention?
a. customer needs/wants
b. production
c. product
d. promotion
e. distribution

_____ 25. Diana's job is to decide whether her company's advertising money will be spent on television, radio, newspaper, or direct mail. To which of the four P's do Diana's duties relate?
a. publicity
b. price
c. promotion
d. place
e. product

_____ 26. Albert must make a quick change to his marketing plan to boost sales, so he should change the element of the marketing mix?
a. product
b. place
c. price
d. promotion
e. publicity

9 Understand why implementation, evaluation, and control of the marketing plan is necessary

_____ 27. Becky's Bolt Supply has set up a management committee that is arranging the delegation of authority and responsibility for marketing strategies, determining a time frame for completion of tasks, and overseeing resource allocation. The task of this committee is:
a. market planning
b. strategic analysis
c. alternative control
d. implementation
e. strategic planning

28. The managers at Unicorn Research realize that implemented plans do not always lead to the desired results. The managers feel they should develop a mechanism for correcting actions that are not efficiently aiding the firm in reaching its objectives. Unicorn's concerns centre around:
    a. control
    b. implementation
    c. objectives
    d. planning
    e. budgeting

29. A planning manager from corporate headquarters finds that his eastern region has no effective method of allocating resources or evaluating goals and performance of the marketing organization. He suggests that the region should prepare a:
    a. service audit
    b. tactical plan
    c. marketing audit
    d. market share analysis
    e. response intervention

10   Identify several techniques that help make strategic planning effective

30. Effective strategic planning requires:
    a. a General Electric planning matrix
    b. management to stay out of the process
    c. a designated single time frame during the year
    d. the planner to challenge existing company assumptions
    e. a stringent and narrow mission statement for guidelines

31. Ethan, the owner of a hobby store, is concerned that his employees are not seriously embracing the marketing concept. You are his friend and a marketing expert. You would suggest all of the following ideas EXCEPT:
    a. a clear declaration of intent and support for the new policies by Ethan
    b. an increased authority for individual employees to make customer-related decisions as problems occur
    c. getting everyone who will be affected by changes in policies and procedures involved in the planning process
    d. slowly implementing new policies that encourage a focus on the customer
    e. concentrating on creating a specific marketing department focused on this problem

Check your answers to these questions before proceeding to the next section.

SCENARIO

After reading the marketing scenario, answer the questions that follow.

The fictitious Strawberry Computer Company has been a leading provider of many generations of computers for over twenty years. The company started out producing large mainframe computers in the 1980s, and while sales have all but diminished in the 21st century, a few customers still buy them from time to time. Strawberry's most profitable business today is in laptop and personal computers, which generate large amounts of money that can be reinvested in other growth businesses, such as subnotebook and hand-held computers. The company has also been dabbling with integrated phone and palm devices. These products have not yet paid off, but they may become big in the future unless new technology makes them obsolete.

Strawberry is entering its marketing planning season and is getting ready to allocate resources to each of its product lines for the coming year. Obviously, resources will not be allocated evenly, as some products show more promise than others.

_____ 1. Strawberry's subnotebook and hand-held computers represent the company's cash cows.

_____ 2. The company should eliminate the mainframe computer line.

_____ 3. The subnotebook and hand-held computers should get more than their share of company resources.

Multiple Choice:

_____ 4. Which of the following best describes the company's line of laptop and personal computers?
   a. Stars.
   b. Cash cows.
   c. Question marks.
   d. Dogs.
   e. Solid products.

_____ 5. Which of the following best describes the company's line of integrated phone and palm devices?
   a. Stars.
   b. Cash cows.
   c. Question marks.
   d. Dogs.
   e. Problem cow.

_____ 6. Which of the following strategies would be most appropriate for the laptop and personal computers?
   a. Harvest: increase the short-term cash return but don't focus too many resources.
   b. Build: pour resources into these products to make them grow further.
   c. Divest: eliminate the product line altogether since they will soon become obsolete.
   d. Hold: preserve market share but don't pour too many resources into this area, as they may become obsolete products.
   e. Flexible growth: pour resources into these products whenever it looks like they might begin to fail.

_____ 7. Which of the following strategies would be most appropriate for the subnotebook and hand-held computers?
   a. Harvest: increase the short-term cash return but don't focus too many resources.
   b. Build: pour resources into these products to make them grow further.
   c. Divest: eliminate the product line altogether since they will soon become obsolete.
   d. Hold: preserve market share but don't pour too many resources into this area, as they may become obsolete products.
   e. Flexible growth: pour resources into these products whenever it looks like they might begin to fail.

Short Answer:

8. List two advantages and two disadvantages of using the portfolio matrix as a basis for resource allocation.

Check your answers to these questions before proceeding to the next section.

1.   What are the elements of the marketing plan?

2.   What is a marketing objective? State four criteria that marketing objectives should have, and write a good example of an objective that has these criteria.

3.   What is a target market? List three general strategies for selecting target markets and give an example for each one.

4. The Boston Consulting Group (BCG) portfolio matrix is a technique that managers can use to classify SBUs. Using the following matrix, label the horizontal and vertical axes with the SBU classifications used by the BCG and label each quadrant. Then describe each quadrant and include the basic tactic followed in each category.

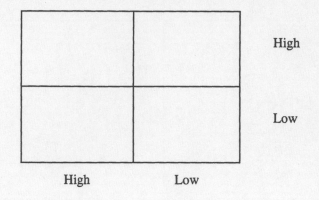

High

Low

High   Low

5. The marketing mix refers to a unique blend of marketing variables known as the four P's. Using a new breakfast cereal as an example, name and briefly describe each of the four P's.

APPLICATION #1

The objective of this assignment is to conduct a thorough SWOT analysis of a company. Select a well-known company or non-profit organization that has a good Web site and for which plenty of recent articles have been written. The company should be facing some critical issues due to the external environment, such as a tobacco, an airline or telecommunication company. Conduct a SWOT analysis of the company using the following chart. List at least five items in each area.

Note: A good place to find information on a famous company's external environment is through a periodicals search through the college's library database. The company's Web site may or may not contain much information on the external environment.

Strengths	Weaknesses
Opportunities	**Threats**

APPLICATION #2

The objective of this assignment is to describe what kinds of competitive advantage a company can have. Use the Internet or your own knowledge to provide examples of companies that represent the following types of competitive advantage in the following industries.

Airline Industry:

- Who has the cost competitive advantage? How do you know?

- Who has product/service differentiation? What makes the company different?

- Who uses a niche competitive advantage? How do you know?

Deep Discount Stores:

- Who has the cost competitive advantage? How do you know?

- Who has product/service differentiation? What makes the company different?

- Who uses a niche competitive advantage? How do you know?

CHAPTER 3: THE MARKETING ENVIRONMENT AND MARKETING ETHICS

LEARNING OBJECTIVES

1 Discuss the external environment of marketing and explain how it affects a firm

The external environmental variables of marketing are the uncontrollable factors that continually mold and reshape the target market. The firm and its customers are affected by social, demographic, economic, technological, political and legal, and competitive factors. The monitoring and evaluating of these environments is a task called environmental scanning.

2 Describe the social factors that affect marketing

The social factors, which include the values and lifestyles of a population, strongly influence the attitudes and desires of target markets. These are perhaps the most difficult variables for marketers to forecast or influence.

3 Explain the importance to marketing managers of current demographic trends

Demographic trends are trends in the vital statistics of a population such as birth rates, death rates, age group totals, and locations. These trends are important for marketers as they attempt to forecast demand and changes in the composition of their markets.

4 Explain the importance to marketing managers of multiculturalism and growing ethnic markets

Multiculturalism occurs when all major ethnic groups in an area are roughly equally represented. Growing multiculturalism makes the marketer's tasks more challenging. Niches within ethnic markets may require micro marketing strategies. An alternative to a niche strategy is maintaining a core brand identity while straddling different languages, cultures, ages, and incomes with different promotional campaigns. A third strategy is to seek common interests, motivations, or needs across ethnic groups.

5 Identify consumer and marketer reactions to the state of the economy

Economic factors in the environment affect consumer demand. Marketers follow trends in consumer income to forecast what type of products will be demanded. Inflation, a period of rising prices, tends to make consumers less brand loyal and likely to stock up on sale items.

6 Identify the impact of technology on a firm

Changes in technological and resource factors can have a momentous effect on an entire industry. The use of a new technology can assist a firm in coping with the detrimental effects of many of the other environmental factors. Not taking advantage of a new technology may cause customers to move to more innovative products and firms.

7 Discuss the political and legal environment of marketing

Federal and provincial laws establish many rules for operating a business. These regulations affect every aspect of the marketing mix. The Competition Bureau is the federal department charged with administering most marketplace laws.

8 Explain the basics of foreign and domestic competition

The competitive environment refers to the number of competitors a firm must face, the relative size of the competitors, and the degree of interdependence within the industry. The nature of a firm's competition is beyond the control of management, yet the marketing mix, particularly the element of pricing, is clearly affected by the type and amount of competition facing the firm. International competition is a growing concern for most businesses in Canada for two reasons: Numerous Canadian firms must consider going international as a growth strategy, and more and more foreign firms entering Canada to do business compete on quality as well as price.

9 Describe the role of ethics and ethical decisions in business

Business ethics may be viewed as a subset of the values of society as a whole. As members of society, marketing managers are morally obligated to consider the ethical implications of their decisions. Many companies develop codes of ethics as a guideline for their employees.

10 Discuss corporate social responsibility

Social responsibility in business refers to a firm's concern for the way its decisions affect society. One theorist suggests that total corporate social responsibility consists of four components: economic (to be profitable), legal (to obey the law), ethical (to be ethical), and philanthropic (to be a good corporate citizen) responsibilities. This model is known as the Pyramid of Corporate Responsibility.

Answer the following questions to see how well you understand the material. Re-take it after you review to check yourself.

1.   What is a target market?

2.   Give three examples of social factors that affect marketing.

3.   What is demography?

4.   Name four generations that are often used as target markets. Describe key characteristics of each generation.

5.   List and briefly describe at least four types of legislation that impact marketing.

1 Discuss the external environment of marketing and explain how it affects a firm

I. The External Marketing Environment

A. The defined group of consumers that managers feel is most likely to buy a firm's product is the **target market**, and it is this group for which the marketing mix is designed.

    External environmental factors are:
1. Social
2. Demographic
3. Economic
4. Technological
5. Political and Legal
6. Competitive

B. Understanding the External Environment

A critical task for the firm is the process of environmental scanning, the collection and interpretation of information about forces, events, and relationships that may affect the future of an organization. An organization's environmental scanning is performed by a group of specialists who collect and evaluate environmental data on a continuing basis.

C. Environmental Management

Although marketing managers consider the external environment to be uncontrollable, they may be able to influence certain aspects. A company may attempt to influence evolving external factors with **environmental management**, the implementation of strategies that attempt to shape the external environment within which a firm operates.

2 Describe the social factors that affect marketing

II. Social Factors

A. Canadian Values

1. A **value** is a strongly held and enduring belief. Four basic values define Canada:

a. Self-sufficiency: Every person should stand on his or her own feet.
b. Upward mobility: Success should come to anyone who gets an education, works hard, and plays by the rules.
c. Work ethic: Hard work, dedication to family, and frugality are moral and right.
d. Conformity: No one should expect to be treated differently from everybody else.

2. Values influence buying habits. Canadian consumers rank characteristics of product quality as: 1) reliable; 2) durable; 3) easy to maintain; 4) easy to use; 5) trusted brand name; and 6) low price.

B. "Poverty of Time" has influenced the:

1. Value of having more control over their lives

2. Decrease time people spend doing things they dislike

3. Growth in home-based self-employment

C. Growth of Component lifestyles

Component lifestyles are the result of choosing products and services that meet diverse needs and interests rather than conforming to traditional stereotypes.

1. Increase the complexity of consumers' buying habits

2. Require a different marketing mix

D. The Changing Role of Families and Working Women

1. Approximately 65 percent of all females between sixteen and sixty-five are in the work force.

2. Women's level of expertise, experience and authority are growing

3. Two-career families have greater household incomes but less available time for family activities. Their purchase roles are changing, as well as their purchase patterns. Women are the principle buyers for over 40 percent of all cars and trucks sold in Canada.

4. Increased demand for new household services and timesaving devices

3   Explain the importance to marketing managers of current demographic trends

III. Demographic Factors

Demographic characteristics are strongly related to consumer buyer behaviour in the marketplace and are good predictors of how the target market will respond to a specific marketing mix.

Demography is the study of a population's vital statistics such as age, race and ethnicity, and location. Demographic factors are an extremely important indicator of composition and change in a market.

III. A. Generation Y

1. The "Y" generation is composed of about 6.4 million Canadians born between 1979 and 1994. This group likes customized products such as clothes, travel planning, computers, and electronics. They have grown up in an even more media-saturated, brand conscious world than their parents.

2. About 84 percent do not currently own a home, but 37% expect to buy one within 2 years.

B. Generation X

1. Generation X-ers represent a market of over 7 million consumers born between 1965 and 1978.

2. This group of consumers doesn't mind indulging and is willing to spend on movies, eating out, clothing, and electronic items. They tend to be more materialistic than past generations.

C. Baby Boomers

1. **Baby Boomers** comprise nearly 9 million consumers born between 1946 and 1964 and represent a huge market.

2. The importance of individualism among baby boomers has led Canada to become a **personalized economy** that delivers products at a good value on demand.

3. Successful products in a personalized economy share three characteristics: custom-designed for small target markets, immediacy of delivery, and value.

4. As today's average consumer moves toward 40, this group focuses on family, health, convenience, finances, and reading materials.

D. Older Consumers: Not Just Grandparents

1. The age fifty+ consumers are healthier, wealthier, and better educated than earlier generations. This group represents a tremendous marketing opportunity.

2. This group tends to be brand loyal.

3. There is a need for products that help older consumers overcome physical limitations.

4 Explain the importance to marketing managers of multiculturalism and growing ethnic markets

IV. Growing Ethnic Markets

A. Canada is becoming a multicultural society with 3 in 10 Canadians that are not of French or British descent. About 13% of Canadians are" visible minorities" with the largest groups from China, Southeast Asia, Hong Kong, India and Africa.

B. Ethnic and Cultural Diversity

1. **Multiculturalism** occurs when all major ethnic groups in an area are roughly equally represented.

2. Growing multiculturalism makes the marketer's tasks more challenging. Niches within ethnic markets may require micro marketing strategies.

3. An alternative to a niche strategy is maintaining a core brand identity while straddling different languages, cultures, ages, and incomes.

C. The Internet is becoming more multicultural, leading to the creation of targeted multicultural Web cites.

5 Identify consumer and marketer reactions to the state of the economy

V. Economic Factors

A. Rising Incomes

1. About 55 percent of all Canadian households earn a "middle-class" income, between $30,000 and $75,000. In 2003, almost half the households were in the upper end of that income range.

2. Today over 14 percent of households earn over $75,000. The trend toward dual-income families contributes heavily to this phenomenon.

3. The rise in consumer income provides more discretionary income (income after taxes and necessities) for higher-quality, higher-priced goods and services.

B.   Inflation

Inflation is a general rise in prices resulting in decreased purchasing power. Inflation generally causes consumers to do two things:

1.   Decrease their brand loyalty as they search for the lowest prices, taking advantage of coupons and sales to stock up on items

2.   Unwillingness to pay more for a product than the subjective value placed on it

C.   Recession

A **recession** is a period of economic activity when income, production, and employment tend to fall--all of which reduce demand for goods and services. The effects of reduced demand can be countered by:

1.   Improving existing products and introducing new ones.

2.   Maintaining and expanding customer services.

3.   Emphasizing top-of-the-line products and promoting product value.

6   Identify the impact of technology on a firm

VI.   Technological and Resource Factors

A.   Changes in technological and resource factors can have a momentous effect on an entire industry. New technology can assist a firm in coping with many of the other environmental factors. For example, new processes can reduce production costs and help a firm fight inflation and recession.

B.   **Basic** or pure **research** attempts to expand the frontiers of knowledge.

C.   Applied research attempts to develop new or improved products from the results of basic research. Canada is improving its track record in applied research.

D.   Technology's impact on productivity in Canada is seen in the areas of information technology and the growth of e-commerce.

7   Discuss the political and legal environment of marketing

VII. A.   Federal laws have impacted on marketing:

Most of the consumer and business protection legislation in Canada is enforced by the Competition Bureau of Industry Canada:

The Competition Act, The Consumer Packaging and Labelling Act, The Motor Vehicle Safety Act, The Food and Drug Act, and many others…

The Competition Bureau is responsible for enforcing the laws covering bankruptcy, trade practices, competition, credit, labelling and packaging, copyrights, hazardous products, patents, pensions, precious metals, trademarks, and food inspection.

B. Provincial laws pose difficulties:

The laws vary from province to province and therefore managers must be aware of any legislation that directly affects their business.

C. Self-Regulation also impacts on marketing as some business make efforts to police themselves.

   i.   The Canadian Code of Advertising Standards, for example, was established by Canada's largest advertising agencies to monitor honesty and fairness in advertising.
   ii. The Canadian Broadcasting Association has also developed its own code of ethics.
   iii. The Canadian Direct Marketing Association has established guidelines to protect consumers' privacy and right not to be contacted.

D. NAFTA: The North American Free Trade Agreement

Since 1988 Canada has had a free trade agreement with its US trading partner. With NAFTA, Mexico was brought in and the world's largest free trade zone was created.

NAFTA has brought about new business opportunities for Canadian companies by lowering trade barriers between the NAFTA countries (Canada, US, and Mexico).

8 Explain the basics of foreign and domestic competition

VIII. Competitive Factors

A. Competition for Market Share and Profits

Regardless of the form of the competitive market, as population growth slows, costs rise, and available resources tighten, firms find they must work harder to maintain their profits and market share.

B. Global Competition

Global competition is a growing facet of Canadian business. Not only do Canadian firms consider going international as a growth strategy, but also more and more foreign firms are entering Canada to do business.

1. In the past, foreign firms entered Canadian markets by emphasizing price, but today the accent is on quality.

2. Canadian companies often battle one another in global markets just as intensively as they battle in the domestic market.

9 Describe the role of ethics and ethical decisions in business

IX. Ethical Decision Making

A. Morality and Business Ethics

1. **Ethics** refers to moral principles or values that generally govern the conduct of an individual or a group.

2. **Morals** are rules or habits, typically stated as good or bad, that people develop as a result of cultural values and norms.

3. Business ethics are actually a subset of the values held by society as a whole. These values are acquired through family, and through educational and religious institutions.

4. Ethics can be very situation-specific and time-oriented.

5. There are three levels of morality:

   a. *Preconventional morality* is childlike in nature, calculating, self-centred, and selfish.
   b. *Conventional morality* is concerned with the expectations of society. Loyalty and obedience are paramount.
   a. *Postconventional morality* represents the morality of the mature adult. People at this level are concerned with how they see and judge themselves and their acts over the long run.

B. Ethical Decision Making

The following factors influence ethical decision making and judgments:

1. The extent of ethical problems within the organization

2. Top-management actions on ethics

3. Potential magnitude of the consequences

4. Social consensus within managerial peers

5. Probability of a harmful outcome

6. Length of time between the decision and the onset of consequences

7. Number of people to be affected

C. Ethical Guidelines

1. Many firms have developed a specific **code of ethics** to help employees make better decisions. The Canadian Marketing Association has such a code.

   An explicit code helps

   a. Identify acceptable business practices
   b. Internally control behaviour
   c. Reduce employee confusion in decision making
   d. Facilitate discussion about right and wrong in issues that may arise

2. Although many companies have issued policies on ethical behaviour, marketing managers must put them into effect. These managers must address the "matter of degree" issue in many situations.

10 Discuss corporate social responsibility

X. Corporate Social Responsibility

A. **Corporate social responsibility** is business's concern for society's welfare. Specifically, this concern is demonstrated by managers who consider the long-range best interests of the company and the company's relationship to the society within which it operates.

B. Despite arguments to the contrary, most large corporations feel that their social responsibility extends beyond simply earning profits.

   1. Today a firm must also develop environmental controls, provide equal employment opportunities, create a safe workplace, produce safe products, and do much more.

   2. Four types of social responsibility make up the **pyramid of corporate social responsibility**:

      a. Economic
      b. Legal
      c. Ethical
      d. Philanthropic

   3. Multinational companies also have important social responsibilities and in some cases can be a dynamic force for social change in host countries.

VOCABULARY PRACTICE

Fill in the blank(s) with the appropriate term or phrase from the alphabetized list of chapter key terms.

applied research
baby boomers
basic research
code of ethics
component lifestyle
Competition Act
Competition Bureau
corporate social responsibility
demography
environmental management
ethics

Generation X
Generation Y
inflation
morals
multiculturalism
personalized economy
poverty of time
pyramid of corporate social responsibility
recession
target market

1 Discuss the external environment of marketing and explain how it affects a firm

1. The marketing mix is designed by marketing managers to appeal to a specific group of potential buyers, known as the _____. This group is most likely to buy the firm's product.

2. When a team of specialists is created to collect and evaluate environmental information, the process is called environmental scanning. When a company decides to implement strategies that attempt to shape the external environment within which it operates, they are engaging in _____.

2 Describe the social factors that affect marketing

3. Dual career families who can do nothing but work, eat, and sleep suffer from _____.
In addition, many people choose goods and services to meet diverse needs and interests rather than conforming to a single way of life. This is known as piecing together a _____.

3 Explain the importance to marketing managers of current demographic trends

4. A university found that their students were on average twenty-eight years old, married, working, and sixty percent female. These statistics are part of the study of _____.

5. The group of people born between 1965 and 1978 are termed _____. The group of people born between 1946 and 1964, known as _____, value home life and convenience. This latter group insists that marketers deliver goods and services at a good value upon demand. This has created a _____. Consumers born between 1979 and 1994, which have grown up in an even more media-saturated, brand conscious world than their parents, are called _____.

4 Explain the importance to marketing managers of multiculturalism and growing ethnic markets

6. When all ethnic groups in an area are roughly equally represented, such as in a city, county, or census metropolitan area, _____ occurs. This has not occurred equally in Canada.

5 Identify consumer and marketer reactions to the state of the economy

7. A general rise in prices, called _____, results in decreased purchasing power for people whose income does not also rise. A period of economic activity when income, production, and employment all tend to fall is called a (n) _____ and is characterized by a reduction in demand.

6 Identify the impact of technology on a firm

8. Canada often engages in the type of research and development that attempts to expand the frontiers of knowledge. This is known as pure or _____, which does not emphasize commercial viability. In contrast, _____ attempts to specifically develop new or improved products.

7 Discuss the political and legal environment of marketing

9. Most of the consumer and business protection legislation in Canada (such as the Competition Act and the Food and Drug Act) is enforced by the _____ of Industry Canada. This federal department is charged with administering most marketplace laws.

9 Describe the role of ethics and ethical decisions in business

10. When moral principles or values generally govern the conduct of an individual or a group, this refers to _____. Rules or habits typically stated as good or bad are _____.

11. Many firms have developed an explicit set of guidelines to help employees make better decisions. This set of guidelines is a (n) _____.

10 Discuss corporate social responsibility

12. The concern of a business for the long-range best interests of the company and its relationships to the society within which it operates is termed _____.

13. One theory defines four kinds of social responsibilities: economic, legal, ethical, and philanthropic. This theory is known as the _____.

Check your answers to these questions before proceeding to the next section.

TRUE/FALSE QUESTIONS

Mark the statement **T** if it is true and **F** if it is false.

1 Discuss the external environment of marketing and explain how it affects a firm

_____ 1. A firm's target market is the group of consumers a marketer thinks will be most likely to buy the firm's product.

_____ 2. To be successful, marketers should control the elements in the external environment and the four P's of the marketing mix.

2 Describe the social factors that affect marketing

_____ 3. Most Canadians today define themselves primarily by profession – what they do for a living.

3 Explain the importance to marketing managers of current demographic trends

_____ 4. Demography is the study of people's vital statistics, such as age, income, and ethnic grouping.

_____ 5. The generation that followed the Baby Boomers is called Generation Y.

_____ 6. Baby Boomers are defined as the population that is married with children and have professional careers.

_____ 7. Today's youngest demographic group who are influenced by humour and irony are called Generation Y.

4 Explain the importance to marketing managers of multiculturalism and growing ethnic markets

_____ 8. Marketers have learned that it is important to treat the entire market as a mass market than to segment it into different ethnic groups.

5 Identify consumer and marketer reactions to the state of the economy

_____ 9. Inflation causes consumers to be less brand loyal.

8 Explain the basics of foreign and domestic competition

_____ 10. Marketing managers should be concerned with competition because most marketing firms exist in a purely competitive environment.

9 Describe the role of ethics and ethical decisions in business

_____ 11. The business ethics we see today shape the values held by society.

10 Discuss corporate social responsibility

_____ 12. PetroCanada contributes its resources to local communities to help preserve nature and wildlife. By being a good corporate citizen, PetroCanada is fulfilling its philanthropic responsibilities on the pyramid of corporate social responsibility.

Check your answers to these questions before proceeding to the next section.

AGREE/DISAGREE QUESTIONS

For the following statements, indicate reasons why you may agree and disagree with the statement.

1. There is really no difference in attitudes between Baby Boomers and Generation X; when Baby Boomers were younger, they had the same attitudes and opinions that Generation X-ers have today.

   Reason(s) to agree:

   Reason(s) to disagree:

2. Canada is a "multicultural" society.

   Reason(s) to agree:

   Reason(s) to disagree:

3. The most important environmental factors that affect marketing efforts are economic factors.

Reason(s) to agree:

Reason(s) to disagree:

Most corporations practice conventional morality; that is, they make ethical decisions only because it may translate into more profits in the long-term.

Reason(s) to agree:

Reason(s) to disagree:

MULTIPLE CHOICE QUESTIONS

Select the response that best answers the question, and write the corresponding letter in the space provided.

1 Discuss the external environment of marketing and explain how it affects a firm

_____ 1. Hilton Resorts, Inc., focuses much of its marketing effort on Baby Boomers who have large disposable incomes and young children. The company offers a large variety of services, including the traditional sporting and leisure services as well as creative child care services. Baby Boomers would be considered Resorts International's:
   a. market quiche
   b. environment
   c. target market
   d. market segmentation
   e. external environment

_____ 2. Beth Wheeler is the Director of Marketing Planning for Visionary Electronics Systems. She has been examining the social factors that may affect the way in which Visionary Electronics does business with consumers in the next decade. Which of the following social factors might affect the way her firm does business?
   a. The population is growing older
   b. The income levels will rise in the next decade
   c. More products will be made with high-tech ceramics
   d. Today's shoppers are environmentalists
   e. Fewer babies are being born

_____ 3. The manufacturer of New Wave Clothing has a marketing department that keeps track of current external environmental changes. Although some information is relatively easy to collect, analyzing and forecasting _____ trends is extremely difficult, yet these trends may be the most important factor for this company.
   a. social
   b. economic
   c. legislative
   d. technological
   e. demographic

_____ 4. The Dispozall Company produces disposable toiletries (razors, combs, curlers, and so on) designed for the busy person who wants simplicity, ease of use, and the convenience of disposable products. Which current environmental trend(s) may pose a major new threat to this company?
   a. social factors that are increasing are an interest in the environment and recycling
   b. technological factors that are automating production
   c. demographic factors that demonstrate a decrease in the birthrate
   d. many large competitors in the same industry
   e. product safety legislation currently under review by the Consumer Product Safety Commission

_____ 5. Scott is a helicopter pilot for the forestry service. He is also a computer programmer, stock portfolio manager, and breeder of pedigreed sable ferrets. His other interests include reading, woodworking, and jazz. Marketers would describe Scott's needs for goods and services as:
   a. fitting into a well-educated segment
   b. a component lifestyle
   c. inappropriate in all segments
   d. the typical pilot target segment
   e. a conforming lifestyle

3 Explain the importance to marketing managers of current demographic trends

_____ 6. This demographic target market was "born to shop." Entire industries, such as children's software, children's versions of adult clothing (such as Baby Gap), and creative educational products have spawned to target this group of people. The target market described above is:
   a. Generation X
   b. Generation Y
   c. grandparents
   d. Baby Boomers
   e. Generation A

_____ 7. You will be marketing to "Generation X" and know that all of the following facts about this group will affect your marketing plan EXCEPT:
   a. this group is non-materialistic
   b. Generation X-ers spend lots of money on eating out and electronic items
   c. this group is the first generation of latchkey children because of dual career households
   d. Generation X-ers are the most likely group to be underemployed
   e. members of Generation X do not mind indulging themselves with movies, clothing, and alcoholic beverages

_____ 8. The number one trait that parents of baby boomers wanted to drive into their children was:
   a. optimism
   b. "me first"
   c. conformity
   d. to think for themselves
   e. materialism

4 Explain the importance to marketing managers of multiculturalism and growing ethnic markets

_____ 9. Which of the following statements about multiculturalism in Canada is false?
   a.   About 3 in 10 Canadians are not of French or British descent.
   b.   The largest degree of multiculturalism is found in the large census metropolitan areas.
   c.   About 13% of Canadians are "visible minorities".
   d.   The trend is towards greater multiculturalism.
   e.   About 5 in 10 Canadians are not of French or British descent..

5 Identify consumer and marketer reactions to the state of the economy

_____ 10. Jorge is a marketing manager faced with planning marketing strategies during times of inflation. He should be aware that inflation causes consumers to:
   a.   purchase counselling and stress management training services
   b.   decrease their brand loyalty to products they have traditionally used
   c.   buy in small quantities until inflation is over
   d.   consume more meals away from home
   e.   put more money into savings accounts because prices are too high

_____ 11. Harold, the owner of a luxury car dealership, is very worried because sales of his luxury cars have declined dramatically. He has read that unemployment is up, that consumer spending is down, and consumer income is also down. Which of the following best describes the current economy?
   a.   recession
   b.   inflation
   c.   stagnation
   d.   price escalation
   e.   depression

6 Identify the impact of technology on a firm

_____ 12. Your company has just allotted $25 million to research and development, with a goal of solving the specific problem of removing fats from meat products while keeping taste. This way, "fat-free" burgers can be marketed in fast-food restaurants. Your company is engaging in:
   a.   basic research
   b.   product introduction
   c.   pure research
   d.   fundamental development
   e.   applied research

7 Discuss the political and legal environment of marketing

_____ 13. Ms. Ashley Timber is Vice President of Marketing for Grand Appliances, Inc. She wants her firm to develop newer and better consumer appliances, but knows they must conform to existing legislation. Which of the following agencies would most likely provide information that would affect how her firm develops new appliances?
   a.   Better Business Bureau
   b.   Food and Drug Act
   c.   Competition Bureau of Industry Canada
   d.   Department of Commerce
   e.   Consumer Product Safety Act

8 Explain the basics of foreign and domestic competition

____ 14. Danny finds that his start-up company, a distributor of cordless telephones, has been seriously affected by the number of competitors in this area. In particular, one area of his marketing mix, _____, is dependent upon the competition.
   a. product
   b. price
   c. promotion
   d. distribution
   e. production

9 Describe the role of ethics and ethical decisions in business

____ 15. Brad's Butcher Shop sells meat that has not been inspected by FDA inspectors. This meat could possibly carry harmful diseases. However, Brad's can buy the meat extremely cheaply from an out-of-province wholesaler, and the meat will help bring in a larger profit. Brad's Butcher Shop is operating at a level of:
   a. conventional immorality
   b. pre-conventional morality
   c. social responsibility
   d. unconventional morality
   e. post-conventional morality

____ 16. A local beer distributor is concerned with whether it is ethical to run an ad in the local college newspaper. Community attitudes toward alcohol are changing, and it may not be acceptable to advertise to young people. What level of morality is the beer distributor adopting?
   a. unconventional morality
   b. conventional morality
   c. social responsibility
   d. pre-conventional morality
   e. post-conventional morality

____ 17. The pesticides company that questions the long-term effects of its products on the environment is operating at what level of morality?
   a. unconventional
   b. pre-conventional
   c. post-conventional
   d. conventional
   e. disconventional

10 Discuss corporate social responsibility

____ 18. Lighthouse Industries has a policy of hiring blind people whenever possible. Not only is this good business, it is also:
   a. mandated by legislation
   b. environmental marketing
   c. a moral obligation
   d. an ethical job orientation
   e. socially responsible

____ 19. Like most other large corporations, the Bizby Corporation feels that its social responsibility:
   a. is the province of marketing managers
   b. may encourage more government regulation
   c. is secondary to earning
   d. is inversely proportional to profits
   e. extends beyond simply earning profits

20. The pyramid of corporate social responsibility assumes that _____ responsibility is the foundation, without which the other responsibilities could not exist.
   a. economic
   b. ethical
   c. moral
   d. philanthropic
   e. legal

Check your answers to these questions before proceeding to the next section.

SCENARIO

After reading the marketing scenario, answer the questions that follow.

With the success of Disneyland Tokyo and the learning garnered from Disneyland Paris, Disney has decided to open a new amusement park in Hong Kong. The park is scheduled to open in 2005.

As with many large ventures, Disneyland faces an interesting external environment. Unlike in free-market countries, Disney must share ownership with Hong Kong's government (a special administrative region of China). The agreement allows the joint venture to share equity shares to private investors, but the owners have not yet sought out these investors. The park is expected to draw its attendance from three core markets: Hong Kong residents (one-third), mainland China resident (one-third), and other Southeast Asian nations (one-third). Though the Chinese government has a history of restricting its residents from going to Hong Kong, it has more recently allowed the flow of mainland residents into Hong Kong, which should have a major impact on the park's success. Currently, Hong Kong's Ocean Park – a small-scale amusement park that is located in a highly developing area of Hong Kong – is expected to benefit from Disneyland.

(Adapted from "Disney Tradition to Carry On at Hong Kong Park," by Natasha Emmons, *Amusement Business*, January 22, 2001.)

True/False:

1. The requirement for Disneyland Hong Kong to be a joint venture is an example of the economic environment.

2. Ocean Park will be a competitor to Disneyland Hong Kong.

3. As described above, Disney's target market is based on demographics.

Multiple Choice:

4. Which of the following external environments is *not* reflected in the above scenario?
   a. Political and legal factors.
   b. Social factors.
   c. Economic factors.
   d. Competition.
   e. Technological factors.

5. Allowing mainland Chinese residents to enter Hong Kong is an example of which of the following external environments?
   a. Political and legal factors.
   b. Social factors.
   c. Economic factors.
   d. Competition.
   e. Technological factors.

_____ 6. The existence of Ocean Park is an example of which of the following external environments?
   a. Political and legal factors.
   b. Social factors.
   c. Economic factors.
   d. Competition.
   e. Technological factors.

_____ 7. The pool of private investors available to buy equity shares in Disneyland Hong Kong, should they be offered, is an example of which of the following external environments?
   a. Political and legal factors.
   b. Social factors.
   c. Economic factors.
   d. Competition.
   e. Technological factors.

Short Answer:

8. List the other external environmental factors that were not mentioned in the scenario and give some example of how these factors could impact Disneyland Hong Kong.

ESSAY QUESTIONS

1. List the six elements of the external environment and provide an example of each element that would affect most businesses.

2. List three demographic trends apparent in Canada in the 21st century. For each trend, describe one way that the trend affects marketing.

3. Ethical development can be thought of as having three levels of morality. Name and briefly define the three levels. Assume that you are a salesperson for Bolt, a highly addictive beverage that, if consumed regularly, can cause death in children, brain damage in teenagers, and mere disorientation for adults. The product sells well and is extremely profitable. Taking on the role of this salesperson, describe the types of thoughts that might occur at each level of morality.

4. The Internet is dramatically changing how and where companies do business. Outline ways companies are using the Internet to boost productivity.

5. What is the pyramid of corporate social responsibility? What are the different levels that should be achieved?

While marketing managers can control the marketing mix, they cannot control the elements in the external environment that continually mold and reshape the target market. Assume you are a movie studio that wants to create a live-action movie for children ages seven to fourteen. Name six elements of the external environment, and briefly describe how each factor might affect the marketing of your movie.

CHAPTER 4: CONSUMER DECISION MAKING

1 Explain why marketing managers should understand consumer behaviour

An understanding of consumer behaviour is essential to marketers who endeavour to satisfy the needs and wants of their customers and wants to communicate effectively with them. Understanding consumer behaviour reduces uncertainty when creating the marketing mix.

2 Analyze the components of the consumer decision-making process

The consumer decision-making process begins with a stimulus that triggers problem recognition, revealing an unmet need or want. The next step is to determine whether additional information is needed to make the decision. Next, the alternatives are evaluated, and purchase decision rules are established. A purchase decision is then made. Postpurchase evaluation, including the important concept of cognitive dissonance, is based on the evaluation of the outcomes.

3 Explain the consumer's postpurchase evaluation process

Postpurchase evaluation weighs a consumer's satisfaction with the purchase. The outcome of a purchase may be positive, negative, or neutral. Cognitive dissonance, which is an internal tension that the consumer experiences due to doubts about the decision, is an extremely important concept to marketers who try to provide customer satisfaction.

4 Identify the types of consumer buying decisions and discuss the significance of consumer involvement

Consumers face three basic categories of decision making: (1) routine response behaviour, used for frequently-purchased, low-cost items that require very little decision effort; (2) limited decision making, used for products that are purchased occasionally; and (3) extensive decision making, used for products that are unfamiliar and expensive or infrequently bought.

The levels of consumer involvement in the purchase task signify the economic and social importance of the purchase to the consumer. Depending on the level of consumer involvement, the extensiveness of the purchase process will vary greatly.

5 Identify and understand the cultural factors that affect consumer buying decisions

The underlying elements of every culture are the values, language, myths, customs, rituals, and laws that shape the behaviour of the cultures, as well as the artifacts, or products, of that behaviour as they are transmitted from one generation to the next. Culture is pervasive, encompassing all the things consumers do without conscious choice. It is functional, giving order to society. It is learned from parents, teachers, and peers. It is dynamic, adapting to changing needs.

6 Identify and understand the social factors that affect consumer buying decisions

Social factors include family, reference groups, opinion leaders, social class, life cycle, culture, and subculture. Consumers may use products or brands to identify with or become a member of a reference group. Opinion leaders are members of reference groups who influence others' purchase decisions. Family members also influence purchase decisions; children tend to shop in patterns like their parents'. Marketers often define their target markets in terms of consumers' life cycle stage, social class, culture, and subculture; consumers with similar characteristics generally have similar consumption patterns.

7 Identify and understand the individual factors that affect consumer buying decisions

Personal/individual factors include gender, age, and family life cycle stage, personality, self-concept, and lifestyles.

8 Identify and understand the psychological factors that affect consumer buying decisions

An individual's buying decisions are further influenced by psychological factors: perceptions, motivation, learning, and beliefs and attitudes. These factors are what consumers use to interact with their world.

PRE-TEST

Answer the following questions to see how well you understand the material. Re-take it after you review to check yourself.

1. List and briefly describe the five steps of the consumer decision-making process.

2. List five factors influence the involvement with which a consumer has in the decision-making process.

---

3. List and briefly describe three cultural factors that influence consumer decision-making.

4. List and briefly describe three social factors that influence consumer decision-making.

5. List and briefly describe three individual factors that influence consumer decision-making.

6. List and briefly describe four psychological factors that influence consumer decision-making.

1 Explain why marketing managers should understand consumer behaviour

I. The Importance of Understanding Consumer Behaviour

Consumer behaviour describes the manner in which consumers make purchase decisions, and how they use and dispose of the purchased goods or services.

2 Analyze the components of the consumer decision-making process

II. The Consumer Decision-Making Process

The **consumer decision-making process** is a step-by-step method used by consumers when buying goods or services.

A. **Need recognition** occurs when consumers are faced with an imbalance between actual and desired states.

   1. A **stimulus** is any unit of input affecting the five senses. Stimuli can be either internal or external.

      a. *Internal stimuli* are a person's normal needs.
      b. *External stimuli* stem from sources outside one's self.

   2. A **want** exists when someone has an unfulfilled need and has determined which product will satisfy it.

   3. Consumers recognize unfulfilled wants in a number of ways. Recognition occurs when the consumer:

      a. Has a current product that isn't performing properly
      b. Is about to run out of a product that is generally kept on hand
      c. Sees a product that appears to be superior to the one currently being used

B. Information search can occur internally, externally, or both.

   1. **Internal information search** is the process of recalling information stored in the memory.

   2. **External information search** seeks information in the outside environment.

      a. **Nonmarketing-controlled information sources**, such as personal experience, personal sources such as friends, and public sources (Canadian Standards Association, Consumer Reports), are product information sources that are not associated with advertising or promotion.
      b. **Marketing-controlled information sources**, such as mass media advertising, sales promotion, salespeople, and product labels and packaging, are biased toward a specific product because they originate with marketers promoting the product.

   3. The factors influencing an external search are the consumer's perceived risk, knowledge, prior experience, and interest level in the good or service.

   4. The search yields an **evoked set** (also called a consideration set), a group of brands resulting from the information search from which a buyer can choose.

C.   Evaluation of Alternatives and Purchase

Evaluation involves the development of a set of criteria. These standards help the consumer evaluate and compare alternatives.

1.   Consumers often set minimum or maximum levels of an attribute (cut-offs) that determine whether a product will be considered as a viable choice.

2.   Adding new brands to an evoked set affects the consumer's evaluation of the existing brands in that set.

3   Explain the consumer's postpurchase evaluation process

III.   Postpurchase Behaviour

A.   When buying products, consumers expect certain outcomes from the purchase. How well these expectations are met determines whether the consumer is satisfied or dissatisfied with the purchase.

B.   **Cognitive dissonance** is a state of inner tension felt when consumers are aware of a lack of consistency between their values or opinions and their behaviour. Consumers can reduce cognitive dissonance by:

1.   Finding new information that reinforces positive ideas about the purchase

2.   Avoiding information that contradicts their decision

3.   Revoking the original decision by returning the product

4   Identify the types of consumer buying decisions and discuss the significance of consumer involvement

IV.   Types of Consumer Decision Behaviour and Consumer Involvement

A.   **Involvement** refers to the amount of time and effort a buyer invests in the search, evaluation, and decision processes of consumer behaviour.

B.   **Routine response behaviour** is used for frequently purchased, low-cost goods and services that require very little decision effort. These can also be called low-involvement products.

C.   **Limited decision-making** typically occurs when a consumer has previous product experience, but is unfamiliar with the current brands available. It is also associated with lower levels of involvement.

D.   **Extensive decision-making** is used for an unfamiliar, expensive, or infrequently bought item. It is the most complex type of consumer buying decision and is associated with high involvement on the part of the consumer.

E.   Factors Determining the Level of Consumer Involvement

Five factors affect involvement level:

1.   Previous experience: Previous experience tends to lead to low involvement.

2.   Interest: A high level of interest in a product leads to high-involvement decision-making.

---

3. Perceived risk of negative consequences: The higher the perceived risk of making the decision, the more involved the consumer will be.

4. Situation: The circumstances of the situation may change a low-involvement situation into a high-involvement situation because of increased risks.

5. Social visibility: Involvement increases as the social visibility of the product increases.

F. Involvement Implications for the Marketing Manager

1. Marketing managers must offer extensive and informative promotion for high-involvement products.

2. In-store promotion is important for low-involvement products.

3. Linking a low-involvement product to a higher-involvement issue is another tactic that can increase sales.

5 Identify and understand the cultural factors that affect consumer buying decisions

V. Cultural Influences on Consumer Buying Decisions

Cultural factors exert the broadest and deepest influence over a person's consumer behaviour and decision-making.

A. Culture and Values

1. **Culture** is the essential character of a society that distinguishes it from other cultural groups.

2. Elements of culture are values, language, myths, customs, rituals, and laws as well as artifacts or products.

3. Culture is pervasive, functional, learned, and dynamic.

4. **Values** are the enduring beliefs shared by a society that a specific mode of conduct is personally or socially preferable to another mode of conduct. Values represent what is most important in people's lives.

5. The personal values of consumers have important implications for marketers as they seek to target their message more effectively.

B. Understanding Culture Differences

1. Underlying core values can vary.

2. Products have cultural values and rules that influence their perception and use. Elements such as the meaning of colours and language can affect the perceptions of a product.

C. A **subculture** is a homogeneous group of people who share elements of the overall culture as well as cultural elements unique to their own group.

1. Aside from French Canadian being the dominant subculture, there are estimated to be more than 80 other ethnic groups in Canada (Chinese, Blacks, South Asians, Arabs and West Asians, Filipinos, Latin Americans and Southeast Asians).

2. More than 75% of ethnic Canadians live in the four major metropolitan areas (Toronto, Vancouver, Montreal, and Calgary/Edmonton.

D. A **social class** is a group of people who

1. Are nearly equal in status or community esteem

2. Regularly socialize among themselves

3. Share behavioural norms

E. Social class is typically measured as a combination of occupation, income, education, wealth, and other variables.

6 Identify and understand the social factors that affect consumer buying decisions

VI. Social Influences on Consumer Buying Decisions

Social factors include all effects on buyer behaviour that result from interactions between a consumer and the external environment.

A. Reference Groups

Reference groups are all of the formal and informal groups in society that influence an individual's purchasing behaviour.

1. Reference groups are an important concept to marketers because consumers may use products to establish identity with a group or to gain membership into it. Reference groups are also an information source for consumption behaviour.

2. Direct membership groups are face-to-face membership groups that touch people's live s directly.

   a. **Primary membership groups** are reference groups with which people interact regularly in an informal, face-to-face manner, such as family, friends, and co-workers.
   b. **Secondary membership groups** are reference groups with which people associate less consistently and more formally, such as clubs, professional groups, and religious groups.

3. Indirect membership groups are groups of which one is not a member.

   a. **Aspirational group** are groups one would like join. To gain membership one must conform to group **norms** (the attitudes and values deemed acceptable by the group).
   b. **Nonaspirational reference groups** (dissociative groups) are groups with which an individual does not want to associate or be identified.

4. An **opinion leader** is an individual who influences the opinion of others.

   a. An opinion leader may not be influential across product categories.
   b. The product endorsement of an opinion leader is most likely to succeed if an association between the spokesperson and the product can be established.

   Opinion leaders are often the first to try new products and services.

B. The Family

The family is the most important social institution for many consumers; it strongly influences our values, attitudes, self-concept, and socialization process (the passing down of cultural values and norms to children).

Not all family decisions are jointly made. Some decision roles are specific to a product or user. Trends in the Canadian family are having a strong influence on decision-making roles.

1. Purchase and information roles within the family:

    a. Instigators: suggest, initiate, or plant the seed for the purchase process
    b. Influencers: provide valued opinions
    c. Decision makers: makes the decision to buy or not to buy
    d. Purchasers: exchange money for the product
    e. Consumers: the actual users

Children today have a great influence over the purchase decisions of their parents.

7 Identify and understand the individual factors that affect consumer buying decisions

VII.   Individual Influences on Consumer Buying Decisions

A person's buying decisions are also influenced by personal characteristics that are unique to each individual.

A. Gender

B. Age and Family Life Cycle Stage

1. Consumer tastes in food, clothing, cars, furniture and recreation are often age related.

2. The *family life cycle* defines an orderly series of stages through which consumer's attitudes and behavioural tendencies evolve. The family life cycle is often used as an indicator of consumer purchase priorities.

C. Personality, Self-Concept, and Lifestyle

1. **Personality** is a way of organizing and grouping the consistencies of an individual's reactions to situations.

2. Personality includes a person's underlying dispositions, their most dominant characteristics.

3. **Self-concept** is how a consumer perceives himself or herself in terms of attitudes, perceptions, beliefs, and self-evaluations. Self-concept provides for consistent and coherent behaviour.

    a. The **ideal self-image** is the way an individual would like to be.
    b. The **real self-image** is the way an individual actually perceives himself or herself.
    c. Another important component of self-concept is *body image*, the perception of one's own physical features.

4. **Lifestyle** is a person's mode of living as identified by activities, interests, and opinions.

    a. *Psychographics* is the analytic technique used to examine consumer lifestyles and to categorize consumers.

8 Identify and understand the psychological factors that affect consumer buying decisions

VIII. Psychological Influences on Consumer Buying Decisions

A. Perception

Perception is the process by which people select, organize, and interpret stimuli to create a meaningful and coherent picture. Perception is how we recognize that we have a consumption problem.

1. **Selective exposure** is the process whereby a consumer notices certain stimuli (such as advertisements) and ignores other stimuli.

2. **Selective distortion** is the process whereby a consumer changes or distorts information that conflicts with his or her feelings or beliefs

3. **Selective retention** is the process whereby a consumer remembers only the information that supports his or her personal feelings or beliefs.

B. Motivation

1. **Motives** are the driving forces that cause a person to take action to satisfy specific needs.

2. **Maslow's hierarchy of needs** is a method of classifying human needs and motivations into five categories (in ascending order of importance):

   a. *Physiological needs*: food, water, shelter
   b. *Safety needs*: security, freedom from pain and discomfort
   c. *Social needs*: love, sense of belonging
   d. *Self-esteem needs*: self-respect, accomplishment, prestige, fame, recognition of one's accomplishments
   e. *Self-actualization*: self-fulfillment, self-expression

C. Learning

Learning is the process that creates changes in behaviour, immediate or expected, through experience and practice.

1. *Experiential learning* is learning by doing.
2. *Conceptual learning* is learning by applying previously learned concepts to a new situation.
3. Reinforcement and repetition boost learning.
4. **Stimulus generalization** occurs when one response is extended to a second stimulus similar to the first.
5. **Stimulus discrimination** is the learned ability to differentiate among stimuli.
6. *Product differentiation* is a marketing tactic designed to distinguish one product from another.

D. Beliefs and Attitudes

1. Beliefs

   a. **Beliefs** are organized patterns of knowledge that individuals hold as true about their world.
   b. Consumers tend to develop a set of beliefs about a product's attributes and through these beliefs, form a *brand image*, a set of beliefs about a particular brand.

---

2. Attitude

    An **attitude** is a learned tendency to respond consistently toward a given object. Beliefs help form the basis for attitudes, as do values.

    Often the marketer's goal is to change attitudes toward a brand. This goal might be accomplished in three ways:

    a. Changing beliefs about the brand's attributes
    b. Changing the relative importance of these beliefs
    c. Adding new beliefs

VOCABULARY PRACTICE

Fill in the blank(s) with the appropriate term or phrase from the alphabetized list of chapter key terms.

aspirational reference group	nonmarketing-controlled information source
attitude	norm
belief	opinion leader
cognitive dissonance	perception
consumer behaviour	personality
consumer decision-making process	primary membership group
culture	real self-image
evoked set	reference group
extensive decision making	routine response behaviour
external information search	secondary membership group
ideal self-image	selective distortion
internal information search	selective exposure
involvement	selective retention
learning	self-concept
lifestyle	social class
limited decision making	socialization process
marketing-controlled information source	stimulus
Maslow's hierarchy of needs	stimulus discrimination
motive	stimulus generalization
need recognition	subculture
nonaspirational reference group	value
	want

1 Explain why marketing managers should understand consumer behaviour

1. Marketers study the processes final consumers use to make purchase decisions, as well as the use and disposal of their product or service. This is known as the study of _____, which also includes the analysis of factors that influence purchase decisions and product usage.

2 Analyze the components of the consumer decision-making process

2. When buying products, consumers follow a series of steps called the _____. The first step in the process is when the consumer is faced with an imbalance between actual and desired states. A unit of input that affects any of the five senses is known as a(n) _____ and starts these conditions under which the consumer experiences _____.

3. A marketing manager cannot create a need, but tries to create a(n) _____ during the problem recognition stage.

4. A consumer can explore alternative sources of information during the information search stage. This information search should ultimately yield a group of brands called the buyer's _____, or consideration set. When a person tries to recall past information stored in his or her memory, the person is conducting a(n) _____. Alternatively, when a person consults a friend or an advertisement, a(n) _____ is being used. Getting information from an advertisement would be considered using a(n)_____, while getting the information from a friend would be using a(n) _____.

3 Explain the consumer's postpurchase evaluation process

5. After buying a product, a consumer may start to feel an inner tension due to an inconsistency among values, opinions, and behaviour. This phenomenon is known as _____.

4 Identify the types of consumer buying decisions and discuss the significance of consumer involvement

6. The amount of time and effort a consumer gives to the search, evaluation, and decision process is known as _____.

7. Consumers have different levels of decision-making. When buying things like soft drinks, milk or gum, the consumer generally uses _____. When a consumer seeks out information about an unfamiliar brand in a familiar product category, the consumer is using _____. Finally, when the consumer is buying an unfamiliar, expensive product, or an infrequently bought item, _____ is used.

5 Identify and understand the cultural factors that affect consumer buying decisions

8. The set of values, norms, and attitudes that shape human behaviour is called _____. This can be divided into smaller sets on the basis of unique elements. This smaller set is _____.

6 Identify and understand the social factors that affect consumer buying decisions

9. A group in society that influences the purchasing behaviour of an individual is a(n) _____. Direct groups can have two forms: The group of people with whom we interact in a regular, informal, and face-to-face manner is the _____. The group of people we interact with on a less consistent and more formal basis is the _____. Groups that one would like to be a member of is a(n) _____, while a group that one would like to avoid is a(n) _____. A value or attitude deemed acceptable by a group is a(n) _____. Individuals who influence or convince others, are called a(n) _____. Marketers are very interested in having these individuals buy their products and services.

10. The process by which families influence consumers by passing down cultural values and norms to each generation is known as _____.

11. A group of people who are considered nearly equal in community esteem and share behavioural norms is called a(n) _____.

7 Identify and understand the individual factors that affect consumer buying decision

12. A broad concept that can be thought of as a way of organizing and grouping the consistencies of an individual's reactions to situations is called _____. An individual's attitudes, perceptions, beliefs, and evaluations about himself or herself as a person make up that individual's _____, which is actually a combination of two facets. The way a person would like to be is their _____, while how a person actually perceives himself or herself is their _____.

13. A person's mode of living as identified by activities, interests, and opinions is called a(n) _____. The analysis technique used to measure this is called psychographics.

8 Identify and understand the psychological factors that affect consumer buying decisions

14. The process by which we select, organize, and interpret stimuli is called _____. Consumers decide which stimuli to notice or ignore. This is known as _____. Two concepts are related to this phenomenon. First, when consumers change information that is in conflict with their feelings or beliefs, _____ takes place. Second, when a consumer remembers only that information that supports personal feelings or beliefs, _____ happens.

15. A driving force that causes a person to take action to satisfy specific needs is a(n)
_____. These forces are described as physiological, safety, social, esteem, and
self-actualization needs in _____. The process that creates changes in
behaviour through experience and practice is known as _____. A key strategy
used in promotion to increase the amount of this process is repetition. A related concept is when one response is
extended to a second similar stimulus, known as _____. Alternatively, some
marketers strive for differentiation between stimuli, known as _____.

16. An enduring belief that a specific mode of conduct is personally or socially preferable to an alternative mode of
conduct is a(n) _____. An organized pattern of knowledge that an individual
holds to be true about the world is a(n) _____. A learned tendency to respond in a
consistently favourable or unfavourable manner toward an object is a(n) _____.

Check your answers to these questions before proceeding to the next section.

TRUE/FALSE QUESTIONS

Mark the statement **T** if it is true and **F** if it is false.

2 Analyze the components of the consumer decision-making process

_____ 1. Amanda's computer is five years old, and she is becoming annoyed by how slowly it operates. This
scenario is an example of need recognition.

_____ 2. After searching for information on TVs, Hugh is about to choose one of the following brands: Sony,
Toshiba, or Mitsubishi. This group of TV brands makes up Hugh evoked set.

4 Identify the types of consumer buying decisions and discuss the significance of consumer involvement

_____ 3. In routine response behaviour, consumers take considerable time and effort evaluating
information and choices.

_____ 4. Ken is familiar with digital cameras and photography accessories. While shopping for a new camera
bag, Ken came across a brand he had never heard of or seen before. Acquiring information about this
unfamiliar brand could be called extensive decision making on Ken's part.

_____ 5. Sandra perceives the purchase of blue jeans to be a socially risky decision because she thinks
people will judge her by the jeans she wears. Violetta, however, does not perceive jeans as a
particularly risky behaviour. As a result, buying jeans will be a high involvement activity for
Sandra, but not for Violetta.

5 Identify and understand the cultural factors that affect consumer buying decisions

_____ 6. The entire Canada would be an example of a global subculture.

_____ 7. Canada, like most other countries, has a social class structure with clear delineations of whom
fits into upper, middle, and lower classes.

6 Identify and understand the social factors that affect consumer buying decisions

_____ 8. Cindy follows all the latest fashion trends at her Beverly Hills high school. Her friends greatly influence the ways she dresses. Cindy's friends are an example of her primary membership group.

8 Identify and understand the psychological factors that affect consumer buying decisions

_____ 9. Adaptability, aggressiveness, and affordability are all personality traits.

_____ 10. Jon Austin is a staunch Liberal. He was just given a pamphlet about the positive aspects of the Progressive party. Jon reads this pamphlet and then throws it away. By the next day, he has forgotten the points made in the pamphlet. This is an example of selective distortion.

_____ 11. Maslow's hierarchy of needs categorizes human needs into five levels: physiological needs, safety needs, social needs, esteem needs, and self actualization needs.

_____ 12. Values, beliefs, and attitudes are closely interrelated concepts, although beliefs are often about entire brands, while attitudes are often concerned with specific attributes.

Check your answers to these questions before proceeding to the next section.

AGREE/DISAGREE QUESTIONS

For the following statements, indicate reasons why you may agree and disagree with the statement.

1. No matter how important or trivial the decision, consumers go through all five steps of the consumer decision-making process.

   Reason(s) to agree:

   Reason(s) to disagree:

2. The same basic cultural values cut across all social classes.

   Reason(s) to agree:

   Reason(s) to disagree:

3. Most firms use aspirational reference group association to get consumers to buy their products.

Reason(s) to agree:

Reason(s) to disagree:

4. Perception is reality. The way a consumer perceives something is more important than what is the truth.

Reason(s) to agree:

Reason(s) to disagree:

MULTIPLE CHOICE QUESTIONS

Select the response that best answers the question, and write the corresponding letter in the space provided.

2 Analyze the components of the consumer decision-making process

_____ 1. Brenda watches a TV commercial that promotes a new fat-free line of snack products and decides that she will buy a few the next time she goes to the grocery store. The TV commercial is a(n):
   a. problem recognition
   b. internal stimulus
   c. external stimulus
   d. subliminal manipulation
   e. cognitive dissonance

_____ 2. Dan is a prestige oriented shopper and will only buy and wear clothing that has a little embroidered polo pony. This illustrates the:
   a. physiological drive
   b. satisfaction of a need
   c. satisfaction of a belief
   d. satisfaction of a want
   e. need motivator

_____ 3. David is trying to decide what kind of new car he is going to buy. He relies on *Consumer Reports*, other car magazines, and the advice of car mechanics. David is using:
   a. marketing controlled information sources
   b. nonmarketing controlled information sources
   c. demographic information sources
   d. secondary data sources
   e. internal search sources

3 Explain the consumer's postpurchase evaluation process

_____ 4. If you were attempting to reduce postpurchase anxiety for your brand of large home appliances, which of the following methods might you attempt to use?
   a. send letters to your customers thanking them for their purchase
   b. produce products that emphasize the attributes customers want from larger appliances
   c. provide warranties to assure customers of the appliances' reliability
   d. conduct follow-up phone calls from the appliance manufacturer assuring customers that if they are not completely satisfied, the manufacturer will do what is necessary to make the customer happy
   e. all of these techniques could be employed to reduce cognitive dissonance

4 Identify the types of consumer buying decisions and discuss the significance of consumer involvement

_____ 5. When Steve goes to the grocery store every other week, he buys the same brands of coffee, milk, cereal, and dog food. This type of buying behaviour is called:
   a. routine response behaviour
   b. extensive decision making
   c. motivational response
   d. limited decision making
   e. situation convenience

_____ 6. When Jill went to purchase nail polish to wear at her wedding, she went to four stores, spent three hours, and looked at over two hundred colour shades before selecting the perfect one. This nail polish (which cost $1.25) is properly designated a high involvement product because of:
   a. brand loyalty
   b. trial investment
   c. financial risk
   d. cognitive dissonance
   e. situational factors

_____ 7. You are the brand manager of a new candy bar. Marketing research shows that consumers do not usually make planned purchases for candy bars and buy on impulse instead. Given the research, which of the following strategies would be most appropriate?
   a. Run numerous TV commercials to "pull" consumers into the grocery stores.
   b. Price the candy very low to encourage children to buy the product.
   c. Determine the important choice criteria the customer uses to shop for candy purchases and then appeal to those criteria when the consumer undertakes alternative evaluation.
   d. Place the candy bars at the point-of-purchase within good view of shoppers.
   e. Match the lifestyles of the target market to the messages used in the advertising.

5 Identify and understand the cultural factors that affect consumer buying decisions

_____ 8. A homogeneous group of people who share elements of the overall culture as well as unique elements of their own group is called a(n):
   a. culture.
   b. society.
   c. social class.
   d. Generation X.
   e. subculture.

_____ 9. Joe has a masters in electrical engineering degree from an Ivy League university and works as a hardware specialist in Silicon Valley. Joe is most likely a part of the:
   a. capitalist class
   b. upper middle class
   c. middle class
   d. working class
   e. working poor

6 Identify and understand the social factors that affect consumer buying decisions

_____ 10. Erika competes on the college swim team and is working hard to qualify for her first college conference competition. She subscribes to all the swimming magazines and reads them as soon as they arrive each month. Past Olympic champion swimmers and divers are often used in the advertisements in the magazines. The ads are quite effective because these champions are a(n) _____ group for Erika.
   a. secondary reference
   b. primary reference
   c. direct reference
   d. dissociative
   e. aspirational

_____ 11. Donna feels that the only type of consumer who would wear a fur coat is wasteful and materialistic, and she would never consider owning one herself. The people who typically buy fur coats are in Donna's _____ group for that type of purchase.
   a. out reference
   b. nonaspirational reference
   c. ex membership
   d. integrated
   e. low aspiration

_____ 12. Reference group influence would be weakest for determining which brand of _____ to buy.
   a. car
   b. clothing
   c. frozen corn
   d. beer
   e. cigarettes

_____ 13. Ethan tends to buy the same brands of mouthwash and toilet paper as his _____, which is often the strongest source of group influence upon the individual for many product purchases.
   a. family
   b. social class
   c. psychographic group
   d. subculture
   e. dissociative group

_____ 14. A baby food manufacturer has spent a large amount of money on packaging, advertising, and store displays. After a successful introduction with sales higher than expected, sales suddenly dropped off dramatically. Subsequent research revealed that many babies refused to eat it. The baby food manufacturer forgot that babies also play an important role in the family decision process as a(n):
   a. instigator
   b. consumer
   c. decision maker
   d. purchaser
   e. selector

7 Identify and understand the individual factors that affect consumer buying decision

_____ 15. Jill, a new junior executive, feels that she is a trendy, upwardly mobile professional woman and wants to project an impression of competence and independence. She carefully shops for suits like the kind worn by the two women vice presidents at her firm. Jill admires the vice presidents and strives to be like them. She is dressing to fit her:

   a. status seeking image
   b. social compliant orientation
   c. real self image
   d. ideal self image
   e. personality

_____ 16. John's purchase behaviour is influenced by his hobbies of antique firearms, working out, and computers; his interest in scuba diving, music, and swimming; and his deeply held political and cause related opinions. All of these things are part of the personal influence factor called:

   a. lifestyle
   b. personality
   c. beliefs
   d. attitude
   e. values

8 Identify and understand the psychological factors that affect consumer buying decisions

_____ 17. Julie, an accounting major, read an article that states that accounting majors receive the highest starting salary offers for business majors. The article also states that marketing majors start with lower salaries but surpass all other majors' salaries within ten years. Julie doesn't remember reading this last part of the article, just the first part. This is an example of:

   a. selective distortion
   b. selective exposure
   c. selective retention
   d. perception retention
   e reinforcement

_____ 18. Universal Alarm Systems uses advertisements that depict a young mother with her baby at home alone at night. A prowler has been stalking the house, but he suddenly leaves when he notices the presence of the alarm system. These advertisements are designed to appeal to the consumers':

   a. self esteem needs
   b. safety needs
   c. economic needs
   d. physiological needs
   e. social needs

_____ 19. When Lever Brothers introduced the new Lever 2000 body soap, they gave away over one million bars of soap for consumers to try in order encourage:

   a. selective perception
   b. learning
   c. consumer needs
   d. psychographics
   e. problem recognition

20. Leonard has used and liked Colgate toothpaste for years, so when the company introduced Colgate mouthwash, he bought some. This is an example of:
    a. stimulus discrimination
    b. selective retention
    c. product reinforcement
    d. social learning
    e. stimulus generalization

21. Jesse has certain opinions about personal computers. She thinks that they are complex and expensive, but are high-quality, reliable products. This is a description of one consumer's _____ about a certain class of product.
    a. values
    b. attitudes
    c. beliefs
    d. facts
    e. motives

22. Ralph Creamden is the brand manager for Top Stuff Clothing Products. His marketing research shows that his targeted audience does not hold favourable attitudes towards his products. If you were an advisor to Mr. Creamden, which of the following actions might you suggest?
    a. changing the belief(s) about the brand attributes
    b. changing the relative importance of these beliefs
    c. adding new beliefs to the ones already possessed by consumers
    d   any of these might stimulate attitude change towards his brand
    e. none of these, because attitudes are all but impossible to change

Check your answers to these questions before proceeding to the next section.

SCENARIO

After reading the marketing scenario, answer the questions that follow.

Daniela has been an avid photographer since she was ten years old. She has always used single lens reflex (SLR) cameras with automatic features but has recently realized that she should get into digital photography to stay current in her art. Many of her friends have already converted to digital photography.

Daniela started conducting some research on different digital cameras on the Internet. She found that digital cameras came in all price ranges – from $200 to several thousand dollars – and came with all kinds of features. Since she is a college student, Daniela knew she couldn't afford much more than $700 for a decent camera. She started searching on C-Net.com, a Web site that specializes in computing and technology products, and in on-line magazines like *Consumer Reports*. She also searched several electronics vendor Web sites – such as Best Buy, Kits Cameras, and Circuit City – to read consumer reviews of the various products. After the research, she decided to buy an Olympus Camedia C-3040 Zoom with 3.3 megapixels for $580.

Later, Daniela got together with her photographer friends to show off her camera. Many complimented her on her choice, but some indicated that she could have gotten a new Canon Powershot camera with 4 megapixels for $200 more. When she left her friends, she wondered if she had made the right choice.

True/False:

1. All the steps of the consumer decision-making process are reflected in the above scenario.

2. Daniela's photographer friends provided the initial stimulus for her need recognition.

3. Daniela used only nonmarketing-controlled information sources for her product search.

_____ 4. C-Net.com and *Consumer Reports* are good examples of:
    a. internal information search sources.
    b. stimuli.
    c. nonmarketing-controlled information sources.
    d. marketing-controlled information sources.
    e. government-controlled information sources.

_____ 5. Daniela's research on the Internet reflects what stage of the consumer decision-making process?
    a. Need recognition.
    b. Information search.
    c. Purchase.
    d. Post-purchase behaviour.
    e. None of these.

_____ 6. Daniela's self-doubt at the end of the scenario is an example of:
    a. denial.
    b. cognitive dissonance.
    c. need reversal.
    d. evoked set.
    e. indecision.

_____ 7. Which of the following best describes Daniela's purchase involvement?
    a. Extensive decision-making.
    b. Limited decision-making.
    c. Short-term decision-making.
    d. Routine response behavior.
    e. Lifetime decision-making.

Short Answer:

8. If you were Daniela, what would you do differently? Would this have affected the product that you purchased?

ESSAY QUESTIONS

1. What is consumer behaviour? Why is it important for consumer marketing managers to understand consumer behaviour?

2. List three types of consumer buying decisions (three levels of involvement) and provide common examples of when each type would be used.

3. List and define each level of Maslow's hierarchy of needs.

4. What is a reference group? Name and describe four types of reference groups as they may relate to your purchase of a new wardrobe.

5. Apply the three methods of changing attitudes about brands to the marketing activities of the company that makes your brand of toothpaste.

APPLICATION #1

You are a senior in college and are planning to continue your studies in graduate business school. You have a high grade point average and know that many good schools would be ready to accept you. List each phase of the consumer decision-making process and describe how you will go about deciding which school you'll attend.

APPLICATION #2

Assume that you have been trying to become a member of a prestigious campus club and have finally been invited to join. The members of this club typically wear extremely expensive style athletic shoes. List and briefly describe four factors that could influence your level of involvement in the purchase of these shoes. How involved will you be in this purchase and why?

CHAPTER 5: BUSINESS MARKETING

LEARNING OBJECTIVES

1 Describe business marketing

Business marketing is the marketing of goods and services to individuals and organizations for purposes other than personal consumption. Business products include those that are used to manufacture other products, that become part of other products, that aid in the normal operations of an organization, or that are acquired for resale without any substantial change in form. The key characteristic distinguishing business products from consumer products is intended use, not physical characteristics.

2 Describe the role of the Internet in business marketing

Businesses use the Internet for many purposes. It is used to communicate product information including attributes, price and availability. The Internet is used as a means of ordering and tracking products. It can be used as a means of soliciting bids.

3 Discuss the role of relationship marketing and strategic alliances in business marketing

Relationship marketing is the name of the strategy that entails seeking and establishing strategic alliances or partnerships with customers. Relationship marketing is driven by strong business forces: quality, cost, speed, cost-effectiveness, and new design technique.

A strategic alliance is a cooperative agreement between business firms. It may take the form of a licensing or distribution agreement, joint venture, R&D consortium, or multinational partnership. Companies form strategic alliances for a variety of reasons, and some fail miserably. The keys to success appear to be choosing partners carefully and creating conditions where both parties benefit. Some benefits may be shared R&D costs, provision of capital, shared production expertise or capacity, ability to penetrate global markets, and reduction of the threat of competition.

Three common problems of strategic alliances are: a) coordination problems which result when the partners are organized quite differently for making marketing and product design decisions; b) partners' inability to effectively use their skills in other countries; c) and the inability of one partner to continue meeting their partner's needs, which is often due to rapid technological change.

4 Identify the four major categories of business market customers

The business market consists of four major categories of customers: producers, resellers, governments, and institutions.

1. The producer segment of the business market is quite large. It consists of individuals and organizations that buy goods and services to produce other products, to become part of other products, or to facilitate the organization's daily operations.
2. The reseller market consists of retail and wholesale businesses that buy finished goods and resell them for a profit.
3. Government organizations include one federal, ten provincial, and three territorial units, as well as the MASH sector (Municipal, Academic, Social, and Hospitals) comprised of thousands of purchasing units. Together these government buyers account for the largest single market for goods and services with $440 billion in expenditures for 2002-03.
4. The fourth major segment of the business market consists of institutions seeking to achieve goals that differ from such ordinary business goals as profit, market share, and return on investment. Excluding the MASH sector, this segment includes churches, labour unions, fraternal organizations, civic clubs, foundations and private nonprofit organizations.

5   Explain the North American Industry Classification System

The North American Industrial Classification System (NAICS) is a system, developed jointly by Canada, the United States and Mexico, which provides a common industry classification system for use by all the NAFTA partners.

6   Explain the major differences between business and consumer markets

Business demand is different from consumer demand in that business demand is derived from the demand for other products, is often price inelastic, may be jointly tied to other products, and is more volatile than consumer demand.

The business market has some other important characteristics: large purchase volume, large number of customers, geographically concentrated customers, direct distribution, professional buyers, negotiation of purchasing prices and terms, the practice of reciprocity, leasing, and the emphasis on personal selling.

7   Describe the seven types of business goods and services

Business products generally fall into one of the following seven categories, depending on how they are used.

Major equipment includes such capital goods as large or expensive machines, mainframe computers, blast furnaces, generators, airplanes, and buildings. These goods are often leased, custom-designed, sold direct, and depreciated over time.

Accessory equipment is generally less expensive, standardized, and shorter-lived than major equipment and includes items such as power tools, word processors, and fax machines.

Raw materials are unprocessed extractive or agricultural products, such as mineral ore, lumber, wheat, vegetables, or fish, which become part of the final product.

Component parts are either finished items ready for assembly or products that need very little processing before they become part of some other product. Examples include spark plugs, tires, and electric motors. There is also a replacement market for component parts.

Processed materials are used directly in the production of other products, but unlike raw materials, they have had some processing. They do not retain their original identity in the final product. Examples include sheet metal, lumber, chemicals, and plastics.

Supplies are inexpensive, standardized, consumable items that do not become part of the product. Examples include lubricants, detergents, paper towels, pencils, and paper.

Services are expense items that do not become part of a final product. Businesses retain outside providers to perform such tasks as advertising, janitorial, legal, maintenance, or other services.

8   Discuss the unique aspects of business buying behaviour

A buying centre includes all those persons in an organization who become involved in the purchase decisions of that organization. Membership and relative influence of the participants in the buying centres vary widely from organization to organization. Buying centres do not appear on the formal organization chart, and many people may have informal yet important roles. In a lengthy decision-making process, people may move in and out of the buying centre. Buying centre roles include initiators, influencers/evaluators, gatekeepers, deciders, purchasers, and users.

There are three typical buying situations in business marketing. In a new-buy situation, a good or service is purchased when a new need arises. A modified rebuy is normally less critical and time-consuming than new-buy purchasing. In a modified-rebuy situation, the purchaser wants something new or something added to the original good or service. In a straight rebuy the order is placed on a routine basis, and the goods or services are provided just as in previous orders.

The business purchase process is a multiple-step procedure that begins with the recognition of a need, the subsequent definition of the type of product that will fill the need, and the development of product specifications. Next, various potential suppliers/vendors are contacted, and proposals are sought. Vendor analysis is the comparison of various alternative suppliers.

After analyzing alternative vendors, selecting a source of supply, and negotiating the terms of the purchase, the buying firm issues a purchase order. After the products are received, inspected, and checked into inventory, the payment process begins. After completion of the transaction, the supplier's performance is periodically monitored to determine whether future purchases should be made with this vendor.

Answer the following questions to see how well you understand the material. Re-take it after you review to check yourself.

1. What is business marketing?

2. What is a strategic alliance?

3. List and briefly describe the four major categories of business market customers.

4. List and briefly describe the seven types of business goods and services.

5. List and briefly describe five important aspects of business buying behaviour.

CHAPTER OUTLINE

1   Describe business marketing

I. What is Business Marketing?

Business marketing is the marketing of goods and services to individuals and organizations for purposes other than personal consumption. Often referred to as B2B.

  A. Business products include those that:

     1. Are used to manufacture other products
     2. Become part of another product
     3. Aid the normal operations of an organization
     4. Are acquired for resale without substantial change in form

  B. The key characteristic distinguishing business products is intended use, not physical characteristics.

2   Describe the role of the Internet in business marketing

II. Business Marketing on the Internet

Business marketing on the Internet offers tremendous opportunities for firms to increase efficiency, reduce costs, improve customer service, create one-to-one relationships, introduce new products, and expand markets.

  A. Two Success Stories

     1. Carrier Corp., the world's largest manufacturer of air conditioners, sells of $1 billion worth of products through its web site. Customers from Brazil have reduced the time to get an air conditioner from 6 days to 6 minutes.

     2. Montreal based BCE, parent company of Bell Canada, has developed a virtual marketplace for small and medium sized business called BellZinc.ca. Membership on BellZinc is free and is promoted as "Canada's leading web destination for businesses, you can take advantage of a host of products and services designed to help save time, save money, and increase sales."

  B. Potential Unrealized

    Worldwide, business internet market represents trillions of dollars of sales potential per year. It has currently reached only a fraction of its potential.

C.   Benefits of Business Marketing on the Internet

    1.   Lower prices

    2.   Greater selection of products and vendors

    3.   Access to customer and product sales data

    4.   Around-the-clock ordering and customer service

    5.   Lower costs

    6.   Customized products

3   Discuss the role of relationship marketing and strategic alliances in business marketing

III.   Relationship Marketing and Strategic Alliances

A.   Relationship marketing entails seeking and establishing strategic alliances or partnerships with customers. It has become an important business marketing strategy as customers have become more demanding and competition has become more intense.

B.   Strategic Alliances

A **strategic alliance (strategic partnership)** is a cooperative agreement between firms. It may take the form of licensing or distribution agreements, joint ventures, R&D consortia, or multinational partnerships.

C.   Relationships in Other Cultures

Businesses in other countries rely on personal relationships to facilitate exchange between firms. Reciprocity and personal relationships contribute to *"amae"*, which is the feeling of nurturing concern for, and dependence upon another.

4   Identify the four major categories of business market customers

IV.   Major Categories of Business Customers

A.   Producers

The producer segment is quite large and consists of individuals and organizations that buy goods and services used in producing other products, incorporating into other products, or facilitating the organization's daily operations.

B.   Resellers

The reseller market consists of retail and wholesale businesses that buy finished goods and resell them for a profit.

Many retailers and most wholesalers carry large numbers of items.

C.   Governments

Government organizations include one federal, ten provincial, and three territorial units, as well as the MASH sector (Municipal, Academic, Social, and Hospitals) comprised of thousands of buying units. Together these government buyers account for the largest single market for goods and services with $440 billion in expenditures for 2002-03.

1. The Senior Government

The Canadian federal government is the nation's largest customer, spending about $187 billion in 2003. The provincial and territorial governments spent $242 billion in 2003, with health, social services, and education expenses representing the lion's share of these expenditures.

2. The MASH sector

The MASH sector (Municipal, Academic, Social, and Hospitals) is comprised of thousands of buying units. Municipal governments in Canada spent $82 billion in 2003, colleges and universities spent $22.2 billion, schools spent $35 billion, healthcare organizations spent $49 billion, and social services spent $5 billion.

D.   Institutions

The fourth major segment of the business market consists of institutions seeking to achieve goals that differ from such ordinary business goals as profit, market share, and return on investment.

Excluding the MASH sector, this segment includes churches, labour unions, fraternal organizations, civic clubs, foundations and nonprofit organizations.

5   Explain the North American Industry Classification System

V.   Classifying Business and Government Markets

The North American Industrial Classification System (NAICS) is an industry classification introduced in 1997 to replace the standard industrial classification system (SIC).

A.   Provides a common industry classification system for the NAFTA partners.
B.   A valuable tool for business marketers in analyzing, segmenting, and targeting markets.

6   Explain the major differences between business and consumer markets

VI.   Business Versus Consumer Markets

Many characteristics of business markets are different from those of consumer markets. Thus marketing strategies are dissimilar.

A.   Demand

1.   Derived Demand

Derived demand is the demand for business products that results from the demand for consumer products.

Because demand for business products is derived, business marketers must carefully monitor demand patterns and changing preferences in final consumer markets.

2. Inelastic Demand

Inelastic demand means that an increase or a decrease in the price of a product will not significantly affect demand for it.

The demand for many business products is inelastic because the price of many products used in the production of a final product has an insignificant effect on the total price of the final consumer product. The result is that demand for the final consumer product is not affected.

3. Joint Demand

Joint demand occurs when two or more items are used together in a final product. An increase in demand for the final product will affect all of the jointly demanded products.

4. Fluctuating Demand

The demand for business products tends to be more volatile than the demand for consumer products.

A small increase or decrease in consumer demand produces a much larger change in demand for the facilities and equipment needed to manufacture the consumer product. This is known as the **multiplier effect** or **accelerator principle**.

B. Purchase Volume

Business customers buy in much larger quantities than consumers.

C. Number of Customers

Business marketers typically have far fewer customers than consumer marketers.

1. Business marketers may have an advantage in identifying prospective customers, monitoring their needs, and providing personal attention.

2. The reduced number of customers can also be a disadvantage, because each customer is so overwhelmingly important to the business.

D. Location of Buyers

Business customers tend to be much more geographically concentrated than consumers.

Most of Canada's buyers are located in the major metropolitan urban areas of Toronto, Montreal, and Vancouver.

E. Distribution Structure

Direct channels are much more common in business marketing than in consumer marketing.

F. Nature of Buying

Business buyers, who are often professionally trained purchasing agents or buyers, normally take a more formal approach to buying compared to consumers.

G. Nature of Buying Influence

More people are usually involved in a single business purchase decision than in a consumer purchase decision.

Some purchase decisions rest with a buying centre, which is a panel of experts from a variety of fields within an organization.

H. Type of Negotiations

Negotiation of price, product specifications, delivery dates, payment terms, and a variety of other conditions of sale is common in business marketing.

I. Use of Reciprocity

Business purchasers often choose to buy from their own customers, a practice known as **reciprocity**. Reciprocity is neither illegal nor unethical unless one party coerces the other; it is generally considered a reasonable business practice.

J. Use of Leasing

Consumers normally buy products rather than lease them. But businesses commonly lease expensive equipment, such as computers, construction equipment and vehicles, and automobiles.

K. Primary Promotional Method

Personal selling tends to be emphasized by business marketers in their promotion efforts.

Many business products are expensive, require customization, are ordered in large volumes, or involve intricate negotiations. All these situations necessitate a great deal of personal contact.

7 Describe the seven types of business goods and services

VII. Types of Business Products

A. Major Equipment

Major equipment (installations) consists of capital goods, such as large or expensive machines, mainframe computers, blast furnaces, generators, airplanes, and buildings.

1. Major equipment is also called an **installation**.

2. Major equipment always depreciates over time.

3. Major equipment is often leased, custom-designed, and sold direct from the producer.

B. Accessory Equipment

Accessory equipment is generally less expensive and shorter-lived than major equipment. It consists of goods such as portable tools and office equipment.

C. Raw Materials

Raw materials are unprocessed extractive or agricultural products, such as mineral ore, lumber, wheat, vegetables, and fish, which become part of the final product.

D. Component Parts

Component parts are either finished items ready for assembly or products that need very little processing before becoming part of some other product; examples include spark plugs, tires, and electric motors.

E. Processed Materials

Processed materials are used directly in manufacturing other products; unlike raw materials, they have had some processing. Examples include sheet metal, lumber, chemicals, corn syrup, and plastics.

D. Supplies

Supplies are consumable items that do not become part of the final product, such as lubricants, detergents, paper towels, pencils, and paper.

G. Business Services

Business services are expense items that do not become part of a final product. Businesses retain outside providers to perform such tasks as advertising, janitorial, payroll, legal, market research, maintenance, or other services.

8 Discuss the unique aspects of business buying behaviour

VIII. Business Buying Behaviour

A. Buying Centres

A **buying centre** includes all those persons in an organization who become involved in the purchase decision. Membership in the buying centre and relative influence of the participants vary widely from organization to organization. Buying centres do not appear on the formal organizational chart, and members play informal yet important roles. In a lengthy decision process people may move in and out of the buying centre.

1. Roles in the Buying Centre

   a. The *initiator* is the person who first suggests making a purchase.
   b. *Influencers* or evaluators often define specifications for the purchase or provide information for evaluating options.
   c. *Gatekeepers* regulate the flow of information about the purchase to the deciders and others.
   d. The *decider* is the person who possesses formal or informal power to choose or approve the selection of the supplier or brand.
   e. The *purchaser* is the person who actually negotiates the purchase.
   f. *Users* are the members of the organization who will actually use the product.

2. Implications of Buying Centres for the Marketing Manager

   Vendors need to identify and interact with the true decision makers. Other critical issues are each member's relative influence and the evaluative criteria used by each member.

B. Evaluative Criteria

The three most important and commonly used criteria are quality, service, and price--in that order.

1. *Quality* refers to technical suitability, the salesperson, and the salesperson's firm.

2. *Service* may range from pre-purchase needs surveys to installation to dependability of supply.

3. *Price* is extremely important in most business purchases.

C. Buying Situations

Often business firms must decide whether to make a certain item or to buy it from an outside supplier. Essentially, this is an economic decision, concerning price and use of company resources.

If a firm does choose to purchase a product, it will do so under one of three basic conditions: new buy, modified rebuy, or straight rebuy.

1. New Buy

    A **new buy** situation requires the purchase of a product for the first time.

    a. A new buy situation is the greatest opportunity for a new vendor to sell to a business purchaser because no previous relationship with a vendor has been established.

    b. New buys often result from **value engineering**, a systematic search for less-expensive substitute goods or services.

2. Modified Rebuy

    A **modified rebuy** is normally less critical and time-consuming than a new buy.

    a. In a modified rebuy situation, the purchaser wants some change in the original good or service.
    b. In some cases the purchaser just works with the original vendor, but in other cases the modified rebuy is opened to outside bidders.

3. Straight Rebuy

    a. In a **straight rebuy**, the purchaser reorders the same goods or services without looking for new information or investigating other suppliers.
    b. One common technique in a straight rebuy is the use of a purchasing contract for items that are purchased often and in high volume, which further automates the purchase process.

D. Purchasing Ethics

The ethics of business buyer and seller relationships are often scrutinized and sometimes criticized by superiors, associates, other prospective suppliers, the general public, and the news media.

E. Customer Service

Business marketers are increasingly recognizing the benefits of developing a formal system to monitor customer opinions and perceptions of the quality of customer service.

Fill in the blank(s) with the appropriate term or phrase from the alphabetized list of chapter key terms.

accessory equipment
business marketing
business services
buying centre
component parts
derived demand
joint demand
keiretsu
major equipment
modified rebuy

multiplier effect (or accelerator principle)
new buy
North American Industry Classification System (NAICS)
Original Equipment Manufacturer (OEM)
processed materials
raw materials
reciprocity
straight rebuy
strategic alliance (strategic partnership)
supplies

1 Describe business marketing

1. The marketing of goods and services to individuals and organizations for purposes other than personal consumption is termed _____.

3 Discuss the role of relationship marketing and strategic alliances in business marketing

2. A cooperative agreement between business firms is a(n) _____.

3. A _____ is the term for the Japanese system of interlocking directorates, creating strong relationships among firms within an industry.

5 Explain the North American Industry Classification System

4. The _____ is used by the United States, Canada and Mexico to provide a common system for grouping business organizations according to their primary economic activity.

6 Explain the major differences between business and consumer markets

5. Demand characteristics in business markets are different from those in consumer markets. Organizations purchase products to be used in producing consumer products. This is termed _____. Additionally, the demand for many business products is not sensitive to price changes; it is inelastic. When two or more items are used in combination in a final product, _____ occurs. Finally, the demand for business products tends to be unstable, which is called fluctuating demand. A small percentage change in consumer demand can produce a much larger change in demand for the facilities and equipment needed to manufacture the consumer product. Economists refer to this as the _____.

6. Business purchasers often choose to buy from their own customers, a practice known as _____. This is generally considered a reasonable business practice.

7 Describe the seven types of business goods and services

7. Business products fall into several categories, depending on their use. Capital goods, such as large and/or expensive machines, are called _____. Items that are less expensive and shorter-lived, such as office equipment or hand tools, are called _____. Unprocessed extractive or agricultural products are termed _____ and become a part of finished products. If goods are finished and ready for assembly into the final product, they are called _____ and needs very little or no processing. One of the most important markets for this is the _____ market, which buy business goods that they incorporate into the products that they produce for final sale. If products require some processing, they are termed _____ and are used directly in the manufacturing of other products; they do not retain their identity in the final product. Consumable items that do not become part of the final product are called _____. Finally, _____ are expense items that do not become part of the final product and are tasks performed by outside providers.

8 Discuss the unique aspects of business buying behaviour

8. All those persons in an organization who become involved in the purchase decision-making process make up the _____.

9. If a firm decides to buy a product rather than make it, it will do so under three different types of buying situations. The first situation requires the purchase of a product or service for the first time and is called a(n) _____. The second buying situation is one in which the purchase is normally less critical and time-consuming. In this case, the purchaser may want something new or added to the original goods or services. This is termed a(n) _____. Finally, there are purchases in which the purchaser is not looking for new information or at other suppliers, and the order is consistently placed with the same provider on a routine basis. This is called a(n) _____.

Check your answers to these questions before proceeding to the next section.

TRUE/FALSE QUESTIONS

Mark the statement **T** if it is true and **F** if it is false.

1 Describe business marketing

_____ 1. Hitsui is a manufacturer of HDTVs. Hitsui sells its TVs through electronics retailers, which in turn sell the TVs to households. Because Hitsui does not sell directly to the consumer, Hitsui is engaged in business marketing.

2 Describe the role of the Internet in business marketing

____ 2. General Electric's Internet consumer sales far exceed those of its business markets since consumers have found more uses than business for the Internet.

3 Discuss the role of relationship marketing and strategic alliances in business marketing

____ 3. A strategic alliance allows two or more companies to share resources and penetrate global markets.

4 Identify the four major categories of business-market customers

____ 4. Producers must, by definition, sell goods and not services.

____ 5. The reseller market includes both wholesalers and retailers.

____ 6. Institutions are in business to make money.

5 Explain the North American Industry Classification System

____ 7. NAICS is an industry classification system used by most nations of the world.

6 Explain the major differences between business and consumer markets

____ 8. Roundo Company manufactures ball bearings for the aerospace industry. Roundo's marketing director noticed a dramatic increase in the price of ball bearings only slightly reduced quantity demand. This is an example of fluctuating demand.

____ 9. Channels of distribution for consumer products are often direct, unlike business product channels of distribution, which usually have several intermediaries.

____ 10. In the business purchase process, unlike in consumer purchase processes, personal selling plays one of the most important roles.

7 Describe the seven types of business goods and services

____ 11. Bertha sells fresh brewed coffee in her diner and purchases her coffee beans from a roaster in the same town. To the roaster, the coffee beans are considered to be raw materials.

8 Discuss the unique aspects of business buying behaviour

____ 12. For the last five years, the Michigan Jams company has bought its birch bark gift baskets from Woodside, Inc. Michigan Jams wants a new kind of handle and decorative ribbons added to the largest type of basket. This is an example of a new buy.

Check your answers to these questions before proceeding to the next section.

For the following statements, indicate reasons why you may agree and disagree with the statement.

1. Strategic alliances are more important in business marketing than in consumer marketing.

    Reason(s) to agree:

    Reason(s) to disagree:

2. Because business customers are fewer and geographically more concentrated, business marketing is easier than consumer marketing.

    Reason(s) to agree:

    Reason(s) to disagree:

3. Businesses use basically the same process for purchase decision making as consumers but on a more formal scale.

    Reason(s) to agree:

    Reason(s) to disagree:

4. Selling to business markets would be more rewarding than selling to consumer markets.

    Reason(s) to agree:

    Reason(s) to disagree:

5. E-commerce benefits everyone.

    Reason(s) to agree:

    Reason(s) to disagree

MULTIPLE CHOICE QUESTIONS

Select the response that best answers the question, and write the corresponding letter in the space provided.

1   Describe business marketing

_____ 1. You have decided that your firm will enter the business market arena. You have been a consumer-products producer selling directly to consumers previously, so you have little knowledge about this new marketing opportunity. Which of the following possible transactions might fit this new arena of business?
   a. sales of products that are used to manufacture other products
   b. sales of products that are to become parts of other products
   c. sales of products that facilitate the normal operations of an organization
   d. sales of products that are acquired for resale without any substantial change in form
   e. all of these are possible transactions that might fit this new arena of business

2   Describe the role of the Internet in business marketing

_____ 2. Which of the following is NOT likely to happen with the emergence of the Internet?
   a. increase in competition
   b. target markets become global
   c. increase in the number of vendors evaluated
   d. consumer markets become larger and more powerful than business markets
   e. efficiency in data exchange

---

3 **Discuss the role of relationship marketing and strategic alliances in business marketing**

_____ 3. Benefits of strategic alliances could include all of the following EXCEPT:
   a. allowing companies to share research and development ideas and costs
   b. reducing the threat of competition, and providing capital
   c. guaranteeing a technologically sophisticated partner in the long-term
   d. allowing firms to share production expertise or capacity
   e. increasing quality and service levels

4 **Identify the four major categories of business-market customers**

_____ 4. Maya Industries owns and operates a metal ore mining operation, a trucking company, and an insurance firm. For classification purposes, Maya Industries would be which type of business customer?
   a. government
   b. wholesaler
   c. reseller
   d. institution
   e. producer

_____ 5. Sysco Foods purchases truckload quantities of consumer products such as frozen foods, cereals, and paper towels from manufacturers. Sysco then breaks down the items into case quantities and distributes them to restaurants and grocery stores. Sysco would be best classified as a(n):
   a. inventory carrier
   b. producer
   c. institution
   d. reseller
   e. transportation company

_____ 6. A manager has decided her company should sell to the government market. What is one common procedure for trying to get a government contract?
   a. The government offers a publication of what it is willing to pay for certain goods, and companies offer to supply them for that price.
   b. The company submits a sealed bid that states price and delivery terms.
   c. The company advertises the availability of its product and has the government contact it.
   d. It is difficult to get a government contract because once a business is a supplier for the government, it will have that contract for the life of the company.
   e. The company submits a quotation, and if the quoted price is in the midrange of all quotes received, it will probably be selected as the fairest and most average supplier.

_____ 7. Brian's Paper Company specializes in serving institutions. Brian would probably have all of the following as customers EXCEPT:
   a. convenience stores
   b. labour unions
   c. churches
   d. MS Foundation
   e. Sun Youth organization

5 Explain the North American Industry Classification System

_____ 8. Which of the following is false regarding the North American Industry Classification System (NAICS)?
   a. In spite of its name, NAICS is also used to classify firms in other regions, such as Europe or Asia.
   b. A code can identify whether a firm is based in the United States, Canada, or Mexico.
   c. The more digits in a NAICS code, the more homogenous the group is.
   d. NAICS facilitates trade among firms in NAFTA countries.
   e. NAICS can help firms identify the number, size, and geographic dispersion of potential business customers.

_____ 9. The North American Industry Classification System is currently uses a _____ digit classification system.
   a. 2
   b. 20
   c. 6
   d. 1
   e. 100

6 Explain the major differences between business and consumer markets

_____ 10. When the demand for beer grew by 10 percent in one year, the demand for aluminium cans and glass bottles grew also. The aluminium and glass industries are enjoying the effects of:
   a. joint demand
   b. inelastic demand
   c. derived demand
   d. fluctuating demand
   e. elastic demand

_____ 11. The Houston Electric Company increased its rates to business customers by 12 percent. Though customers complained, the company saw very little change in the volume of electricity used. The demand for electricity can be described as
   a. inelastic
   b. derived
   c. joint
   d. elastic
   e. resistant

_____ 12. 3M manufactures 3.5-inch computer diskettes. Each disk is made from four components: the magnetic media, the plastic casing, a metal hub, and a metal slide. The supplies purchaser at 3M has noticed that each time the case order for magnetic media increases, so does the case order for plastic casings, metal hubs, and metal slides. This is because the products in this situation have:
   a. inelastic demand
   b. derived demand
   c. elastic demand
   d. fluctuating demand
   e. joint demand

_____ 13. The Wisconsin Wild Rice Company has slowly changed its customer base. They used to sell small bags of rice to retail walk-in consumers, but now they deliver rice to grocery stores and restaurants. The company should develop:
   a. more customers
   b. a greater reliance on advertising to gain new customers
   c. a smaller order size
   d. a more formal purchasing process
   e. less use of reciprocity

_____ 14. Geni owns her own computer repair firm. She decided that she needed a photocopier for her business, and she checked her customer list first for copier dealers. She found three copier dealers that were regular customers, and she shopped only at those dealers. Geni's actions are:
a. a normal business practice called reciprocity
b. an example of illegal influence
c. an example of nested demand
d. unethical because of competitive discouragement
e. a business practice called circular buying

7   Describe the seven types of business goods and services

_____ 15. Charlie purchases tuna fish directly from fishing fleets daily and then processes and cans the tuna. The fish are an example of:
a. OEM parts
b. supplies
c. component parts
d. processed materials
e. raw materials

_____ 16. Models Inc. uses pre-assembled engines in its radio-controlled model airplanes. These engines are classified as:
a. raw materials
b. component parts
c. accessory equipment
d. processed materials
e. supplies

_____ 17. Manufacturers of CDs such as TDK or Sony sell their products to software developers, such as Microsoft, to be used to store software programs. Microsoft would be considered a(n):
a. replacement part market
b. processed materials market
c. finished goods market
d. accessory equipment market
e. OEM market

8   Discuss the unique aspects of business buying behaviour

_____ 18. When Mike visited a potential customer, he found that the manager was too busy to meet with him. The secretary offered to look through Mike's brochures and pass them on to the manager if it was a product that the firm could use. Which role in the buying center does the secretary have?
a. gatekeeper
b. influencer
c. purchaser
d. decider
e. user

_____ 19. Hitec Corp is selecting a supplier for unusual parts used in its recently developed highly technical machine tooling equipment. Which of the following buying processes will most likely be employed?
a. extensive buying process
b. low-involvement buying process
c. new-buy process
d. modified-rebuy process
e. straight-rebuy process

_____ 20. The local university buys many desk calculators each year and has an ongoing relationship with a local supplier. The accounting department secretary finds that he needs a calculator with more functions than his current one has, and the university buyer discusses the specifications with the supplier. This is an example of a:
   a. modified rebuy
   b. value engineering task
   c. straight rebuy
   d. new task
   e. derived rebuy

_____ 21. A new edition of a marketing textbook has just been released. The marketing professor at Beaufort University has always liked the textbook and authorizes the purchase of the new edition without even looking at other textbooks. This is an example of a:
   a. modified rebuy
   b. value engineering task
   c. straight rebuy
   d. new task
   e. derived rebuy

Check your answers to these questions before proceeding to the next section.

SCENARIO

After reading the marketing scenario, answer the questions that follow.

Ryan is a sales representative for the fictitious Burke Pharmaceutical which makes prescription drugs for ailments such as ulcers, high cholesterol, and asthma. As a sales professional, Ryan calls on large accounts, such as hospitals, doctor's offices, and drugstores, on a regular basis.

Ryan's largest client is New Hope Hospital. He typically visits doctors, nurses, and even front office personnel to tell them about new pharmaceuticals that his company is developing and to handle any other product problems the account has. Burke has a patent on its ulcer medicine and enjoys the leading market share because of it. As a result, Ryan has little difficulty selling it to New Hope. The cholesterol medicine, however, is another story. Burke is one of many competitors in this market and has the fifth leading market share, so Ryan has not been as successful at selling this medicine to the hospital.

At New Hope Hospital, the purchasing manager handles the actual ordering of Ryan's pharmaceuticals. However, the doctors tell the purchasing manager what pharmaceuticals they prefer to carry at the hospital.

True/False:

_____ 1. Burke Pharmaceutical would be considered a producer.

_____ 2. New Hope Hospital would be considered a reseller.

_____ 3. Ryan is performing a marketing function.

Multiple Choice:

_____ 4. Ryan's drugstore accounts would be considered what type of business market?
   a. Producers.
   b. Resellers.
   c. Government.
   d. Institutions.
   e. Medical.

5. Which of the following types of demand does Burke's ulcer medicine most likely have?
    a. Inelastic demand.
    b. Elastic demand.
    c. Joint demand.
    d. Fluctuating demand.
    e. Independent demand.

6. The purchasing manager at New Hope Hospital represents which type of buying center role?
    a. Influencer.
    b. Decider.
    c. Purchaser.
    d. User.
    e. Initiator.

7. The doctors at New Hope Hospital represent which type of buying center role?
    a. Influencers.
    b. Gatekeepers.
    c. Purchasers.
    d. Initiators.
    e. Users.

Short Answer:

8. Describe the three buying situations for Burke's ulcer medicine.

ESSAY QUESTIONS

1. What is a strategic alliance? Why are strategic alliances becoming more important in business marketing?

2. Briefly describe the four major categories of customers in business marketing. Give examples of companies or organizations in each category.

3. Name and briefly describe eight major differences between business and consumer markets. Are there any ways that business purchasing behaviour is similar to consumer buying behaviour?

4. What are the benefits of Internet marketing?

5.   What is NAICS? Why is it important?

6.   Pike's Print Shop has decided to purchase some colour copying machines. Identify the three possible buying situations and describe the conditions under which each would take place.

APPLICATION

Assume that you are the vice-president of marketing in a small firm that includes the following departments: marketing, finance, purchasing, and management. The sales force manager has mentioned to you that one of the salespersons thought that cellular telephones would help the sales force become more efficient. The manager requests that eight such phones be purchased. Illustrate the six buying decision roles that would take place for the purchase of these cellular phones.

CHAPTER 6: SEGMENTING AND TARGETING MARKETS

LEARNING OBJECTIVES

1   Describe the characteristics of markets and market segments

A market is a group of people or organizations with wants and needs that can be satisfied by particular product categories. This group has the ability to purchase these products, is willing to exchange resources for the products, and has the authority to do so. If a group lacks any of these characteristics, it is not a market.

A market segment is a subgroup of people or organizations sharing one or more characteristics that cause them to have relatively similar product needs. The process of dividing a market into meaningful groups that are relatively similar and identifiable is called market segmentation.

2   Explain the importance of market segmentation

The purpose of segmentation is to enable the marketer to tailor marketing mixes to meet the needs of one or more specific segments. Market segmentation assists marketers in developing more precise definitions of customer needs and wants.

3   Discuss criteria for successful market segmentation

To be useful, a segmentation scheme must produce segments that meet four basic criteria: substantiality, measurability, accessibility, and responsiveness.

A selected segment must be substantial, or large enough, to justify the development and maintenance of a special marketing mix. The marketer must be able to profit by serving the specific needs of this segment, whatever its size. The segments must be identifiable and their size measurable. The target market must be accessible by the firm's customized marketing mixes. A market segment must respond differently to some aspect of the marketing mix than other segments do.

4   Describe bases commonly used to segment consumer markets

A segmentation base (or variable) is a characteristic of individuals, groups, or organizations used to divide a market into segments. Many different characteristics can be used. Some common bases are geographic, demographic, psychographics, benefits offered by product, and usage rate by consumers.

5   Describe the bases for segmenting business markets

Business markets can be segmented three general bases. First, businesses segment markets based on company characteristics, such as customer's geographic location, type of company, company size, and product use. Second, companies may segment customers based on the buying processes those customers use. Third, companies are increasingly basing marketing segmentation on the type of relationship they have with their customers.

6   List the steps involved in segmenting markets

Six steps are involved when segmenting markets: (1) Select a market or product category for study; (2) choose a basis or bases for segmenting the market; (3) select segmentation descriptors; (4) profile and analyze segments; (5) select target markets; (6) design; implement; and maintain appropriate marketing mixes.

7   Discuss alternative strategies for selecting target markets

There are three general strategies for selecting target markets. A firm using an undifferentiated targeting strategy essentially adopts a mass-market philosophy, viewing the world as one big market with no individual segments. It formulates only one marketing mix and assumes that the individual customers in the market have relatively similar needs.

A concentrated targeting strategy entails focusing marketing efforts on one segment of a market. Because the firm is appealing to a single segment, it can concentrate on understanding the needs, motives, and satisfactions of the members of that segment and develop a highly specialized marketing mix. The term *niche targeting strategy* is sometimes used to describe this strategy.

When a firm chooses to serve two or more well-defined market segments and develops distinct marketing mixes for each, it is practicing multisegment targeting. A firm can use various methods to achieve this goal. Some companies have very specialized marketing mixes, including specialized products for each segment; other companies may only customize the promotional message that is directed to the various target markets.

8   Explain how and why firms implement positioning strategies and how product differentiation plays a role

Positioning is the development of a specific marketing mix to influence potential customers' overall perception of a brand, product line, or organization in general. The term *position* refers to the place a product, brand, or group of products occupies in consumers' minds relative to competing offerings. Firms use the elements of the marketing mix to clarify their position or to reposition the product in the consumers' minds.

The purpose of product differentiation is to distinguish one firm's products from another's. The differences can be real or perceived. The marketer attempts to convince customers that a brand is significantly different from the others and should therefore be demanded over competing brands.

9   Discuss global market segmentation and targeting issues

The key tasks in market segmentation, targeting, and positioning are the same whether the selected target market is local, regional, or multinational. The main differences are the variables used by marketers in analyzing markets and assessing opportunities and the resources needed to implement strategies.

Answer the following questions to see how well you understand the material. Re-take it after you review to check yourself.

1. What is a market? A market segment?

2. List four basic criteria for segmenting markets.

3. Name and briefly describe five bases for segmenting consumer markets.

4. Name and briefly describe two bases for segmenting business markets.

5. List the six steps in segmenting a market.

6. List and describe three strategies for selecting target markets.

7. What is positioning?

1   Describe the characteristics of markets and market segments

I.   Market Segmentation

    A.   A **market** is people or organizations with needs or wants and with the ability and the willingness to buy.

    B.   A **market segment** is a subgroup of people or organizations sharing one or more characteristics that cause them to have similar product needs.

    C.   **Market segmentation** is the process of dividing a market into meaningful groups that are relatively similar and identifiable.

2   Explain the importance of market segmentation

II.   The Importance of Market Segmentation

    A.   Market segmentation developed in the 1960s in response to growing markets with a variety of needs and in response to increasing competition.

    B.   Market segmentation assists marketers in developing more precise definitions of customer needs and wants. Segmentation helps decision-makers more accurately define marketing objectives and better allocate resources.

3   Discuss criteria for successful market segmentation

III.   Criteria for Successful Segmentation

    A.   *Substantiality:* A selected segment must be large enough to justify the development and maintenance of a special marketing mix. Serving the specific needs of this segment, whatever its size must be profitable.

    B.   *Identifiability and measurability*: The segments must be identifiable and their size measurable.

    C.   *Accessibility:* The firm must be able to reach members of targeted segments with customized marketing mixes.

    D.   *Responsiveness*: A market segment must respond differently to some aspect of the marketing mix than do other segments.

4   Describe the bases commonly used to segment consumer markets

IV.   Bases for Segmenting Consumer Markets

A **segmentation base** (or **variable**) is a characteristic of individuals, groups, or organizations that is used to divide a total market into segments. Markets can be segmented using a single or multiple variables.

    A.   Geographic Segmentation

        1.   **Geographic segmentation** is a method of dividing markets based on the region of the country or world, market size, market density (number of people within a unit of land), or climate.

        2.   Climate is frequently used because of its dramatic impact on residents' needs and purchasing behaviour.

---

3. Regional marketing, using specialized marketing mixes in different parts of the country, has become prevalent among consumer goods companies for four principal reasons:

    a. Firms need to find ways to generate sales in sluggish markets
    b. Scanner technology helps manufacturers better pinpoint which brands sell better where
    c. Regional brands appeal to regional preferences
    d. A regional approach allows a faster response to competition

B. Demographic Segmentation

Demographic segmentation is the method of dividing markets on the basis of demographic variables, such as age, gender, income, ethnic background, and family life cycle.

Marketers use demographic information to segment markets because it is widely available and often related to consumers' purchasing and consuming behaviour.

1. Age segmentation: Specific age groups are tremendously attractive markets for a variety of product categories.

2. Gender segmentation: Marketers of many items, such as clothes, footwear, personal care items, magazines, and cosmetics, commonly segment by gender.

3. Income segmentation: Income level influences consumers' wants and determines their buying power.

4. Ethnic Segmentation: Many companies are segmenting their markets by ethnicity and/or visible minority status. Canadian marketers are aware of the multicultural makeup of the Canadian market, and in particular, the Chinese market.

5. Family life cycle segmentation: The **family life cycle (FLC)** is a series of life stages, which are defined by a combination of age, marital status, and the presence or absence of children.

C. Psychographics Segmentation

Psychographics segmentation is the method of dividing markets based on personality, motives, lifestyle, and geodemographics.

1. *Personality*: Individual characteristics reflect traits, attitudes, and habits.

2. *Motives*: Consumers have motives for purchasing products. Marketers often try to appeal to such motives as safety, rationality, or status.

3. *Lifestyles*: Lifestyle segmentation divides individuals into groups according to activities, interests, and opinions. Often certain socioeconomic characteristics, such as income and education, are included.

4. Geodemographics: **Geodemographic segmentation** is the method of dividing markets on the basis of neighbourhood lifestyle categories and is a combination of geographic, demographic, and lifestyle segmentation.

5. Claritas PRIZM: PRIZM Lifestyle segmentation divides Americans into 62 "clusters," or consumer types based on a combination of basic demographic data (age, income, ethnicity) and psychographics information (lifestyle). Some categories are:

    a. "Kids and Cul-de-Sacs:" upscale, suburban families with a median household income of $68,900 and who tend to shop on-line.
    b. "Bohemian Mix:" professionals aged 25 to 44 with a median income of $38,500 who are likely to shop at the Gap.

D. Benefit Segmentation

Benefit segmentation is the method of dividing markets on the basis of benefits consumers seek from the product.

1. By matching demographic information to interest in particular types of benefits, typical customer profiles can be built.

2. Customer profiles can be matched to certain types or times of media usage to develop promotional strategies for reaching these target markets.

E. Usage Rate Segmentation

Usage rate segmentation is the method of dividing a market based on the amount of product purchased or consumed.

1. The most common usage-rate categories are former users, potential users, first-time users, light users, medium users, and heavy users.

2. The **80/20 principle** is a business heuristic (rule of thumb) stating that 20 percent of all customers generate 80 percent of the demand. Although the percentages are not always exact, a close approximation of this rule is often true. This principle reinforces the concept that heavy users, usually the most important and profitable part of a business, are actually a small percentage of the total number of customers.

5   Describe the bases for segmenting business markets

V. Bases for Segmenting Business Markets

The business market consists of producers, resellers, institutions, and government. Business market segmentation can be based on company characteristics, buying processes, and customer relationships.

A. Company Characteristics

1. Company characteristics, such as geographic location, type of company, company size, and product can be used as segmentation variables.

B. Buying Processes

1. Business markets can also be segmented on the basis of how they buy. This can include the profiles of the buyer (strategies used for buying) and the personal characteristics of the buyers themselves.
2. Two purchasing strategies are:

a. **Satisficers** usually contact familiar suppliers and place an order with the first to satisfy product and delivery requirements.
b. **Optimizers** consider numerous suppliers, both familiar and unfamiliar, and then solicit bids and analyze options.

C. Customer Relationship

Business markets can also be segmented on the basis of the type of relationship that marketers have with their customers. These segments can include: client accounts, customer accounts, and buyer accounts.

---

6   List the steps involved in segmenting markets

VI.   Steps in Segmenting a Market

The purpose of market segmentation is to identify marketing opportunities (and eventually target markets) for existing or potential markets.

A.   *Select a market or product category* for study, whether it is an existing, related, or new market.

B.   *Choose a basis or bases for segmenting the market*

    1.   The decision is a combination of managerial insight, creativity, and market knowledge; no scientific procedure has been developed for selecting segmentation variables.

    2.   The number of segmentation bases is limited only by the decision-maker's imagination and creativity.

C.   Select segmentation descriptors

    Descriptors are the specific segmentation variables to be used. For example, if demographics are the chosen base, age could be a descriptor variable.

D.   Profile and evaluate segments

    A profile should include a segment's size, expected growth rates, purchase frequency, current brand usage, brand loyalty, and overall long-term sales and profit potential.

    The analysis stage can rank potential market segments by profit opportunity, risk, and consistency with the organizational mission and objectives.

E.   Select target markets

F.   Design, implement, and maintain appropriate marketing mixes

7   Discuss alternative strategies for selecting target markets

VII. Strategies for Selecting Target Markets

A **target market** is a group of people or organizations for which an organization designs, implements, and maintains a marketing mix to fit the needs of that group or groups, resulting in mutually satisfying exchanges.

A.   Undifferentiated Targeting

    The **undifferentiated targeting strategy** is a marketing approach based on the assumption that the market has no individual segments and thus requires a single marketing mix. It is a mass-market philosophy, viewing the world as one big market with no individual segments.

    1.   There is only one marketing mix with an undifferentiated strategy.

    2.   It assumes that individual customers have similar needs.

    3.   The first firm in an industry sometimes uses this targeting strategy, because no competition exists.

4. With this strategy, production and marketing costs are often at their lowest.

5. This strategy leaves opportunities for competitors to enter the market with more specialized products and appeals to specific parts of the market.

B. Concentrated Targeting

The **concentrated targeting strategy** is a marketing approach based on appealing to a single segment of a market.

1. It focuses a firm's marketing efforts on a single segment or market niche.

2. A firm can concentrate on understanding the needs, motives, and satisfactions of the members of one segment and on developing and maintaining a highly specialized marketing mix.

3. A concentrated strategy allows small firms to be competitive with very large firms because of a small firm's expertise in one area of the market.

4. The dangers associated with this type of strategy include changes in the competitive environment, which could destroy the only segment targeted.

C. Multisegment Targeting

The **multisegment targeting strategy** is a marketing approach based on serving two or more well-defined market segments, with a distinct marketing mix for each.

1. Some companies have very specialized marketing mixes for each segment, including a specialized product; other companies may only customize the promotional message for each target market.

2. The multisegment strategy offers many benefits, including potentially greater sales volume, higher profits, larger market share, and economies of scale in marketing and manufacturing.

3. This strategy also includes many extra costs, such as:

✓ Product design costs
✓ Production costs
✓ Promotion costs
✓ Inventory costs
✓ Marketing research costs
✓ Management costs
✓ **Cannibalization**, which occurs when sales of a new product cut into sales of a firm's existing products.

8 Explain how and why firms implement positioning strategies and how product differentiation plays a role

VIII. Positioning

Positioning is the development of a specific marketing mix to influence potential customers' overall perception of a brand, product line, or organization in general.

The term **position** refers to the place a product, brand, or group of products occupies in consumers' minds relative to competing offerings.

A. Product Differentiation

Product differentiation is a positioning strategy designed to distinguish one firm's products from another's. The aim of differentiation is to convince customers that a brand is significantly different from the others and should therefore be demanded over competing brands

B. Perceptual Mapping

Perceptual mapping is a means of displaying or graphing, in two or more dimensions, the location of products, brands, or groups of products in the minds of present or potential customers.

C. Positioning Bases

1. A product is associated with an attribute, product feature, or customer benefit.

2. The position may stress high price as a symbol of quality or low price as an indicator of value.

3. Stressing uses and applications can be an effective means of positioning a product.

4. Another base may focus on a personality or type of user.

5. One position is to associate the product with a particular category of products.

6. Positioning against competitors is often a part of any positioning strategy.

D. Repositioning

Repositioning is changing consumers' perceptions of a brand in relation to competing brands.

9   Discuss global market segmentation and targeting issues

IX. Global Issues in Market Segmentation and Targeting

A. Two divergent trends, toward global marketing standardization and toward micromarketing in global markets, are occurring at the same time.

B. The steps in global market segmentation and targeting are the same as in local marketing; the main difference is the segmentation variables commonly used.

VOCABULARY PRACTICE

Fill in the blank(s) with the appropriate term or phrase from the alphabetized list of chapter key terms.

benefit segmentation	niche
cannibalization	optimizer
concentrated targeting strategy	perceptual mapping
demographic segmentation	position
80/20 principle	positioning
family life cycle (FLC)	product differentiation
geodemographic segmentation	psychographic segmentation
geographic segmentation	repositioning
market	satisficer
market segment	segmentation bases (variables)
market segmentation	target market
multisegment targeting strategy	undifferentiated targeting strategy
	usage rate segmentation

1   Describe the characteristics of markets and market segments

1. People or organizations with needs or wants and with the ability, and the willingness, to buy are a(n) _____.

2. A subgroup of people or organizations sharing one or more characteristics that cause them to have similar product needs is a(n) _____. The process of dividing a market into meaningful, relatively similar, and identifiable groups is called _____.

4   Describe the bases commonly used to segment consumer markets

3. Characteristics of individuals, groups, or organizations that are used to divide a total market into segments are called _____.

4. Dividing markets based on region of the country or world, market size, market density, or climate is referred to as _____.

5. Marketers can segment markets according to age, gender, income, and ethnic background. This is called _____. Another common basis for this type of segmentation is a series of stages that uses a combination of age, marital status, and the presence or absence of children. This is known as the _____.

6. Market segmentation based on personality, motives, or lifestyles, is known as _____. One type of segmentation that combines geographic, demographic, and lifestyle variables to cluster potential customers into neighbourhood lifestyle categories is called _____.

7. The process of dividing a market according to different benefits customers seek from the product is called _____. Dividing the market based on the amount of product purchased or consumed is called _____. Segmenting in this manner allows marketers to concentrate on heavy users. Heavy users account for a disproportionate share of the total consumption of many products as stated by the _____.

5   Describe the bases for segmenting business markets

8. One way businesses segment their market is by purchasing strategies. Two purchasing profiles have been identified. The first type contacts familiar suppliers and places an order with the first to satisfy product and delivery requirements. This type is called a(n) _____. The second type considers numerous suppliers, both familiar and unfamiliar, solicits bids, and examines all alternatives carefully. This type is called a(n) _____.

7   Discuss alternative strategies for selecting target markets

9. A group of people or organizations for which a marketer designs, implements, and maintains a marketing mix intended to meet the needs of that group is called a(n) _____.

10. There are three general strategies for selecting target markets. If a firm adopts a mass-marketing philosophy and views the market as one big market with no segments, the firm is using a(n) _____. If a firm selects one segment of a market for targeting its marketing efforts, it is using a(n) _____, and the one segment is called a(n) _____. Finally, if a firm chooses to serve two or more well-defined market segments and develops a distinct marketing mix for each segment, it is practicing _____. One of the dangers of this last segmenting strategy is that sales of a firm's new product directed at one segment may cause a decline in sales of the firm's other products targeted at existing segments. This is called _____.

8   Explain how and why firms implement positioning strategies and how product differentiation plays a role

11. There are two important marketing strategies related to targeting. The first strategy develops a specific marketing mix to influence potential customers' overall perception of a brand, product line, or organization in general. This strategy is called _____. The strategy assumes that competing products are arranged in consumers' minds along various dimensions. The place a product occupies in consumers' minds relative to competing offerings is the _____. Another strategy is used to distinguish one firm's products from another's. These distinctions can be either real or perceived. This strategy is called _____. A means of displaying these dimensions and locations is known as _____. These can be also used for plans to change consumers' perceptions, a process called _____.

Check your answers to these questions before proceeding to the next section.

TRUE/FALSE QUESTIONS

Mark the statement **T** if it is true and **F** if it is false.

1   Describe the characteristics of markets and market segments

_____   1.   Doggy Dumplings, Inc., has developed a new animal food. The company has identified pet ferrets, skunks, otters, weasels, raccoons, and badgers as animals that would eat the food. These animals make up the market for Doggy Dumplings' new food.

2   Explain the importance of market segmentation

_____   2.   Large companies like Coca-Cola do not practice segmentation because their products are targeted at the mass market.

_____   3.   Market segmentation helps marketers define customer needs and wants more precisely.

3   Discuss criteria for successful market segmentation

_____   4.   It is important for a targeted market segment to be identifiable and measurable because it must sustain long-term sales and profit for the marketer.

4   Describe bases commonly used to segment consumer markets

_____   5.   Levi's produces Dockers clothing designed for the baby boomer generation. Levi's is using the family life cycle as a segmentation variable for Dockers.

_____   6.   The Sharper Image sells a variety of high-tech items through its catalogues and specialty shops. The items are designed to appeal to the wealthy "yuppie" market, especially those consumers who are adventurous and active and have a flair for self-expression. The Sharper Image should use demographic variables for market segmentation.

_____   7.   Targeting a segment of people who are politically conservative is an example of psychographics segmentation.

7   Discuss alternative strategies for selecting target markets

_____   8.   The C&H sugar company does not single out any particular subgroup within the population of sugar users but instead directs one marketing mix at everyone. This is a differentiated targeting strategy.

_____   9.   The Gap targets young adults with its nice quality casual clothes. Baby Gap targets children from newborn to 5 years, while GapKids targets children aged six to teens. Altogether, the Gap stores use a concentrated strategy.

8   Explain how and why firms implement positioning strategies and how product differentiation plays a role

_____   10.   Perceptual maps indicate where firms are trying to position their products.

_____   11.   Product differentiation is a positioning strategy firms used to distinguish their products from those of competitors.

Check your answers to these questions before proceeding to the next section.

AGREE/DISAGREE QUESTIONS

For the following statements, indicate reasons why you may agree and disagree with the statement.

1. Marketers should always practice market segmentation.

    Reason(s) to agree:

    Reason(s) to disagree:

2. The most important criterion for market segmentation is substantiality.

    Reason(s) to agree:

    Reason(s) to disagree:

3. To a certain extent, all firms practice geographic segmentation.

    Reason(s) to agree:

    Reason(s) to disagree:

4. Psychographic segmentation should not be used, as other bases for segmentation (demographic and geographic) are based on more accurate data.

    Reason(s) to agree:

    Reason(s) to disagree:

5. It is better to launch a new product than to reposition an old one.

Reason(s) to agree:

Reason(s) to disagree:

MULTIPLE CHOICE QUESTIONS

Select the response that best answers the question, and write the corresponding letter in the space provided.

1   Describe the characteristics of markets and market segments

_____ 1. Which of the following is NOT necessarily a characteristic of a market?
     a. Willingness to buy the product.
     b. Ability to buy the product.
     c. Awareness of the product.
     d. A group of people or organizations.
     e. Having needs or wants.

_____ 2. Pepper Planes has decided that all of its customers are not similar enough to respond to one marketing mix. In particular, some of its accounts are large corporations that need planes for executive transportation, and others are farmers who need planes for crop dusting. The procedure of dividing this market into identifiable, similar groups is called:
     a. micromarketing
     b. positioning
     c. cannibalization
     d. market segmentation
     e. perceptual mapping

2   Explain the importance of market segmentation

_____ 3. Shirley owns the Coachlight Travel Agency and would like to improve customer satisfaction and increase repeat business. You ask Shirley to describe a typical customer, and she says it is hard to find one kind of customer. With corporate travel, family vacations, retirement cruises, college spring breaks, and honeymoons, it is hard to know how to serve all these accounts. You suggest that it is time for market segmentation because:
     a. Shirley needs to learn how to group these markets together into one market to serve them adequately
     b. Shirley needs to reduce the size of her market served
     c. it will enable Shirley to build an accurate description of the customer needs by group and to design a marketing mix to fit each segment
     d. it will help develop a generalized definition of the market as a whole and the optimal marketing mix for this market
     e. this will position Shirley's company in the minds of her consumers as compared to the competition

_____ 4. The Poquet Company, a manufacturer of hand-held computers, completed a thorough examination and analysis of its business customers two years ago. They grouped the customers into four segments based on size, geographic region, and benefits sought. Would you recommend a new segmentation analysis this year?
   a. Yes, I would recommend one even more regularly because of the rapidly changing nature of most markets.
   b. No, once every five years is about average.
   c. No, business customer markets are not rapidly changing or developing like consumer goods markets.
   d. Yes, but use different bases to get some variety.
   e. No, segmentation is rarely done by business-to-business marketers because it is not useful.

3 Discuss criteria for successful market segmentation

_____ 5. Which of the following factors should a museum consider prior to engaging in segmentation?
   a. ability to identify and measure segments
   b. differentiated responses among segments
   c. ability to reach targeted segments
   d. sufficient size to warrant developing a unique marketing mix
   e. all of these

_____ 6. A manufacturer of photographic equipment segments the camera market by use: family and personal, hobbyists, professional, and scientific. In order for this segmentation scheme to be successful, all of the following criteria must be met EXCEPT:
   a. substantiality
   b. accessibility
   c. identifiability and measurability
   d. responsiveness
   e. complexity

_____ 7. The manager of CritterEats noted that due to an increase in owners of nontraditional pets such as ferrets, the exotic animal feed segment could be classified as having substantiality. This means that it:
   a. has enough special stores, magazines, and other outlets that it will be possible to direct advertisements at this group
   b. is too large and needs to be reduced to a more easily identifiable and measurable size
   c. exhibits a response rate to marketing variables different from the rates of other segments
   d. is large enough to permit a viable market effort toward its members
   e. will be difficult to develop a product to match this group of buyers

_____ 8. Marketers sometimes ignore small market niches—even if they have unfulfilled needs—primarily because these niches lack:
   a. substantiality
   b. identifiability and measurability
   c. responsiveness
   d. accessibility
   e. causality

_____ 9. The Help-U Program will be offering a course to help people become more assertive. It wants to segment the market and to slant its ads based on a consumer's amount of timidity and shyness. The first segmentation criterion problem that would greet this proposal is:
   a. identifiability and measurability
   b. responsiveness
   c. accessibility
   d. substantiality
   e. responsibility

_____ 10. The city of Calsey has a literacy program for migrant farm workers but has had a difficult time reaching this group with information about the program, even though radio and television stations have provided public service announcements free of charge. This is a segmentation problem called:
   a. substantiality
   b. accessibility
   c. responsiveness
   d. identifiability and measurability
   e. causality

_____ 11. The Good Doggie firm has a new training program especially for puppies. After placing fliers around town, the classes filled up within two days. Which segmentation success criterion is in force?
   a. accessibility
   b. identifiability and measurability
   c. responsiveness
   d. substantiality
   e. causality

4 Describe bases commonly used to segment consumer markets

_____ 12. The Merry Maid Home Cleaning Service offers three levels of cleaning: luxury-deluxe service (which includes a pet shampoo and ceiling scrubbing), the moderately priced basic package, and budget quick-clean service (vacuuming and laundry only). The income characteristic that has been used to divide its customers into segments is called the:
   a. accessibility quotient
   b. perceptual map
   c. segmentation base
   d. differentiation rule
   e. 80/20 principle

_____ 13. A new sport utility vehicle is targeting people who want the option to drive in regions with rugged terrain, such as the desert or mountainous areas. This is an example of:
   a. topographic segmentation
   b. geographic segmentation
   c. demographic segmentation
   d. benefit segmentation
   e. geodemographic segmentation

_____ 14. At an affordable price, the Mitsubishi Eclipse is targeting Generation X. This is an example of:
   a. usage rate segmentation
   b. benefit segmentation
   c. psychographic segmentation
   d. demographic segmentation
   e. geodemographic segmentation

_____ 15. The director of marketing has just completed demographic research on the total market for home improvement supplies. Which of the following is demographic that could be used to develop his market segmentation strategy?
   a. age data about home improvement buyers
   b. lifestyles of home improvement buyers
   c. home improvement usage patterns among buyers
   d. the benefits sought by home improvement buyers
   e. values of home improvement buyers

_____ 16. A new minivan is targeting households with a married couple who have three or more young children. This kind of demographic targeting is based on:
   a. micromarkets
   b. the family life cycle
   c. the VALS program
   d. geodemographics
   e. psychographics

---

17. Rising Hot Air Balloon Company targets adventurous and fun-loving people. This is an example of:
    a. demographic segmentation
    b. usage rate segmentation
    c. benefit segmentation
    d. psychographic segmentation
    e. family life cycle segmentation

18. Wrigley's Chewing Gum ran an advertising campaign that targeted heavy smokers. The pitch was "when you can't smoke, chew Wrigley's." This is an example of what type of segmentation?
    a. geodemographic
    b. benefit
    c. demographic
    d. psychographic
    e. usage rate

19. The Parker Pen Company manufactures several different categories of writing instruments: inexpensive disposable ballpoints, pens with erasable ink, pens specifically designed for artwork, and expensive executive pens. The Parker Pen Company is using which type of segmentation?
    a. benefit
    b. usage rate
    c. demographic
    d. psychographic
    e. geodemographic

20. When Jon opened his music store he noticed that he sold most of his cassette tapes to the same small group of customers (about eighty people), even though his sales records showed that he had over 400 regular cassette tape purchasers. This is a marketing phenomenon called the:
    a. optimizer principle
    b. music loyalty rule
    c. 80/20 principle
    d. cannibalization rule
    e. majority fallacy

5 Describe the bases for segmenting business markets

21. The Teletech Telephone Supply Company has categorized its business customers by their purchasing strategy used. Teletech has found that it is much easier to serve the customer that prefers to recontact familiar suppliers and place an order immediately if product and delivery requirements are acceptable. These customers can be described as:
    a. experiencers
    b. satisficers
    c. optimizers
    d. strugglers
    e. actualizers

22. Segmenting a business market by how customers would use the product uses which of the following segmentation bases?
    a. Company characteristics
    b. Customer relationship
    c. Industry type
    d. Buying processes
    e. Company size

23. Industry-Quip has decided to enter the industrial heating and air-conditioning market, and all the current competitors in that market use a differentiated product market strategy. Which strategy would make the LEAST sense for Industry-Quip?
    a. product differentiation strategy
    b. specialized product strategy
    c. concentrated or niche targeting strategy
    d. undifferentiated targeting strategy
    e. multisegment targeting strategy

24. Which of the following marketers is most likely to be able to practice undifferentiated marketing?
    a. the owner of the only hardware store in a small rural town located in Quebec City
    b. the owner of a three-store chain of budget outlets in the eastern part of Ontario
    c. the owner of a print-shop in Vancouver
    d. the administration of a small private college in Montreal
    e. the operator of a year-round resort in Mont-Tremblant, Quebec

25. Left-Out, Inc., manufactures knives, scissors, and other utensils specifically designed for left-handed consumers. Left-Out is using which type of strategy?
    a. concentrated or niche targeting
    b. undifferentiated targeting
    c. multisegment marketing
    d. universal product coding
    e. specialized marketing

26. When Procter & Gamble introduced Liquid Tide to a new segment, consumers in the traditional powdered detergent segment switched to the liquid product. Rather than real sales growth, P&G simply experienced the shifting of existing customers to a new product. This drawback of a multisegment targeting strategy is called:
    a. shift fallacy
    b. perceptual confusion
    c. undifferentiation
    d. repositioning
    e. cannibalization

8   Explain how and why firms implement positioning strategies and how product differentiation plays a role

27. A producer of teas commissioned a large research project on different brands of tea. The result was a graphical display of how consumers viewed these brands. Some brands were viewed as being "for iced tea," while others were considered as "hot teas." Also, some brands were viewed as traditional, while others were considered to have a variety of flavours. This is an example of:
    a. a positioning map
    b. cannibalization
    c. a segmentation study
    d. a perceptual map
    e. target marketing

____ 28. In the late 1980s, Oldsmobile tried to change its image from being a car for older people to being a car for younger people by using an advertising campaign, "This is Not Your Father's Oldsmobile." This effort is an example of:
   a. reimaging
   b. perceptual mapping
   c. resegmenting
   d. market segmentation
   e. repositioning

9 Discuss global market segmentation and targeting issues

____ 29. You are a marketing manager wanting to segment European and Asian food markets. Which of the following segmentation variables could be used?
   a. per capita GDP
   b. psychographics
   c. religion
   d. culture
   e. all the variables

Check your answers to these questions before proceeding to the next section.

SCENARIO

Read the marketing scenario and answer the questions that follow.

Claire has created a new, healthy snack product called VeggieChip. VeggieChip is similar to a potato chip but is made from other vegetables such as sweet potatoes, spinach, tomatoes, and zucchini. VeggieChip is baked with a minimum of canola oil for taste and contains sodium. It is low in fat and relatively low in calories but provides high "crunch" and good taste.

Claire came up with the product idea when she saw a market gap for a salty, healthy snack. She is targeting her snack toward women aged 14 to 25 who are active, health-conscious, and enjoy snacking between meals. She chose this target market because she knows she can identify them, reach them easily through magazine advertising and because they would be responsive to her product.

True/False:

____ 1. Claire engaged in some type of market segmentation before selecting her target market.

____ 2. Claire's strategy for selecting a target market is called undifferentiated marketing.

____ 3. Claire's choice to target "active, health-conscious" people is based on demographics.

Multiple Choice:

____ 4. Which of the following bases for segmentation are NOT being used by Claire?
   a. Geographic.
   b. Demographic.
   c. Psychographic.
   d. Benefits sought.
   e. All of these are being used.

____ 5. The choice of marketing to women aged 14 to 25 is based on which segmentation variable?
   a. Geographic.
   b. Demographic.
   c. Psychographic.
   d. Benefits sought.
   e. Usage-rate.

6. Which of the following criteria for successful segmentation has not been considered by Claire?
   a. Substantiality.
   b. Indentifiability.
   c. Accessibility.
   d. Responsiveness.
   e. Complexity.

7. Which of the following steps has Claire NOT yet accomplished?
   a. Choosing the bases for segmentation.
   b. Design, implement, and maintain an entire marketing mix.
   c. Select a target market.
   d. Select a market or product for study.
   e. Preliminary promotion ideas.

Short Answer:

8. Discuss the three strategies for selecting a target market and whether each strategy would make sense for VeggieChip.

ESSAY QUESTIONS

1. What is the difference between a market and a market segment? Why is segmentation so important?

2. Head and Shoulders Shampoo has targeted a new segment of people with dry scalps. To be useful, a segmentation scheme must produce segments that meet four basic criteria. Name and briefly describe each of these four criteria, and assess whether a dry scalp segment meets these criteria.

You would like to market a line of aromatherapy candles that not only provide light but also help people relax. Using all five variables for segmenting consumer markets, describe a target market for your products.

3. For toothpaste, list eight benefits that might be sought by consumers. For each benefit, give an existing brand name that best exemplifies segmentation according to that benefit.

4. You would like to start a new food store concept that sells only wholesome and organic foods. Describe three possible target markets for your new concept, using the three strategies for targeting markets.

6. What is a perceptual map? How can marketers use these maps?

7. Put the following list of steps in segmenting markets in the logical order for a marketer to proceed.

    — select target markets
    — profile and evaluate segments
    — select a market or product category
    — select segmentation descriptors
    — design, implement, and maintain appropriate marketing mixes
    — choose a basis or bases for segmenting the market

APPLICATION #1

You are given the following limited information about a market consisting of ten people. Describe all the possible ways to segment this market.

Age Group	Geographic Region
Adult	Northeast
Child	South
Child	South
Adult	West
Child	South
Adult	South
Adult	Northeast
Adult	West
Child	West
Child	West

You are the marketing manager for Propel Fitness Water, a thirst-quenching product that is a cross between highly flavoured sports drinks (such as Gatorade) and bottled water. Propel is vitamin-enhanced and contains only 10 calories, as opposed to Gatorade, which contains much more sugar and calories. However, it is lightly flavoured and has a better taste than water.

Do some research on the following brands. Then "map" each product on the following perceptual map according to how you perceive the product.

Aquafina
Coca-Cola
Dasani
Evian
Gatorade
Pepsi-cola
Powerade
Propel

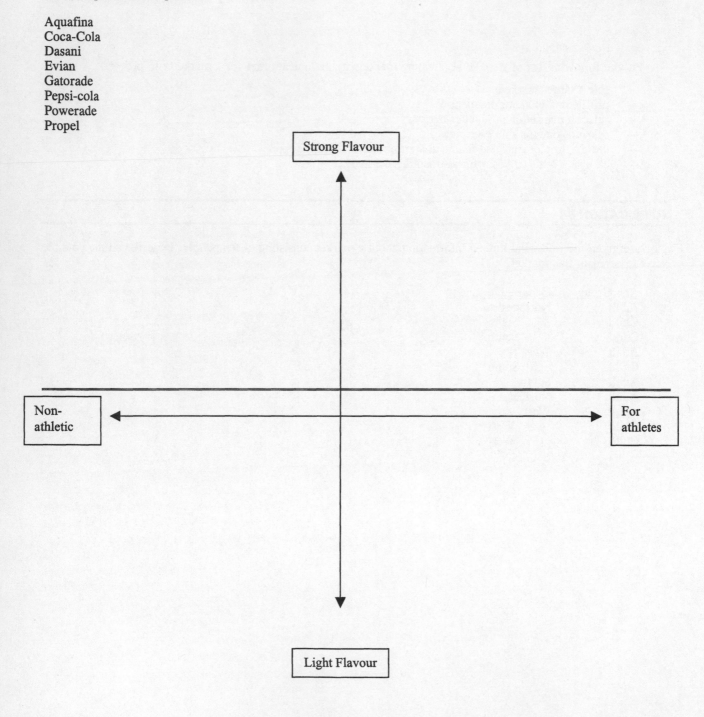

CHAPTER 7: DECISION SUPPORT SYSTEMS AND MARKETING RESEARCH

LEARNING OBJECTIVES

1   Explain the concept and purpose of a marketing decision support system

A decision support system (DSS) is an interactive, flexible information system that enables managers to obtain and manipulate information as they are making decisions. A DSS bypasses the information-processing specialist and lets managers instantly access data from their terminals. Successful use of a DSS allows the firm to respond quickly and creatively to marketing trends and opportunities.

2   Define marketing research and explain its importance to marketing decision making

Marketing research is the planning, collection, and analysis of data relevant to marketing decision-making. The results of this analysis are then communicated to management. Marketing research provides managers with data on the effectiveness of the current marketing mix and provides insights for changes. It is an important tool for reducing uncertainty in decision-making.

3   Describe the steps involved in conducting a marketing research project

The first step is to define the problem or questions that this research needs to examine. The next step, planning the research design, specifies the method that will be used to collect data. Then the sampling procedures that best fit this situation are selected. Next, the data is collected, often by an outside firm. Then data analysis takes place, and the results are interpreted. Subsequently, a report is drawn up and presented to management. A follow-up on the usefulness of the data and the report is the final step.

4   Discuss the profound impact of the Internet on marketing research

The Internet has vastly simplified the secondary data search process, placing more sources of information in front of researchers than ever before. Internet survey research is surging in popularity. Internet surveys can be created quickly and reported in real time. They are also relatively inexpensive and can be easily personalized. Often researchers can contact respondents who are difficult to reach via the Internet. The Internet can also be used to distribute research proposals and reports and to facilitate collaboration between the client and the research supplier. Clients can access real-time data and analyze it as the collection process continues.

5   Discuss the growing importance of scanner-based research

A prominent goal of marketing research is to develop an accurate, objective picture of the direct causal relationship between different kinds of sales and marketing efforts and actual sales. Single-source research is bringing marketers closer to that goal. Single-source research gathers information from a single panel of respondents by continuously monitoring the advertising, promotion, and pricing the panel is exposed to and what it subsequently buys.

Two electronic tools help to manage the single-source research system: television meters and laser scanners that read the UPC codes on products. These tools allow researchers to observe what advertisements reach a home and what products are purchased by the home.

6   Explain the concept of competitive intelligence

Competitive intelligence (CI) is the creation of an intelligence system that helps managers assess their competition and their vendors in order to become more efficient and effective competitors. Intelligence is analyzed information, and it becomes decision-making intelligence when it has implications for the organization.

Answer the following questions. After you finish, check your answers with the solutions at the back of this Study Guide.

1. What is marketing research? List and explain the three roles of marketing research.

2. List the seven steps of the marketing research process.

3. What are five advantages to Internet-based marketing research?

4. What is scanner-based research?

5. What is the purpose of competitive intelligence?

1 Explain the concept and purpose of a marketing decision support system

I.   Marketing Decision Support Systems

   A.   Accurate and timely information is the lifeblood of marketing decision- making. **Marketing information** is everyday information about developments in the marketing environment that managers use to prepare and adjust marketing plans. The system for gathering marketing intelligence is called a *marketing decision support system (DSS)*.

   B.   A **marketing decision support system (DSS)** is an interactive, flexible information system that enables managers to obtain and manipulate information as they are making decisions.

      1.   DSS bypasses the information-processing specialist and gives managers access to the data from their own desks.

      2.   The four characteristics of a DSS are that it is interactive, flexible, discovery-oriented, and accessible.

      3.   Perhaps the fastest growing use of DSS is for database marketing which is the creation of a large computerized file of customers' and potential customers' profiles and purchase patterns.

2 Define marketing research and explain its importance to marketing decision making

II.   The Role of Marketing Research

   A.   **Marketing research** is the planning, collection, and analysis of data relevant to marketing decision- making. It plays a key role in the marketing system. It:

      1.   provides managers with data on the effectiveness of the current marketing mix

      2.   provides insights for changes

      3.   is the primary data source for management information systems (MIS) and DSS

   B.   Roles of Marketing Research

      1.   Descriptive: gathering and presenting statements of fact.

      2.   Diagnostic: explaining data

      3.   Predictive: attempting to estimate the results of a planned marketing decision

   C.   Management Uses of Marketing Research

      1.   Marketing research improves the quality of marketing decision- making.

      2.   Marketing research is also used to discover what went wrong with a marketing plan.

      3.   Marketing research is used to retain customers by having an intimate understanding of their needs.

      4.   Marketing research helps managers understand what is going on in the marketplace and take advantage of opportunities.

3   Describe the steps involved in conducting a marketing research project

III. Steps in a Marketing Research Project

Virtually all firms that have adopted the marketing concept engage in marketing research, which can range from a very formal study to an informal interview with a few customers.

The marketing research process is a scientific approach to decision-making that maximizes the chance for getting accurate and meaningful results.

A. Problem/Opportunity Identification and Formulation

1. The research process begins with the recognition of a marketing problem or opportunity. It may be used to evaluate product, promotion, distribution or pricing alternatives, and/or find and evaluate new market opportunities.

2. The **marketing research problem** involves determining what information is needed and how that information can be obtained efficiently and effectively.

3. The **marketing research objective** is to provide insightful decision-making information. This requires specific pieces of information needed to answer the marketing research problem.

4. The **management decision problem** is broader in scope and far more general. It is action oriented.

5. **Secondary data** are data previously collected for any purpose other than the one at hand.

   a. The use of secondary data represents a savings in time and money.
   b. Disadvantages include the lack of fit between this unique problem and the data that have already been collected, and the difficulty of assessing the quality and accuracy of secondary data.

6. The Internet provides a new source of secondary data.

   a. Search engines contain collections of links to documents throughout the world. You can use the search engine to locate sites that include information that meets your requirements. You can also use subject directories on the Web to explore a topic.

   b. Discussion Groups include **newsgroups** that function much like bulletin boards for a particular topic or interest.

   c. Databases (periodical, newspaper, and book databases) on CD ROM include segmentation and demographic studies and mapping.

B. Planning the Research Design and Gathering Primary Data

1. The **research design** specifies which research questions must be answered using primary data, how and when the data will be gathered, and how the data will be analyzed.

2. **Primary data** are pieces of information collected for the first time and used for solving the particular problem under investigation.

   a. Must be collected if the specific research question cannot be answered by available secondary data. It is designed to answer specific questions, is current, is gathered using methodology specified by the researcher, and can be gathered in such a way as to maintain accuracy and secrecy.

b. A major disadvantage of primary data collection is the expense

3. Techniques for primary data collection include surveys, observation, and experiments.

   a. The most popular technique for gathering primary data is **survey research**, in which a researcher interacts with people to obtain facts, opinions, and attitudes.

   b. In-home interviews often provide high-quality information, offer the opportunity to gain in-depth responses, but are extremely expensive because of the interviewer's time and mileage.

   c. Mall intercept interviews are a survey research method that involves interviewing people in the common areas of shopping malls. They must be briefer than in-home interviews, often do not provide a representative sample of consumers, provide an overall quality of information similar to that of telephone interviews, and are less costly than in-home interviews.

   d. Another technique is **computer-assisted personal interviewing**, with the interviewer reading the questions from a computer screen and entering the respondent comments. A second approach is **computer-assisted self-interviewing**.

   e. Telephone interviews offer the advantage of lower cost than personal interviews, and have the potential for the best sample among interview types. Sometimes interviews are conducted from the interviewer's home, but most often are executed from a **central-location telephone (CLT) facility**, which is a specially designed room for conducting telephone interviews for survey research. These facilities have a number of phone lines and monitoring equipment in one location. Many CLT facilities offer **computer-assisted interviewing**, in which responses are input directly into the computer.

   f. Mail surveys, have relatively low costs, eliminate interviewees and field supervisors, centralize control, provide (or promise) anonymity for respondents, and produce low response rates.

   g. Mail panels consist of a sample of households recruited to participate by mail for a given period, responding repeatedly over time.

   h. Executive interviewing is used by marketing researchers to conduct the industrial equivalent of door-to-door interviewing.

   i. **Focus groups** are groups of seven to ten people with desired characteristics who participate in a group discussion about a subject of interest to a marketing organization. The **group dynamics** and interaction are essential to the success of this method

4. All forms of survey research require a questionnaire to ensure that all participants are asked the same series of questions.

   a. **Open-ended questions** are those worded to encourage unlimited answers phrased in the respondent's own words.

   b. **Closed-ended questions** are those in which the respondent is provided with a list of responses and is requested to make a selection from that list. These questions may be dichotomous (only two possible answers) or multiple choice.

   c. A **scaled-response question** is a closed-ended question designed to measure the intensity of a respondent's answer.

    d.   Qualities of good questionnaires include clearness, conciseness, objectiveness, and reasonable terminology.

    e.   Care should be taken to ask only one question at a time

    f.   The purpose of the survey and expectations of the participants' behaviour should be stated up front

5. **Observation research** is a research method that relies on three types of observation: people watching people, people watching an activity, and machines watching people.

    a.   People watching people is one form of observation research. Mystery shoppers are researchers posing as customers to observe the quality of service being offered.

    b.   One-way mirror observations are used to see how consumers use and react to products.

6. In an **experiment**, the researcher changes one or more variables (such as price or package design) while measuring the effects of those changes on another variable (usually sales).

C. When specifying the sampling procedures, the **sample** or subset of the larger population to be drawn for interviewing must be determined.

    ✓   First, the population from which a sample is drawn, or **universe** of interest, must be defined.
    ✓   Next, the researcher must determine if the sample for this study should be representative of the population as a whole.
    ✓   If yes, then a probability sample is called for.

1. With a **probability sample**, every element in the population has a known nonzero probability of being selected. Scientific rules are used to ensure that the sample represents the population.

    a.   A **random sample** is set up so that every element of the population has an equal chance of being selected as part of the sample.
    b.   Often a random sample is selected by using random numbers from a table found in statistics books.

2. A **nonprobability sample** is any sample in which little or no attempt is made to get a representative cross section of the population.

    a.   A **convenience sample** uses respondents who are readily accessible to the researcher.
    b.   Nonprobability samples are frequently used in market research, because they cost less than probability samples.

3. Several types of errors are associated with sampling.

    a.   **Measurement error** occurs when the information desired by the researcher differs from the information provided by the measurement process.
    b.   **Sampling error** occurs when a sample is not representative of the target population in certain respects.

        1)   Nonresponse error occurs when certain members of the sample refuse to respond and their responses may have differed from the sample as a whole.
        2)   **Frame error** arises if the sample drawn from a population differs from the target population.
        3)   **Random error** occurs when the selected sample does not represent the overall population.

D. Collecting the Data

    1. Primary data collection is done mostly by field service firms.

        a. **Field service firms** specialize in interviewing respondents on a subcontract basis.
        b. Field service firms also conduct focus groups, mall intercepts, retail audits, and other data-collection services.

E. Analyzing the Data

    1. Three types of analysis are common in marketing research.

        a. One-way frequency counts are the simplest, noting how many respondents answered a question a certain way. This method provides a general picture of the study's results.
        b. **Cross tabulations** relate the responses to one question to the responses to one or more other questions.
        c. Statistical analysis, the most sophisticated type, offers a variety of techniques for examining the data.

F. Prepare and Present the Report

The research must communicate the conclusions and recommendations to management. Usually both oral and written reports are required.

G. Follow Up

The researcher should determine if management followed the recommendations and why or why not.

Market research is not always the correct solution to a problem. In several situations it may be best not to conduct market research:

    a. When decision-making information already exists
    b. When the costs of conducting research are greater than the benefits.

4 Discuss the profound impact of the Internet on marketing research

IV. The Profound Effect of the Internet on Marketing Research

It has been predicted that Internet marketing research will account for about 50 percent of all marketing research revenue in North America by 2005.

A. Reasons for the success of Internet marketing research include; better and faster decision making through more rapid access to business intelligence, improves the ability to respond quickly to customer needs and market shifts, makes the conducting of follow-up studies and longitudinal research easier and more fruitful, and cuts time and labour costs.

B. Advantages of Internet surveys include speed, low cost, creation of longitudinal studies, cost effectiveness of short surveys, the ability to reach large audiences, and eye appeal.

C. Disadvantages if Internet surveys include the unrepresentativeness of the sample, security, the respondents are self-selecting, and respondents may complete the survey more than once.

D. Other uses of the Internet by marketing researchers includes the distribution of requests for proposals, collaborative projects, data management and on-line analysis, the publication and distribution of reports, and oral presentations to widely scattered audiences.

5   Discuss the growing importance of scanner-based research

V.   Scanner-based Research

Scanner-based research is a system for gathering information from a single group of respondents by continuously monitoring the advertising, promotion, and pricing panel to which members are exposed and the things they buy.

    A.   Two electronic tools help to manage the single-source system: television meters and laser scanners, which read the bar codes on products.

    B.   The two major suppliers of single-source research are Information Resources Incorporated (IRI) and the A.C. Nielsen Company.

        1.   IRI offers information collected through its **BehaviorScan** program, a single-source research program that tracks the purchases of 3,000 households through store scanners. Household purchasing is monitored, as well as exposure to such marketing variables as TV advertising and consumer promotions.

        2.   Another IRI product, **InfoScan**, is a scanner-based national and local sales-tracking service for the consumer packaged-goods industry. Retail sales, detailed consumer purchasing information, and promotional activity are monitored and evaluated for bar-coded products.

6   Discuss the concept of competitive intelligence

VI.   Competitive Intelligence

    A.   Competitive intelligence is the creation of a system that helps managers assess their competitors and their vendors in order to become a more efficient and effective competitor.

        1.   Advantages of using competitive intelligence

            a.   helps managers assess their competition and their vendors
            b.   allows managers to predict changes in business relationships
            c.   helps identify marketplace opportunities
            d.   helps guard against threats
            e.   forecasts a competitor's strategy
            f.   discover new or potential competitors
            g.   learn from the success or failure of others
            h.   learn about new technologies
            i.   learn about the impact of government regulations

        2.   Promotes effective and efficient decision-making, which should lead to greater profitability.

Fill in the blank(s) with the appropriate term or phrase from the alphabetized list of chapter key terms.

BehaviorScan
central-location telephone (CLT) facility
closed-ended question
competitive intelligence
computer-assisted personal interviewing
computer-assisted self interviewing
convenience sample
cross-tabulation
data base marketing
decision support system (DSS)
executive interviews
experiment
field service firms
focus group
frame error
group dynamics
InfoScan
mall intercept interview
management decision problem
marketing information
marketing research
marketing research objectives

marketing research problem
measurement error
mystery shoppers
newsgroups
nonprobability sample
observation research
open-ended question
primary data
probability sample
random error
random sample
recruited Internet sample
research design
sample
sampling error
scaled-response question
scanner-based research
screened Internet sample
secondary data
survey research
universe
unrestricted Internet sample

1 Explain the concept and purpose of a marketing decision support system

1. Everyday information about developments in the marketing environment that managers use to prepare and adjust marketing plans is called _____. An interactive, flexible system that enables managers to obtain and manipulate information as they are making decisions is called a _____.

2. Perhaps the fastest-growing use of decision support systems is for _____, which is the creation of large, computerized files of customers' and potential customers' profiles and purchasing patterns.

2 Define marketing research and explain its importance to marketing decision making

3. The process of planning, collecting, and analyzing data relevant to marketing decision-making defines _____.

3 Define marketing research and explain its importance to marketing decision making

4. The first step in the research process is defining the _____. Once this step has been completed, the researcher should determine what specific pieces of information are needed and will formulate _____. Marketing research may provide managers with enough information to determine the _____, which tends to be broader in scope and more action oriented.

5. One important type of information used for decision making in the marketing research process is _____, which are data previously collected for any purpose other than the one at hand. The Internet is a good source for many types of this data. One good Internet source may be _____, which function like electronic bulletin boards that focus on a particular topic.

6. Upon completing the situation analysis, researchers may conclude that secondary data does not answer the research question. This means that _____ must be collected, which is information gathered for the first time. The _____ specifies the research questions to be answered, where and when these data will be gathered, and how the data will be analyzed.

7. The most popular technique for gathering primary data is through _____, in which a researcher interacts with people to obtain information. One technique is using in-home interviews. Another technique involves interviewing people in the common areas of shopping malls. This is called a(n) _____.

8. Marketing researchers are applying new technology in mall interviewing. One technique allows researchers to conduct in-person interviews by reading questions from a computer and keying responses into the computer. This method is known as _____. Another method is to allow respondents to key their own responses into the computer themselves. This is known as _____.

9. Most telephone interviewing is conducted from a specially designed phone room called a(n) _____.

10. Marketing researchers may also use _____, a survey that involves interviewing businesspeople at their offices. This is often done for industrial products or services.

11. One type of personal interviewing involves a small group of qualified consumers who participate in a group discussion led by a moderator. This type of survey research is called a(n) _____. The interaction provided by the group of respondents is called _____ and is crucial to the success of this research.

12. There are a variety of question types that can be used on a survey questionnaire. To encourage unlimited answer choices phrased in the respondent's own words requires a(n) _____. Alternatively, a respondent may be asked to make a selection from a limited list of responses, which is called a(n) _____. A type of this second kind of question that measures the intensity of a respondent's answer is called a(n) _____.

13. In contrast to survey research, an alternative type of research does not rely on direct interaction with people. This technique is called _____ and takes three forms: people watching people, people watching an activity, and machines watching people. In addition to one-way mirror observation, retailers often use _____ who pose as customers to gather observational data about a store.

14. In another method that researchers use to gather primary data, the researcher alters one or more variables (such as price, advertising, or packaging) while observing the effects of those alterations on another variable (usually sales). This is called a(n) _____.

15. Once the primary data collection technique has been determined, the sampling procedures must be selected. First, a population, of interest must be defined. A(n) _____ is a subset of that population. This population is called the _____.

16. After the population is defined, the researcher must then decide if the sample must be representative of the population. If the sample must be representative, a(n) _____ is needed. One type of this kind of sample is arranged in such a way that every element of the population has an equal chance of being selected as part of the sample. This is called a(n) _____. If population representativeness is not required, a(n) _____ can be used. A common form of this type of sample is based on using respondents who are readily accessible to the researcher. This is called a(n) _____.

17. Whenever a sample is used in marketing research, two major types of error occur. When there is a difference between the information desired by a researcher and the information provided by the measurement process, _____ has occurred. The other major type of error occurs when the sample is not representative of the target population. This is known as _____. This second type of error can be categorized into several components. If the sample drawn from a population differs from the target population, _____ has occurred. Finally, if the sample is an imperfect representation of the overall population, _____ has occurred.

18. After specifying sampling procedures, the data must be collected. Most data collection is performed by _____ that specialize in interviewing respondents on a subcontract basis. After data collection, data analysis takes place. One method of analysis allows the analyst to look at responses to one question in relation to responses to one or more other questions. This is called a(n) _____. Other types of analysis include one-way frequency counts and statistical analysis.

4   Discuss the profound impact of the Internet on marketing research

19. Though there are many advantages to conducting surveys through the Internet, there are also some disadvantages. One disadvantage occurs when anyone who desires completes a survey, creating an unrestricted sample that may not be representative of targeted respondents. One solution is to select respondents by specific characteristics, such as gender or geographic region, resulting in a(n) _____. If researchers wish to adjust for the unrepresentativeness of the Internet population, they may use a(n) _____, which uses quotas based on desired sample characteristics. Another solution maintains even more control over the sample. Researchers call, e-mail, or write to potential respondents and ask them to participate in a survey. This sample is called a _____.

5   Discuss the growing importance of scanner-based research

20.   One type of marketing research gathers its information from a single panel of respondents by continuously monitoring the advertising, promotion, and pricing the panel is exposed to and its subsequent purchases. This is called _____. A company called Information Resources, Inc. (IRI) offers single-source data of two types. The first type uses panel members who shop with an ID card so that purchases can be tracked. This is called a(n) _____. The second product tracks sales of consumer packaged goods by scanning UPC codes. This is known as _____.

6   Explain the concept of competitive intelligence

21. The creation of a system that helps managers assess their competitors and vendors is called a system.

Check your answers to these questions before proceeding to the next section.

TRUE/FALSE QUESTIONS

Mark the statement **T** if it is true and **F** if it is false.

1   Explain the concept and purpose of a marketing decision support system

_____   1.   Marketing intelligence is a measure of the skills and education levels of employees in a marketing department.

2   Define marketing research and explain its importance to marketing decision making

_____   2.   Marketing research is but one component in a decision support system (DSS).

_____   3.   Marketing research focuses on gathering information about environmental trends and communicating that information to marketing managers.

3   Describe the steps involved in conducting a marketing research project

_____   4.   Cosmic Bowling has experienced a decline in sales over the past five years. Management at the bowling alley has defined the problem and would like to get started with some marketing research. The next step in the research process is to determine which methodology to use to gather information.

_____   5.   Greg and Amy run an errand service. They would like to find out what services they'd like to offer. Amy suggests they use the results of a survey they conducted last year because they were asking some similar questions then. Amy is suggesting they use primary research data.

_____   6.   Brett is researching the effects of advertising dessert products during primetime TV programming. The major advantage of using primary data is that this is probably the only way he could get questions about such a specific topic answered.

_____   7.   The Internet can be used for both primary and secondary research.

_____   8.   When Mars wondered whether a bigger bar sold at the same price would increase sales enough to offset the higher ingredient costs, it maintained the same marketing mix but varied the size of the bar in three different markets, the company was most likely conducting an experiment.

_____   9.   Rebecca needs twenty people to fill out a survey for her marketing class project. She stands outside the library and hands the survey to the first twenty people who come out. Rebecca is using a random sample.

Check your answers to these questions before proceeding to the next section.

For the following statements, indicate reasons why you may agree and disagree with the statement.

1. Secondary data rarely provide enough information for decision-making.

    Reason(s) to agree:

    Reason(s) to disagree:

2. Focus groups should not be used as a sole tool for making marketing decisions.

    Reason(s) to agree:

    Reason(s) to disagree:

3. There is no such thing as perfect information in marketing research.

    Reason(s) to agree:

    Reason(s) to disagree:

4. Competitive intelligence is an ethical part of marketing research.

    Reason(s) to agree

    Reason(s) to disagree

Select the response that best answers the question, and write the corresponding letter in the space provided.

1 Explain the concept and purpose of a marketing decision support system

_____ 1. Decision support systems have all the following characteristics EXCEPT:
   a. flexibility
   b. accessibility
   c. interactive features
   d. difficult to learn
   e. discovery orientation

_____ 2. Which of the following is the best example of the interactivity of a decision support system?
   a. Managers who are not skilled with computers can use the system.
   b. Managers give simple instructions to the system and see immediate results.
   c. Managers can create "what if" scenarios.
   d. The system can manipulate data in various ways.
   e. The system is not costly.

_____ 3. The creation of a large computerized file of customers' and potential customers' profiles and purchase patterns is known as:
   a. a decision support system (DSS)
   b. a marketing decision support system
   c. database marketing
   d. the Internet
   e. customer relationship marketing

2 Define marketing research and explain its importance to marketing decision making

_____ 4. The manager for Slurp Soda has requested marketing research to find out why a recent rebate offer failed to generate much response or any increase in sales. This type of research is:
   a. descriptive
   b. predictive
   c. historical
   d. normative
   e. diagnostic

_____ 5. An advertising agency is researching consumer attitudes toward a TV commercial that promotes a cellular phone service. This type of research is:
   a. descriptive
   b. predictive
   c. historical
   d. normative
   e. diagnostic

_____ 6. Which of the following best illustrates the predictive role of marketing research?
   a. Exit poll research has found that 60 percent of voters voted for the incumbent senator.
   b. A survey concludes that nine out of ten dentists recommend Brite toothpaste.
   c. Consumers in a focus group explain why they like the new product.
   d. Research has found that consumers do not like the new product improvement.
   e. Research has found that increasing a product's price 20 percent will result in a sales decrease of 35 percent.

_____ 7. The manager of a video rental store is worried about her store's performance. Sales have declined steadily over the past two years, and she cannot explain why. She would like to do some research. What should her first step in the market research process be?
   a. collect the data
   b. plan the research design
   c. analyze the marketplace
   d. recognize the marketing problem
   e. specify the sampling plan

_____ 8. The President of Clone Clothing stores has seen her chain of stores experience a decline in sales. She disliked the recent advertising campaign and thinks the campaign caused the sales decline. Her informal research showing potential customers were not enthusiastic toward the ads for Clone Clothing. Which of the following actions should be taken?
   a. conduct an experiment to show which of several alternative advertising campaigns are most appealing to potential Clone customers
   b. perform a survey to see how knowledgeable potential customers are with Clone Clothing
   c. investigate to reveal the exact problem with the advertising and why it caused sales to decline
   d. do a survey first to see if an experiment would be cost effective
   e. investigate the potential causes of the sales decline

_____ 9. Which of the following is the best example of a marketing research objective?
   a. To determine why sales have decreased over the past three years.
   b. To create a print advertisement emphasizing customer service.
   c. To determine what role children have in influencing family decisions about vacation destinations.
   d. To increase sales by 10 percent.
   e. To develop a method to track consumer attitudes.

_____ 10. The Play-It-Again used sporting equipment outlet cannot afford to collect primary data and has decided to use secondary data to answer some research questions. Play-It-Again should realize the potential disadvantages of secondary data, which include:
   a. the difficulty of holding certain variables constant while varying one factor of interest
   b. the high cost of collecting secondary data
   c. the information may not be timely to address the needs of the research problem
   d. the measurement error that can occur during the collection process
   e. the length of time it takes to collect secondary data

_____ 11. When assessing the quality of secondary data, it is:
   a. necessary to know who collected the data in the first place
   b. important to be able to have easy access to the data
   c. important to know when the data were collected
   d. important to know the purpose for which the data were originally collected
   e. important to assess all of these

_____ 12. You would like to find some annual sales figures of a major competitor as part of your secondary data research. You have decided to use the World Wide Web as your source. Which of the following is the most direct way of finding out this information?
   a. Type the words "sales" and the competitor's name in a search engine.
   b. Type the URL (Uniform Reference Locator) of the competitor and search through annual reports.
   c. Type the competitor's name in a search engine and scan for sales information.
   d. Type the URL (Uniform Reference Locator) of a trade association to which you both belong.
   e. Type the word "sales" in a search engine and scan for the competitor's name.

_____ 13. One of the disadvantages to using focus groups to collect data is:
   a. the cost is relatively high compared to other research methods.
   b. the time it takes to organize focus group is very long.
   c. the sample size is not large enough to be quantitatively measured.
   d. the marketer cannot show concepts or story boards to focus groups.
   e. there is very little control over the focus group moderator.

14. One disadvantage of primary data is:
    a. high cost compared to secondary data
    b. accessibility only through complex computerized data bases
    c. being nonsecure data because of its availability to any interested party for use
    d. potential irrelevance to the problem at hand
    e. not providing a realistic picture of the marketplace

15. The Acme Marketing Department is collecting data on consumers' spending habits and their attitudes toward environmental legislation, using one questionnaire. This is an example of a(n):
    a. piggyback study
    b. multiple-source study
    c. dual-probe experiment
    d. dichotomous question
    e. experiment

16. The Robo-Vac company wants to get consumer feedback about the style, features, and operation of its prototype automatic mini-vacuum cleaner, all while giving a demonstration of the product. What form of survey would allow them to do this?
    a. mall intercept
    b. mail questionnaire
    c. telephone interview
    d. observation study
    e. laboratory experiment

17. A local political party has decided to use telephone interviews to help predict the next election primarily because this technique offers:
    a. speed in gathering data
    b. few nonresponses
    c. a potential for census rather than sample data
    d. the ability to collect complex and large amounts of data
    e. the least amount of sampling error

18. The biggest disadvantage of Internet surveys is that:
    a. the cost is prohibitive.
    b. it has a lower response rate than mail or telephone surveys.
    c. the respondents are not representative of the population as a whole.
    d. research firms can only communicate with respondents during business hours.
    e. the respondents may not provide accurate answers to questions.

19. You have been hired to view store customers through a video camera and record the number of times a shopper pauses beside the special display case. You are engaging in:
    a. survey sampling research
    b. experimental research
    c. observation research
    d. focus group research
    e. panel research

20 Cox's Department Stores wanted to learn more about its customers and their shopping habits in Cox's stores. After considering several different methods, Cox's decided on observation research because:
    a. biases from the interviewing process are eliminated
    b. it relies on the respondent's willingness to provide the desired data
    c. it has a relatively high response rate
    d. attitudes and motivations are clearly demonstrated in observation research
    e. it is actually an experiment using natural environments

21. A research manager decides to have his telephone interviewers dial every tenth number in the telephone directory. This is a:
    a. convenience sample
    b. probability sample
    c. stratified sample
    d. quota sample
    e. nonprobability sample

_____ 22. TeleResearch, Inc., is conducting a telephone survey to determine the brand recall of a particular TV commercial that ran the night before. TeleResearch is calling every one-hundredth person that is listed in the Toronto phone book. This is an example of:
   a. field service sample
   b. random sample
   c. nonprobability sample
   d. regular sample
   e. convenience sample

_____ 23. Jerome has to interview eighty people for his marketing research class project and decides to use his fellow dorm residents. This is a:
   a. convenience sample
   b. probability sample
   c. simple random sample
   d. field service sample
   e. multirespondent sample

4   Discuss the profound impact of the Internet on marketing research

_____ 24. Behaviour Research Company is calling several people to determine who would be appropriate respondents to a long Internet survey it would like to administer. The people who agree to take the survey are then directed to a Web site that contains a link to the survey. The respondents taking the Internet survey are an example of:
   a. a recruited Internet sample.
   b. a screened Internet sample.
   c. an Internet focus group.
   d. an unrestricted Internet sample.
   e. a mass market sample.

_____ 25. The Internet has greatly enhanced marketing researchers by:
   a. facilitating the distribution of requests for proposals
   b. allowing easier collaboration among researchers geographically separated
   c. providing data management and on-line analysis capabilities
   d. expanding publication and distribution of reports
   e. all of these

5   Discuss the growing importance of scanner-based research

_____ 26. Pietro's Pasta Products gathers weekly information from the same consumers. Pietro's continuously monitors the advertising the consumers are exposed to and records their purchases. Pietro's uses cable TV to send different commercials to different areas, and it keeps a record of all consumers' grocery purchases in return for a fee. This is a:
   a. television meter investigation
   b. scanner-based research
   c. CLT interview
   d. laser scanner study
   e. one-way TV observation

Check your answers to these questions before proceeding to the next section.

Read the marketing scenario and answer the questions that follow.

Canine Country Day School (CCDS) is a premium daycare centre for dogs. Its target market is dog owners who have "guilt" about leaving behind their beloved best friend when they go to work every day. CCDS offers several basic services for dogs, including walks with each dog twice a day, monitored "playtime" on the large grassy area at the school, obedience training, nutritious lunches, and naptime.

CCDS would like to find out what additional services it can offer to dog owners and how it can increase its business. It has hired Michael Dogbert, a marketing researcher, to conduct some research. After interviewing the owners at the company, Michael determined that the company should start with some focus groups, simply selected from among the company's best customers. The focus groups were used to determine what additional types of services customers would like to see offered and how much they were willing to pay for them. Then Michael got permission from a local pet store chain to "intercept" customers and survey them on their needs and what they did with their dogs while at work. All customers who walked into the stores between 10AM and 2PM on two consecutive Saturdays were screened to determine if they were dog owners and then asked if they would complete the survey.

True/False:

_____ 1. Michael has conducted all the steps of the marketing research process.

_____ 2. The marketing research problem or opportunity was identified.

_____ 3. Michael has collected only primary data in this scenario.

Multiple Choice:

_____ 4. Which of the following steps of the marketing research process has NOT been conducted?
   a. Problem or opportunity identification.
   b. Collecting the data.
   c. Analyzing the data.
   d. Sampling procedures.
   e. Setting objectives.

_____ 5. A good example of secondary data that was collected is:
   a. the focus groups.
   b. the surveys at pet stores.
   c. the interview with CCDS owners.
   d. conversations with the owners.
   e. none; secondary data was not collected.

_____ 6. Which of the following sampling procedures was used for the focus groups?
   a. Probability sampling.
   b. Random sampling.
   c. Convenience sampling.
   d. Experimental sampling.
   e. Nonprobability market sampling

_____ 7. What other type of research would be appropriate for this marketing research problem?
   a. Telephone interview that screens for dog owners who work full-time.
   b. Mall-intercept interviews with shoppers who may or may not own dogs.
   c. Mass market mail survey given to all households in five zip codes that are near the school.
   d. An experiment involving interactions between current customers with their dogs.
   e. BehaviorScan tracking of current customers.

8.   If you were Michael, how would you finish up the research process?

ESSAY QUESTIONS

1.   What is marketing research? Name and briefly describe the three functional roles of marketing research. Then discuss two possible benefits of marketing research to managers.

2.   What are the steps of the marketing research process?

3.   Your boss has asked you to get consumer feedback on a recent gourmet cookbook your company has published. He is thinking of using an Internet survey but is unsure. Write your boss a memo detailing the advantages and disadvantages to conducting a survey on the Internet. Tell him what can be done to avoid getting an unrestricted sample on the Internet.

---

4. What is competitive intelligence? Discuss at least five advantages to having a competitive intelligence system.

APPLICATION

A marketing researcher has many options when designing a questionnaire. However, some questions are better than others for obtaining responses. Match each survey question example with its definition by placing the matching letter in the blank to the left of the example. Each letter is used only once.

A. Open-ended question
B. Closed-ended dichotomous question
C. Closed-ended multiple-choice question
D. Scaled-response question
E. Ambiguous question
F. Two questions in one
G. Biased/leading question

_____ What is your favourite brand of athletic shoe?
_____ Nike _____ L.A. Gear _____ Reebok _____ Other

_____ Do you currently own a pair of athletic shoes?
_____ YES _____ NO

_____ What are your opinions about owning a pair of Nike shoes?

_____ Do you think Nikes and Reeboks are good quality shoes?

_____ Why do you think Nikes are such excellent shoes?

_____ Now that you know about Nike athletic shoes, would you ...
_____ Definitely buy
_____ Probably buy
_____ Might or might not buy
_____ Probably not buy
_____ Definitely not buy

_____ If you are thinking of buying a pair of Nikes, will you be buying soon?
_____ YES _____ NO

CHAPTER 8: PRODUCT CONCEPTS

1   Define the term "product"

A product may be defined as everything, both favourable and unfavourable, that one receives in an exchange. It can be a tangible good, a service, an idea, or a combination of these things.

2   Classify consumer products

Consumer products can be differentiated from business products according to intended use.

Consumer products are purchased to satisfy an individual's personal wants. The most widely used classification approach has four categories: convenience products, shopping products, specialty products, and unsought products. This approach classifies products on the basis of the amount of effort that is normally expended in the shopping process.

3   Define the terms "product item," "product line," and "product mix"

A product item is a specific version of a product that can be designated as.a distinct offering among an organization's products. A product line is a group of closely related products offered by the organization. An organization's product mix includes all the products it sells.

Marketing strategies and mixes may be built around individual product items, product lines, or the entire product mix. Product line and mix decisions can affect advertising economies, packaging strategies, standardization of components, and efficiency of the sales and distribution functions.

4   Describe marketing uses of branding

Branding is the major tool marketers have to distinguish their products from those of the competition. A brand is a name, term, symbol, design, or combination thereof that identifies a seller's products and differentiates them from competitors' products. Branding has three main objectives: identification, repeat sales, and new product sales.

5   Describe marketing uses of packaging and labelling

Packaging is an important strategic part of the marketing mix. The product and its package are often inseparable in the consumer's mind. Subtle changes in packaging can dramatically alter the consumer's perception of the product. A package should communicate an image to the consumer that will help achieve the positioning objectives of the firm.

An integral part of any package is its label. Labelling strategy generally takes on one of two forms. Persuasive labelling focuses on a promotional theme or logo, with information for the consumer taking secondary importance. Informational labelling is designed to help consumers in making proper product selections and to lower cognitive dissonance after the purchase.

6   Discuss global issues in branding and packaging

In addition to brand piracy, international marketers must address a variety of concerns regarding branding and packaging, including choosing a brand name policy, translating labels and meeting host-country labelling requirements, making packages aesthetically compatible with host-country cultures, and offering the sizes of packages preferred in host-countries.

7   Describe how and why product warranties are important marketing tools

One part of the product is its warranty, a protection and information device for consumers. A warranty guarantees the quality or performance of a good or service. An express warranty is made in writing; an implied warranty is an unwritten guarantee that a good or service is fit for the purpose for which it was sold. All sales in Canada carry an implied warranty but warranties do vary from province to province.

Answer the following questions to see how well you understand the material. Re-take it after you review to check yourself.

1. What is a product? Name and briefly describe four types of consumer products.

2. Define the terms "product item," "product line," and "product mix." Give an example of each.

3. What is a brand? Name and briefly describe three branding strategies.

4. List and briefly describe three different branding strategies when entering international markets.

5. What are the three most important functions of packaging?

6. Why are warranties important as marketing tools?

1   Define the term "product"

I.   What Is a Product?

    A.   A **product** may be defined as everything, both favourable and unfavourable, that one receives in an exchange.

    B.   It can be a tangible good, a service, an idea, or a combination of these things.

2   Classify consumer products

II.   Types of Consumer Products

Products are classified as either business or consumer products depending on the buyer's intentions for the product's use.

    A.   A **business product** (industrial product) is used to manufacture other goods or services, to facilitate an organization's operations, or to resell to other customers.

    B.   A **consumer product** is purchased to satisfy an individual's wants. It can be classified on the basis of the amount of effort that is normally expended in the shopping process.

        1.   A **convenience product** is an inexpensive item that requires little shopping effort. These products are purchased regularly, usually with little planning, and require wide distribution.

        2.   A **shopping product** requires comparison-shopping because it is usually more expensive than convenience products and is found in fewer stores. Consumers usually compare items across brands or stores.

            a.   *Homogeneous* shopping products are products that consumers see as being basically the same, and consumers shop for the lowest price.
            b.   *Heterogeneous* shopping products are seen by consumers to differ in quality, style, suitability, and lifestyle compatibility. Comparisons between heterogeneous shopping products are often quite difficult because they may have unique features and different levels of quality and price.

        3.   A **specialty product** is searched for extensively, and substitutes are not acceptable. These products may be quite expensive, and often distribution is very limited.

        4.   An **unsought product** is a product that is not known about or not actively sought by consumers. Unsought products require aggressive personal selling and highly persuasive advertising

3   Define the terms "product item," "product line," and "product mix"

III.   Product Items, Lines, and Mixes

A **product item** is a specific version of a product that can be designated as a distinct offering among an organization's products.
A **product line** is a group of closely related product items.
An organization's **product mix** includes all the products it sells.

A. Why Form Product Lines?

1. *Advertising economies* occur when several products can be advertised under the umbrella of the line.

2. *Package uniformity* increases customer familiarity, and the different items actually help to advertise one another.

3. Product lines provide an opportunity for *standardizing components*, thus reducing manufacturing and inventory costs.

4. Product lines facilitate efficient *sales and distribution*, leading to economies of scale for managing the sales force, warehousing, and transportation.

5. Product lines based on a brand name help consumers *evaluate quality*. Consumers usually believe that all products in a line will be of similar quality.

B. Width and Depth

1. **Product mix width** refers to the number of product lines that an organization offers. Firms increase product mix width to:
   a. Spread risk across multiple lines
   b. Capitalize on established reputations

2. **Product line depth** is the number of product items in a product line. Firms increase product line depth to:
   a. Attract buyers with widely different preferences
   b. Capitalize on economies of scale
   c. Increase sales and profits by further segmenting the market
   d. Even out seasonal sales patterns

C. Adjustments to Product Items, Lines, and Mixes

1. Modifying Existing Products

   Product modification involves changing one or more of a product's characteristics.

   a. A *quality modification* entails changing a product's dependability or durability.
   b. A *functional modification* is a change in a product's versatility, effectiveness, convenience, or safety.
   c. A *style modification* is an aesthetic product change rather than a quality or functional modification. **Planned obsolescence** is the practice of causing products to become obsolete before they actually need replacement. It is often implemented through style modifications.

4 Describe marketing uses of branding

IV. Branding

A. Branding is the major tool marketers have to distinguish their products from those of the competition.

1. A **brand** is a name, term, symbol, design, or combination thereof that identifies a seller's products and differentiates them from competitors' products.

2. A brand name is that part of the brand that can be spoken, including letters, words, and numbers.

---

3. The **brand mark** is the element of the brand that cannot be spoken, such as symbols.

B. Benefits of Branding

1. Identification is the most important objective. The brand allows the product to be differentiated from others and serves as an indicator of quality to consumers.

    a. The term **brand equity** refers to the value of company and brand names.

2. Branding helps customers identify products they are satisfied with, promoting *repeat sales*. Brand loyalty, a consistent preference for one brand over all others, is quite high in some product categories.

    The term **global brand** refers to a brand that sell at least 20% outside of its home country. Examples of global brands are Coca-Cola, Microsoft, IBM, and McDonald's.

C. Branding Strategies

1. **Generic products** vs. branded products

    a. **Generic products** are typically no-frills, no-brand-name, low-cost products that is identified by their product category
    b. Are sold for 30 to 40 percent less than manufacturers' brands and 20 to 25 percent less than retailer-owned brands
    c. Are obtaining substantial market shares in some product categories, such as pharmaceuticals

2. Manufacturer's brands vs. private brands

    a. A **manufacturer's brand** strategy is used when manufacturers use their own name on their products.
    b. A **private brand** is a brand name that a wholesaler or retailer uses for the products it sells.

3. Individual brands vs. family brands

    a. **Individual branding** is the practice of using a different brand name for each product.
    b. Individual brands are used when products differ greatly in use or in performance, quality, or targeted segment
    c. A company that markets several different products under the same brand name is using a **family brand**.

4. Co-branding

    a. **Co-branding** entails placing two or more brands names on a product or its package

       1) *Ingredient branding* identifies the brand of a part that makes up the product.
       2) *Cooperative branding* is where two brands receiving equal treatment borrow each other's brand equity.
       3) *Complementary branding* is where products are advertised or marketed together to suggest usage.

D. Trademarks

1. A **trademark** is a legal term indicating the owner's exclusive right to use the brand or part of the brand. Others are prohibited from using the brand without permission. A **service mark** performs the same functions for service businesses.

---

a. Many parts of a brand (such as phrases and abbreviations) and symbols associated with product identification (such as shapes and colour combinations) qualify for trademark protection.

b. The mark has to be used continuously to be protected.

c. Rights to a trademark continue for as long as it is used.

2. Companies must guard against the unauthorized use of their brands, slight alterations to the brand by mimics, and counterfeit merchandise that is labelled with the brand.

a. In Canada, trademarks are registered under the Trademarks Act, and these rights last as long as the mark is used.

b. Companies that fail to protect their trademarks face the problem of their product names becoming generic. A **generic product name** identifies a product by class or type and cannot be trademarked.

5   Describe marketing uses of packaging and labelling

V. Packaging

A. Packaging is a container for protecting and promoting a product. Packaging has traditionally been viewed as a means of holding contents together and as a way of protecting the physical good as it moves through the distribution channel.

B. Packaging Functions

1. Containing and Protecting Products

a. Some packaging has to be quite sophisticated to protect the product from spoilage, tampering, or children.

2. Promoting Products

a. Packaging can differentiate a product from the competition by its convenience and utility.

b. Packages are the last opportunity marketers have to influence buyers before they make purchase decisions.

c. Packages are very important in establishing the brand image.

3. Facilitating Storage, Use, and Convenience

a. Wholesalers and retailers prefer packages that are easy to ship, store, and stock on shelves. They also like packages that protect the product, prevent spoilage or breakage, and extend shelf life.

b. Customers seek items that are easy to handle, open, and reclose.

c. Packaging is often used to segment markets, particularly by offering different sizes for different segments.

4. Facilitating Recycling and Reducing Environmental Damage

a. An important recent issue is the compatibility of the package and environmental concerns.

b. Many consumers demand recyclable, biodegradable, and reusable packages.

C. Labelling

1. **Persuasive labelling** focuses on a promotional theme or logo, and consumer information is secondary.

2. **Informational labelling** is designed to help consumers in making proper product selections and lower cognitive dissonance after the purchase.

3. The Consumer Packaging and Labelling Act and the Food and Drug Act state the minimum information that must appear on food products and set the standards for health claims on food packaging.

4. The **Universal Product Codes (UPC)** that appear on most items found in supermarkets and other high-volume outlets were first introduced in 1974. Computerized optical scanners read the bar codes that appear as a series of thick and thin vertical lines.

6 Discuss global issues in branding and packaging

VI. Global Issues in Branding and Packaging

A. Branding

When entering a foreign market, a firm has three options for handling the brand name.

1. One brand name everywhere
2. Adaptations and modifications
3. Different brand names in different markets

B. Packaging

Three aspects of packaging are especially important in international marketing.

1. *Labelling* - which must have accurate translations.
2. *Aesthetics* - which are attuned to cultural traits in the host countries.
3. *Climate* - which affects shipping concerns and packaging decisions.

7 Describe how and why product warranties are important marketing tools

VII. Product Warranties

A. Another part of the product is its warranty, a protection and information device for consumers.

1. A **warranty** confirms the quality or performance of a good or service.

2. An **express warranty** is made in writing; an **implied warranty** is an unwritten guarantee that a good or service is fit for the purpose for which it was sold.

Fill in the blank(s) with the appropriate term or phrase from the alphabetized list of chapter key terms.

brand	persuasive labelling
brand equity	planned obsolescence
brand loyalty	private brand
brand mark	product
brand name	product item
business (industrial) product	product line
co-branding	product line depth
consumer product	product line extension
convenience product	product mix
express warranty	product mix width
family brand	product modification
generic product	service mark
generic product name	shopping product
global brand	specialty product
implied warranty	trademark
individual branding	universal product code (UPC)
informational labelling	unsought product
manufacturer's brand	warranty

1 Define the term "product"

1. Everything, both favourable and unfavourable, that a person receives in an exchange, is a(n) _____. This may take the form of a tangible good, a service, an idea, or any combination of these three.

2 Classify consumer products

2. Products can be classified in two ways, depending on the intended use of the product. If a product is used to manufacture other goods or services, to facilitate an organization's operations, or is resold to other customers, it is called a(n) _____, or industrial product. If the product is purchased to satisfy an individual's personal wants, it is a(n) _____.

3. Consumer products can be classified into four categories. A product like gum or gasoline that is relatively inexpensive and requires little shopping effort is called a(n) _____. A product that is more expensive and found in fewer stores is called a(n) _____; these products can be homogeneous or heterogeneous. A product that consumers search for extensively and that is usually expensive is called a(n) _____. Finally, a product unknown to the potential buyer or a known product that the buyer does not actively seek is referred to as a(n) _____.

3 Define the terms "product item," "product line," and "product mix"

4. A specific version of a product that can be designated as a distinct offering among an organization's products is called a(n) _____. A group of closely related products offered by the organization is called a(n) _____. Finally, all the products that an organization sells is called the _____.

5. The number of product lines that an organization offers is referred to as _____. The number of product items in one product line is _____.

6. One job of the marketing manager is to decide when and if to alter existing products by changing one or more of a product's characteristics. This alteration procedure is _____, and can change functional, style, or quality attributes. Frequent product modifications can cause products to become outdated before they actually need replacement. This practice describes _____.

7. Adding additional products to an existing product line to compete more broadly in the industry is called _____.

4 Describe marketing uses of branding

8. A name, term, symbol, or design that identifies a seller's products and differentiates them from competitors' products is a(n) _____. The elements that can be spoken make up the _____, and the elements that cannot be spoken are called the _____.

9. When a company owns a brand name that is extremely familiar to consumers, the dollar value of the company is raised. This value of brand names is _____. A brand where at least 20 percent of its sales are sold outside the home country is called a _____. If a customer consistently prefers one brand over all others and is a repeat purchaser, the consumer has _____.

10. Firms face a variety of branding decisions, the first of which is whether to brand at all. A no-brand name, low-cost product is a(n) _____. If a firm chooses to brand, it has several options. The manufacturer's name used as a brand name is called a(n) _____, sometimes called a national brand. If the brand name is owned by a wholesaler or retailer, the brand is a(n) _____. If a firm has products that vary substantially in use or performance, it should use different brand names for different products, a strategy called _____. Alternatively, if the company markets several different products under the same brand name, it is using a(n) _____. If two or more brands names are placed on a product or its package, _____ is being used.

11. A legal term indicating the owner's exclusive right to use a product brand name or other identifying mark brand is a(n) _____. A(n) _____ performs the same legal function for services. If companies do not sufficiently protect their brand names, the name could become a(n) _____, which identifies a product by class or type and cannot be trademarked.

5 Describe marketing uses of packaging and labelling

12. The container for protecting and promoting a product is its package. An integral part of this is the label. Labelling strategy can take one of two forms. The first form focuses on a promotional theme or logo, and is known as _____. The second form is designed to help consumers make proper product selections and lower cognitive dissonance after the purchase; this is known as _____. A numerical code that appears on many product labels is the _____ for reading by computerized optical scanners.

7 Describe how and why product warranties are important marketing tools

13. When a company wants to guarantee the quality or performance of a good or service, it uses a(n) _____, which protects the buyer and gives essential information about the product. If it is in the form of a written guarantee, it is a(n) _____. If it is unwritten, a(n) _____ is being used; all sales have this.

Check your answers to these questions before proceeding to the next section.

TRUE/FALSE QUESTIONS

Mark the statement **T** if it is true and **F** if it is false.

1 Define the term "product"

_____ 1. When consumers purchase a sports drink, they are interested in the chemical composition of the product.

2 Classify consumer products

____ 2. Tammy considers her eye makeup to be very important. She spends considerable time comparing the prices and colour options available at various cosmetic counters in department stores. For Tammy, makeup is a convenience product.

____ 3. Joe Foxhunter makes unique silver jewellery. Loyal customers drive from miles around to buy the jewellery, which is sold only in his workshop. This jewellery is a specialty product.

3 Define the terms "product item," "product line," and "product mix"

____ 4. Sony makes a variety of products, all under the Sony brand name. These products include CD players, televisions, and computer diskettes. These products represent Sony's product line.

____ 5. Marketers should always add line extensions to their products to make the product line stronger.

____ 6. Ultra-Comp produces a high-quality, expensive line of executive laptop computers. Recently, it introduced another line of computers with fewer features and a lower price, but which still carried the Ultra-Comp brand name. This is an example of a line extension.

4 Describe marketing uses of branding

____ 7. The "rainbow-coloured apple" that Apple Computer puts on its machines is part of the company's branding strategy.

____ 8. Colgate-Palmolive makes Colgate toothpaste and has recently introduced Colgate mouthwash and Colgate toothbrushes. This is an example of family branding.

5 Describe marketing uses of packaging and labelling

____ 9. The most important functions of packaging are to contain and protect products; promote products; facilitate product storage, use, and convenience; and facilitate recycling.

Check your answers to these questions before proceeding to the next section.

AGREE/DISAGREE QUESTIONS

For the following statements, indicate reasons why you may agree and disagree with the statement.

1. Branding is dead. Consumers make purchase decisions on price more than any other feature.

   Reason(s) to agree:

   Reason(s) to disagree:

2. Because they are typically less expensive, lower income consumers purchase private brands.

    Reason(s) to agree:

    Reason(s) to disagree:

3. Global marketers should adapt their products (including brand) to local markets instead of using global strategies.

    Reason(s) to agree:

    Reason(s) to disagree:

4. It is better for marketers to use family branding than to use individual branding.

    Reason(s) to agree:

    Reason(s) to disagree:

MULTIPLE CHOICE QUESTIONS

Select the response that best answers the question, and write the corresponding letter in the space provided.

1 Define the term "product"

_____ 1. The creation of a product is the starting point for the marketing mix because:
  a. the production department must know what to produce first
  b. the product is the first of the four P's in the marketing mix
  c. the product does not have to be the starting point--distribution or promotional strategies could also be the starting point
  d. product development takes the longest amount of time to complete
  e. determination of the price, promotional campaign, and distribution network cannot begin until the product has been specified

2 Classify consumer products

_____ 2. David has wanted to purchase a Mercedes most of his adult life. He has done extensive research into different Mercedes models. Finally, at age 50, he has achieved the income level to be able to purchase one. The Mercedes is an example of a(n):
   a. specialty product
   b. consumer product
   c. convenience product
   d. business product
   e. unsought product

_____ 3. Zack decides to purchase a filing cabinet. He watches television and newspaper ads until he sees one at a low price. For Zack, the filing cabinet is a(n):
   a. convenience product
   b. shopping product
   c. component product
   d. unsought product
   e. specialty product

_____ 4. Joe jumps out of his truck and runs into a 7-Eleven store to grab a drink. While he is paying for his drink, he notices the candy bars at the counter and grabs one to buy. The candy bar in this case is considered to be a(n):
   a. specialty product
   b. consumer product
   c. convenience product
   d. business product
   e. unsought product

3 Define the terms "product item," "product line," and "product mix"

_____ 5. In the Helidyne Industries' product portfolio, there is a list of all the product items that the company manufactures and markets. This list includes several types of helicopter engines, nuts, bolts, washers, rotor blades, and instrument systems. This is a description of its:
   a. product mix
   b. product line
   c. marketing mix
   d. line depth
   e. mix consistency

_____ 6. PepsiCo makes a variety of soft drinks, including Pepsi, Pepsi One, and Sierra Mist. This is an example of:
   a. product line width
   b. product mix
   c. marketing mix
   d. product mix consistency
   e. product line depth

_____ 7. A laptop manufacturer recently added a metal case and shock mountings to its laptop computers to make them more durable. It has not changed its prices. This is a modification.
   a. quality
   b. style
   c. functional
   d. repositioning
   e. minor

_____ 8. A manufacturer of car batteries has added a handle and an emergency reserve switch to its batteries. The manufacturer has not changed its prices. This is a(n) modification.
   a. style
   b. functional
   c. quality
   d. repositioning
   e. upward extension

9. Frequent style modifications by product manufacturers can also be called planned obsolescence. All the following statements are true about planned obsolescence EXCEPT:
    a. planned obsolescence describes the practice of causing products to become obsolete before they actually need replacement
    b. opponents of planned obsolescence argue that the practice is wasteful and unethical
    c. marketers contend that consumers decide when styles are obsolete
    d. marketers ignore quality, safety, and functional modifications to incorporate planned obsolescence into their marketing plans
    e. consumers favour style modifications because they like changes in the appearance of goods such as clothing and cars

10. Kentucky Fried Chicken (KFC) has added several items to its menu, including Hot Wings, chicken wraps, and chicken nuggets. This is an example of:
    a. product line width
    b. portfolio expansion
    c. product line extension
    d. contraction
    e. repositioning

4 Describe marketing uses of branding

11. Coca-Cola is the best known brand name in the world. The name has a high perceived quality and high brand loyalty among soft drink users. The company has developed the brand name for over 100 years. Coca-Cola has a valuable:
    a. line extension
    b. logo
    c. private brand
    d. package
    e. brand equity

12. Pizza Hut has restaurants in many different areas of the world. As such, this makes Pizza Hut a:
    a. trademarked brand
    b. brand equity
    c. global brand
    d. generic brand
    e. family brand

13. The Safeway supermarket chain sells a brand of cookies, pasta, and other products under the name "Safeway Select." This is an example of a:
    a. master brand
    b. family brand
    c. brand grouping
    d. generic brand
    e. private brand

14. Fastop convenience stores sell only manufacturer's brands of snack foods. You explain to the manager that there are disadvantages to selling only manufacturer's brands such as:
    a. a well-known manufacturer's brand will not enhance store image
    b. manufacturers typically offer a lower gross margin than a dealer could earn on a private label
    c. manufacturers rarely spend money advertising the brand name to consumers
    d. manufacturers force stores to carry large inventories
    e. relying on the manufacturer to deliver a national brand quickly is optimistic at best

15. General Mills offers brands such as Bisquick pancake mix, Gold Medal flour, Betty Crocker cake mixes, and Yoplait yogurt. General Mills appears to be using a(n) strategy.
    a. equity brand
    b. individual brand
    c. private brand
    d. family brand
    e. dealer brand

16. Many personal computer manufacturers, such as Compaq and Dell, sell computers with the words "Intel inside" written on the central processing unit. This is an example of:
   a. dealer branding
   b. brand grouping
   c. private branding
   d. generic branding
   e. co-branding

17. Your boss has just told you to work on getting trademark protection for a new product brand the firm has developed, the "Zipper," which has a unique logo. You tell your boss that this protection will be difficult because:
   a. brand logo designs, even as unique as yours, cannot be trademarked
   b. of the catchy phrase used to promote your new brand
   c. you also use abbreviated versions of your brand name, "Zip" and "Zipp"
   d. your brand is considered a generic product name
   e. the shape of your new and unusual product cannot be legally protected

5 Describe marketing uses of packaging and labelling

18. Which of the following is NOT one of the major functions of packaging?
   a. guarantees product quality
   b. contains the product
   c. protects the product
   d. promotes the product
   e. facilitates storage and use of the product

6 Discuss global issues in branding and packaging

19. Companies considering global marketing should consider all of the following global aspects of branding and packaging EXCEPT:
   a. whether to use one brand name with no adaptation to local markets, or whether to use one name but adapt and modify it for each local market
   b. problems with brand imitations, brand piracy, and product counterfeits
   c. whether to use different brand names in different markets for the same products
   d. different currencies in each country, exchange rates, and final retail prices
   e. product labelling, package aesthetics, and climate considerations

7 Describe how and why product warranties are important marketing tools

20. The label on a can of Elmo's glue that states "100 percent satisfaction guaranteed" is _____ warranty.
   a. a descriptive
   b. an express
   c. an implied
   d. a limited
   e. not a

21. Realizing that their product needed a warranty to gain rapid market acceptance, the managers of Risktakers, Inc. produced:
   a. a statement for salespeople to read to prospective buyers
   b. an acknowledgement of company responsibilities for salespeople to build into presentations
   c. a label stating that the product is the highest quality and backed by years of experience
   d. an advertisement stating that buyers would not perceive the purchase of this product as risky
   e. a written guarantee that the product would work as promised and that it is fit for the purpose it was sold

____ 22. Greta purchased an electric can opener last week and attempted to open a can of soup with it this weekend for the first time. However, the blade on the can opener was too dull and succeeded only in denting the can, rather than cutting it. Given that there is the _____, she has a right to demand that the machine perform the job for which it was purchased.
   a.   implied warranty
   b.   Product Liability Act
   c.   Trademarks Act
   d.   Federal Communications Code
   e.   Package Labelling Act

Check your answers to these questions before proceeding to the next section

SCENARIO

Read the marketing scenario and answer the questions that follow.

George is the group product manager at a major large company that makes many different toiletries products, including bar soap, liquid soap, deodorant, and hair care products. His company markets three brands of bar soap called Dune, Scrub, and Swish, with Dune having the highest market share. The company also markets a Dune deodorant and a line of hair care products (shampoos, conditioners, hair sprays, and styling aids) called Silky Soft.

George has been working closely, with his Dune brand manager on a new product called Liquid Dune, which will compete in the liquid hand soap category. Since Dune bar soap has high brand loyalty, the launch of Liquid Dune is thought to have high potential.

True/False:

_____ 1.   Dune is an example of a private label brand.

_____ 2.   Dune probably has strong brand equity.

_____ 3.   Dune's offering of a bar soap, a deodorant, and a liquid hand soap is an example of a product item.

Multiple Choice:

_____ 4.   All of the products that George's company offers are called the:
   a.   product items.
   b.   product line.
   c.   product depth.
   d.   product mix.
   e.   product width.

_____ 5.   Dune, Scrub, and Swish bar soaps represent:
   a.   a product line.
   b.   a product mix.
   c.   product depth.
   d.   line extensions.
   e.   product versions.

_____ 6.   Liquid Dune is an example of:
   a.   brand equity.
   b.   a line extension.
   c.   repositioning.
   d.   a private label brand.
   e.   a family brand.

_____ 7. If George's company made a line of bar soaps for Wal-Mart under Wal-Mart's "Sam's" brand, this would be an example of:
   a. generic branding.
   b. family branding.
   c. private label branding.
   d. cobranding.
   e. pairs branding

Short Answer:

8. What is the importance of Dune's brand equity? Why should the company protect the brand name?

ESSAY QUESTIONS

1. Name and briefly define four categories of consumer products. For each category, list three specific examples of products that would most likely be classified in that category.

2. What is the difference between a product item, a product line, and a product mix?

3. You are a marketing manager for Gillette, a manufacturer of razors, blades, and various personal care items. You have been asked by the Vice-President of marketing to some up with some branding strategies for a new line of men's toiletries to be launched by the company. These toiletries will include shaving cream, deodorant and anti-perspirant, shampoo and conditioner, and disposable razors. List all the branding strategies you would use and list one advantage and one disadvantage to each strategy. Which one would you choose?

4. List and describe four ways to adjust a product line. Provide examples using products marketed by the Coca-Cola company.

APPLICATION #1

The Kauphy Coffee Company's product portfolio is shown below:

Coffees	Appliances	Desserts
Fresh roast beans	Coffeemaker	Coffee ice cream
Fresh ground	Espresso maker	Coffee cakes
Instant	Coffee grinder	
Decaffeinated		
Gourmet		

What is the product mix width? What is the product line depth? What options does this company have to adjust its product lines or its mix as a whole?

You are the brand manager of the family of Q-T-Pie custom-shaped pies that are distributed in Canada. The products include a wide variety of pie flavours, ingredients, and shapes. The brand is a favourite among gourmet gift givers and dessert aficionados. Your firm would like to enter several foreign markets. Write a proposal to your boss naming and describing the major alternative brand name choices for this global strategy and identifying the best one.

CHAPTER 9: DEVELOPING AND MANAGING PRODUCTS

LEARNING OBJECTIVES

1 Explain the importance of developing new products and describe the six categories of new products

New products can be classified as new-to-the-world products (discontinuous innovations), new product lines, additions to existing product lines, improvements to or revisions of existing products, repositioned products, or lower-cost products.

The product life cycle concept reminds us that developing and introducing new products is vital to business growth and profitability. Major manufacturers expect new products to account for a substantial portion of their total sales and profits.

2 Explain the steps in the new-product development process

Most companies use a formal new product development process, which usually begins with identifying the firm's new product strategy. Each stage in the process acts as a screen, filtering out ideas that should not be considered further. After setting a new product strategy, the steps are as follows: idea generation, screening, business analysis, development, testing, and commercialization.

3 Explain why some products succeed and others fail

The most important factor in determining the success of a new product is the extent to which the product matches the needs of the market. Good matches are frequently successful. Poor matches are not.

4 Discuss global issues in new-product development

A marketer with global vision seeks to develop products that can easily be adapted to suit local needs. The goal is not simply to develop a standard product that can be sold worldwide. Smart marketers also look for good product ideas worldwide not just in their home country.

5 Explain the diffusion process through which new products are adopted

The diffusion process is the spread of a new product idea from its producer to the ultimate adopters. An adopter is a consumer who was sufficiently satisfied with his or her trial experience with a product to use it again. Adopters in the diffusion process belong to five categories: innovators, early adopters, early majority, late majority, and laggards. Product characteristics that affect the rate of adoption include product complexity, compatibility with existing social values, relative advantage over substitutes, observability, and trialability. The diffusion process is facilitated by word-of-mouth promotion among consumers and communication from marketers to consumers.

6 Explain the concept of product life cycles

The product life cycle (PLC) is one of the most familiar concepts in marketing and a prevalent marketing management tool. The product life cycle has been adopted as a way to trace the stages of a product's acceptance from its introduction to its demise. The stages are introduction, growth, maturity, and decline. The length of time a product spends in any one stage of the product life cycle may vary dramatically, from a few weeks to decades. The life cycle concept does not predict how long a product will remain in any one stage; rather, it is an analytical tool to help marketers understand where their product is now, what may happen, and which strategies are normally appropriate.

Answer the following questions to see how well you understand the material. Re-take it after you review to check yourself.

1. What are the six categories of new products?

2. List the seven stages of new product development.

3. List at least five reasons why new products may fail.

4. What is diffusion? List and briefly describe five categories of product adopters.

5. List and briefly describe the four stages of the product life cycle.

1 Explain the importance of developing new products and describe the six categories of new products

I. The Importance of New Products

A **new product** can be new-to-the-world, to the market, to the producer or seller, or to some combination of these.

A. Categories of New Products

1. *New-to-the-world products* are also called discontinuous innovations. The product category itself is new.

2. *New product lines* are products the firm has not offered in the past that allow it to enter an established market.

3. *Additions to existing product lines* are new products that supplement a firm's established line.

4. *Improvements or revisions* of existing products result in new products.

5. *Repositioned products* are existing products and targeted at new markets or market segments.

6. *Lower-priced products* are products that provide similar performance to competing brands at a lower cost.

2 Explain the steps in the new-product development process

II. The New Product Development Process

A. A **new product strategy** links the new product development process and the objectives of the marketing department, business unit, and corporation. All these objectives must be consistent.

B. Idea Generation

New product ideas can come from a many sources:

1. *Customers*: The marketing concept suggests that customers' needs and wants should be the springboard for developing new products.

2. *Employees*: Because of their involvement in and analysis of the marketplace, employees who are not in the research and development department often come up with new product ideas.

3. A *distributor* is often more aware of customer needs than the manufacturer because the distributor or dealer is closer to end-users.

4. *Competitors* may have new products that can or should be a source of new product ideas.

5. **Research and development (R&D)** may be a source of new product ideas and innovation. R&D is carried out in four ways:

a. Basic research is scientific research aimed at discovering new technologies.
b. Applied research attempts to find useful applications for new technologies.
c. **Product development** is the process of converting applications for new technologies into marketable products.
d. Sometimes research and development involves *product modification*, cosmetic changes in products or functional product improvements.

6. *Consultant groups* are available to examine a business and recommend product ideas.

A variety of approaches and techniques have been used to stimulate creative thinking and generate product ideas:

a. **Brainstorming** is a process for getting a group to think of unlimited ways to vary a product or solve a problem.
b. Excellent new product ideas are often generated by focus groups. These interviews usually consist of seven to ten consumers interacting in a structured discussion.

C. Idea Screening

Screening is the first filter in the product development process, which eliminates ideas that are inconsistent with the organization's new product strategy or are obviously inappropriate for some other reason.

1. Most new product ideas are rejected at this stage.

2. Concept tests are often used to rate concept (product) alternatives. A **concept test** is the evaluation of a new product idea, usually before a prototype has been created.

D. Business Analysis

The **business analysis** is the second stage of the screening process where preliminary figures for demand, cost, sales, and profitability are calculated.

At the end of this stage, management should have a good idea of the market potential for the product.

E. Development

In the **development stage** of the product development process, a prototype is developed and a marketing strategy is outlined.

Costs increase dramatically as the new product idea moves into the development stage.

1. In the early stages of development, the research and development or engineering department may develop a prototype or working model.

2. Decisions such, as packaging, branding, and labelling will be made. Preliminary promotion, price, and distribution strategies should be established.

3. During the development stage, the technical feasibility of manufacturing the product at a reasonable cost is thoroughly examined, and the product may be modified.

4. Laboratory tests subject products to much more severe or critical treatment than is anticipated by end users.

5. Many products that test well in the laboratory are next subjected to use tests, in which they are placed in consumers' homes or businesses for trial.

6. The development process works best when all the involved areas (departments) work together rather than sequentially. This process is called parallel engineering, **simultaneous product development**, or concurrent engineering.

F. Test Marketing

After products and marketing programs have been developed, they are usually tested in the marketplace.

1. **Test marketing** is a limited introduction of a product and a marketing program to determine the reactions of potential customers in a market situation.

2. Selection of test market cities should ensure that they reflect market conditions in the new product's projected market area. There is no one "perfect" city that reflects the market as a whole, and selecting a test market city is a very difficult task.

3. Costs of test marketing are very high. Some companies choose to forgo this procedure altogether, especially for line extensions of well-known brands. Test marketing can take twelve to eighteen months and cost in excess of $1million.

4. Many firms are looking for cheaper or faster alternatives to test marketing.

   a. Supermarket scanner testing (single-source data) keeps track of the sales response to marketing mix alternatives.
   b. Another alternative is **simulated (laboratory) market tests**, which usually entail showing members of the target market advertising for a variety of products. Purchase behaviour, in a mock or real store, is then monitored.

5. One drawback of test marketing is that the product and its marketing mix are exposed to competitors before its introduction. Competitors may sabotage the test or rush an imitation of the new product to market.

6. Despite the problems associated with test marketing, most firms still consider it essential for new products. The high price of failure prohibits the widespread introduction of a product that might fail.

3 Explain why some products succeed and others fail

III. Product Success and Failure

A. Products fail for many reasons

1. They do not offer any discernible benefit
2. Poor match between product features and customer desires
3. Overestimation of market size
4. Incorrect positioning
5. Incorrect pricing
6. Inadequate distribution
7. Poor promotion
8. Inferior product

B. Degrees of failure

    1. Absolute failure when a company actually loses money

    2. Relative failure when marketing goals are not met, but the product returns a profit

C. The most important factor in successful new-product introduction is a good match between the product and market needs.

4   Discuss global issues in new-product development

IV. Global Issue in New Product Development

A. A firm that starts with a global strategy is better able to develop products that are marketable worldwide.

B. Some global marketers design their products to meet regulations and other key requirements in their major markets and then, if necessary, meet smaller markets' requirements country by country.

5   Explain the diffusion process through which new products are adopted

V. The Spread of New Products

An **adopter** is a consumer who was happy enough with his or her trial experience with a product to use it again.

A. Diffusion of Innovation

    1. An **innovation** is a product perceived as new by a potential adopter.

    2. **Diffusion** is the process by which the adoption of an innovation spreads.

B. Five categories of adopters participate in the diffusion process:

    1. *Innovators* are eager to try new ideas and products, have higher incomes, and are better educated than non-innovators, and represent the first 2.5 percent of all those who will adopt.

    2. *Early adopters* represent the next 13.5 percent to adopt the product. Early adopters are much more reliant on group norms, are oriented to the local community, and tend to be opinion leaders.

    3. The *early majority*, the next 34 percent to adopt, collects more information and evaluates more brands than do early adopters. This group relies on friends, neighbours, and opinion leaders for information and norms.

    4. The *late majority*, the next 34 percent to adopt, does so because most of their friends have already done so. For them, adoption is the result of pressure to conform. This group is older than the others and tends to be below average in income and education.

    5. *Laggards*, the final 16 percent to adopt, are similar to innovators in that they do not rely on the norms of the group. They are independent, however, because they are tradition-bound. Laggards tend to have the lowest socio-economic status, are suspicious of new products, and are alienated from a rapidly advancing society.

C. Product Characteristics and the Rate of Adoption

Five product characteristics to predict and explain the rate of acceptance and diffusion of new products.

1. *Complexity* refers to the degree of difficulty involved in understanding and using a new product. The more complex the product, the slower its diffusion.
2. *Compatibility* refers to the degree to which the new product is consistent with existing values and product knowledge, past experiences, and current needs. Incompatible products diffuse more slowly than compatible products.

3. *Relative advantage* is the degree to which a product is perceived to be superior to existing substitutes.

4. *Observability* refers to the degree to which the benefits and other results of using a new product can be observed by others and communicated to target customers.

5. *Trialability* is the degree to which a product can be tried on a limited basis.

D. Marketing Implications of the Adoption Process

1. Two types of communication, *word-of-mouth communication* among consumers and *communication directly from the marketer to potential adopters*, aid the diffusion process.

2. The effectiveness of different messages and appeals depends on the type of adopter targeted.

6 Explain the concept of product life cycles

VI. Product Life Cycles

A. The product life cycle is a concept that provides a way to trace the stages of a product's acceptance from its introduction to its decline.

1. The product life cycle refers to the life of the product category, which includes all brands that satisfy a particular type of need.

2. The length of time a product category spends in any one stage of the product life cycle may vary dramatically, from a few weeks to decades.

3. The life cycle concept does not predict how long a product category remains in any one stage, rather, it is an analytical tool to help marketers understand where their product is, what may happen, and which strategies are appropriate.

B. Stages in the Product Life Cycle

1. Introductory Stage

   a. The **introductory stage** of the product life cycle represents the full-scale launch of a new product into the marketplace.
   b. The introductory stage is typified by a high failure rate, little competition, frequent product modification, and limited distribution
   c. The introductory stage usually has high marketing and production costs and negative profits as sales increase slowly

---

    d. Promotion strategy in this stage focuses on developing product awareness and informing
        customers of product benefits. The aim is to stimulate primary demand for the product
        category
    e. Intensive personal selling to retailers and wholesalers is required.

2. Growth Stage

    a. The **growth stage** of the life cycle is characterized by: sales growing at an increasing rate, the
        entrance of competitors into the market, market consolidation, and healthy profits.
    b. Promotion in the growth stage emphasizes heavy brand advertising and the differences
        between brands.
    c. Gaining wider distribution is a key goal in this stage.
    d. Toward the end of the growth stage, prices normally fall and profits reach their peak.
    e. Development costs have been recovered by the end of the growth stage, and sales volume has
        created economies of scale.

3.   Maturity Stage

    a. The **maturity stage** of the life cycle is characterized by declining sales growth rates, markets
        approaching saturation, annual product changes that are more cosmetic that substantial, and a
        move toward the widening or extension of the product line.
    b. During the maturity stage, marginal competitors begin dropping out of the market. Heavy
        promotions to both the dealers and consumers are required. Prices and profits begin to fall.
    c. Emergence of "niche marketers" that target narrow, well-defined, under-served segments of a
        market.

4.   Decline Stage

    a. A long-run drop in sales signals the decline stage.
    b. The rate of decline is governed by how rapidly consumers' tastes change or how rapidly
        substitute products are adopted.
    c. Falling demand forces many competitors out of the market, often leaving a few small specialty
        firms manufacturing the product.

C.   Implications for Marketing Management

    Strategies used by marketing managers to prevent products from slipping into the decline stage
    include

    a. Promoting more frequent use of the product by current customers
    b. Finding new target markets for the product
    c. Finding new uses for the product
    d. Pricing the product below the market
    e. Developing new distribution channels
    f. Adding new ingredients or deleting old ingredients
    g. Making a dramatic new guarantee.

Fill in the blank(s) with the appropriate term or phrase from the alphabetized list of chapter key terms.

adopter	maturity stage
brainstorming	new product
business analysis	new product strategy
commercialization	product category
concept test	product development
decline stage	product life cycle
development	screening
diffusion	simulated (laboratory) test marketing
growth stage	simultaneous product development
innovation	test marketing
introductory stage	

1 Explain the importance of developing new products and describe the six categories of new products

1. Discontinuous innovations, new product lines, additions to existing product lines, and improvements/revisions all describe categories of a(n) _____.

2 Explain the steps in the new-product development process

2. The strategy that links the new product development process with marketing, business unit, and corporate objectives is the _____.

3. If managers create new products for present markets by converting applications for new technologies into marketable products, _____ has taken place. If cosmetic or functional changes are made to products to improve them, product modification has taken place.

4. One option for generating new product ideas is to have a groupthink of unlimited ways to vary a product or solve a problem. This is called _____.

5. After new ideas are generated, they pass through the first filter in the product development process. This stage, called _____, eliminates new product ideas that are inappropriate. One tool that may be used in this stage evaluates a new product idea, usually before any prototype has been created. This tool is a(n) _____ and is considered a relatively good predictor of product success.

6. New product ideas that survive the screening process progress to the _____ stage, when preliminary demand, costs, sales, and profitability estimates are made. If financial estimates are favourable, then a prototype product may be developed and a marketing strategy sketched out. These activities occur during the _____ stage.

7. A limited introduction of a product and a marketing program to determine the reactions of potential customers in a market situation is _____. An alternative to this method is a test that exposes consumers to the marketing mix and records subsequent purchasing behaviour. This is called _____. If these tests are successful, the product goes to the final stage in the new product development process, _____.

8. To shorten the new product development process and to reduce cost, all relevant functional areas and outside suppliers participate in all stages of the development process. This approach is called

_____.

5 Explain the diffusion process through which new products are adopted

9. If a person buys a new product, is satisfied, and becomes a repeat purchaser, that person is a(n) _____. A product that is perceived as new by this person is a(n) _____. The process by which the adoption of innovation spreads is _____.

6 Explain the concept of product life cycles

10. A marketing management tool that provides a way to trace the stages of a product's acceptance from its birth to its death is the _____. These phases are generally done for a class of products that satisfy a particular need, which is a(n) _____. The four stages, listed in the order from birth to death, begin with the _____, continue with the _____, along to the _____, and end with the _____.

Check your answers to these questions before proceeding to the next section.

TRUE/FALSE QUESTIONS

Mark the statement **T** if it is true and **F** if it is false.

1 Explain the importance of developing new products and describe the six categories of new products

_____ 1. Ben & Jerry's addition of new ice cream flavours would not be considered new products since the company was already making ice cream. They would simply be called line extensions.

2 Explain the steps in the new-product development process

_____ 2. If a firm adopts the marketing concept, then during the idea generation stage of the new product development process, the logical starting place should be the customers of the firm.

_____ 3. The employees at Genco are all in a room together, shouting out potential ideas. The ideas are written down and evaluated as they are generated, with everyone voting on which ideas to accept or discard. This is an example of brainstorming.

_____ 4. During the business analysis stage of the new product development process, it is appropriate to use concept tests.

_____ 5. During the development stage of the new product process, the product may undergo laboratory tests.

_____ 6. Line extensions of well-established brands are often not test-marketed because of the high cost of test markets.

_____ 7. The Wheelsport Company has developed a new type of inline skateboard. The company has already gone through several stages of the new product development process, including screening, development, and testing. Assuming the results are consistent with profit and cost expectations, the most likely next step is commercialization.

5 Explain the diffusion process through which new products are adopted

_____ 8. The process by which the adoption of an innovation spreads is called the adoption process.

_____ 9. Early adopters of a new product are generally opinion leaders who often influence the adoption by the early and late majority.

_____ 10. Carol loves romantic comedy movies and is among the first 2.5 percent to see a new movie when it is released. She either tries to see it in a preview showing or else goes during the first weekend launch. Carol is an example of an early adopter.

6 Explain the concept of product life cycles

_____ 11. The Kitchen-Pro Company is about to introduce a new kitchen gadget that combines a food processor with a toaster oven. As with other products of this type, Kitchen-Pro can expect sales of this new product to follow a bell-shaped curve over the next ten to fifteen years as it follows the product life cycle.

Check your answers to these questions before proceeding to the next section.

AGREE/DISAGREE QUESTIONS

For the following statements, indicate reasons why you may agree and disagree with the statement.

1. Following each step of the new product process is arduous and only delays a product launch.

   Reason(s) to agree:

   Reason(s) to disagree:

2. New product ideas that are based on a sound positioning will not fail.

   Reason(s) to agree:

   Reason(s) to disagree:

3. New product ideas are not the sole responsibility of a new products committee or department; they should be the responsibility of the entire organization.

Reason(s) to agree:

Reason(s) to disagree:

4. The product life cycle concept is old and not applicable to all products.

Reason(s) to agree:

Reason(s) to disagree:

MULTIPLE CHOICE QUESTIONS

Select the response that best answers the question, and write the corresponding letter in the space provided.

1 Explain the importance of developing new products and describe the six categories of new products

_____ 1. The artificial sweetener NutraSweet (aspartame), when first introduced, was a new-to-the-world product--a method of sweetening products with few calories and no bad aftertaste. This type of new product was a:
a. diffusion
b. discontinuous innovation
c. moderate innovation
d. venture product
e. specialty product

_____ 2. Gerber has introduced a new plastic bottled for its single-serve bottled juices for babies. Is this a new product?
a. yes, additions to the product line are new products
b. no, bottled juices cannot be considered an innovation
c. no, it is only a product addition
d. yes, this is a discontinuous innovation
e. no, this is not a product improvement

_____ 3. Recently, the Cheez Whiz cracker spread product has been featured in promotions as a cheese sauce for the microwave oven. This is an example of:
a. revising existing products
b. lowering costs
c. repositioning
d. segmenting existing product lines
e. reformulation

4. Klean Laundry detergent was just replaced with a "new and improved" Klean that makes clothes smell good as well as gets them clean. This new product is an example of:
   a. revising an existing product
   b. lowering costs
   c. repositioning
   d. a new-to-the-world product
   e. a line extension

2 Explain the steps in the new-product development process

5. Veronica is the new products manager at a packaged foods company. She would like to put together a brainstorming team to generate ideas about new food products. She should consider inviting people from the following areas EXCEPT:
   a. account executives from her advertising agency
   b. a couple of big customers
   c. lawyers from the company's law firm
   d. a couple of large distributors
   e. sales people who have access to competitive intelligence

6. The first step in the new products process is:
   a. concept testing
   b. generating ideas ("brainstorming")
   c. developing the new product
   d. developing a new-product strategy
   e. test marketing

7. Fabrique, Inc. invented a fabric that was fireproof, tearproof, but also edible. The week after the product was invented, a group of the firm's employees got together and listed ways the product might be used. This is an example of:
   a. an unfocus group
   b. concept testing
   c. brainstorming
   d. venture group activities
   e. screening

8. After the research team at Epsilon Corporation had generated a dozen new product ideas for gasoline additives, a committee of company executives met to analyze whether the product ideas were consistent with the organization's new product strategy. This is called:
   a. screening
   b. commercialization
   c. business analysis
   d. test marketing
   e. idea generation

9. After Revvin' Cosmetics evaluated many new product ideas, the company selected three ideas to present to consumers. Before any prototype had been created, researchers presented the product ideas to groups of consumers for evaluation. This stage of new product development is called:
   a. screening
   b. market testing
   c. concept testing
   d. simulated market testing
   e. use testing

10. As the Slimmy Company continued the development of its new product idea, diet fat, a group was assigned the task of estimating preliminary demand for the product, costs, sales, and future profitability. This is the _____ stage in product development.
    a. test marketing
    b. idea generation
    c. concept testing
    d. screening
    e. business analysis

---

11. When Philips developed a new extra-long life halogen light bulb, the company installed one hundred bulbs at no charge in the homes of fifty consumers and monitored the bulbs for one year. This is a:
    a. laboratory test
    b. use test
    c. concept test
    d. market test
    e. diffusion test

12. Sigma-Sunco is introducing its new sunscreen eye drops in only two cities so that it can closely monitor the reactions of potential customers to the product and marketing program. This is called:
    a. diffusion analysis
    b. use test
    c. concept test
    d. test marketing
    e. laboratory test

13. All of the following factors should be considered when choosing a test market EXCEPT:
    a. the city's large population
    b. the city's relative isolation from other cities
    c. the city's good record as a test city, but not overly used
    d. availability of retailers that will cooperate in the test market
    e. similarity to planned distribution outlets

14. Gramma's Treats tested consumers' reactions to a new dessert by getting consumers to look through a newspaper with grocery store ads, make out a grocery list, and then "shop" in a mock store filled with real products, including the new dessert. This is a:
    a. real test market
    b. simulated (laboratory) market test
    c. concept test
    d. use test
    e. cable/scanner test

15. SunGlass has ordered production materials and equipment for its new polarized auto windshields for all of its manufacturing plants. SunGlass is entering the _____ stage of new product development.
    a. business analysis
    b. commercialization
    c. product testing
    d. product prototypes
    e. market testing

3 Explain why some products succeed and others fail

16. In the long run, products fail because of a poor match between:
    a. advertising and personal selling
    b. limited resources and unlimited consumer wants
    c. the marketing mix and physical distribution
    d. prices and consumer demand
    e. product characteristics and consumer needs

5 Explain the diffusion process through which new products are adopted

17. In an attempt to understand its target markets better, Carrot Personal Computers has been studying the product adoption stages and strategies. Carrot can expect to find all of the following EXCEPT that:
    a. early adopters may also be opinion leaders
    b. there are three categories of consumers who will adopt computer products
    c. laggards are the last consumers to adopt a new product
    d. early triers of a product are generally heavy users of that product
    e. innovators were the first to purchase home computers

18. In a meeting with Sony corporate officials, you (a leading marketing consultant) are asked if the new digital tape technology will be quickly accepted and sought by the Canadian consumer. You tell them that this depends on many product characteristics, including all of the following EXCEPT:
    a. how similar it is to existing tape players in use and fulfilling needs
    b. the degree of difficulty involved in understanding and using it
    c. how much of a relative advantage it has over current tape players
    d. the "buy Canadian" movement in Canada
    e. its degree of trialability

6 Explain the concept of product life cycles

19. Wilderness, Inc., sells a tent that collapses down into a roll the size of one roll of toilet paper. The tent can be easily carried in a backpack. The tent has been in the market for two years, and the company is spending a lot on advertising. The tent is in which stage of the product life cycle?
    a. maturity stage
    b. introduction stage
    c. innovation stage
    d. growth stage
    e. early majority stage

20. Pepsi and Coca-Cola have been battling in the "cola war" for years. Both products have been in the market for nearly one hundred years and spend much of their marketing budgets on short-term promotions to steal market share from each other. Pepsi and Coca-Cola are in which stage of the product life cycle?
    a. maturity stage
    b. decline stage
    c. promotional stage
    d. growth stage
    e. late majority stage

21. The Acme Slide Rule Company has seen most of its competition slip away, and it now holds 90 percent of the market share for slide rules and other mechanical calculation devices. Acme's own sales totals are slowly decaying, and it spends little on promotion. Acme's products are in which stage of the product life cycle?
    a. maturity stage
    b. decline stage
    c. downfall stage
    d. decay stage
    e. laggard stage

22. At what stage in the product life cycle are product line extensions generally launched?
    a. maturity stage
    b. decline stage
    c. downfall stage
    d. decay stage
    e. laggard stage

Check your answers to these questions before proceeding to the next section.

Read the marketing scenario and answer the questions that follow.

Nintendo Co., Ltd., of Kyoto, Japan, is a leading worldwide marketer of interactive entertainment. The company manufactures both hardware and software for video game systems and has created many new products over its century-old existence. In 1989, Nintendo launched the world's first portable, hand-held game system – Game Boy – and took the market by storm. Over the next several years, Game Boy underwent some improvements. In 1996, Nintendo introduced Game Boy Pocket, a smaller and sleeker version of the original Game Boy. In 1998, Game Boy Colour was launched along with accessories, Game Boy Camera and Printer. Finally, in 2001, Nintendo launched the heavily anticipated Game Boy Advance, with a better screen and vastly better games. The product sold out immediately.

(Source: Nintendo Web Site (**www.nintendo.com**).

<u>True/False:</u>

_____ 1. The original Game Boy was considered a discontinuous innovation.

_____ 2. Game Boy Advance is probably in the maturity stage of the product life cycle.

_____ 3. All the versions of Game Boy are considered to be new products.

<u>Multiple Choice:</u>

_____ 4. Game Boy Pocket, Game Boy Colour, and Game Boy Advance are examples of what kind of new product?
   a. New product lines.
   b. Additions to existing product lines.
   c. Improvements or revisions of existing products.
   d. Repositioned products.
   e. Discontinuous innovations.

_____ 5. The Game Boy Camera and Printer are examples of:
   a. new product lines.
   b. additions to existing product lines.
   c. improvements or revisions of existing products.
   d. repositioned products.
   e. new product depth

_____ 6. The new generations of Game Boy were most likely launched during the:
   a. introductory stage of the previous generation.
   b. growth stage of the previous generation.
   c. maturity stage of the previous generation.
   d. decline stage of the previous generation.
   e. a period of technological innovation.

_____ 7. When Game Boy Advance was launched, what strategy did Nintendo most likely follow?
   a. It dropped the price of the Game Boy Colour to force out distribution.
   b. It advertised Game Boy Colour more heavily before the launch of the new generation product.
   c. It maintained the same price on Game Boy Colour product to keep up profits.
   d. It heavily promoted the Game Boy Advance to get people to buy it.
   e. It harvested Game Boy to focus on its newer products.

Short Answer:

8.   If you were the product manager of Game Boy Advance, how would you describe each of the five types of adopters of the product? Approximately when would each adopter buy the product?

ESSAY QUESTIONS

1.   There are several correct definitions of the term "new product." Name and describe six categories of new products. For each category, give a specific real-life example of a product that fits into that category.

2.   The multiple-step new product development process is an essential ingredient in new product development. List the steps of this process.

---

3. You are in charge of test marketing your company's new brand of non-alcoholic wine. List ten criteria you should consider when choosing a good test market city. What is an advantage for your company of using test marketing? What is a disadvantage of using test marketing?

4. Draw the sales line and the profit line of the product life cycle in the following diagram, and label each line. Indicate the names of the four stages of the product life cycle in the blanks provided. Then list the four stages of the product life cycle. For each stage, list five typical characteristics of that stage.

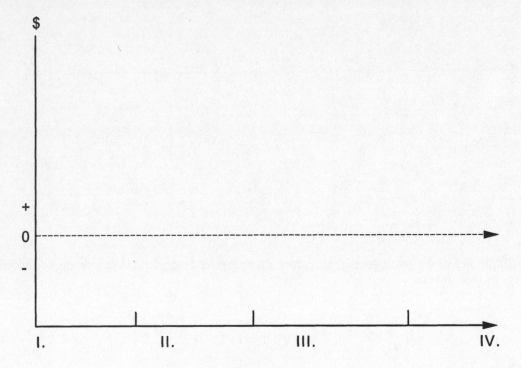

5. Name and briefly describe each of these five categories in the product adoption process. Using the launch of a new movie as an example, tell what each adopter might do.

APPLICATION

You are manager of new products at a toy company. You have spent the last several months working with Product Development to create a new, interactive robotic puppy that obeys commands from the owner's voice. The robotic puppy is targeted at kids aged five to ten. You are ready to put the new product into test market and are trying to determine which two markets you should use. Using various sources on the Internet, select two test market cities in Canada, based on the following criteria:

- Population: Medium-sized cities
- Media: Isolated media markets
- Diversity: Population should closely resemble that of the entire Canadian population in terms of age, ethnicity, etc.
- Income levels: Population should closely resemble income levels that mirror the Canadian population
- Distribution: The cities should have adequate distribution outlets for toys

What two cities match these criteria? How well do they match them?

CHAPTER 10: SERVICES AND NONPROFIT ORGANIZATION MARKETING

LEARNING OBJECTIVES

1   Discuss the importance of services to the economy

The service sector plays a crucial role in the Canada economy, employing roughly 75 percent of the work force and accounting for about 70 percent of the gross domestic product.

2   Discuss the differences between services and goods

Services are distinguished from goods by four characteristics. Services are intangible performances in that they lack clearly identifiable physical characteristics, making it difficult for marketers to communicate their specific benefits to potential customers. The production and consumption of services occur simultaneously. Services are heterogeneous because their quality depends on elements such as the service provider, the individual consumer, location, and so on. Finally, services are perishable in the sense that they cannot be stored or saved.

3   Describe the components of service quality and the gap model of service quality

The improvement of service quality is one of the most critical challenges facing business leaders today. Customers evaluate service quality along the dimensions of reliability, responsiveness, assurance, empathy, and tangibles. Overall service quality is measured by combining customers' evaluations for all five components.

4   Develop marketing mixes for services

In contrast to positioning goods, positioning services favourably in the eyes and minds of potential customers is more difficult. This is because of services' unique characteristics of intangibility, inseparability, heterogeneity, and perishability. Positive strategies to deal with these characteristics include carefully designed and implemented market analysis and customer targeting, along with careful decision making about product, price, promotion, and distribution.

5   Discuss relationship marketing in services

Relationship marketing involves attracting, developing, and retaining customer relationships. There are three levels of relationship marketing: Level 1 focuses on pricing incentives; level 2 uses pricing incentive and social bonds with customers; and level 3 uses pricing, social bonds, and structural bonds to build long-term relationships.

6   Explain internal marketing in services

Internal marketing means treating employees as customers and developing systems and benefits that satisfy their needs. Employees who like their jobs and are happy with the firm they work for are more likely to deliver good service. Internal marketing activities include competing for talent, offering a vision, training employees, stressing teamwork, giving employees freedom to make decisions, measuring and rewarding good service performance, and knowing employees' needs.

7   Discuss global issues in services marketing

Competition in the global market for services is increasing rapidly. Many Canadian service industries (such as financial institutions, construction and engineering, and insurance) can easily enter the global marketplace because of existing competitive advantages.

8   Describe nonprofit organization marketing

Individuals and organizations also conduct marketing to achieve goals other than profit, market share, and return on investment. Nonprofit organization marketing facilitates mutually satisfying exchanges between nonprofit organizations and their target markets.

Answer the following questions to see how well you understand the material. Re-take it after you review to check yourself.

1.   List and briefly describe four characteristics of service products that make them different from goods.

2.   What are five components of service quality?

3.   List five "gaps" that can occur in service quality.

4.   What is internal marketing?

5.   Briefly describe the unique aspects of objectives, target markets, product, distribution, and promotion for nonprofit organization marketing.

1   Discuss the importance of services to the economy

I.   The Importance of Services

A **service** is the result of applying human or mechanical efforts to people or objects.

A.   The basic marketing process is the same for all products and organizations. However, services and nonprofit businesses have many unique characteristics that affect marketing strategy.

B.   The service sector substantially influences the Canadian economy, accounting for nearly 70% of the Canadian gross domestic product.

2   Discuss the differences between services and goods

II.   How Services Differ from Goods

Services are distinguished from products by four unique characteristics. They are intangible performances, they are produced and consumed simultaneously, they have greater variability in outputs, and they are perishable.

A.   Services as Intangible Performances

The fundamental difference between services and goods is that services are intangible performances. **Intangibility** means that services cannot be touched, seen, tasted, heard, or felt in the same manner that goods can be sensed.

1.   Services cannot be stored and can often be easily duplicated.

2.   Evaluating the quality of services is more difficult than evaluating the quality of goods.

    a.   Services exhibit fewer **search qualities**, characteristics that can be easily assessed before purchase.
    b.   Services have more **experience qualities**, characteristics that can only be assessed after use.
    c.   Services also have **credence qualities**, characteristics that cannot be easily assessed even after purchase and experience.

B.   Services Are Produced and Consumed Simultaneously

1.   Services are often sold and then produced and consumed at the same time.

2.   The consumer of services is usually involved at the time of production. Services cannot be produced in a centralized location and consumed in decentralized locations.

C.   Services Have Greater Variability

1.   Consistency and quality control are often hard to achieve, because services are labour-intensive and vary by employee.

2. Consistency and reliability are strengths that many service firms actively pursue through mechanization of the process, standardization, and training.

    D. Services Are Perishable

        1. Services cannot be stored, warehoused, or inventoried.

        2. One of the most important challenges in many service industries is finding ways to synchronize supply and demand. Such techniques as differential pricing during nonpeak periods may help.

3   Describe the components of service quality and the gap model of service quality

III. Service Quality

Because of the four unique characteristics of services, service quality is difficult to define and measure. Customers evaluate services along 5 dimensions.

    A. These dimensions are:

        1. **Reliability** is the ability to perform the service dependably, accurately, and consistently.

        2. **Responsiveness** is the ability to provide prompt service.

        3. **Assurance** is the knowledge and courtesy of employees and their ability to convey trust.

        4. **Empathy** is caring, individualized attention to customers.

        5. **Tangibles** are the physical evidence of the service.

    B. The Gap Model of Service Quality

A model of service quality called the **gap model** identifies five gaps that can cause problems in service delivery.

        1. Gap 1: the gap between what customers want and what management thinks customers want.

        2. Gap 2: the gap between what management thinks customers want and the quality specifications that management develops to provide the service.

        3. Gap 3: the gap between the service quality specifications and service that is actually provided.

        4. Gap 4: the gap between what the company provides and what the customer is told it provides.

        5. Gap 5: the gap between the service that customers receive and the service they want.

4   Develop marketing mixes for services

VI. Marketing Mixes for Services

Elements of the marketing mix need to be adjusted to meet the special challenges posed by the unique characteristics of services.

A. Product (Service) Strategy

The development of a product strategy requires that the business focus on the service process itself.

1. What Is Being Processed

    a. *People processing*
    b. *Possession processing*
    c. *Information processing*

2. Core and Supplementary Services

    The service product can be viewed as a bundle of activities that include the **core service**, which is the most basic benefit the customer is buying, and a group of **supplementary services** that support or enhance the core service.

3. Mass Customization

    a. Customized services are more flexible and responsive to individual customer needs but also cost more.
    b. Standardized services are more efficient and cost less.
    c. An emerging strategy is called **mass customization**, which uses technology to deliver customized services on a mass basis.

4. The Service Mix

    a. Most service organizations offer more than one service. A service firm must understand it is managing a portfolio of services that include opportunities, risks, and challenges.
    b. Service marketing strategy includes deciding what new services to introduce to which target markets, what existing services to maintain, and what services to eliminate from the portfolio.

B. Distribution Strategy

1. Distribution strategies for service organizations focus on convenience, number of outlets, direct vs. indirect distribution, location and scheduling.
2. Management must set objectives for the distribution system and select operation type (usually direct or franchise), location, and scheduling.

C. Promotion Strategy

1. Four promotional strategies for dealing with the unique features of services are

    a. *Stressing tangible cues,* which are a concrete symbol for the service offering.
    b. *Using personal information sources* which are people consumers are familiar with, such as celebrities.
    c. *Creating a strong organizational image* by managing the physical environment, employee appearance, and tangible items.
    d. *Engaging in postpurchase communication* through follow-up activities such as phone calls and surveys.

D. Price Strategy

The unique characteristics of services present some special pricing challenges.

1. It is important to define the unit of service consumption.

2. For services that are composed of multiple elements, the issue is whether each element should be priced separately.

3. Several trends, such as increased competition and deregulation, have changed pricing from a passive to an active component of firms' marketing strategies in services (such as banking, telecommunications, and transportation).

4. Three categories of pricing objectives have been suggested:

    a. *Revenue-oriented pricing* focuses on maximizing the surplus of income over costs.

    b. *Operations-oriented pricing* seeks to match supply and demand by varying prices to ensure maximum use of productive capacity at any specific point in time.

    c. *Patronage-oriented pricing* attempts to maximize the number of customers using the service.

5. In practice, a firm may use more than one objective in setting prices, often trying to blend the objectives to best fit the type of business.

5   Discuss relationship marketing in services

V. Relationship Marketing in Services

Relationship marketing is a means for attracting, developing, and retaining customer relationships to build strong customer loyalty.

A. Relationship marketing is important in service businesses that involve a process of continuous interaction.

B. Relationship marketing can be practiced at three levels:

1. Financial: pricing incentives, such as frequent-flier programs; low customization

2. Financial and social: adds social bonds, staying in touch; medium customization

3. Financial, social, and structural: adds value-added services that are not available from other firms; high customization

6   Explain internal marketing in services

VI. Internal Marketing in Service Firms

Internal marketing means treating employees as customers and developing systems and benefits that satisfy their needs.

A. Happy employees are more likely to deliver high-quality service.

B. Internal marketing activities include competing for talent, offering a vision, training, stressing teamwork, giving employees freedom to make decisions, measuring and rewarding quality, and learning about employee needs.

7   Discuss global issues in services marketing

VII. Global Issues in Services Marketing

Canada is a growing exporter of services.

A. Services that are exported include financial, credit card, construction, engineering, education, and insurance.

B. The marketing mix for each service usually has to be designed to meet the specific needs of each country.

8   Describe nonprofit organization marketing

VIII. Nonprofit Organization Marketing

A **nonprofit organization** is an organization that exists to achieve some goal other than the usual business goals of profit, market share, or return on investment.

Nonprofit organizations account for nearly 20 percent of the economic activity in Canada.

A. What Is Nonprofit Organization Marketing?

    1. **Nonprofit organization marketing** is the effort of public and private nonprofit organizations to bring about mutually satisfying exchanges with their target markets.

       a. Nonprofit organizations include government organizations as well as private museums, theatres, schools, and churches.

       b. Many nonprofit organizations do not realize that their functions and activities, such as choosing a target market, setting prices, and communication, involve marketing.

       c. Nonprofit organizations may believe that marketing is only appropriate in commercial, profit-seeking organizations.

B. Unique Aspects of Nonprofit Marketing Strategy

Differences between business and nonprofit marketers create unique challenges for nonprofit managers in setting marketing objectives, selecting target markets, and developing appropriate marketing mixes.

    1. Setting Objectives

Without a profit motive to guide them, many nonprofit organizations have a multitude of vague, diverse, intangible, and often-conflicting objectives. Still, goals must be set, and measures must be established.

2. Target Markets

    a.   Nonprofit organizations often have *apathetic or strongly opposed* targets as recipients of their services.

    b.   Many nonprofit organizations are *pressured* to adopt undifferentiated segmentation strategies to serve the maximum number of people or to achieve economies of scale.

    c.   Nonprofit organizations are often expected to *complement rather than compete* against private-sector organizations.

3. Product Decisions

    a.   *Benefit complexity:* Nonprofit organizations often market complex behaviours or ideas.

    b.   *Benefit strength:* The benefit strength of many nonprofit offerings is quite weak or indirect for the individual.

    c.   *Involvement:* Many nonprofit products elicit either very low involvement ("Prevent forest fires") or very high involvement ("Stop smoking").

4. Distribution Decisions

Distribution for nonprofit products is usually direct from producer to consumer.

    a.   A nonprofit organization's capacity for distributing its service offerings to potential customer groups when and where they are needed is typically a key variable in determining the success of those service offerings.

    b.   Many nonprofit services are not facility-dependent and have the freedom to go to the clients.

    c.   Soliciting funds and donations of goods also requires good channels of distribution.

5. Promotion Decisions

    a.   *Professional volunteers* can assist organizations in developing and implementing promotion strategies. Advertising agencies may donate their services.

    b.   *Sales promotion activities* are increasingly being used by nonprofit organizations.

    c.   *A public service advertisement* (PSA), also called a public service announcement, is an announcement that promotes programs, activities, or services of federal, state, or local governments or the programs, activities, or services of nonprofit organizations. The media donates the time and space for a PSA.

6. Price Decisions

Five key characteristics distinguish nonprofit organization pricing decisions from profit-sector pricing decisions.

    a.   *Pricing objectives* are generally concerned with covering costs partially or fully or equitably distributing resources.

    b.   Nonprofit services may have *non-financial prices* consisting of the costs of waiting time, embarrassment, or effort.

    c.   *Indirect payment* by consumers of nonprofit services through taxes is common.

    d.   *Separation between payers* (often those in a good financial situation) *and users* (in a poor economic situation) is common for many charitable organizations.

    e.   Many nonprofit organizations use *below-cost pricing*.

Fill in the blank(s) with the appropriate term or phrase from the alphabetized list of chapter key terms.

assurance	nonprofit organization
core service	nonprofit organization marketing
credence quality	public service advertisement (PSA)
empathy	reliability
experience quality	responsiveness
gap model	search quality
intangibility	service
internal marketing	supplementary service
mass customization	tangibles

1 Discuss the importance of services to the economy

1. The result of applying human or mechanical efforts to people or objects and involves a deed, performance, or effort that cannot be physically possessed is a _____.

2 Discuss the differences between services and goods

2. The fundamental difference between services and goods is that services cannot be touched, seen, tasted, heard, or felt in the same manner in which goods can be sensed. This is the characteristic of _____.

3. Evaluating the quality of services is more difficult than evaluating the quality of goods. Goods exhibit characteristics such as colour or size that can be easily assessed before purchase. Most services, however, do not exhibit a(n) _____. A characteristic that can only be assessed after use is a(n) _____ and could characterize restaurant or travel services. A characteristic that cannot be easily assessed even after the purchase and experience is a(n) _____. Medical and consulting services exemplify this quality.

3 Describe the components of service quality, and the gap model of service quality

4. Customers evaluate service quality by five components. The ability to perform the service dependably, accurately, and consistently is known as _____. The ability to provide prompt service is called _____. When employees are knowledgeable and courteous, customers have great _____ in the service provider. _____ indicates the caring, individualized attention given to customers. Finally, the physical evidence of the service is known as _____.

5. The _____ identifies five gaps that can cause problems in service delivery.

4 Develop marketing mixes for services

6. The service offering can be viewed as a bundle of activities. These activities include the most basic benefit the customer is buying, which is the _____. The activities also include support or enhancement services, known as the _____.

7. Instead of choosing to either standardize or customize a service, a firm may incorporate elements of both by adopting an emerging strategy called _____.

6 Explain internal marketing in services

8. The quality of a firm's employees is an important part of service quality. Firms that treat employees as customers and develop systems and benefits that satisfy their needs are practicing _____.

8 Describe nonprofit organization marketing

9. An entity that exists to achieve some goal other than profit, market share, or return on investment is a(n) _____. These entities practice _____.

10. An announcement, free of charge, that promotes programs, activities, or services of governments or nonprofit organizations is a(n) _____.

Check your answers to these questions before proceeding to the next section.

TRUE/FALSE QUESTIONS

Mark the statement **T** if it is true and **F** if it is false.

1 Discuss the importance of services to the economy.

_____ 1. Services represent about half of the gross domestic product of Canada.

3 Describe the components of service quality, and the gap model of service quality

_____ 2. Martha is a customer service agent at a department store. When a customer calls with a complaint about merchandise purchased at the store, she calls the customer back immediately and resolves the issue as quickly as possible. This is an example of the reliability component of services.

4 Develop marketing mixes for services

_____ 3. Ian runs a restaurant that serves excellent barbecue. He also has karaoke night, when customers are invited to come up on stage and sing country-and-western songs. The karaoke is considered to be a supplementary service to the restaurant.

---

6 Explain internal marketing in services

_____ 4. IBM offers its employees flexible work hours, work-at-home programs, on-site childcare, and travel benefits that reward quality performance. IBM is practicing relationship marketing.

7 Discuss global issues in service marketing

_____ 5. You cannot export a service; only goods can be exported.

8 Describe nonprofit organization marketing

_____ 6. Target markets are generally easier to persuade in nonprofit organization marketing because they are not asked to "buy" anything.

_____ 7. The characteristics of for-profit services and nonprofit organizations suggest that their distribution channels should be direct.

_____ 8. Paid advertisements that promote programs, activities, or services of nonprofit agencies or governments are called PSAs (public service advertisements or announcements).

_____ 9. Consumers in nonprofit situations pay prices not in dollars but in other ways such as time or opportunity costs.

Check your answers to these questions before proceeding to the next section.

AGREE/DISAGREE QUESTIONS

For the following statements, indicate reasons why you may agree and disagree with the statement.

1. Employees who work for firms selling services must be trained better in customer service than employees who work for firms selling goods.

   Reason(s) to agree:

   Reason(s) to disagree:

2. The "gap model" of service quality could also be used for the marketing of goods.

   Reason(s) to agree:

   Reason(s) to disagree:

3. Service providers should use promotion to build a strong organizational image rather than advertise their products.

Reason(s) to agree:

Reason(s) to disagree:

4. Target markets are easier to identify for nonprofit organizations than for for-profit organizations.

Reason(s) to agree:

Reason(s) to disagree:

MULTIPLE CHOICE QUESTIONS

Select the response that best answers the question, and write the corresponding letter in the space provided.

2 Discuss the differences between services and goods

_____ 1. Randy left his marketing job at a large company in order to consult to small businesses. Consulting proves to be a much more difficult than marketing goods because consulting is:
   a. intangible
   b. unknowable
   c. tangible
   d. amortizable
   e. elusive

_____ 2. Which of the following is NOT true of services?
   a. Services are produced and consumed simultaneously.
   b. Services are intangible.
   c. Services are difficult to evaluate.
   d. Services have greater variability.
   e. Services are perishable.

_____ 3. You walk into an electronics store to purchase a computer. Even before you purchase, you are pleased with the service of the store's sales associates, who seem knowledgeable and helpful. The service provided by the sales associates is an example of:
   a. credence quality
   b. internal marketing
   c. experience quality
   d. search quality
   e. dependency

4. Yesterday, you went to your favourite brunch restaurant with a friend and are now suffering from a bad case of food poisoning. This is example of:
   a. credence quality
   b. internal marketing
   c. experience quality
   d. search quality
   e. dependency

5. Ingrid recently went to the dentist, who filled one of her cavities. She didn't have any pain, but she really has no idea if the dentist did a good job or not because she is far from being a medical expert. This is an example of:
   a. credence quality
   b. internal marketing
   c. experience quality
   d. search quality
   e. dependency

3 Describe the components of service quality, and the gap model of service quality

6. Kentucky Fried Chicken once measured its managers' success by how little chicken was thrown away at the end of the night. Customers who came into stores late at night either had to wait for chicken to be cooked or to settle for chicken that was cooked several hours before. This is an example of a gap between:
   a. what customers want and what management thinks customers want.
   b. the service quality specifications and the service that is actually provided.
   c. what the company provides and what the customer is told it provides.
   d. what management thinks what customers want and the quality specifications that management develops to provide the service.
   e. the service that customers receive and the service they want.

7. Sylvia runs a day care centre for the children of professional parents. In order to enrolment in her centre, Sylvia lowered tuition but had to increase the number of children that each teacher would care for. Sylvia was surprised when some of the parents pulled their children out of the centre, especially when the tuition had been lowered. This is an example of a gap between:
   a. what customers want and what management thinks customers want.
   b. the service quality specifications and the service that is actually provided.
   c. what the company provides and what the customer is told it provides.
   d. what management thinks what customers want and the quality specifications that management develops to provide the service.
   e. the service that customers receive and the service they want.

8. A major airline once advertised that passengers should fly the airline because of the "respect" that airline personnel gave to passengers. However, passengers were always disappointed by the lack of respect that the personnel gave them. This is an example of a gap between:
   a. what customers want and what management thinks customers want.
   b. the service quality specifications and the service that is actually provided.
   c. what the company provides and what the customer is told it provides.
   d. what management thinks what customers want and the quality specifications that management develops to provide the service.
   e. the service that customers receive and the service they want.

_____ 9. In addition to the sale of the basic computer hardware, Gateway Computer now offers services such as maintenance and troubleshooting and its own Internet service. Gateway likely does this in order to:
   a. differentiate itself from other computer companies.
   b. gain loyalty from its customer base.
   c. gain a competitive advantage over other computer companies.
   d. None of these.
   e. All of these.

4 Develop marketing mixes for services

_____ 10. British Airways' first-class passengers sit in a semi-private pear-wood berth that converts into a bed, thus providing more comfort on long flights. This service is an example of the airline's:
   a. standardized service.
   b. core service.
   c. customized service.
   d. supplementary service.
   e. component service.

_____ 11. You are opening your first hair-styling salon and are concerned with the development of your distribution mix decision. Which of the following reflects the key issue in your distribution decision?
   a. considerations of the storage of the service
   b. the development of a long channel of intermediaries
   c. standardizing the service
   d. intensity of distribution
   e. the location of your service for customer convenience

_____ 12. You have recently opened a specialty service that cleans, stores, and insures valuable jewelry. Your shop is exquisitely decorated, and the keys to the storage vaults are solid gold. Each time a customer visits the store to make a deposit or withdrawal, free champagne is offered. After each customer contact, the customer is mailed a thank-you note, handwritten on expensive stationery. The thank-you note is a(n):
   a. skimming strategy
   b. prestige prompt
   c. tangible cue
   d. intangible cue
   e. pricing strategy

_____ 13. Long-distance telephone companies have more expensive rates during peak usage times (weekdays) and discount rates for slower times (evenings and weekends). This illustrates the _____ pricing objective.
   a. peak profitability
   b. operations-oriented
   c. patronage-oriented
   d. supply-demand
   e. revenue-oriented

5 Discuss relationship marketing in services

_____ 14. The Xerox Corporation stays in touch with its customers with phone calls and greeting cards, periodically sends out needs-assessment questionnaires, and designs new services to meet new needs. This is an example of relationship marketing based on:
   a. financial bonds
   b. service delivery
   c. social bonds
   d. internal bonds
   e. structural bonds

7 Discuss global issues in services marketing

_____ 15. Many Canadian services industries have the potential for globalization because of their existing competitive advantages. Industries that possess distinct advantages include all of the following EXCEPT:
   a. insurance
   b. construction and engineering
   c. computer microchip manufacturing
   d. credit card operations
   e. banking

8 Describe nonprofit organization marketing

_____ 16. Green Canada is a nonprofit organization and therefore has:
   a. no need to develop an understanding of pricing
   b. a marketing orientation
   c. the same organizational structure as profit-making firms
   d. no impact on nonbuyers
   e. a need for marketing skills

_____ 17. What is one of the consequences of the nonprofit orientation of the Humane Society?
   a. The Humane Society does not have to worry about revenues and costs.
   b. The Humane Society will not make as much money as a profit-oriented firm.
   c. The success of the Humane Society cannot be measured in financial terms.
   d. The Humane Society is not expected to be as efficient as a for-profit firm.
   e. The Humane Society's success is based on how much money is donated to it.

_____ 18. Cancel Cocaine is a not-for-profit organization with the goal of providing low-cost assistance to cocaine addicts who do not have health insurance. To raise funds, it distributes pamphlets and videos to local businesses and wealthy homeowners, who encourage the donation of money. Cancel Cocaine is most likely to face the target market issue of:
   a. pressure to adopt undifferentiated segmentation strategies
   b. lack of bottom-line objectives
   c. complementary positioning
   d. apathetic or strongly opposed targets
   e. benefit complexity and strength

_____ 19. A local church formed a committee to provide aid to the homeless. The church applied to the city and local governments for funding but was denied when it could not adequately state what the services would include. In this case the committee failed because it had not defined the:
   a. user market
   b. product to be offered
   c. sponsoring organizations
   d. donor market
   e. target market

Check your answers to these questions before proceeding to the next section.

Read the marketing scenario and answer the questions that follow.

Leilani is the concierge at a posh resort in Maui, Hawaii. The resort provides many amenities to its guests, including oversized rooms with ocean views and kitchenettes, fitness centre and health spa, three restaurants including a five-star restaurant, sports activities such as tennis and golf, and a variety of other activities. Leilani's job as concierge is very important, as guests at the resort are highly discriminating. Leilani provides accurate information about Maui and its sites. She also responds to guest requests as quickly as possible and has been known to call contacts in the middle of the night to accommodate her guests. As a result, the resort's guests have entrusted her with their itineraries. Leilani is always professionally groomed, wears well-tailored tropical suits, and has a warm smile.

True/False:

_____   1.   The resort where Leilani works is considered a service business.

_____   2.   The service that Leilani provides as concierge lasts forever since guests have memories of their stay.

_____   3.   Leilani's well-groomed appearance is an example of a tangible feature of the resort's service.

Multiple Choice:

_____   4.   The guests' rooms are considered to be the resort's:
    a.   line extension.
    b.   supplementary service.
    c.   product mix.
    d.   core service.
    e.   value proposition

_____   5.   The restaurants, sports activities, and spa are examples of the resort's:
    a.   line extensions.
    b.   supplementary services.
    c.   product line.
    d.   core services.
    e.   new products

_____   6.   Which of the components of service quality is represented by Leilani's willingness to go to lengths to meet her guests' wishes?
    a.   Empathy.
    b.   Responsiveness.
    c.   Assurance.
    d.   Tangibles.
    e.   Patience.

_____   7.   Which of the following best explains the type of service processing that the resort provides?
    a.   People processing.
    b.   Possession processing.
    c.   Mental stimulus processing.
    d.   Information processing.
    e.   Project processing.

8. Is Leilani engaged in relationship marketing? Why or why not?

ESSAY QUESTIONS

1. Services have four unique characteristics that distinguish them from goods. Name and briefly define each of these four characteristics. These characteristics can make the marketing of services more difficult. Use the example of a restaurant to help describe each of the four characteristics.

2. Discuss service strategies for each of the four Ps in the marketing mix.

3. What is internal marketing? Why is it so important for employees at service firms to engage in this?

APPLICATION

You are the marketing manager at an organization that has the goal of decreasing the incidence of smoking among teen-agers. Describe unique issues that you will encounter in each of the four Ps in achieving your organizational goals.

CHAPTER 11: MARKETING CHANNELS AND SUPPLY CHAIN MANAGEMENT

LEARNING OBJECTIVES

1 Explain what a marketing channel is and why intermediaries are needed

A marketing channel is a business structure of interdependent organizations which reach from the point of product origin to the consumer with the purpose of physically moving products to their final consumption destination, representing "place" in the marketing mix and encompassing the processes involved in getting the right product to the right place at the right time. Members of a marketing channel create a continuous and seamless supply chain that performs or supports the marketing channel functions. Channel members provide economies to the distribution process in the form of specialization and division of labour; overcoming discrepancies in quantity, assortment, time and space; and providing contact efficiency.

2 Describe the channel structures for consumer and business-to-business products and discuss alternative channel arrangements

Marketing channels for consumer and business-to-business products vary in degree of complexity. The simplest consumer product channel involves direct selling from producers to consumers. Businesses may sell directly to business or government buyers. Marketing channels grow more complex as intermediaries become involved. Consumer product channel intermediaries include agents, brokers, wholesalers, and retailers. Business product channel intermediaries include agents, brokers, and industrial distributors.

Marketers often use alternative channel arrangements to move their products to the consumer. With dual distribution or multiple distribution, they choose two or more different channels to distribute the same product. Nontraditional channels help differentiate a firm's product from the competitor's or provide a manufacturer with another avenue for sales. Finally, strategic channel alliances are arrangements that use another manufacturer's already established channel.

3 Define supply chain management and discuss its benefits

Supply chain management coordinates and integrates all of the activities performed by supply chain members in a seamless process from the source to the point of consumption. The responsibilities of a supply chain manager include developing channel design strategies, managing the relationships of supply chain members, sourcing and procurement of raw materials, scheduling production, processing orders, managing inventory and storing product, and selecting transportation modes. The supply chain manager is also responsible for managing customer service and the information that flows through the supply chain.

The benefits of supply chain management include reduced costs in inventory management, transportation, warehousing, and packaging; improved service through techniques like time-based delivery and make-to-order; and enhanced revenues, which result from such supply chain-related achievements as higher product availability and more customized products.

4 Discuss the issues that influence channel strategy

When determining marketing channel strategy, the marketing manager must determine what market, product, and producer factors will influence the channel selected. The manager must also determine the appropriate level distribution intensity.

5 Explain channel leadership, conflict, and partnering

To achieve control, a channel member assumes channel leadership and exercises authority and power over other members of the channel. Inequitable channel relationships often lead to channel conflict, which is a result of a clash of goals and methods among the members of a distribution channel. Channel partnering is the joint effort of all channel members to create a supply chain that serves customers and creates a competitive advantage.

6   Describe the logistical components of the supply chain

The logistics supply chain consists of several interrelated and integrated functions: 1) processing supplies and raw materials; 2) scheduling production; 3) processing orders; 4) managing inventories of raw materials and finished goods; 5) warehousing and materials handling; and 6) selecting modes of transportation.

7   Discuss new technology and emerging trends in supply chain management

Several technological advances and trends affect the logistics today. Technology and automation has linked intermediaries in information networks. Concern for the environment is also affecting physical distribution. Another trend is the use of third-party carriers and a quest for quality in transportation. Finally, the need to understand global logistics has assumed greater importance for many companies.

8   Discuss channels and distribution decisions in global markets

Global marketing channels are important to Canadian companies that export their products or manufacture abroad. Manufacturers introducing products in foreign countries must decide what type of channel structure to use. Should the product be marketed through direct channels or through foreign intermediaries? Foreign intermediaries must be chosen very carefully because they will affect the brand image. Also, channel structures in other countries may be very different from those in Canada.

9   Identify the special problems and opportunities associated with distribution in service organizations

Managers in service industries use the same skills, techniques, and strategies to manage logistics functions as managers in goods-producing industries. The distribution of services focuses on three main areas: minimizing wait times, managing service capacity, and improving service delivery.

Answer the following questions to see how well you understand the material. Re-take it after you review to check yourself.

1. What is a marketing channel?

2. List and briefly describe three intensities of distribution.

3. What is channel conflict? Channel leadership? Channel partnering?

4. What are the six major functions of the supply chain?

1 Explain what a marketing channel is and why intermediaries are needed

I.   Marketing Channels

A.   The term *channel* is derived from the Latin word *canalis*, which means canal. A marketing channel can be viewed as a canal or pipeline for products.

B.   A **marketing channel** or **channel of distribution** is the set of interdependent organizations that facilitate the transfer of ownership as products move from producer to business user or consumer.

C.   Many different types of organizations participate in marketing channels.

   1.   **Channel members**, also called intermediaries, resellers, and middlemen negotiate with one another, buy and sell products, and facilitate the change of ownership between buyer and seller.

   2.   The **supply chain** is the connected chain of all of the business entities that perform or support the marketing channel functions.

D.   Providing Specialization and Division of Labour

   Essentially producers hire channels members to perform tasks and activities (such as transportation or selling to the consumer) that the producer is not prepared to perform or that the intermediary is better prepared to perform.

E.   Overcoming Discrepancies

   1.   A **discrepancy of quantity** is the difference between the amount of product produced and the amount an end user wants to buy.

   2.   A **discrepancy of assortment** is the lack of all the items necessary to receive full satisfaction from a product or products. A manufacturer may produce only one product, yet it may require the addition of several more products to actually use the first product.

   3.   A **temporal discrepancy** is created when a product is produced and a consumer is not ready to purchase it.

   4.   A **spatial discrepancy** is the difference between the location of the producer and the location of widely scattered markets.

F.   Providing Contact Efficiency

   Marketing channels simplify distribution by reducing the amount of transactions required to get products from manufacturers to consumers. Retailers assemble a selection of merchandise so that one contact (buying trip) can result in the purchase of many different items.

2 Describe the channel structures for consumer and business-to-business products and discuss alternative channel arrangements

II. Channel Structures

The appropriate configuration of channel members to move a product from the producer to the end user may differ greatly by product.

A. Channels for Consumer Products

1. One channel is the **direct channel**, which entails producers selling directly to consumers. This includes telemarketing, mail order, and catalogue shopping and forms of electronic retailing.

2. The longest typical channel found for consumer products is the *agent/broker channel*, in which agents or brokers bring manufacturers and wholesalers together for negotiation. Ownership then passes from one or more wholesalers to retailers, and finally retailers sell to the consumer.

a. A *retailer channel* is used when the retailer is large and can buy in large quantities direct from the manufacturer.

b. A *wholesaler channel* is often used for low-cost, frequently purchased items such as candy and gum. The wholesalers purchase large quantities and break it into smaller lots, which are sold to retailers.

B. Channels for Business-to-Business and Industrial Products

1. Channels for business and industrial markets are usually characterized by fewer intermediaries.

2. Many producers sell directly, in large quantities, to the large manufacturers that are their customers.

3. The channel from producer to government buyers is direct. This is usually because of specialized products and bidding.

4. For standardized items of moderate or low value, an intermediary is often used. This is usually an industrial distributor or manufacturers' representative.

5. The Internet is increasingly being used in business-to-business channels as a more direct and efficient means of purchasing and selling supplies and raw materials.

C. Alternative Channel Arrangements

1. Some producers select two or more channels to distribute the same products to target markets, a practice called **multiple distribution** or **dual distribution**. A variation of this practice is the marketing of similar products using different brand names.

2. Often *nontraditional channel* arrangements help differentiate a firm's product from that of the competition.

3. **Strategic channel alliances** are sometimes formed to use another manufacturer's already established channel.

---

3   Define supply chain management and discuss its benefits

III. Supply Chain Management

The goal of supply chain management is to coordinate and integrate all of the activities performed by supply chain members into a seamless process, from the source to the point of consumption.

A. Philosophy that seeks to unify the competencies and resources of business functions both within the firm and outside in the firm's allied channel partners.

B. Completely customer driven

C. Flow of demand changed from "push" to "pull".

    1. Supply chain management is a communication of customer demand

    2. Supply chain management is a physical flow process

4   Discuss the issues that influence channel strategy

IV. Making Channel Strategy Decisions

Supply chain channel strategy is substantially influenced by channel objectives, which in turn should reflect marketing objectives and organization objectives.

The marketing manager faces two important issues: what factors will influence the channel(s) and what level of distribution intensity will be appropriate.

A. Factors Affecting Channel Choice

    1. Market Factors

    These include target customer profiles and preferences, geographic location, size of market, and competition.

    2. Product Factors

    These include whether products are complex, customized, standard, the price, stage of product life cycle, and delicacy of the product.

    3. Producer Factors

    Producer factors that impact channel choice include size of managerial, financial, and marketing resources, number of product lines, and desire for control of pricing, positioning, brand image, and customer support.

B. Levels of Distribution Intensity

    1. **Intensive distribution** is distribution aimed at having a product available in every outlet where target consumers might want to buy it.

       a. Many convenience goods and supplies have intensive distribution.
       b. Low-value, frequently purchased products may require a long channel of distribution.

---

2. **Selective distribution** is distribution achieved by screening dealers to eliminate all but a few in any single area.

    a.   Selective distribution strategies often hinge on a manufacturer's desire to maintain superior product image to be able to charge a premium price.

    b.   Shopping goods usually have selective distribution, as do some specialty products.

G. Transportation

The five major modes of transportation are railroads, motor carriers, pipelines, water transportation, and airways.

Supply chain managers choose a mode on the basis of:

1. **Cost:** total amount a specific carrier charges to move the product from the point of origin to the destination.
2. **Transit time:** total time a carrier has possession of goods.
3. **Reliability:** consistency with which the carrier delivers goods on time and in acceptable condition.
4. **Capability:** ability of the carrier to provide the appropriate equipment and conditions for moving goods.
5. **Accessibility:** carrier's ability to move goods over a specific route or network.
6. **Traceability:** relative ease with which a shipment can be located and transferred.

7   Discuss new technology and emerging trends in supply chain management

VII. Trends in Supply Chain Management

A. Technology

Computer technology has dramatically boosted the efficiency of logistics with tools such as automatic identification systems using bar coding and radio frequency technology, and supply chain software systems that help synchronize the flow of goods and information with customer demand.

B. Outsourcing Logistics Functions

1. In **outsourcing or contract logistics**, a manufacturer or supplier turns over the entire function of buying and managing transportation to a third party.

2. Third-party contact logistics allows companies to cut inventories, locate stock at fewer plants and distribution centres, and still provide the same level of service or better.

C. Electronic Distribution

Electronic distribution is the most recent development in the physical distribution arena.

1. This will include any product or service that can be distributed electronically, whether through traditional cable or through satellite transmission.

8   Discuss channel structure and distribution decisions in global markets

VIII. Channels and Distribution Decisions for Global Markets

    A.   Developing Global Marketing Channels

       Manufacturers introducing products in global markets must determine what type of channel structure to use.

       1.   Channel structure abroad may not be very similar to channels in the United States.

       2.   Channel types available in foreign countries usually differ as well.

       3.   Marketers must be aware of grey - marketing channels in which products are distributed through unauthorized channel intermediaries.

       4.   Internet channels are becoming more common for legitimate and unauthorized product distribution.

    B.   Global Logistics and Supply Chain Management.

       1.   One critical issue is the legalities of trade in other countries.

       2.   A second factor is the transportation infrastructure.

9   Identify the special problems and opportunities associated with physical distribution in service organizations

IX. Channels and Distribution Decisions for Services

The fastest-growing part of the Canadian economy is the service sector. The same skills, techniques, and strategies used to manage inventory can be used to manage service inventory.

    A.   Service Industries' Distribution Opportunities

       1.   Service distribution means getting the right service and the right people and the right information to the right place at the right time.

       2.   Production and consumption are simultaneous

       3.   Service distribution attempts to minimize wait times, manage service capacity, and improve delivery through new distribution channels

       4.   The Internet is fast becoming an alternative channel through which to deliver services

Fill in the blank(s) with the appropriate term or phrase from the alphabetized list of chapter key terms.

channel conflict
channel control
channel leader (channel captain)
channel members
channel partnering (channel cooperation)
channel power
direct channel
discrepancy of assortment
discrepancy of quantity
distribution resource planning (DRP)
dual distribution (multiple distribution)
electronic data interchange (EDI)
electronic distribution
exclusive distribution
horizontal conflict
intensive distribution
inventory control system

just-in-time (JIT) production system
logistics information system
marketing channel (channel of distribution)
mass customization
materials-handling system
materials requirement planning (MRP)
order processing system
outsourcing (contract logistics)
selective distribution
spatial discrepancy
strategic channel alliance
supply chain
supply chain management
supply chain team
temporal discrepancy
vertical conflict

1   Explain what a marketing channel is and why intermediaries are needed

1. A set of interdependent organizations that ease the transfer of ownership as products move from producer to business user or consumer is a(n) _____. All the parties involved that negotiated with one another, buy and sell products, and facilitate the change of ownership in course of moving the final product to the consumer are known as _____.

2. Channel members are often included between producers and consumers because they help overcome discrepancies. The difference between the amount of product produced and the amount an end user wants to buy is a(n) _____; this is overcome by making products available in the amounts buyers desire. The lack of all the items necessary to provide full satisfaction to a buyer is a(n) _____; to overcome this discrepancy, channels assemble varieties of products that buyers want available at one place. When a product is produced but a consumer is not ready to purchase it, a(n) _____ is created; channels overcome this discrepancy by maintaining inventories. Markets are usually scattered over large geographic regions, creating a(n) _____; channels overcome this discrepancy by making products available in convenient locations.

2   Describe the channel structures for consumer and business-to-business products and discuss alternative channel arrangements

3. If a producer sells to consumers with no intermediaries, it is using a(n) _____.

4. Producers often devise alternative marketing channels to move their products. Some producers select two or more different channels to distribute the same products to target markets. This practice is known as _____. A producer may elect to use another manufacturer's already-established channel for distribution by forming a(n) _____.

4   Discuss the issues that influence channel strategy

5.   Distribution aimed at maximum market coverage is _____. If products are distributed to a limited number of dealers in a particular region, _____ is taking place. The most restrictive form of market coverage is _____, which entails only one or a few dealers within a given area.

5   Explain channel leadership, conflict, and partnering

6.   A channel member's capacity to control or influence the behaviour of other channel members is known as _____. When one channel member affects another member's adaptive behaviour, it exercises _____ by assuming the position of _____.

7.   When a clash of goals and methods among members of a distribution channel occurs, this is known as _____. Conflict that occurs among channel members on the same level, such as two retailers, is known as _____, while conflict that occurs between different levels in a marketing channel, such as between the manufacturer and wholesaler, is known as _____.

8.   _____ is the joint effort of all channel members to create a supply chain that serves customers and creates a competitive advantage.

9.   The process of strategically managing the efficient flow and storage of raw materials, in-process inventory and finished goods from point of origin to point of consumption is known as _____. The connected chain of all the business entities, both internal and external to the company, that perform the logistics function is a _____. All activities performed by members of the chain must be coordinated and integrated, and this process is known as _____.

6   Describe logistical components of the supply chain

10.   A _____ is information technology that integrates and links all of the logistics functions of the supply chain. The entire group of individuals who orchestrate the movement of goods, services and information from the source to the consumer is known as a(n) _____.

11.   A production method whereby products are not made until an order is placed by the customer and where products are made according to customer specifications is known as _____. Another important service that suppliers offer to their customers is _____, whereby the supplier delivers raw materials just when they are needed on the production line. This helps the manufacturer to reduce inventory costs.

12.   The _____ processes the requirements of the customer and sends the information to the supply chain via the logistics information system. These systems are becoming more automated, and many firms use _____ to reduce the amount of paper documents needed for transactions, such as purchase orders and invoices.

13. The physical distribution subsystem that develops and maintains an adequate assortment of products to meet customers' demands is the _____. Managing inventory from the supplier to the manufacturer is called _____. Systems that manage the finished goods inventory from the manufacturer to end user are called _____. A(n) _____ moves inventory into, within, and out of the warehouse.

7   Discuss new technology and emerging trends in supply chain management

14. The most recent development in physical distribution includes any kind of product or service that can be distributed by fibre optic cable or through satellite transmission of electronic signals. This is known as _____. Another trend in logistics is _____ which occurs when a manufacturer uses an independent third party to manage an entire function of the logistics system, such as transportation, warehousing, or order processing.

Check your answers to these questions before proceeding to the next section.

TRUE/FALSE QUESTIONS

Mark the statement **T** if it is true and **F** if it is false.

1   Explain what a marketing channel is and why intermediaries are needed

_____ 1. The marketing channel is the same as the supply chain.

_____ 2. David stopped by the convenience store to buy a can of soda pop. He is glad that he can buy one can at a time, instead of having to buy the thousands of gallons of soda the manufacturer produces every day. For David, the convenience store overcomes a discrepancy of quantity.

_____ 3. Jill would like to put some kiwifruit in her fruit salad. Fortunately, she does not have to hop on an airplane and fly to New Zealand to buy one; she can buy a kiwifruit at the neighbourhood grocery store. In this case, marketing channels have helped to overcome a spatial discrepancy.

2   Describe the channel structures for consumer and business-to-business products and discuss alternative channel arrangements

_____ 4. Company Alpha sells cotton balls for consumers to use. Company Zeta sells cotton for the fabric industry to make clothing. It is more likely that Company Zeta will use a direct channel because the direct channel is used more often in business markets than in consumer markets.

_____ 5. Agents and brokers are commonly used in markets that have few, large manufacturers and powerful retailers.

_____ 6. Volvo united with Federal Express Logistics to overcome its problem getting replacement parts where needed for emergency roadside repairs. This is an example of a strategic channel alliance.

3   Define supply chain management and discuss it benefits

_____ 7. One of the primary benefits of supply chain management is increased revenue.

_____ 8. Supply chain management seeks to unify the competencies and resources of business functions both within and outside in the firm's allied channel partners.

---

4 Discuss the issues that influence channel strategy

_____ 9. The objective of selective distribution is to achieve mass market selling.

_____ 10. The D'Or Galleries sells its solid gold picture frames at only five stores in the United States. D'Or promotes the frames intensively to those retailers and performs much cooperative advertising. This is an example of intensive distribution.

_____ 11. Mini-Micro Company manufactures miniature microwave ovens suitable for campers, dorm rooms, and small kitchens. The company's marketing research indicates that consumers are willing to look around for miniature microwaves but may not be willing to search or travel extensively to acquire the product. Mini-Micro should use selective distribution.

5 Explain channel leadership, conflict, and partnering

_____ 12. Savings Mart is a large discount retailer that requires its suppliers to provide the lowest possible cost and to adhere to a just-in-time inventory system. Wholesalers and manufacturers generally yield to the authority of this giant retailer. Savings Mart exercises channel power.

_____ 13. Fred's Mart and Josephine's Foods are two independent grocery stores that are claiming that a large manufacturer is treating them unfairly because they are small. This is an example of vertical conflict within the marketing channel.

6 Describe the logistical components of the supply chain

_____ 14. The supply chain team is not responsible for transportation; this is the job of wholesalers.

_____ 15. U-Build-It Computer Company specializes in providing computers built-to-order to its customers. This is an example of mass customization.

_____ 16. Fiske's Disks, Inc., produces computer diskettes and has just changed its assembly method. The diskettes are produced on an assembly line, and suppliers deliver the needed parts in five small daily shipments directly to the line. Fiske's has noticed a dramatic decrease in carrying costs but a sharp increase in delivery costs because the company must pay more for the added delivery convenience. Fiske's Disks uses just-in-time (JIT) production.

_____ 17. Nancy Gordon orders office supplies from a local retailer through her computer. The computer program is set up to transmit purchase orders and invoices between customers and the retailer. The retailer then delivers the products to her office. This is an example of electronic distribution.

7 Discuss new technology and emerging trends in supply chain management

_____ 18. The use of outsourcing has resulted in firms using more carriers, but demanding less from them.

8 Discuss channels and distribution decisions in global markets

_____ 19. Small firms are less likely to enter global markets because of uncertainty in logistics.

Check your answers to these questions before proceeding to the next section.

For the following statements, indicate reasons why you may agree and disagree with the statement.

1. Marketing channels are far too complex. The best channel is direct: to go from manufacturer to retailer.

    Reason(s) to agree:

    Reason(s) to disagree:

2. When a channel leader emerges, there will inevitably be channel conflict.

    Reason(s) to agree:

    Reason(s) to disagree:

3. It is better to use intensive distribution, rather than selective or exclusive distribution, because a larger number of outlets means increased sales.

    Reason(s) to agree:

    Reason(s) to disagree:

4. There is no such thing as a marketing channel for services.

    Reason(s) to agree:

    Reason(s) to disagree:

Select the response that best answers the question, and write the corresponding letter in the space provided.

1 Explain what a marketing channel is and why intermediaries are needed

_____ 1. Which of the following is NOT a function of a marketing channel?
a. To provide specialization
b. To achieve economies of scale in production
c. To divide labour
d. To provide contact efficiency
e. To overcome discrepancy of assortment

_____ 2. The Hit-the-Beach Store purchases swimsuits, sunscreen products, towels, beach toys, beach chairs, and surf boards from a variety of manufacturers and brings these items to its large store in a large California coastal city. The store's goal is to provide every amenity needed for a trip to the beach, so Hit-the-Beach is aiding consumers by overcoming the:
a. discrepancy of assortment
b. discrepancy of quantity
c. spatial discrepancy
d. temporal discrepancy
e. contact discrepancy

_____ 3. The Howlin' Halloween Company operates its manufacturing facilities year-round, but the sales season for Halloween costumes and party decorations is usually September 1 through November 1. However, sales remain steady all year as the company sells to wholesale distributors that stock the product. The wholesale distributors are helping to overcome a:
a. discrepancy of assortment
b. temporal discrepancy
c. contact discrepancy
d. discrepancy of quantity
e. spatial discrepancy

2 Describe the channel structures for consumer and business-to-business products and discuss alternative channel arrangements

_____ 4. The Gusto-Lift Company manufactures customized, high-tech elevator shelving systems for specialized automated warehouses. For distribution, you would expect Gusto-Lift to use a:
a. network of facilitating agents
b. horizontally integrated channel
c. long channel
d. vertical marketing system
e. direct channel

_____ 5. General Electric sells large home appliances both through independent retailers (department stores and discount houses) and directly to large housing-tract builders. This is an example of:
a. intensive distribution
b. intermediary distribution
c. selective distribution
d. alternative distribution
e. dual distribution

4 **Discuss the issues that influence channel strategy**

_____ 6. Life Savers candy is sold in grocery stores, service stations, convenience stores, drugstores, discount stores, and vending machines. This is a(n) _____ distribution strategy.
   a. circular
   b. franchising
   c. selective
   d. intensive
   e. horizontal

_____ 7. Lennox Air Conditioners carefully screens its dealers to ensure a quality dealer image and service ability. Only a few dealers are chosen in any single geographic area. This is an example of:
   a. selective distribution
   b. intensive distribution
   c. exclusive distribution
   d. dual distribution
   e. premier distribution

_____ 8. Rolls Royce has a restrictive policy of only establishing one or two dealers within a given large geographic area. Buyers of this type of expensive car will travel to acquire the product, so this form of distribution, _____, is appropriate for the product.
   a. prestige
   b. intensive
   c. selective
   d. dual
   e. exclusive

5 **Explain channel leadership, conflict, and partnering**

_____ 9. As the largest retailer in the world, Wal-Mart exerts great power over its suppliers, who provide the best possible prices. In the marketing channel, Wal-Mart would be considered a:
   a. channel authority
   b. channel member
   c. channel leader
   d. channel team
   e. merchant wholesaler

_____ 10. American Booksellers Association, a group of small independent bookstores, filed a suit against the large chains Barnes & Noble and Borders, alleging that they violated antitrust laws by using their buying power for deeper discounts on books. This is an example of:
   a. horizontal channel conflict
   b. lateral channel conflict
   c. retailer conflict
   d. vertical channel conflict
   e. channel conspiracy

_____ 11. The joint effort of all channel members to create a supply chain that serves customers and creates a competitive advantage is known as:
   a. channel conflict
   b. logistics system
   c. strategic alliance
   d. channel partnering
   e. channel conspiracy

12. Spiffy Spices is trying to decide on a location for its new warehouse and should consider all of the following EXCEPT:
    a.   the cost and quality of industrial land
    b.   transportation costs and distances to customers
    c.   the stage of the product life cycle
    d.   the location of production facilities
    e.   the availability of transportation modes

13. A university commissions a computer manufacturer to produce three hundred computers that would be tailored to the school's specific needs. This is an example of:
    a.   JIT production
    b.   auto ID
    c.   EOQ
    d.   mass customization
    e.   procurement

14. The PorterCo Company can no longer afford expensive storage facilities for its inventory. Furthermore, its computer products need to be built as soon as customers place orders. PorterCo should establish a(n) _____ system.
    a.   UPC
    b.   auto ID
    c.   EOQ
    d.   JIT
    e.   TQM

15. The Limited clothing store can immediately transmit orders for new clothing to its suppliers in Asia. The Asian suppliers can electronically transmit back to the Limited information about in-stock items and shipping dates. This is an example of:
    a.   UPC
    b.   EDI
    c.   EOQ
    d.   JIT
    e.   ROP

16. The Megabit Company experiences much damage and loss when moving its computer products from the manufacturing plant to the storage facilities. The company should consider reducing the number of times an item is moved in the warehouse by installing a(n):
    a.   inventory control system
    b.   order-processing system
    c.   safety procedure
    d.   materials-handling system
    e.   transportation system

17. Massachusetts Mining harvests timber and mines metal ores and coals. This company is most likely to use _____ for transportation to customers.
    a.   railroads
    b.   airplanes
    c.   truck lines
    d.   water transportation
    e.   pipelines

18. The Prime Cut Cattle Company has determined that its chief priority for choosing a transportation mode in the United States is transit time because meats must be fresh. However, this must be tempered by practical cost considerations. Prime Cut should use to ship their meats.
    a.   railroads
    b.   airplanes
    c.   motor carriers
    d.   water transportation
    e.   pipelines

_____ 19. Florida Greenhouses, Inc. promises its customers fresh-cut tropical flower arrangements with premium service (at a premium price). Florida Greenhouses most likely uses:
   a. railroads
   b. airways
   c. motor carriers
   d. water transportation
   e. pipelines

_____ 20. Some Canadian car buyers save money by purchasing Mercedes-Benz cars in Germany and adding Canada required emission systems while the car is in transit. The most likely transportation mode is:
   a. water carrier
   b. motor carrier
   c. railroad
   d. air
   e. ocean pipeline

_____ 21. The marketing division of ExxonMobil developed SpeedPass to accelerate the process of pumping and paying for gasoline. This is an example of:
   a. managing service capacity
   b. improving contact efficiency
   c. minimizing wait times
   d. reducing slack time
   e. improving service delivery

7   Discuss new technology and emerging trends in supply chain management

_____ 22. Remex Diesel recognizes its main business strengths as efficient manufacturing procedures, an excellent dealer network, extensive market research, and an experienced marketing staff. The company has never developed a strong physical distribution system because it is not a focus of the business. Remex should use:
   a. private warehousing
   b. intermodal sourcing
   c. distribution centre systems
   d. freight forwarding
   e. contract warehousing

8   Discuss channels and distribution decisions in global markets

_____ 23. Celestial Seasonings, a Canadian tea manufacturer, would like to sell its herbal teas in China and Russia. Given the product and market characteristics, Celestial Seasonings should probably:
   a. use a direct-mail wholesaler
   b. establish an overseas company sales force
   c. use independent foreign intermediaries for distribution
   d. establish a vertical marketing system and act as channel leader
   e. purchase the services of an industrial distributor

Check your answers to these questions before proceeding to the next section.

Read the marketing scenario and answer the questions that follow.

<u>Note</u>: *The following case incorporates theory from both chapter 11 (Marketing Channels) and Chapter 12 (Retailing and Wholesaling) and may be best covered after completion of chapter 12.*

Ralph has just purchased a small business that manufactures sunglasses for people who play sports. The previous owner of the business sold the sunglasses through the Internet to directly to consumers. Despite the high quality of the sunglasses and the market demand, the business did not succeed, due mostly to the limited growth and lack of exposure of the sunglasses to the target market.

Ralph would like to expand distribution of the sunglasses by going through more traditional channels other than the Internet and mail. He has considered the following options: 1) selling directly to retailers; 2) selling to a sporting goods wholesaler; or 3) using an agent or broker who could sell to a wholesaler. Each option has its advantages and disadvantages. His ultimate distribution goal is to get sporting goods stores and other specialty athletic shops to carry the sunglasses, as they are quite expensive and should retail around at around $200.

<u>True/False:</u>

_____ 1. Before Ralph purchased the business, the sunglasses business used a wholesaler channel.

_____ 2. Ralph's business dilemma is due solely to distribution.

_____ 3. If Ralph continues to sell his sunglasses through the Internet and adds another channel option, he will be engaging in dual distribution.

<u>Multiple Choice:</u>

_____ 4. What would most likely lead Ralph to reject option #1 (selling directly to retailers)?

     a. Retailers of sporting goods are not plentiful.
     b. Ralph's business is too small to transport his products directly to retailers.
     c. Retailers have no power in the marketing channel.
     d. Salespeople don't like calling on retailers.
     e. None of these are reasons to reject selling directly to retailers

_____ 5. What is the major advantage of option #3 for Ralph (using an agent or broker)?

     a. This option is the least expensive.
     b. Agents and brokers take title to the goods and, therefore, assume liability.
     c. Agents and brokers match small manufacturers with small retailers.
     d. The channel is much more direct.
     e. Agents and brokers don't charge commissions, so Ralph will have higher margins

_____ 6. Distribution to sporting goods stores and specialty athletic shops is an example of what level of distribution intensity?

     a. Extensive
     b. Intensive
     c. Exclusive
     d. Prestige
     e. Selective

_____ 7. Which of the following would most likely NOT be considered by Ralph as he selects his marketing channel?

     a. The type of product he is selling (expensive and specialized).
     b. The branding strategy he's planning to use.
     c. The market he's targeting (athletes) and its size.
     d. The size and capability of this own business.
     e. Ralph will consider all of these as he selects his marketing channel.

Short Answer:

8.   Which channel should Ralph choose? Why?

ESSAY QUESTIONS

1.   Channel members, such as wholesalers and retailers, are often included between producers and business users or consumers for three important reasons. Name and describe each of these reasons.

2.   Assume you are an instructor of marketing. Explain to your class what the three options concerning distribution intensity are. Give examples of three specific products that may be distributed at each level.

3.   What is channel conflict? Name two types of channel conflict, describe them, and provide an example for each.

4.   Name and describe six functions of a supply chain.

5.   One important subsystem of physical distribution is transportation. Name the different modes of transportation. For each mode, list two examples of cargo typically carried. Distribution managers select different transportation modes based on several distinct criteria. List and briefly define five of these criteria, and name the best and worst transportation mode for each criterion.

Trace the distribution of coffee beans, grown in Colombia, to a cup of coffee served at a gourmet coffee house in your hometown. Discuss all the channels of distribution that may be involved, modes of transportation that are used, and any other distribution issues that are relevant to this product. Use the Internet, the library, and other resources to help in your research.

Chapter 11 ■ *Marketing Channels and Supply Chain Management*

CHAPTER 12: RETAILING

LEARNING OBJECTIVES

1   Discuss the importance of retailing in the Canadian economy

Retailing is a huge and visible portion of marketing. Retailing is one of the largest employers, with over 1.46 million people employed by over 240,000 Canadian retailers. At the store level, retailing is still considered a mom-and-pop business, with almost 7 out of 10 retail establishments employing fewer than four employees. Although most retailers are quite small, a few large retail chains tend to dominate their categories.

2   Describe the nature of retail operations

Many different kinds of retailers exist. They can be differentiated on the basis of ownership, level of service, product assortment, and general price levels. On the basis of ownership, retailers can be broadly differentiated as independent retailers, chain stores, or franchise outlets. The level of service retailers provide can be classified along a continuum of high to low. Retailers also classify themselves by the breadth and depth of their product assortment; some retailers have concentrated product assortments whereas others have extensive product assortments. Last, general price levels also classify a store, from discounters offering low prices to exclusive specialty stores where high prices are the norm. Retailers use the latter three variables to position themselves in the marketplace.

3   List the major tasks involved in developing a retail marketing strategy

Retailers must develop marketing strategies based on overall goals and strategic plans. The key tasks in retail strategy are defining and selecting a target market and developing the six Ps of the retailing mix to successfully meet the needs of the chosen target market.

The first task in developing the retail strategy is to define the target market. This process begins with market segmentation. The markets are often defined on demographic, geographic, and lifestyle or psychographic dimensions.

The six Ps of the retailing mix consist of those elements controlled by the retailer that are combined together in varying degrees and forms and directed as a single retailing method to the target market. The six Ps include product, place, promotion, price, personnel, and presentation, and together these items project the store's image.

The presentation of a retail store to its customers helps determine the store's image. The most predominant aspect is the store's atmosphere - the store's overall impression established by the physical layout or decor.

Personnel and customer service are a prominent aspect of retailing. Most retail sales involve a customer-salesperson interaction.

4   Discuss the challenges of expanding retailing operations into global markets

Canadian and U.S. retailers feel that now there is a great opportunity to expand into global markets. Reasons for this include the spread of communication networks and mass media, which has homogenized tastes and product preferences to some extent. However, retailers must still do their homework. They must keep their core strengths while making adjustments to the marketing mix to suit the culture of the individual market.

5   Describe future trends in retailing

Three major trends are evident in retailing today. First, adding entertainment to the retail environment is one of the most popular strategies in retailing in recent years. Second, retailers of the future will offer more convenience and efficiency to consumers as consumers become more precise on their shopping trips. Staples won't be sold in stores, but instead delivered directly to the consumer freeing shoppers to visit stores for products they enjoy buying. Advances in technology will make it easier for consumers to obtain the products they want. Last, more and more retailers are using the information they collect about their customers at the point of sale to develop customer management programs, including customer relationship marketing, loyalty programs, and clienteling.

6   Discuss the importance of wholesaling in the Canadian economy

Wholesalers are important intermediaries in the distribution of goods and services. Wholesaler revenues are higher than retail revenues because wholesalers sell to industry and farmers and also other wholesalers, who in turn resell. Since products may move through multiple levels of intermediaries before reaching the final consumer, wholesalers have a major impact on pricing in the marketplace.

7   Identify the major types of wholesalers

Merchant wholesalers are those organizations that facilitate the movement of products and services from the manufacturer to producers, resellers, governments, institutions, and retailers. Agents and brokers do not take title to goods and services they market, but they do facilitate the exchange of ownership between sellers and buyers.

8   List the major functions that wholesalers perform

Channel intermediaries (retailers and wholesalers) perform three basic types of functions. Transactional functions include contacting and promoting, negotiating, and risk-taking. Logistical functions performed by channel members include physical distribution storing, and sorting functions. Finally, channel members may perform facilitating functions, such as researching and financing.

9   Describe future trends in wholesaling

Future trends in wholesaling include: a focus on improving productivity of operations, improving customer service, seizing international opportunities, and integrating forward from wholesale into retail operations.

Answer the following questions to see how well you understand the material. Re-take it after you review to check yourself.

1. What is retailing?

2. List ten types of stores.

3. List and briefly describe four types of nonstore retailing.

4. List and briefly describe the six Ps of retailing.

5. List and briefly describe two types of wholesalers?

1   Discuss the importance of retailing in the Canadian economy

I.   The Role of Retailing

Retailing is all activities directly related to the sale of goods and services to the ultimate consumer for personal, non-business use.

    A.   Retailing is one of the largest employers, with over 1.46 million people employed by over 240,000 Canadian retailers.

    B.   Although most retailers are quite small, a few large retail chains tend to dominate their categories.

2   Describe the nature of retailer operations

II.   Nature of Retail Operations

    A. Retailers can be differentiated on the basis of ownership, level of service, product assortment, and price.

    1.   Ownership

    Retailers can be broadly classified by form of ownership: independent, part of a chain, or a franchise outlet.

        a.   **Independent retailers** are owned by a single person or partnership. They are not operated as part of a larger retail institution.
        b.   **Chain stores** are owned and operated as a group by a single organization.
        c.   Franchises are owned and operated by individuals but are licensed by a larger supporting organization. A **franchise** is the right to operate a business or sell a product.

    2.   Level of Service

    Various services provided by retailers can be classified along a continuum from full-service (such as exclusive clothing stores) to self-service (such as factory outlets and warehouse clubs).

    3.   Product Assortment

    Another basis for positioning or classifying stores is by the breadth and depth of their product line.

        1.   Specialty stores may be very narrow in product lines but offer great depth within that area.

        2.   Discounters such as Wal-Mart and Zellers are just the opposite. They have a wide array of products with limited depth.

    4.   Price

    Some stores such as department stores typically charge full price, while other stores emphasize their discounting or outlet pricing. **Gross margin** shows how much a retailer makes. It is expressed as a percentage of sales after the cost of goods sold is subtracted.

B. Major Types of Retail Operations

1. Department Stores

   a. With several departments under one roof, a **department store** carries a wide variety of shopping and specialty goods, including apparel, cosmetics, housewares, electronics, and sometimes furniture.

   b. Each department is usually headed by a **buyer**, a department head that selects the merchandise for his or her department and may also be responsible for promotion and personnel.

   c. The majority of department store sales are made by national chains (Wal-Mart, Sear, Zellers and The Bay).

   d. To protect themselves from powerful new specialty retailers, discounters, outlets, and other price cutters, department store managers are using several strategies.

      i. Many department stores are repositioning themselves as specialty outlets with a "store-within-a-store" format, dividing departments into mini boutiques.
      ii. Department stores view their high level of service as the one unique benefit they offer to consumers. Emphasizing service rather than price enables them to compete with discounters.
      iii. Expansion and renovation of existing stores allows growth in new market areas and changes in merchandising directions and images.

2. Specialty Stores

   a. A **specialty store** is not only a type of store but also a method of retail operations that specializes in a given type of merchandise.

   b. A typical specialty store carries a deep but narrow assortment of merchandise and offers attentive customer service and knowledgeable sales clerks.

   c. Price is usually of secondary importance to customers of specialty stores.

3. Supermarkets

   a. Canadians spend 11.25 percent of their total expenditures on food in **supermarkets**, which are large, departmentalized, self-service retailers that specialize in food and some nonfood items.

   b. With razor-thin profit margins (1 to 2 percent) and the slow annual population growth (less than 1 percent), supermarkets have had to discover and exploit several demographic and lifestyle trends in order to prosper.

   c. *Superstores* offer foods, non-foods, and services in a store, which is usually twice the size of supermarkets.

   d. Offering a wide variety of nontraditional goods and services under one roof is **scrambled merchandising**. These superstores offer one-stop shopping for many food and nonfood needs, and may include pharmacies, flower shops, bookstores, salad bars, takeout food sections, dry cleaners, photo processing, health food sections, and banking.

   e. *Loyalty marketing programs* reward loyal customers with discounts or gifts.

4.   Drugstores

     Drugstores stock pharmacy-related products and services as their main draw.
     a.   Customers are most attracted by the pharmacist, convenience, and acceptance of third party prescription drug plans

     b.   Drugstores have developed value-added services in order to compete with growing competition.

5.   **Convenience stores** carry a limited line of high-turnover convenience goods and resemble miniature supermarkets. Prices are higher than supermarkets because the stores offer so many conveniences such as location, long hours, and fast service.

6.   Discount Stores

     Discount stores are retail stores that are able to compete on the basis of low prices, high turnover, and high volume.

     a.   **Full-line discounters, also called mass merchandisers**, carry a broad assortment of nationally branded hard goods (broader than a department store) and offer customers few services. Very similar to department stores in many respects, the mass merchandising shopping chains have wide product assortments, yet their sheer size in sales volume, promotion budgets, and number of stores sets them apart.

     b.   **Mass merchandising** is the strategy of setting moderate to low prices on large quantities of products, coupled with big promotional budgets, to stimulate high inventory turnover.

     c.   Several different hybrids of the full-line discounters have appeared:

          i.   **Hypermarkets** are even larger than the largest supermarket and discount store, with between 200,000 and 300,000 square feet. They must generate a huge volume to compensate for very low gross margins. This concept has had limited success in the Canada and the United States.
          ii.   **Supercentres** combine groceries and general merchandise goods with a wide range of services including pharmacy, dry cleaning, photo finishing, optical shops, and hair salons. (Loblaws).
          iii.   The *extreme-value retailer* is characterized by a narrow selection of basic merchandise and rock bottom prices (Dollar Store).

     d.   **Discount specialty stores** are single-line stores offering merchandise such as sporting goods, electronics, auto parts, office supplies, or toys (Office Depot, Rona) .

          i.   **Specialty discount stores** offer a nearly complete selection of one line of merchandise and use self-service, discount prices, high volume, and high-turnover merchandise to their advantage.
          ii.   They are often termed **category killers** because they so heavily dominate their narrow segment.

     e.   **Warehouse membership clubs** are limited-service merchant wholesalers that offer a limited selection of brand-name appliances, household items, and groceries, usually in bulk on a cash-and-carry basis to members only (Costco).

     f.   **Off-price discount retailers** sell at prices that are 25 percent or more below traditional department store prices because these retailers pay cash for their stock, and usually don't ask for return privileges.

i. The **off-price retailers** purchase goods at cost or less from manufacturers' overruns, bankruptcies, irregulars, and unsold end-of-season output. An example is Winners.

   ii. **Factory outlets** are a type of off-price retailer with one big difference: They are owned and operated by manufacturers and carry one line of merchandise (their own).

7. Restaurants

   Restaurants straddle the line between a retailing establishment and a service establishment. Tangible products are food and drink. Service elements are food preparation and food service.

   a. Food away from home accounts for 30 percent of the household food budget, and it is expected to grow.

   b. The restaurant industry remains one of the most entrepreneurial of businesses and one of the most competitive.

   c. More restaurants are now competing directly with supermarkets by offering take-out and delivery in an effort to capture more of the home replacement market.

C. Nonstore Retailing

Nonstore retailing refers to shopping without visiting a store and is currently growing faster than in-store shopping because of the consumer demand for convenience.

1. **Automatic Vending** is a form of nonstore retailing that uses automated machines offer products for sale.

   a. Vending machine and coffee retailers yield sales of $700, with the majority coming from food and beverages.

   b. Trends include branching out into different types of merchandise and a debit card system.

2. **Direct retailing** occurs in a home setting. It includes door-to-door sales and party plan selling, and the trend is toward party-plans rather than cold door-to-door canvassing. The sales of direct retailers have suffered as more women have entered the work force, and the direct retailers have had to become more creative in reaching women. Due to declining U.S. sales, many direct retailers are exploring opportunities in other countries.

3. **Direct marketing**, sometimes called **direct-response marketing**, describes a variety of techniques such as telephone selling, direct mail, catalogues, and newspaper, television, or radio ads that invite the shopper to buy from their homes

   a. Direct Mail can be the most or least efficient retailing method, depending on the quality of the mailing list and the effectiveness of the mailing piece. Direct mail can be very precise in targeting customers according to demographics, geographics, and even psychographics.

   b. Catalogues and Mail Order make it possible for consumers to buy just about anything through the mail.

   c. **Telemarketing** is the use of the telephone to sell directly to consumers. It consists of outbound sales calls, usually unsolicited, and inbound calls, that is, taking orders through toll-free 800 numbers or fee-based 900 numbers.

      i. *Outbound* telemarketing is an attractive direct-marketing technique because of rising postage rates and decreasing long-distance phone rates.

      ii. *Inbound* telemarketing programs are mainly used to take orders, generate leads, and provide customer service.

    d. Electronic Retailing

        i. **Shop-At-Home Networks** are a specialized form of direct response marketing. The shop-at-home cable television industry has quickly grown into a billion dollar business with a loyal customer following. Merchandise is displayed and demonstrated on the screen and credit-card orders are taken over toll-free phone lines.

        ii. **On-line retailing or** *e-tailing* is available to users with computers and access to the Internet. On-line retailing has exploded because consumers find it to be convenient and less costly. Retailers are experimenting with ways to make their physical stores, Internet sites, and catalogues work together.

D. Franchising

    1. A *franchise* is a continuing relationship in which a franchiser grants to a franchisee the business rights to operate or to sell a product.

    2. The **franchiser** is the originator of the trade name, product, methods of operation, and so forth that grants operating rights to another party to sell its product.

    3. The **franchisee** is an individual or business that is granted the right to sell another party's product.

    4. Franchising offers many benefits to a person wanting to own and manage a business:

        a. an opportunity to become an independent businessperson with relatively little capital

        b. a product or service that has already been established in the marketplace

        c. technical training and managerial assistance by the franchiser

        d. quality-control standards enforced by the franchiser that will aid in ensuring product uniformity throughout the franchise system

    5. The franchiser obtains benefits also:

        a. company expansion with limited capital investment

        b. motivated store owners

        c. bulk purchasing of inventory

    6. There are two basic forms of franchises: product and trade name franchising, and business format franchising.

3   List the major tasks involved in developing a retail marketing strategy

III. Retail Marketing Strategy

    A. Defining a Target Market

        1. The first task in developing a retail strategy is to define the target market.

        2. This process begins with market segmentation. The markets are often defined by demographics, geographics, and lifestyles or psychographics.

B. Choosing the Retailing Mix

The six Ps of the retailing mix are all variables that can be used in a marketing plan. The six Ps include product, place, promotion, price, personnel, and presentation, and together these items project the store's image.

1. The first element in the retailing mix is the **product offering**, also called the product assortment or merchandise mix, which is the mix of products offered to the consumer by the retailer.

    a. The retailer must determine what to sell, and this is based on research of the target market, past sales, fashion trends, customer requests, and other sources.

    b. The width and depth of the product assortment must be determined. *Width* refers to the assortment of products offered; *depth* refers to the number of different brands offered within each assortment.

    c. Computer technology, through *electronic data interchange* (EDI), is allowing retailers to respond quickly to fashion trends and new merchandise opportunities. EDI aids in producing and buying merchandise. This leads to *efficient consumer response* (ECR) a philosophy of streamlining the way products move to the consumer.

    d. Use of **private brands** that are designed and developed using the retailer's name is an advantage as margins drop and competition intensifies.

2. Retail promotion strategy includes advertising, public relations, publicity, and sales promotion.

    a. The goal of the retailer's promotional strategy is to help position the store in consumers' minds.

    b. Media advertising for retailers is generally concentrated at the local level.

    c. Publicity and public relations are a very important part of the promotional mix.

    d. Many retailers are forgoing media advertising in favour of direct mail or frequent shopper programs

3. The third element in the retail mix is site location. Selecting a proper site is extremely important.

    a. A location is a large and long-term commitment of resources.

    b. Location selection may be based on economic, political, or geographic factors.

    c. Specific site selection is based on neighbourhood socioeconomic characteristics, traffic flows, land costs, zoning regulations, and public transportation.

    d. A decision must be made on whether or not to locate as a freestanding unit or to become a shopping mall tenant.

4. Another important element in the retail mix is price.

    a. Price is also a large part of a retail store's positioning strategy and classification.

    b. A trend has been *everyday low pricing (EDLP),* a move away from sales and discounts.

5. The presentation of a store determines the store's image.

    a. The predominant aspect is the store's **atmosphere**, the store's mood or feeling as established by the physical layout, decor, and surroundings.

    b. The main determinants of a store's atmosphere are:

        i.   *employee type and densi*ty: employee characteristics combined with the number per thousand square feet

        ii. *merchandise type and density*: the typical merchandise carried and how it is displayed add to the atmosphere the retailer is trying to create.

        iii. *fixture type and density*: should be consistent with the general atmosphere the store is trying to create.

        iv. *sound*: can be pleasant or unpleasant to a customer

---

v.   *odours*: smell can either stimulate or distract from sales

vi.   *visual factors*: colours can create a mood or focus attention

6.   Personnel and customer service are a prominent aspect of retailing. Most retail sales involve a customer-salesperson relationship, if only briefly.

   a.   Sales personnel provide their customers with the amount of service prescribed in the retail strategy of the store.
   b.   An important task for retail salespeople is personal selling, persuading shoppers to buy.
   c.   Most salespeople are trained in two common selling techniques: trading-up, which is convincing customers to buy a higher-priced item than they originally intended, and suggestive selling, which seeks to broaden the customer's original purchase with related items.

4   Discuss the challenges of expanding retailing operations into global markets

IV.   Global Retailing

A.   Several events have made expansion across national boundaries more feasible.

1.   Spread of communication networks and mass media has homogenized tastes and product preferences.

2.   The lowering of trade barriers and tariffs, such as with the North American Free Trade Agreement (NAFTA) and the formation of the European Union (EU).

3.   High growth potential in underserved markets.

B.   Prerequisite for going global include:

1.   A secure and profitable position domestically.
2.   A long-term perspective.
3.   A global strategy that meshes with the retailers overall corporate strategy.

5   Describe future trends in retailing

V.   Trends in Retailing

Future trends in retailing include the use of entertainment, a shift toward providing greater convenience and the emergence of customer management programs.

A.   Entertainment

Adding entertainment to the retail environment is one of the most popular strategies in retailing. Entertainment may include anything that enables shoppers to have a good time.

B.   Convenience and Efficiency

Today's consumer is looking for ways to shop quicker and more efficiently. Consumers are visiting stores less often. New technology may offer many innovative solutions for consumers.

C. Customer Management

Through customer management strategies, leading retailers are intensifying their efforts to identify, satisfy, retain, and maximize the value of their best customers. *One-to-one marketing* is the use of database technology to manage customer relationships. More on this topic in Chapter 21.

1. *Customer relationship marketing* (CRM) originated out of the need to more accurately target a fragmented customer base. More on this topic in Chapter 18.

2. Retailers are taking active measures to develop loyalty programs that identify and reward their best customers.

3. *Clienteling* strongly emphasizes personal contact on the part of managers and sales associates with customers.

9   Describe the future trends in wholesaling

IX. Trend in wholesaling

Future trends in wholesaling include: a focus on improving productivity of operations, improving customer service, seizing international opportunities, and integrating forward from wholesale into retail operations.

VOCABULARY PRACTICE

Fill in the blank(s) with the appropriate term or phrase from the alphabetized list of chapter key terms.

agents and brokers	hypermarket
atmosphere	independent retailers
automatic vending	logistics
buyer	mass merchandising
category killers	merchant wholesaler
chain stores	nonstore retailing
convenience store	off-price retailer
department store	on-line retailing
direct marketing (direct response marketing)	private brands
direct retailing	product offering (product assortment)
discount store	retailing
drugstore	retailing mix
factory outlet	scrambled merchandising
franchise	specialty discount store
franchisee	specialty store
franchiser	supercentre
full-line discount store	supermarket
gross margin	telemarketing
	warehouse membership club

1   Discuss the importance of retailing in the Canadian economy

1. All activities directly related to the sale of goods and services to the ultimate consumer for personal, nonbusiness use or consumption can be defined as _____.

2   Describe the nature of retailer operations

2. Retailers can be broadly classified by form of ownership. Retailers than are owned by a single person or partnership are _____. Retailers that are owned and operated as a group by a single firm are _____.

3. One way to classify retailers is according to price. One measure of this is expressed as a percentage of sales less the cost of goods sold. This measure is _____.

4. One method of retail operations carries a wide variety of shopping and specialty goods in several departments under one roof. This defines a(n) _____. The head of each department, or the _____ , selects the merchandise mix and may be responsible for promotion and personnel.

5. As retailers focus more carefully on segmentation and tailor their merchandise to specific target markets, stores may carry a deeper but narrower assortment of merchandise. This type of store would be a(n) _____.

6. A large, departmentalized, self-service retailer that specializes in wide assortments of foodstuffs and limited nonfood items is a(n) _____. Sometimes these retailers offer a wide variety of nontraditional goods and services, which is called _____. A miniature version of this retailer type is a(n) _____ , which carries only a limited line of high-turnover goods. _____ carry a variety of pharmaceutical products—including over-the-counter (OTC) and prescription drugs—and cosmetics, health and beauty care items, and specialty products.

7. A retail chain that competes on the basis of low prices, high turnover, and high volume is a(n) _____. A type of retailer that offers consumers very limited service and carries a much broader assortment of well-known, nationally-branded "hard goods" are known as _____. These retailers use moderate to low prices on large quantities of merchandise, coupled with big promotional budgets, to stimulate high turnover of products, a strategy known as _____.

8. A hybrid form of a full-line discounter combines a supermarket and general merchandise discount store in a large space. This is a _____. Similar to this type is a retailer about half the size, which is a(n) _____.

9. Stores that offer a nearly complete selection of single-line merchandise and heavily dominate their narrow merchandise segment are called _____ or are also known as _____.

10. Limited-service retailers that carry bulk items and sell to members are called _____.

11. If the store sells manufacturers' overruns and irregular merchandise at prices far below that of department stores, the store would be a(n) _____. If the retailer carries one line of discount merchandise, its own, it is called a(n) _____.

12. Shopping without visiting a store is termed _____. A low-profile form of this retailing is _____, which involves consumers making purchases from machines.

13. Another form of retailing involves representatives visiting the customer to sell, which is known as _____. Other techniques used to get consumers to purchase from their home, office, or other nonretail setting. These techniques are known as _____ or _____ and include direct mail, catalogues, and mail order, as well as _____, which involves a systematic use of telephones in the selling process. Today, many consumers use their personal computers to engage in _____.

14. A continuing relation in which a company grants operating rights (trade name, product, operation methods) to another party is a(n) _____. The individual or business granting the business rights is called the _____, and the individual or business granted the right to operate and sell the product or service is called the _____.

3   List the major tasks involved in developing a retail marketing strategy

15. Product, place, promotion, price, personnel, and presentation make up the _____. This first element in this grouping is known as the merchandise mix or _____. Retailers can also choose to sell their own propriety brand name product called _____.

16. The presentation of a retail store to its customers helps determine the store's image. The predominant aspect of a store's presentation is its _____, which refers to how a store's physical layout, decor, and surroundings convey an overall impression.

7   Identify the major types of wholesalers

17. There are two types of wholesalers that help move products from producer to the final customer. The first is _____ who act as salespeople representing producers, retailers, or wholesalers and who do not take title to the goods. The second are _____ who facilitate the movement of product from producers to end user and who take title to the goods. These organizations specialize in warehousing, inventory management and transportation.

Check your answers to these questions before proceeding to the next section.

Mark the statement **T** if it is true and **F** if it is false.

1 Discuss the importance of retailing in the Canadian economy

_____ 1. L.L. Bean sells casual clothing on-line and through catalogues mailed to homes. Because L.L. Bean does not have a store front, it is not considered a retailer.

2 Describe the nature of retail operations

_____ 2. Sales minus the cost of goods sold will give a retailer's gross margin.

_____ 3. Each Aames Store has several departments, including housewares and menswear. Because there are many Aames stores and each store has huge sales volumes, the store would be a mass merchandiser rather than a department store.

_____ 4. The Body Stop is a retail store with a narrow assortment of merchandise (lotions and herbs) and with great depth in its product line. The Body Stop is a specialty store.

_____ 5. Jon Schommer owns a neighbourhood pharmacy. He is considering offering other profitable items that customers sometimes ask for, including snack foods, diapers, cosmetics, greeting cards, and magazines. This would be an example of secular merchandising.

_____ 6. Factory outlets are called "category killers" because they dominate the competition in their narrow merchandise segment.

_____ 7. Cindee sells cosmetics through her Web site and via a 1-800 number. Cindee practices direct-response marketing.

_____ 8. Gloria sells high-end cookware for the Pampered Chef. She throws parties at her friends' houses, where her friends and their friends can buy products. This is known as telemarketing.

_____ 9. The fictitious Burger Queen Corporation sells franchise rights to independent business owners for it hamburger restaurants. Burger Queen itself would be known as the franchiser.

3 List the major tasks involved in developing a retail marketing strategy

_____ 10. The six Ps of retailing are product, price, promotion, place, presentation, and perseverance.

_____ 11. When choosing a retail location, freestanding stores are typically the best for attracting customers.

7 Identify the major types of wholesalers

_____ 12. Merchant wholesalers take title to the goods that they help move through the marketing channel.

Check your answers to these questions before proceeding to the next section.

For the following statements, indicate reasons why you may agree and disagree with the statement.

1. With communication technology, traditional store retailing will yield to nonstore retailing and eventually disappear.

    Reason(s) to agree:

    Reason(s) to disagree:

2. Given the dominance of large retail chains, the small independent store generally has no purpose.

    Reason(s) to agree:

    Reason(s) to disagree:

3. Canadian retailers should always adapt their products to local market when they enter foreign countries.

    Reason(s) to agree:

    Reason(s) to disagree:

Select the response that best answers the question, and write the corresponding letter in the space provided.

1   Discuss the importance of retailing in the Canadian economy

_____   1.   Which of the following statements about retailing is NOT true?
   a.   Retail sales represent about 30 percent of the gross domestic product of Canada.
   b.   Large retail operations represent over 70 percent of all retail sales in the Canada.
   c.   The retailing industry employs about 12 percent of the nation's workers.
   d.   There are over 240,000 Canadian retail establishments.
   e.   The nation's top retailer is Wal-Mart.

2   Describe the nature of retailer operations

_____   2.   A store's gross margin is:
   a.   the final profit after all expenses are subtracted from costs.
   b.   the percentage of sales after cost of goods is subtracted.
   c.   the marketing expenses as a percentage of sales.
   d.   the net sales as a percentage of gross sales.
   e.   the cost of merchandise from suppliers.

_____   3.   Stores that are owned and operated as a group by a single organization are called:
   a.   independent retailers.
   b.   chain stores.
   c.   cooperatives.
   d.   shopping malls.
   e.   franchises.

_____   4.   Stores that are owned and operated by individuals but are licensed by a larger supporting organization are known as:
   a.   independent retailers.
   b.   chain stores.
   c.   cooperatives.
   d.   shopping malls.
   e.   franchises.

_____   5.   Maxies, Metro, IGA, and other supermarkets offer a variety of nontraditional goods and services such as video rental, flower shops, dry cleaning, and banking. This practice is called:
   a.   convenience merchandising
   b.   retail wheeling
   c.   scrambled merchandising
   d.   trade-up positioning
   e.   specialty service

_____   6.   The Muffy Mart utilizes a strategy of setting low prices on large quantities of products and then uses daily television advertisements to stimulate a high turnover of inventory. Muffy Mart also offers a wide variety of product lines. Muffy Mart is a:
   a.   mass merchandiser
   b.   factory outlet
   c.   convenience store
   d.   cash flow retailer
   e.   specialty store

7. Smart-Sam's has opened a new store, even larger than its largest supermarket. This new store is over 200,000 square feet and combines a supermarket and discount department store. The store must generate a volume of over $1,000,000 per week in sales just to break even. This new store is a:
   a. mass merchandiser
   b. warehouse membership club
   c. hypermarket
   d. discount store
   e. factory outlet

8. SoundSensation offers stereo equipment and accessories. It has a deep assortment and low prices. The store is operated on a self-service, no-frills concept. SoundSensation is a:
   a. specialty store
   b. factory outlet
   c. warehouse membership club
   d. discount specialty store
   e. discount store

9. Abby buys many of the office supplies for her income tax preparation business at a retailer that stocks a limited selection of items, which are sold in bulk on a cash-and-carry basis to members only. She browses through a huge store that has a warehouse atmosphere. She buys computer paper, pencils, a small copy machine, and a television for her waiting area. Abby is shopping at a(n):
   a. off-price discount retailer
   b. factory outlet
   c. warehouse membership club
   d. industrial supply warehouse
   e. hypermarket

10. The Waverly Wear clothing company has to find a way to dispose of its overrun and unsold end-of-season clothes. As a marketing consultant, you suggest that they either open a factory outlet or sell the merchandise to a(n):
   a. off-price discount retailer
   b. hypermarket
   c. department store
   d. supermarket
   e. mass merchandiser

11. The Samsonite Company has decided that the most profitable way to dispose of out-of-season and irregular stock would be to open a store and sell its own merchandise in a remote location. This is the retail strategy of:
   a. hypermarkets
   b. mass merchandisers
   c. discount stores
   d. factory outlets
   e. bargain basements

12. Which of the following is NOT an example of nonstore retailing?
   a. An Avon sales person sells cosmetics in an office setting.
   b. L.L. Bean sells clothing through catalogue sales.
   c. A famous chef sells her pasta sauce in her restaurant.
   d. The QVC network sells jewellery through television.
   e. PC Flowers sells flower arrangements on-line.

13. BigFoote sells its hunting and hiking boots through catalogues in the mail. This retailing technique is known as:
   a. on-line retailing
   b. direct marketing
   c. franchising
   d. vending
   e. in-home retailing

14. The Super Shoppe has decided to display products on a cable television channel and encourage shoppers to call a toll-free number to purchase the merchandise with a credit card. This form of retailing is called a(n):
    a. in-store electronic shopping technique
    b. on-line method
    c. electronic point of sale
    d. shop-at-home network
    e. catalogue viewing

15. Brigitte has decided to buy a franchise pet grooming business rather than develop her own independent business. She probably chose the franchise for all of the following reasons EXCEPT:
    a. a management training program
    b. obtaining a well-known product or service name
    c. the individual can try personal, innovative product and service ideas in the business
    d. the established image of the franchise
    e. product uniformity, which is ensured by quality-control standards

3 List the major tasks involved in developing a retail marketing strategy

16. The retailing mix consists of all of the following EXCEPT:
    a. parties
    b. product
    c. presentation
    d. place
    e. price

17. The Greenhouse Exotique has decided that consumers will be drawn to its offering of rare and specialty plants. The store's manager believes that consumers will be willing to drive out of their way to buy these plants. The company needs to keep its overhead costs (such as rent) low and wants to avoid locating near competing nurseries and plant stores. For a location the Greenhouse Exotique will probably choose a:
    a. factory outlet
    b. freestanding store
    c. strip centre
    d. shopping centre
    e. regional mall

18. Alice wants to open a small, specialty toy store and is considering locating it in a regional shopping mall. She should know that:
    a. parking is usually inadequate
    b. the leases required are usually inexpensive
    c. her store could be the mall anchor
    d. the mall atmosphere and other stores will help attract shoppers
    e. there is usually a problem with image because malls have no unified image, as a shopping centre does

19. The Bay and Sears are two anchor stores and therefore:
    a. are most likely large department stores that are located at opposite ends of a mall to create a heavy pedestrian traffic flow
    b. are the stores within the mall that sell services rather than products
    c. probably specialize in high-priced items like furniture
    d. are supermarkets that are located within shopping malls
    e. are retail stores that "drop off" to freestanding locations

20. Beach Bums is a new, trendy store that specializes in swimwear and beach accessories. The store is decorated in neon colours, is full of potted palm trees, has sand on the floor, and plays beach music in the background. These factors are used to create the store's:
   a. cultural impact
   b. merchandise mix
   c. target strategy
   d. atmosphere
   e. promotional strategy

21. When you decide to replace your worn out skis, you go to a local sporting goods store that specializes in winter outdoor activities. Although you only needed skis, you walked out with new boots, a new coat, and some new goggles. The salesperson engaged in effective:
   a. up-selling
   b. cross-selling
   c. persuasion selling
   d. suggestion selling
   e. bundled selling

4 Discuss the challenges of expanding retailing operations into global markets

22. Which of the following statements would least explain why retailing has become global?
   a. Communication technology has accented differences in tastes and preferences throughout the world.
   b. Trade barriers and tariffs have been lowered.
   c. Many markets in the underdeveloped world have little sales potential.
   d. Retailers around the world have been merging and creating global retail chains.
   e. Marketers do not know how to conduct market research in other countries.

23. Sears is interested in global retailing. Sears is most likely to be successful in this endeavour with a:
   a. product and trade name franchise
   b. megamall with multiple department store anchors
   c. mail-order catalogue
   d. specialty store chain
   e. hypermart

5 Describe future trends in retailing

24. When Jamie goes to JosephBeth, a regional independent bookstore, on a Saturday, she takes her preschool-aged children because JoBeth offers puppet shows, storytelling, and story-related crafts. This is example of a trend in retailing called:
   a. advertainment
   b. multiple activity retailing
   c. entertainment retailing
   d. children's retailing
   d. cross-over retailing

7 Identify the major types of wholesalers

25. McKesson Drug purchases large quantities of over-the-counter and prescription pharmaceutical products from manufacturers and sells them to drug stores. McKesson takes title to the products when they are purchased. This company is a(n):
   a. retailer
   b. agent
   c. broker
   d. merchant wholesaler
   e. manufacturer's representative

_____ 26. Murdock and Company represents several health and beauty care products made by small manufacturers that cannot afford their own sales forces. Murdock sells the goods to distributors and retailers and does not carry brands that compete directly with each other. Murdock does not take title to the goods. This company is a(n):
a. retailer
b. distributor
c. merchant wholesaler
d. placement company
e. agent

Check your answers to these questions before proceeding to the next section.

SCENARIO

Read the marketing scenario and answer the questions that follow.

Pottery Barn sells comfortable, casual home furnishings to middle to middle-high income consumers. Consumers can purchase the furnishings one of three ways: by browsing through the many Pottery Barn stores throughout the country, by calling a 1-800 number and ordering furniture found in a company catalogue, and by ordering furniture on-line through the company's Web site. Pottery Barn sells a variety of furnishings, from sofas to dining room tables to wall hangings to decorate the urban dweller's home. Most of the retailer's products are sold under the Pottery Barn name. The stores are set up in an appealing manner to convey comfort, welcoming shoppers as they walk by. It may remind consumers of how their own homes might look with Pottery Barn furniture.

True/False:

_____ 1. Only Pottery Barn stores are considered part of retailing.

_____ 2. Pottery Barn offers a large product width.

_____ 3. Pottery Barn engages in three types of retailing.

Multiple Choice:

_____ 4. Which of the following best describes Pottery Barn's type of retailing?
a. Department store.
b. Warehouse club.
c. Specialty store.
d. Hypermarket.
e. Category killer.

_____ 5. What kind of branding strategy does Pottery Barn use for most of its products?
a. Manufacturer's label.
b. Private label.
c. Control label.
d. Third party label.
e. None of these.

_____ 6. The appealing way in which stores are set up is an example of the store's:
a. atmosphere.
b. target market.
c. personality.
d. product assortment.
e. ambiance.

_____ 7. Pottery Barn can be best described as a(n):
    a.   department store.
    b.   franchise.
    c.   independent retailer.
    d.   chain of stores.
    e.   national niche retailer

<u>Short Answer:</u>

8.   Who are Pottery Barn's competitors in your hometown? How would you categorize these retailers?

ESSAY QUESTIONS

1.   There are several types of retail stores, each offering a different product assortment, service level, and price level, according to the shopping preferences of its customers. Name eight types of retailers. For each type, indicate the level of service, price level, and width of product assortment.

Type of Retailer	Service Level	Assortment	Price Level
1			
2			
3			
4			
5			
6			
7			
8			

2.   Retail strategy involves the six Ps of the retailing mix. Name each of the six Ps, and briefly define elements of each P that are unique to retailing.

3. The Gap stores sell high-end casual clothing for middle class and upper-middle class consumers. Summarize the major strategies used in the Gap's retail mix.

APPLICATION

You are the owner of a new gourmet coffee shop that will compete against large chains such as Starbucks. Name three trends in retailing and describe how you could use each one to compete as a small independent retailer in such a competitive business.

CHAPTER 13: MARKETING COMMUNICATION AND PERSONAL SELLING

LEARNING OBJECTIVES

1   Discuss the role of promotion in the marketing mix

Promotion is communication by marketers that informs, persuades, and reminds potential buyers of a product in order to influence an opinion or elicit a response. Promotional strategy is a plan for the optimal use of the elements of promotion: advertising, personal selling, sales promotion, and public relations. The main function of promotion is to convince target customers that the goods and services offered provide a differential advantage over the competition.

2   Discuss the elements of the promotional mix

The elements of the promotional mix include advertising, public relations, sales promotion, and personal selling. Advertising is a form of impersonal, one-way mass communication paid for by the source. Public relations is the function of promotion concerned with a firm's public image. Firms can't buy good publicity, but they can take steps to create a positive company image. Sales promotion is typically used to back up other components of the promotional mix by stimulating immediate demand. Finally, personal selling typically involves direct communication, in person or by telephone; the seller tries to initiate a purchase by informing and persuading one or more potential buyers.

3   Describe the communication process

The communication process begins when the sender has a thought or idea and wants to share it with one or more receivers. The source then encodes this message and sends it, via a channel, to the receiver(s) for decoding. In turn, the sender receives feedback from the receiver(s) as to whether the message was understood.

4   Explain the goals and tasks of promotion and the AIDA concept

Promotion seeks to modify behaviour and thoughts in some way and to reinforce existing behaviour. There are three tasks for promotion: informing, persuading, and reminding the target market. Informative promotion explains a good's or service's purpose and benefits. Promotions that inform the consumer are typically used to increase demand for a general product category or introduce a new good or service. Persuasive promotion is designed to stimulate a purchase or an action. Promotions that persuade the consumer to buy are essential during the growth stage of the product life cycle, when competition becomes fierce. Reminder promotion is used to keep the product and brand name in the public's mind. Promotions that remind are generally used during the maturity stage of the product life cycle.

The AIDA concept outlines the four basic stages in the purchase decision-making process: attention, interest, desire, and action. These stages are initiated and propelled by promotional activities. The promotional mix needs to recognize and fit the customer's stage in the hierarchy.

5   Describe the factors that affect the promotional mix

Many factors can affect the promotional mix. These factors include the nature of the product, product life cycle stage, target market characteristics, the type of buying decision involved, the availability of funds, and the feasibility of either a push or pull strategy.

6   Discuss the concept of integrated marketing communications

Integrated marketing communications is the method of carefully coordinating all promotional activities - advertising, sales promotion, personal selling, public relations, as well as direct marketing, packaging, and other forms of communication - to produce a consistent, unified, customer-focused message. Marketing managers carefully coordinate all promotional activities to ensure that consumers see and hear one message. Integrated marketing communications has received more attention in recent years due to the proliferation of media choices, the fragmentation of mass markets into more segmented niches, and the decrease in advertising spending in favour of promotional techniques that generate an immediate sales response.

7   Describe personal selling

Personal selling allows salespeople to thoroughly explain and demonstrate a good or service. Salespeople have the flexibility to tailor a sales pitch to the particular needs and preferences of individual customers. Personal selling is more efficient than some other promotion methods because salespeople target qualified prospects and avoid wasting effort on unlikely buyers. Personal selling affords greater managerial control over promotion costs. Finally, personal selling is the most effective method of closing a sale.

8   Discuss the key differences between relationship selling and traditional selling

Relationship selling is the practice of building, maintaining, and enhancing interactions with customers in order to develop long-term satisfaction through mutually beneficial partnerships. Traditional selling, on the other hand, is transaction-focused. That is, the salesperson is most concerned with making one-time sales and moving on to the next prospect. Salespeople practicing relationship selling spend more time understanding a prospect's needs and developing solutions to meet those needs.

9   List the steps in the selling process

The selling process consists of seven basic steps: 1) Generating sales leads; 2) Qualifying sales leads; 3) Making the sales approach; 4) Making the sales presentation; 5) Handling objections; 6) Closing the sale; 7) Following up.

10   Describe the functions of sales management

Sales managers set overall company sales objectives and individual salespeople's quotas. They establish a sales force structure using geographic-, product-, function-, or market-oriented variables. Size of the sales force, compensation plans, recruiting, training, motivation, and evaluation are also functions of the sales manager.

Answer the following questions to see how well you understand the material. Re-take it after you review to check yourself.

1. List and briefly describe four elements of the promotion mix.

2. List and briefly describe the four steps of the communication process.

3. What is AIDA?

4. What is the difference between a push strategy and a pull strategy?

5. What are the advantages of personal selling?

6. List the steps in the sales process.

CHAPTER OUTLINE

1 Discuss the role of promotion in the marketing mix

I. The Role of Promotion in the Marketing Mix

Promotion is communication by marketers that informs, persuades, and reminds potential buyers of a product in order to influence an opinion or elicit a response.

A. **Promotional strategy** is a coordinated plan for the optimal use of the elements of promotion: advertising, personal selling, sales promotion, and public relations.

B. The main function of promotion is to convince target customers that the goods and services offered provide a differential advantage over the competition.

C. A **differential advantage** is a set of unique features of a company and its products that are perceived by the target market as significant and superior to the competition.

---

2 Discuss the elements of the promotional mix

II. The Promotional Mix

A combination of the various promotional tools is called the **promotional mix**. It includes advertising, personal selling, sales promotion, and public relations.

A. Advertising

Advertising is any form of paid communication in which the sponsor or company is identified. It is an impersonal and one-way mass communication vehicle. It may be transmitted via many different media and does not provide direct feedback.

1. Cost per contact is very low because advertising can reach such a large number of people.
2. The total cost to advertise, however, is typically very high

B. Public Relations

Public relations is the marketing function that evaluates public attitudes, identifies areas within the organization that the public may be interested in, and executes a program of action to earn public understanding and acceptance.

1. A good public relations program can generate favourable publicity.

2. **Publicity** is public information about a company, good, or service appearing in the mass media as a news item. Although publicity does not require paid media space or time, costs are generated by public relations employees who organize and distribute news.

C. Sales Promotion

Sales promotion consists of all marketing activities—other than personal selling, advertising, and public relations—that stimulate consumer purchasing and dealer effectiveness.

1. Promotion is used to improve the effectiveness of other ingredients in the promotional mix.
2. Sales promotion can be aimed at the end consumers, trade customers, or a company's employees. Examples include free samples, contests, bonuses, trade shows, and coupons.

D. Personal Selling

Personal selling is a situation in which two people communicate in an attempt to influence each other in a purchase situation.

1. Traditional methods of personal selling include a planned, face-to-face presentation to one or more prospective buyers for the purpose of making a sale.
2. More current notions on the subject of personal selling emphasize the relationship that develops between a salesperson and a buyer.

3 Describe the communication process

III.   Marketing Communication

Communication is the process by which we exchange or share meanings through a common set of symbols.

A.   Categories of Communication

1.   **Interpersonal communication** is direct, face-to-face communication between two or more people.
2.   **Mass communication** refers to communicating to large audiences, usually through a mass medium such as television or newspaper.
3.   For effective communication between two communicators (sender and receiver), common understanding or overlapping frames of reference are required.

B.   The Communication Process

The communication process involves both a sender and a receiver, and begins when the sender has a thought or idea and wants to share it with one or more receivers.

1.   The **sender** is the originator, or source, of the message in the communication process.

   Encoding is the conversion of the sender's ideas and thoughts into a message, usually in the form of words or signs.

2.   Transmission of a message requires a **channel**, such as a voice, gesture, newspaper, or other communication medium.

   Although transmitted, the message may not be received by the desired target audience. **Noise** is anything that interferes with, distorts, or slows the transmission of information.

3.   The **receiver** is the person who decodes the message.

   a.   **Decoding** is the interpretation of the language and symbols sent by the source through a channel.
   b.   Even though the message is received, it may not be properly understood and decoded.

4.   In interpersonal communication, the receiver's response to a message is direct **feedback** to the source.

   Mass communicators are cut off from direct feedback and must rely on market research or sales trends for indirect feedback.

C.   The Communication Process and the Promotional Mix

The four elements in the promotional mix differ in their ability to affect the target audience. The elements also differ in how they interact with the communication process.

---

4   Explain the goals and tasks of promotion and the AIDA concept

IV.   The Goals and Tasks of Promotion

Promotion seeks to modify behaviour and thoughts in some way and to reinforce existing behaviour. Thus, the goal of promotion is to *inform*, *persuade*, and *remind*.

A.   Informative promotion is generally more prevalent during the early stages of the product life cycle, when it can increase demand for a product category.

1.   Informative promotion explains the purpose and benefits of a good or service.

2.   More complex products often require informative promotion that explains technical benefits.

B.   Persuasion, the second promotional task, is simply attempting to motivate a consumer to purchase or use more of a product.

1.   Persuasion normally becomes the primary promotion goal when the product enters the growth stage of the product life cycle.

2.   The aim of persuasion is to convince the customer to buy the company's brand rather than the competitor's.

C.   Reminder promotion is used to keep the product and brand name in the public's min d.

1.   This type of advertising is common during the maturity stage of the product life cycle.

2.   The purpose of these ads is to trigger memory.

IV.   Promotional Goals and the AIDA Concept

A.   A classic model for reaching promotional goals is called the **AIDA concept**, standing for Attention-Interest-Desire-Action. It outlines the stages of consumer involvement with a promotional message.

B.   The AIDA concept assumes that promotion propels consumers along four steps in the purchase-decision process.

1.   The advertiser must first attract the *attention* of the target market to the product.

2.   The next step is to create an *interest* in the product.

3.   The *desire* to purchase the product is the third step in the process.

4.   *Action* is the final step in the purchase decision process.

The promoter's task is to determine where on the purchase ladder most of the target consumers are located and design a promotion plan to meet their needs.

C.   AIDA and the Promotional Mix

Each promotional tool is more effective at certain stages of the hierarchy of effects model.

1.   Advertising is most effective in creating awareness.

---

2. Public relations has the greatest effect in building awareness about the company, good, or service.

3. Sales promotion is most effective in creating strong desire and purchase intent.

4. Personal selling is most effective at creating customer interest for a product and for creating desire.

5   Describe the factors that affect the promotional mix

V. Factors Affecting the Promotional Mix

    A.   Nature of the Product

        1.   The characteristics of the product influence the promotional mix.

            a.   Industrial or business products are often expensive, complex, and customized, requiring personal selling.
            b.   Consumer products are promoted mainly through advertising to create brand familiarity.

        2.   As the costs and risks of the product increase, so does the need for personal selling. Risks can be financial or social.

    B.   Stage in the Product Life Cycle

        The product's stage in its life cycle can also affect the promotional mix.

        1.   During the *introduction* stage in the product life cycle, both advertising and publicity are very important in informing the target audience that the product is available.

        2.   During the *growth stage* of the product life cycle, the promotional strategy is designed to build and maintain brand loyalty. Advertising and public relations continue to be major elements, but sales promotion can be reduced.

        3.   As a product reaches the *maturity stage* of its life cycle, increased competition mandates the emphasis of persuasive and reminder advertising and the increased focus on sales promotion.

        4.   During the *decline stage*, personal selling and sales promotion may be maintained but other forms of promotion, especially advertising, are reduced.

    C.   Target Market Characteristics

        The characteristics of the target market influence the blend of promotion tools.

        Widely scattered markets, highly informed buyers, and brand-loyal repeat purchasers generally respond to a blend of advertising and sales promotion with less personal selling.

    D.   Type of Buying Decision

        The type of buying decision—whether routine or complex—also affects the promotional mix.

        1.   Advertising and sales promotion are most effective for routine decisions.

2. For decisions, which are neither routine nor complex, advertising and public relations help establish awareness.

3. Personal selling is used in complex buying situations.

E. Available Funds

1. Available (or unavailable) funds may be the most important factor in determining the promotional mix.

2. A lack of money may force a firm to rely on publicity or commission-only manufacturers' sales ag ents.

3. When funds are available a firm will generally try to optimize its return on promotion dollars while minimizing the *cost per contact*, the cost of reaching one member of the target market.

F. Push and Pull Strategies

1. Some manufacturers employ a **push strategy**, which uses aggressive personal selling and trade advertising to convince wholesalers and retailers to carry and sell the merchandise.

2. At the other extreme, a **pull strategy** stimulates consumer demand with consumer advertising and special promotions and thus obtains product distribution.

6 Discuss the concept of integrated marketing communications

VI. Integrated Marketing Communications

A. Integrated Marketing Communications

1. Companies are adopting the concept of **integrated marketing communications (IMC)**.

2. IMC is the method of carefully coordinating all the promotional activities to product a consistent, unified message that is customer-focused.

3. Marketing managers work out the roles of the various promotional elements in the marketing mix and monitor results.

B. A disjointed approach to promotion has propelled many marketers toward the idea of **integrated marketing communications**, or the careful coordination of all promotional messages for a product or service.

1. Advantage of IMC are consistency

2. The more integrated the campaign, the more successful it usually is.

3. Movies generally are good examples of IMC (text sites Lord of the Rings, Spiderman, and others)

C.   IIMC is growing in popularity because:

      1.   There is a proliferation of media choices available to the marketer.

      2.   The market is increasingly fragmented.

      3.   Marketers have reduced advertising spending in favour of promotional tools that yield faster results.

7   Describe personal selling

VII.   Personal Selling

A.   **Personal selling** is direct communication between a sales representative and one or more prospective purchasers, for the purpose of making a sale. This can be accomplished through a face-to-face, personal sales call or over the telephone, called telemarketing

B.   Advantages to personal selling include:
      1.   Personal selling can be used to provide a detailed explanation or demonstration of the product.

      2.   The message can be varied by the salesperson to fit the motivations and interests of each prospective customer.

      3.   Personal selling can be directed to specific qualified prospects.

      4.   Personal selling costs can be controlled by adjusting the size of the sales force.

      5.   Personal selling is most effective in obtaining a sale and gaining a satisfied customer.

C.   Certain customer and product characteristics indicate that personal selling might work better than other forms of promotion. In general, personal selling is more important if the product has a high value, the product is custom-made, the product is technically complex, there are few customers, and customers are concentrated.

8   Discuss the key differences between relationship selling and traditional selling

VIII.   Relationship Selling

A.   Traditional selling is transaction-focused. That is, the salesperson is most concerned with making one-time sales and moving on to the next prospect.

B.   **Relationship selling**, or **consultative selling** is a multi-stage process that emphasizes personalization and empathy as key ingredients in identifying prospects and developing them as long-term, satisfied customers.

Salespeople practicing relationship selling spend more time understanding a prospect's needs and developing solutions to meet those needs.

9   List the steps in the selling process

I .   Steps in the Selling Process

The **sales process** or **sales cycle** is the set of steps a salesperson goes through to sell a particular product or service.

The steps of selling follow the AIDA concept

Traditional selling and relationship selling follow the same basic steps. The difference is the relative importance placed on key steps.

A. Generating Leads

    1. **Lead generation**, or **prospecting**, is the identification of those firms and people most likely to buy the seller's o fferings.

    2. Sales leads come from advertising and other media, favourable publicity, direct mail and telemarketing, cold calling, Internet Web sites, client referrals, salesperson networking, trade shows and conventions, and internal company records.

        a. A **referral** is a recommendation from a customer or business associate.
        b. **Networking** is finding out about potential clients from friends, business contacts, coworkers, acquaintances, and fellow members in professional and civic organizations.
        c. **Cold calling** occurs when the salesperson approaches potential buyers without any prior knowledge of the prospects' nee ds or financial status.

B. Qualifying Leads

The next step is **lead qualification**, which determines the prospects that have:

    1. A recognized need

    2. Buying power (ability and authority to purchase)

    3. Receptivity and accessibility

Often the task of lead qualification is handled by a telemarketing group or a sales support person who *prequalifies* the lead for the salesperson.

With more and more companies setting up web sites on the Internet, qualifying online leads has also received some attention.

C. Approaching the Customer and Probing Needs

    1. Prior to approaching the customer, the salesperson should learn as much as possible about the prospects' organization and its buyers. This process is called the **preapproach**.

    2. During the approach, the salesperson's ultimate goal is to conduct a **needs assessment** in which he or she finds out as much as possible about the prospects' situation .

        a. The consultative salesperson must be an expert on his or her product or service.
        b. The salesperson should know more about the customer than they know themselves.
        c. The salesperson must know as much about the competitor's company and products as he or she knows about their own. *Competitive intelligence* includes identifying the competitors, their products and services, advantages and disadvantages, strengths and weaknesses.
        d. The salesperson should be involved in active research concerning the industry.

3.   Creating a *customer profile* during the approach helps salespeople optimize their time and resources.

D.   Developing and Proposing Solutions

A **sales proposal** is a written document or professional presentation that outlines how the company's prod uct or service will meet or exceed the client's needs. The **sales presen tation** is the face-to-face explanation of a product's benefits to a prospective buyer; it is the heart of the selling process

1.   The quality of both the sales proposal and presentation can make or break the sale.

2.   The selling presentation can be enhanced by allowing customers to touch or hold the product, using visual aids, and emphasizing important selling points of the product.

3.   Technology has become an important part to presenting solutions.

E.   Handling Objections

Objections should be viewed positively as a request or need for more information.
Anticipating objections is the best way to prepare for them.

F.   Closing the Sale

1.   At the end of the presentation, the salesperson attempts to close the sale. This requires skill and courage on the part of the salesperson.

2.   **Negotiation** often plays a key role in the closing of the sale. The salesperson offers special concessions at the end of the selling process and uses it in closing the sale. Examples include price cuts, free installation, free service, or trials.

3.   Accepted closing techniques may differ greatly from country to country.

4.   Rarely is a sale closed on the first call.

G.   Following Up
Most businesses rely on repeat sales, and repeat sales depend on thorough **follow-up**. Salespeople must ensure that:

1.   Delivery schedules are met.

2.   Goods or services perform as promised.

3.   The buyer's empl oyees are properly trained to use the products.

10 Describe the functions of sales management

Sales Management

Sales management is one of marketing's most critical areas. It has several important functions.

A.   Defining Sales Objectives and the Sales Process

1.   Overall sales force objectives are usually stated in terms of desired dollar sales volume, market share, or profit level.

2. Individual salespeople are also assigned objectives in terms of quotas. A **quota** is simply a statement of sales objectives, usually based on sales volume but sometimes including key accounts, new accounts, and specific products.

A sales manager needs to formally define the specific procedures salespeople go through to do their jobs, examine the sales process in their business.

B. Determining the Sales Force Structure

1. Sales departments are most commonly organized by geographic regions, by product lines, by marketing function performed, by market or industry, or by individual client or account.

2. Market or industry based structure and key account structures are gaining in popularity with today's emphasis on relationship selling.

C. Compensating and Motivating the Sales Force

Compensation planning is one of the sales manager's toughest jobs.

a. The **straight commission** system provides salespeople with a specified percentage of their sales revenue as income. No compensation is received until a sale is made. This system encourages salespeople to spend as much time as possible selling and may make them reluctant to perform nonselling activities.

b. The **straight salary** system compensates salespeople with a stated salary regardless of sales productivity. It may provide little incentive to produce but is useful in sales situations that require spending a great deal of time on prospecting, doing paperwork, training customers, and performing other nonselling tasks.

c. *Combination systems* offer a base salary plus an incentive, usually a bonus based on sales. This system provides selling incentives while allowing managers to control the activities of their sales forces.

d. Sales incentives: recognition at ceremonies, premiums, awards, merchandise, vacations, and cash bonuses are often used to motivate salespersons.

e. An effective sales manager inspires his or her salespeople to achieve their goals through clear and enthusiastic communications.

D. Evaluating the sales force requires regular feedback. Typical performance measures include sales volume, contribution to profit, calls per order, sales or profits per call or percentage of calls achieving specific goals.

Fill in the blank(s) with the appropriate term or phrase from the alphabetized list of chapter key terms.

advertising	preapproach
AIDA concept	promotion
channel	promotional mix
cold calling	promotional strategy
communication	publicity
decoding	public relations
differential advantage	pull strategy
encoding	push strategy
feedback	quota
follow-up	receiver
integrated marketing communication (IMC)	referral
interpersonal communication	relationship selling
mass communication	sales presentation
lead generation	sales process (sales cycle)
lead qualification	sales proposal
needs assessment	straight commission
negotiation	straight salary
networking	sales promotion
noise	sender
personal selling	

1   Discuss the role of promotion in the marketing mix

1. Communication by marketers that informs, persuades, and reminds potential buyers of a product is _____. A plan for the optimal use of advertising, public relations, sales promotion, and personal selling is the _____. This vital part of the marketing mix helps communicate a set of unique features of a company and its products that are superior to the competition; this is the company's _____.

2   Discuss the elements of the promotional mix

2. A combination of promotional tools makes up the _____, which refers to the amount of funds allocated to each promotional tool and to the managerial emphasis placed on each technique. There are four major tools that make up this combination. The first is a form of impersonal, one-way mass communication paid for by the sponsor and transmitted by many different media; this tool is _____. The second promotional tool performs functions such as evaluating public attitudes and executing programs that earn public understanding and acceptance; this tool is known as _____, and a solid program utilizing this tool can generate favourable _____, which is public information appearing in the mass media as a news item. A third promotional tool includes marketing activities that stimulate consumer purchasing and dealer effectiveness; this tool is called _____ and may include such activities as coupons, contests, bonuses, and samples. The fourth promotional tool involves a planned face-to-face presentation to one or more prospective purchasers for the purpose of making a sale; this tool is _____.

3   Describe the communication process

3. The process by which individuals exchange or share meanings through a common set of symbols is called _____. This can be divided into two major categories. The direct, face-to-face category is called _____, while the category directed to large audiences is called _____.

4. The communication process begins with an originator, or source of a thought or idea, which is called the _____. When these ideas and thoughts are converted into a message, usually in the form of words or signs, _____ has taken place. Then the message is transmitted through a(n) _____, such as a voice on a radio ad or a printed coupon. The message is communicated to a(n) _____ who will interpret the language and symbols of the message. This process is known as _____. When a receiver responds to a message, this gives direct _____ to the source. Anything that interferes with, distorts, or slows this communication process is called _____.

4   Explain the AIDA concept

5. One model for reaching promotional objectives is called the _____, which is an acronym for a sequential process.

5   Describe the factors that affect the promotional mix

6. Manufacturers may use aggressive personal selling and trade advertising to convince a wholesaler or retailer to carry and sell their merchandise; this approach is known as a(n) _____. Alternatively, the manufacturer may wish to promote heavily to the end consumer to stimulate demand; this approach is the _____.

6   Discuss the concept of integrated marketing communications

7. The method of carefully coordinating all promotional activities to produce a consistent, unified message that is customer focused is _____, and is the result of increased fragmentation of mass markets and proliferation of media alternatives.

8   Discuss the key differences between relationship selling and traditional selling

8. The practice of building, maintaining, and enhancing interactions with customers in order to develop long-term satisfaction through mutually beneficial partnerships is called _____.

9   List the steps in the selling process

9. The set of steps a salesperson goes through to sell a product or service is called the _____.

10. The first step in the selling process is the identification of those firms and people most likely to buy the seller's offerings; this is called _____ and can be achieved with several different methods. With one method, the salesperson approaches potential buyers without any knowledge of the prospects' needs or financial status. This unsolicited sales method is _____. A salesperson can also use a recommendation, or _____, from a customer or business associate. The method of using friends, business contacts, co-workers, and acquaintances as a means of meeting new people who could become potential clients is called _____.

11. The second step in the selling process is _____, which determines the prospects who have the authority to buy and can afford to pay for the product or service.

12. During the _____, the salesperson learns as much as possible about the prospect's organization and its buyers. When determining the customer's specific needs and wants and the range of options a customer has for satisfying them, the salesperson in performing a(n) _____.

13. Once the salesperson has identified customer needs, he/she will put together a written document that outlines how the companies product or service will meet the customer's needs, otherwise known as a(n) _____. Once this has been completed, the salesperson will make the _____, which is the formal meeting with the client.

14. At the end of the sales presentation, the salesperson can close the sale if the prospect's objections have been handled properly. Sometimes a salesperson will withhold a special concession until the end of the selling process and use it in closing the sale; this strategy is called _____.

15. One of the most important aspects of the selling process is the last step: the _____. This activity can help repeat sales.

10 ■ Describe the functions of sales management

16. The first task in sales force management is to set sales objectives. Individual salespeople may be assigned objectives in the form of a statement of sales volume, financial achievements, or account goals. This type of stated objective is a(n) _____.

17. There are three basic compensation methods for salespeople. The first method provides salespeople with a specified percentage of their sales revenue, but no compensation is received until after the sale is made; this is a(n) _____ system. The second method compensates people with a stated dollar figure regardless of sales productivity; this is the _____ system. Finally, to achieve the advantages of both of the first two systems, a combination system can be used.

Check your answers to these questions before proceeding to the next section.

Mark the statement **T** if it is true and **F** if it is false.

1 Discuss the role of promotion in the marketing mix

_____ 1. Communication by marketers with the intent of informing, persuading, and reminding potential buyers of a product is known as promotion.

_____ 2. Promotional strategy involves developing an integrated plan to utilize advertising, public relations, personal selling and sales promotion.

_____ 3. The set of unique features of a company and its products as perceived by its target audience is the firm's differential advantage.

2 Discuss the elements of the promotional mix

_____ 4. Advertising evaluates public attitudes, identifies areas within the organization that the public is interested in, and executes a program of action to earn public understanding and acceptance.

_____ 5. Sales promotions are designed to stimulate consumer purchasing and dealer effectiveness.

3 Describe the communication process

_____ 6. The Addle Ad Agency conducted research on a popular television ad and found that people were so caught up in the flashy pictures and catchy music that the message in the ad was not noticed. This is an example of noise in the communications process.

_____ 7. Once an advertisement is seen by a member of the target market, the message is understood as intended.

_____ 8. Encoding is the conversion of a sender's ideas into a software program designed to develop efficient communication plans.

_____ 9. Voice, radio, newspapers are all examples of channels of communication.

_____ 10. Noise is anything that disrupts the concentration of marketers as they develop their marketing communications.

_____ 11. Most elements of the promotional mix are indirect and impersonal when used to communicate with a target audience.

4 Explain the goals and tasks of promotion and the AIDA concept

_____ 12 Promotion can have the basic tasks to inform, persuade, or remind the consumer about a product, even though different types of promotion may be used (personal selling, advertising, sales promotion, or public relations).

_____ 13. Persuasive promotional messages are designed to convert existing needs into wants or to stimulate interest in a new product.

_____ 14. AIDA stands for Action-Investment-Differential advantage-Attention.

_____ 15. Of the four types of promotion, sales promotion is the most effective at getting potential customers to purchase the product (the "action" of AIDA).

5   **Describe the factors that affect the promotional mix**

_____   16.   Tia is trying to develop a promotional mix for her firm's new product, a high-technology solar heating/cooling system. Because her product is complex and carries high economic risk, she should concentrate on personal selling.

_____   17.   Totter Toys uses personal selling and sales promotions to encourage intermediaries to carry and sell its toy products. Totter Toys is using a pull strategy.

6   **Discuss the concept of integrated marketing communications**

_____   18.   Before approving a change in the company's advertising slogan, Rick considers the various media and audiences that will see and hear the new message. This is an example of the importance of integrated marketing communications.

7   **Describe personal selling**

_____   19.   One of the advantages of personal selling is that it can be used to reach many consumers quickly.

_____   20.   Personal selling allows much more message variation than advertising.

_____   21.   Personal selling is more important for low-value, mass-produced products.

8   **Discuss the key differences between relationship selling and traditional selling**

_____   22.   The difference between relationship selling and traditional selling is how well you know the customer when you approach them.

_____   23.   Relationship selling involves a longer follow-up process than traditional selling.

9   **List the steps in the selling process**

_____   24.   The first step in the selling process is qualifying leads.

_____   25.   During the "approach" stage of the selling process, the goal of sales reps is to conduct a needs assessment.

_____   26.   When a sales representative closes the sale, his or her job is done.

10   **Describe the functions of sales management**

_____   27.   Edward earns a 20 percent commission on every sale he makes to supplement his base income of $20,000. This is an example of a straight commission system.

Check your answers to these questions before proceeding to the next section.

For the following statements, indicate reasons why you may agree and disagree with the statement.

1. Advertising is the most important element of the promotional mix.

    Reason(s) to agree:

    Reason(s) to disagree:

2. Advertising alone cannot make customers complete the AIDA process.

    Reason(s) to agree:

    Reason(s) to disagree:

3. Personal selling is the opposite of true marketing.

    Reason(s) to agree:

    Reason(s) to disagree:

4. The selling process as described in the textbook cannot be applied to all products and selling situations.

    Reason(s) to agree:

    Reason(s) to disagree:

MULTIPLE CHOICE QUESTIONS

Select the response that best answers the question, and write the corresponding letter in the space provided.

1   Discuss the role of promotion in the marketing mix

_____ 1. The Rebecca's Popcorn Company manufactures popcorn that is clearly superior to the competition in terms of freshness, variety, and use of organic corn. Rebecca's promotion emphasizes this:
   a. unique selling proposition
   b. comparative advantage
   c. special benefit
   d. differential advantage
   e. promotional theme

2   Discuss the elements of the promotional mix

_____ 2. A local exterminator uses its own fleet of trucks to communicate its service. The trucks are painted yellow and are made to resemble a mouse. This is a form of:
   a. personal selling
   b. advertising
   c. sales promotion
   d. public relations
   e. publicity

_____ 3. Sunee, a native of Thailand, started her own Thai restaurant, which received rave reviews from the food critic of the local newspaper. Sunee's restaurant received:
   a. public relations
   b. personal selling
   c. sales promotion
   d. advertising
   e. publicity

_____ 4. Sally's Security Service has sent a representative to most of the large local corporations to introduce the firm and its services and to explain the rates for corporate customers for after-hours security. This is a form of:
   a. mass communication
   b. implicit communication
   c. public relations
   d. personal selling
   e. telemarketing

_____ 5. Most large warehouse membership clubs give away samples of the packaged foods sold in their stores. This is a form of:
   a. public relations
   b. personal selling
   c. sales promotion
   d. advertising
   e. publicity

_____ 6. Mammoth Oil Company uses radio, television, magazine, and newspaper advertising for its promotion. This form of communication is known as:
   a. reference
   b. factual
   c. mass
   d. interpersonal
   e. public

3 Describe the communication process

_____ 7. All of the following are noise in the communication process EXCEPT:
   a. three competing ads on the same page of a magazine
   b. music, flashing lights, and hot temperatures in the store dressing room
   c. important news stories in the newspaper with bold headlines
   d. two people with a shared frame of reference
   e. a crying child and ringing telephone while you are watching television

_____ 8. PiperCo places its messages on local radio stations and in the yellow pages of the phone book. These communications are directed at the _____, the person who will decode the message.
   a. sender
   b. communicator
   c. encoder
   d. channeler
   e. receiver

_____ 9. Which of the following CANNOT be a channel of communication?
   a. radio
   b. TV
   c. email
   d. noise
   e. voice

_____ 10. The logical order of the marketing communication process is:
   a. encoding, channelling, sending, decoding, receiving
   b. sender, encoding, channelling, decoding, receiving
   c. sender, noise, decoding, receiving, channelling
   d. receiver, decoding, channelling, encoding, sending
   e. channelling, sending, encoding, decoding, receiving

_____ 11. Which of the following is an example of feedback in the marketing communication process?
   a. "I agree."
   b. Nodding
   c. Smiling
   d. Frowning
   e. All of these are types of feedback

_____ 12. _____provides the marketer with the most control over the communication situation.
   a. advertising
   b. public relations
   c. sales promotion
   d. personal selling
   e. infomercials

13. _____ provides the least control over message content.
    a. advertising
    b. public relations
    c. sales promotion
    d. personal selling
    e. infomercials

4   Explain the goals and tasks of promotion and the AIDA concept

14. The Micro-Blaze is a surgeon's tool for microscopic eye surgery and has been on the market for eight years. The advertising agency is writing the ad copy for the Micro-Blaze and has decided on a(n) _____ format because the product is technical.
    a. informative
    b. persuasive
    c. reminder
    d. talkative
    e. influencer

15. Quinn's Quiches has started a new ad campaign aimed at changing negative perceptions of cholesterol-laden eggs (a primary ingredient in quiche). The ads state that eggs are a good source of protein and that Quinn's Quiches are preferred by famous athletes. The message ends by asking viewers to buy Quinn's Quiches for their next special dinner. This promotion has the task of:
    a. informing
    b. persuading
    c. reminding
    d. suppressing
    e. rewarding

16. Coca Cola should use _____ promotion to keep the brand name in the public's mind.
    a. influence
    b. reminder
    c. informative
    d. persuasive
    e. humorous

17. Icellee's Ice Cream is in the maturity stage of the product life cycle. Icellee should probably use _____ promotion.
    a. reminder
    b. amusement
    c. informative
    d. persuasive
    e. influence

18. AIDA stands for:
    a. attention, interest, desire, action
    b. attention, intention, desire, action
    c. awareness, interest, desire, action
    d. awareness, interest, demand, attention
    e. awareness, intention, desire, attention

19. You are the public relations manager for an environmentally friendly paint. You know that public relations will have its greatest impact in the _____ stage of the AIDA model.
    a. awareness
    b. attention
    c. desire
    d. demand
    e. action

20. Displays in grocery stores, coupons, premiums, and trial-size packages are most useful at the _____ stage the AIDA model.
    a. awareness
    b. attention
    c. desire
    d. demand
    e. action

5   Describe the factors that affect the promotional mix

_____ 21. As Freddie's Flour plans its promotion for its new oat-blend flours, all of the following factors can be expected to affect the promotional mix EXCEPT that it is:
    a. just being introduced
    b. targeted at restaurants that will use the flour for their baking
    c. a healthy product
    d. sold by a small company
    e. targeted at home users

6   Discuss the concept of integrated marketing communications

_____ 22. Integrated marketing communications refers to:
    a. efforts to increase diversity in marketing images
    b. careful coordination of all promotional activities
    c. globalization resulting in expanded cultural diversity
    d. efforts to communicate marketing messages through alternative public relations methods
    e. all of the above

_____ 23. Which of the following is NOT a reason for the rising importance of integrated marketing communications?
    a. proliferation of media choices
    b. fragmentation of mass markets into more segmented niche markets
    c. decreased advertising spending
    d. increased use of promotional techniques that generate immediate sales response
    e. Federal requirements for added diversity in marketing communications.

7   Describe personal selling

_____ 24. All the following circumstances describe when personal selling is more important than other forms of promotion EXCEPT:
    a. customers are geographically dispersed
    b. the product has a high value
    c. the product is technically complex
    d. it is a custom-made product
    e. there are few customers

_____ 25. Brown's sells customized oil field drilling equipment in Texas and Oklahoma. You would expect Brown's to rely on _____ to promote their products.
    a. publicity
    b. advertising
    c. personal selling
    d. sales promotion
    e. word-of-mouth

_____ 26. Lucille offers high-priced, customized clothing for women over eighty years of age. Lucille will probably use considerable:
    a. publicity
    b. advertising
    c. personal selling
    d. sales promotion
    e. word-of-mouth

8   Discuss the key differences between relationship selling and traditional selling

_____ 27. Closing sales, limited sales planning and follow-up are all characteristic of:
    a. Traditional relationship selling
    b. Relationship selling
    c. Traditional personal selling
    d. Sales management training
    e. Sales by objectives

_____ 28. Team approach, advice, and assistance are all part of:
    a. relationship selling
    b. traditional personal selling
    c. non-personal advertising sales management
    d. selling communication
    e. all of these choices use team approach, advice, and assistance

9   List the steps in the selling process

_____ 29. The Chem-Gro Company has developed a new type of liquid chemical fertilizer for large lawn areas. The company has purchased mailing lists of landscape contractors, corporate lawn care services, and turf companies to send out brochures with a detachable card that can be sent in for more information. Chem-Gro is involved in:
    a. qualification
    b. the sales approach
    c. a sales presentation
    d. the contact procedure
    e. lead generation

_____ 30. When Sammy began selling Singer sewing machines, he called friends, relatives, former business acquaintances, and members of his neighbourhood club. He asked them if they knew anyone who was looking for a deal on a new sewing machine. This technique is known as:
    a. networking
    b. cold calling
    c. quota driving
    d. qualifying
    e. following up

_____ 31. The SnoGo snowblower salesperson is demonstrating how the snowblower works, letting the potential customer try it personally. This is the _____ stage of the sale.
    a. leading
    b. follow-up
    c. sales presentation
    d. sales approach
    e. closing

32. As Sherri is trying to conclude the sale of the aluminium house siding system to the Renaud family, she finally offers them free gutter cleaning services and six pairs of window shutters for half-price. This is a closing technique called:
   a. summative
   b. assumptive
   c. follow-up
   d. adaptive
   e. negotiation

10 Describe the functions of sales management

33. At the Elica Electronics Store, all salespeople are paid a percentage of their individual sales, and there is no guaranteed minimum pay. This is a(n):
   a. straight commission plan
   b. salary
   c. hourly wage
   d. combination pay plan
   e. bonus plan

Check your answers to these questions before proceeding to the next section.

SCENARIO

Read the following marketing scenario and answer the questions that follow.

Juan has just started his own national monthly magazine targeting Asian men. The magazine features interesting articles about music, men's fashion, lifestyle, and women. Though Juan sells the magazine as a subscription, the lion's share of his revenue comes from advertising. For his first issue, he successfully sold out all his advertising space to toiletries companies, designer fashion brands, TV networks' and movie studios. Juan ran his own ads on the Internet, on late night TV, and in local newspapers.

As an introductory incentive, Juan offered readers a two-month free subscription with a money-back guarantee if readers were not satisfied. He communicated this incentive in his advertisements. He hired a sales agency to get distribution of his magazines at major supermarkets, drugstores, mass merchandisers, and convenience stores.

True/False:

1. Juan is not using any type of sales promotion.

2. Juan's use of a sales agency is an example of a pull strategy.

3. Juan is following the appropriate promotional strategies given the stage of the magazine's life cycle.

Multiple Choice:

4. Which of the following elements of the promotional mix has Juan NOT used so far?

   a. Advertising.
   b. Public relations.
   c. Sales promotion.
   d. Personal selling.
   e. Mass communication

5. Given the introductory nature of Juan's magazine, which goals of promotion is the magazine most likely trying to achieve?

    a. Maintaining consumer awareness.
    b. Encouraging brand switching.
    c. Reminding consumers to buy the product.
    d. Informing consumers of a new product.
    e. Persuading consumers of the magazine's value

6. Which of the following is NOT an example of how Juan is using a pull strategy?

    a. Using a sales agency.
    b. Running ads on network TV.
    c. Running ads on late night TV.
    d. Offering the two-month free subscription.
    e. Offering incentives to newsstands to carry the magazine.

7. If Juan wanted to use integrated marketing communications (IMC) in his promotional efforts, he should:

    a. use all the elements of the promotional mix.
    b. make sure that the message communicated in all his promotions is consistent.
    c. target at least two diverse market segments.
    d. maintain a high level of sales promotion throughout the magazine's introduction.
    e. integrate a loyalty marketing program into his promotional mix.

Short Answer:

8. Is Juan missing anything from his promotional mix? What else would you do if you were Juan?

ESSAY QUESTIONS

1. The promotional mix is made up of a blend of four promotional tools. Name and describe each of these four tools and give specific examples of each tool.

2.   Draw a diagram that illustrates the communication process. Then briefly describe each of the steps in the communication process.

3.   The ultimate objective of any promotion is a purchase or some other activity. One model for reaching promotional objectives is called the AIDA concept. Using the stages of the AIDA model, describe the activities of a salesperson selling an executive cellular telephone.

4.   The nature of the promotional mix depends upon several types of factors. Name five of these factors, and describe how changes in those factors affect the mix of promotional elements.

5.   You are the sales representative for a large computer company that sells to business firms. Name the seven steps of the selling process and describe each step as it relates to selling computers.

6.   You are the new sales manager for the computer company in the last question.
     What type of salary/commission structure would you recommend? Why?

APPLICATION

Select your favourite recent TV commercial that you remember well. Use the AIDA concept to illustrate how the commercial involved you as a consumer.

CHAPTER 14: ADVERTISING, SALES PROMOTION, AND PUBLIC RELATIONS

LEARNING OBJECTIVES

1 Discuss the effect advertising has on market share and consumers

Advertising can help increase or maintain brand awareness and, subsequently, market share. Typically more is spent to advertise new brands with a small market share than to advertise older brands. Advertising affects consumers' daily lives as well as their purchases. Advertising can seldom change strongly held consumer values, but it may transform a negative attitude toward a product into a more positive one. Additionally, when consumers are highly brand loyal, they may buy more of that brand when advertising is increased. Advertising can also change the importance of a brand's attributes to consumers. By emphasizing different brand attributes, advertisers can customize their appeal to respond to changing consumer needs or try to achieve an advantage over competing brands.

2 Identify the major types of advertising

The major types of advertising are institutional advertising and product advertising. Institutional advertising is not product-oriented; rather its purpose is to foster a positive company image among the general public, investment community, customers, and employees. Product advertising is designed primarily to promote goods or services and is classified into three categories: pioneering, competitive, and comparative.

3 Discuss the creative decisions in developing an advertising campaign

Before any creative work can begin on an advertising campaign, it is important to determine what goals or objectives the advertising should achieve. The objectives of a specific advertising campaign often depend on the overall corporate objectives and the product being advertised. Once objectives are defined, creative work can begin on the advertising campaign. Creative decisions include identifying the product's benefits, developing possible advertising appeals, evaluating and selecting the advertising appeals, executing the advertising message, and evaluating the effectiveness of the campaign.

4 Describe media evaluation and selection techniques

Media evaluation and selection make up a crucial step in the advertising campaign process. Major types of advertising media include newspapers, magazines, radio, television, outdoor advertising such as billboards and bus panels, and the Internet. Recent trends in advertising media include fax, video shopping carts, computer screen savers, and cinema and video advertising. Promotion managers choose the advertising campaign's media mix on the basis of the following variables: cost per contact, reach, frequency, characteristics of the larger audience, flexibility of the medium, noise level, and the life span of the medium. After choosing the media mix, a media schedule designates when the advertisement will appear and the specific vehicles it will appear in.

5 Define and state the objectives of sales promotion

The primary objectives of sales promotion are to increase trial purchasing of products, consumer inventories, and repurchasing. Promotion is also designed to support advertising activities.

6 Discuss the most common forms of consumer sales promotion

Consumer sales promotion includes coupons, premiums, contests and sweepstakes, sampling, and point-of-purchase displays.

7 List the most common forms of trade sales promotion

Trade sales promotion includes: some consumer sales promotions, plus trade allowances, push money, training programs, free merchandise, store demonstrations, and meetings, conventions, and trade shows.

---

8   Discuss the role of public relations in the promotional mix

Public relations is a component of the promotional mix. A company fosters good publicity to enhance its image and promote its products. An equally important aspect of public relations is crisis management, or managing bad publicity in a way that is least detrimental to a firm's image.

PRE-TEST

Answer the following questions to see how well you understand the material. Re-take it after you review to check yourself.

1.   Name and briefly describe three types of product advertising.

2.   List the four steps in creating an advertising campaign.

3.   List at least seven different types of media.

4. List six types of consumer sales promotion tools and six types of trade sales promotion tools.

5. List six public relations tools.

CHAPTER OUTLINE

1   Discuss the effect advertising has on market share and consumers

I. Effects of Advertising

Advertising is any form of impersonal, paid communication in which the sponsor or company is identified. The amount of advertising spending in Canada increases annually, with estimated expenditures now at about $10 billion per year.

    A. Advertising and Market Share

        1. New brands with a small market share tend to spend proportionately more for advertising and sales promotion than those with a large market share.

        2. After a certain level of advertising is reached, diminishing returns set in. This phenomenon, known as the **advertising response function**, explains why well-known brands can spend proportionately less on advertising than new brands can.

        3. Advertising requires a certain minimum level of exposure to measurably affect purchase habits.

    B. The Effects of Advertising on Consumers

        1. According to estimates, Canadians are exposed to hundreds of advertisements a day from the various types of advertising media.

---

2. Attitudes and values are deeply rooted within an individual's psychological makeup. Advertising seldom succeeds in changing an attitude that stems from a person's moral code or culture. But advertising does attempt to change attitudes toward brands and to create an attitude toward the advertisement itself.

3. Advertising can affect the way consumers rank a brand's attributes such as colour, taste, smell, and texture.

2 Identify the major types of advertising

II. Major Types of Advertising

The two major types of advertising are institutional advertising and product advertising. **Product advertising** touts the benefits of a specific good or service. **Institutional advertising** is used if the goal of the campaign is to build the image of the company rather than promote a particular product.

A. Institutional Advertising

1. Institutional advertising has four important audiences: the public, the investment community, customers, and employees.

2. A unique form of institutional advertising called **advocacy advertising** is a way for corporations to express their views on controversial issues.

3. Many advocacy campaigns react to criticism or blame, media attacks, or impending legislation.

B. Product Advertising

1. **Pioneering advertising** is intended to stimulate primary demand for a new product or product category.

2. The goal of **competitive advertising** is to influence demand for a specific brand; it is often used when a product enters the growth phase of the product life cycle.

3. **Comparative advertising** compares two or more specifically named or shown competing brands on one or more specific product attributes.

a. Advertisers often make taste, price, and preference claims in reference to the competition.

b. The federal Competition Act prohibits advertisers from falsely describing competitors' products and allows competition to sue if advertised products are presented in an incorrect or false manner.

3 Discuss the creative decisions in developing an advertising campaign

III. Creative Decisions in Advertising

A. The **advertising campaign** is a series of related advertisements focusing on a common theme, slogan, and set of advertising appeals that extends for a defined time period.

1. Before any creative work can begin on an advertising campaign, it is important to determine the **advertising objective**, the specific communication task a campaign should accomplish for a specified target audience during a specified period of time.

2. The DAGMAR approach (Defining Advertising Goals for Measured Advertising Results) is one method that stresses defining the objective as a percent of change.

3. Once objectives are defined, work can begin on the advertising campaign

B. Identifying Product Benefits

1. Marketers strive to identify product benefits – not product attributes – which will be the message to the consumers.

2. Marketing research and creative intuition are usually used to list the perceived benefits of a product and to rank these benefits.

C. Developing and Evaluating Advertising Appeals

1. After identifying product benefits, possible advertising appeals are developed. An **advertising appeal** identifies a reason a person should purchase a product.

   a. Advertising campaigns can focus on one or more appeals, which are developed by the creative people in the advertising agency.
   b. Typical appeals are profit, health, love, fear, convenience, and fun.

2. The next step is to evaluate the proposed appeals. An appeal needs to be desirable, exclusive, and believable.

3. The dominant appeal for the campaign will be the **unique selling proposition**, and it usually becomes the campaign slogan.

D. Executing the Message

1. Message execution is the way the advertisement will be portrayed. Examples of message execution style include fantasy, humour, demonstration, and slice of life.

2. Executional styles for foreign advertising are often quite different from those we are accustomed to in Canada.

3. Global advertising managers are increasingly concerned with the issue of standardization vs. customization.

4 Describe media evaluation and selection techniques

IV. Media Decisions in Advertising

A medium is the channel used to convey a message to the target market. Media planning is the series of decisions advertisers make regarding the selection and use of media to communicate the advertising message to the target audience

A. Media Types

Six major types of advertising media are available: newspapers, magazines, radio, television, outdoor advertising, and the Internet. Marketers can also use alternative media to reach their target market.

1. *Newspaper advertising* has the advantage of geographic flexibility and timeliness. Newspapers reach a very broad mass market.

Cooperative advertising is an arrangement in which the manufacturer and retailer split the costs of advertising the manufacturer's brand.

2. *Magazines* are often targeted to a very narrow market. Although they may offer a very high cost per contact, the cost per potential customer may be much lower.

3. *Radio* can be directed to very specific audiences, has a large out-of-home audience, has low unit and production costs, is timely, and can have geographic flexibility.

4. *Television* can be divided into networks (CBC, and CTV), independent stations, cable television, and direct broadcast satellite television.

   a. In Canada, subscription television services (cable TV systems and satellite TV systems) are among the most highly developed in the world. Subscription TV is often characterized as "narrowcasting" by media buyers because of its targeted channels.
   b. Television reaches a huge market, but both the advertising time and production costs are very expensive.
   c. The **infomercial** is a 30-minute or longer advertisement, popular because of its cheap airtime and relatively small production costs.

5. *Outdoor, or out-of-home*, advertising is a flexible, low-cost medium that may take a variety of forms, such as billboards, skywriting, ads in and on modes of transportation. It reaches a broad and diverse market.

6. The *Internet* has established itself as a solid advertising medium. By 2005, Internet advertising is expected to increase and represent close to 10 percent of total media spending.

   a. Since consumers are more Web savvy, banner ads that have the brand awareness potential have had low-click through rates. Web advertisers are now focusing on new banner formats; the *skyscraper* and *rectangle*, both formats offering more space to include the entire message and thus avoiding the need to click to another site.

   b. Web advertisers are also becoming more targeted with their approach to advertising by studying clickstream data.

7. Alternative media include facsimile (fax) machines, video shopping carts, electronic "place-based" media, interactive computer advertising, and cinema and video advertising.

B. Media Selection Considerations

1. The **media mix** is the combination of media to be used for a promotional campaign. Media decisions are typically based on cost per thousand, reach, and frequency.

   a. **Cost per contact** is the cost of reaching one member of the target market.
   b. **Reach** refers to the number of target consumers exposed to a commercial at least once over a period of time, such as four weeks.
   c. **Frequency** measures the intensity of coverage in a specific medium. Frequency is the number of times an individual is exposed to a brand message during a specific time period.
   d. Another consideration is **audience selectivity**, the medium's ability to reach a precisely defined market.
   e. The *flexibility* of a medium can be extremely important to an advertiser.
   f. *Noise level* is the level of distraction to the target audience in a medium.
   g. *Life span* means that messages can either quickly fade or persist as tangible copy to be carefully studied.

C.   Media Scheduling

After selecting the media, a **media schedule** - which designates the vehicles, the specific publications or programs, and the dates and times - must be set. There are three basic types of media schedules:

1.   With a **continuous media schedule**, advertising runs steadily throughout the advertising period.

2.   With a **flighted media schedule**, the advertiser schedules ads heavily every other time period (such as every other month or every two weeks).

3.   A **pulsing media schedule** combines continuous scheduling with flighting, resulting in a base advertising level with heavier periods of advertising.

4.   A **seasonal media schedule** is used for products that are sold more during certain times of the year.

5   Define and state the objectives of sales promotion

V.   Sales Promotion

Sales promotion is an activity in which a short-term incentive is offered to consumers or channel members to induce the purchase of a particular good or service.

Consumer sales promotion is aimed at the ultimate consumer of a good. **Trade sales promotion** is directed to members of the marketing channel, such as wholesalers and retailers.

A.   Sales promotion objectives centre on immediate purchase. Specific objectives may be to:
1.   Increase trial
2.   Boost consumer inventory
3.   Encourage repurchase
4.   Support and increase the effectiveness of advertising

B.   Sales promotion may also encourage brand switching in some instances (coupons) and brand loyalty in others (*frequent-buyer clubs*).

6   Discuss the most common forms of consumer sales promotion

VI.   Tools for Consumer Sales Promotion

Consumer sales promotion tools are used to create new users of the product, as well as to entice current customers to buy more.

A.   A **coupon** is a certificate that entitles consumers to an immediate price reduction when they purchase the item.

1.   Coupons are effective for product trial and repeat purchase. They are also useful for increasing the amount of product a customer will buy.
2.   Approximately 268 billion coupons are distributed through freestanding newspaper inserts annually, but only about 2 percent are used.
3.   In-store couponing is most likely to affect customer-buying decisions.
4.   **Rebates** offer the purchaser a price reduction but the reward is not as immediate, as the rebate form and proof-of-purchase must be mailed in.

B.   A **premium** is an extra item offered, usually with proof of purchase, to the consumer. Sometimes it may be a small item, such as a T-shirt or coffee mug, or it may be free air travel or hotel stays. Frequent-buyer clubs and programs offer premiums.

C.   **Loyalty marketing programs** or **frequent-buyer programs**, reward loyal consumers for making multiple purchases.

D.   **Contests and sweepstakes** are promotions that give away prizes and awards. A *contest* is based on some skill or ability, but *sweepstakes* rely on chance and luck.

E.   **Sampling** is a way to reduce the amount of risk a consumer perceives in trying a new product. For sampling to be beneficial, the new product must have benefits that are clearly superior to existing products and must have a unique new attribute that the consumer must experience to believe in.

        Distributing samples to specific location types where consumers regularly meet for a common objective or interest is one of the most cost-efficient methods of sampling.

F.   A **point-of-purchase display** is a promotional display set up at the retailer's location to build traffic, advertise the product, or induce impulse buying.

        Point-of-purchase displays include shelf talkers, shelf extenders, ads on grocery carts and bags, end-aisle and floor-stand displays, in-store audio messages, and audiovisual displays.

G.   **On-line sales promotion** has been increasing due to the popularity of the Internet and has proved to be effective and cost-efficient, generating response rates that are three to five times higher than their off-line counterparts.

7   List the most common forms of trade sales promotion

VII.   Tools for Trade Sales Promotion

Trade promotions push a product through the distribution channel. When selling to members of the distribution channel, manufacturers use many of the same sales promotion tools used in consumer promotions. Several tools, however, are unique to intermediaries.

A.   A **trade allowance** is a price reduction offered by manufacturers to intermediaries, such as wholesalers or retailers, in exchange for the performance of specified promotion activities.

B.   Intermediaries receive **push money** as a bonus for pushing the manufacturer's brand. Often the push money is directed at the retailer's salespeo ple.

C.   Sometimes a manufacturer will provide free **training** for the personnel of an intermediary if the product is complex.

D.   Another trade promotion is **free merchandise** offered in lieu of quantity discounts.

E.   **In-store demonstrations** are sometimes provided by manufacturers as a sales promotion for retailers.

F.   **Trade association meetings, conferences, and conventions** are an important aspect of trade promotion and an opportunity to meet and interact with current and potential customers.

8   Discuss the role of public relations in the promotional mix

VIII.   Public Relations

Public relations evaluates public attitudes, identifies issues that may elicit public concern, and executes programs to gain public understanding and acceptance.

Publicity is the effort to capture media attention.

A.   Public relations campaigns strive to achieve and maintain a corporation's positive image in the eyes of the public.

     1.   The first task of public relations management is to set objectives that fit with the corporation's overall marketing program.

     2.   Public relations tools include press relations, product publicity, corporate communication (internal and external), public affairs, lobbying, employee and investor relations, and crisis management.

9   Describe the major public relations activities

IX.   Public Relation Activities

A.   Major Public Relations Tools

     1.   New Product Publicity

     Public relations can help differentiate new products by creating free news stories about the product and its uses, garnering valuable exposure.

     2.   Product Placement

     Marketers can garner publicity by making sure their products appear at special events or in movies and on television shows.

     3.   Consumer Education

     Free seminars and demonstrations help develop more knowledgeable and loyal consumers.

     4.   Event Sponsorship

     Sponsoring events and charities is a popular method of getting positive exposure for the company or a product.

     5.   Issue Sponsorship

     Companies also build awareness and loyalty by supporting their customers' favourite issues such as ecology (green marketing).

     6.   Internet Web Sites

     These sites are an excellent vehicle to post news releases on products, product enhancements, strategic relationships, and financial earnings. It can also be site for feedback and a self-help desk.

B.   Managing Unfavourable Publicity

    1.   **Crisis management** is used by public relations managers to handle the effects of bad publicity.

    2.   It is imperative that firms have plans for fast and accurate communication in times of emergency.

VOCABULARY PRACTICE

Fill in the blank(s) with the appropriate term or phrase from the alphabetized list of chapter key terms.

advertising appeal	loyalty marketing program
advertising campaign	media mix
advertising objective	media planning
advertising response function	media schedule
advocacy advertising	medium
audience selectivity	pioneering advertising
comparative advertising	point-of-purchase display
competitive advertising	premium
continuous media schedule	product advertising
consumer sales promotion	pulsing media schedule
cooperative advertising	push money
cost per contact	reach
coupon	rebate
crisis management	sampling
flighted media schedule	seasonal media schedule
frequency	trade allowance
frequent buyer program	trade sales promotion
infomercial	unique selling proposition
institutional advertising	

1   Discuss the effect advertising has on market share and consumers

1.   After a certain level of advertising is reached, diminishing returns set in. This is known as the

    _____.

2   Identify the major types of advertising

2.   If the goal of an advertising campaign is to build the image of the company or the industry, the advertiser will

use _____. A unique form of this advertising is a means for corporations to

express their viewpoints on various controversial issues; this is _____. In

contrast, if the advertiser wishes to enhance the sales of a specific product, brand, or service,

_____ is used, which can be implemented in one of three forms. Advertising

intended to stimulate primary demand for a new product or product category is

_____. Advertising used to influence demand for a specific brand of a good or

service is _____. Finally, if the advertising compares two or more specifically

named or shown competing brands on one or more specific product attributes,

_____ is being used.

3   Discuss the creative decisions in developing an advertising campaign

3. A series of related advertisements focusing on a common theme, slogan, and a set of advertising appeals is the _____. The first step in developing this series is to set goals for specific communications tasks that should be accomplished for a specified target audience during a specified period of time. These goals are _____.

4. To make creative decisions, the marketer must know which message channel, or _____, will be used. The series of decisions marketers make regarding media selection and use is called _____.

5. Part of making creative decisions involves identifying a reason a person should purchase a product or service; this is the _____ and could take the form of a profit motive, fear, convenience, or concern for health. The dominant form chosen becomes the _____, which then becomes the campaign slogan.

4   Describe media evaluation and selection techniques

6. An arrangement under which the manufacturer and the retailer split the cost of advertising the manufacturer's brand is called _____.

7. A relatively new version of direct-response advertising is in the form of a thirty-minute extended television promotion that resembles a talk show. This is a(n) _____.

8. The cost of reaching one member of a market with advertising is called _____. Another factor that marketing managers evaluate is the volume of advertising that will be conducted with various media, or the _____. The degree of coverage of a total audience through a particular medium is _____, or the number of different target consumers exposed to a commercial at least once during a specific period. The intensity of a specific medium coverage is measured by _____; this is the number of times an individual is exposed to a given message during a specific time period. The ability of a medium to reach a precisely defined market is _____.

9. The designation of vehicles, specific publications or programs, and the insertion dates of the advertising is the _____, which has several basic types. Products that are advertised on a reminder basis use a(n) _____, which allows the advertising to run steadily throughout the advertising period. If the advertiser schedules ads heavily every other month to achieve a certain impact with increased frequency and reach, a(n) _____ has been used. A variation of this is _____, which combines continuous scheduling with flighting. Finally, certain times of the year, such as holidays, the flu season, or summertime call for a(n) _____.

---

10. The series of decisions advertisers make regarding the selection and use of media to communicate the advertising message to the target audience is called _____ .

5   Define and state the objectives of sales promotion

11. A promotional activity in which a short-term incentive is offered to a consumer to induce the purchase of a particular product or service is _____ . If this is targeted at intermediaries or channel members, it is known as _____ .

6   Discuss the most common forms of consumer sales promotion

12. There are many forms of sales promotion. A certificate given to consumers entitling them to an immediate price reduction when they purchase the item is a(n) _____ . A cash refund is called a _____ . A gift item offered, usually with a proof-of-purchase, to the consumer is a(n) _____ . If consumers are rewarded for brand loyalty, a _____ is being used. One of the fastest forms of this type of sales promotion is when consumers are rewarded for making multiple purchases, also known as a(n) _____ . When a consumer can try a product for free, _____ is being used. Finally, a promotional display set up at the retailer's location to build traffic, advertise the product, or induce impulse buying is a(n) _____ .

7   List the most common forms of trade sales promotion

13. A price reduction offered by manufacturers to intermediaries is a(n) _____ . If intermediaries receive a bonus for moving the product through the distribution channel, the intermediary is receiving _____ .

8   Discuss the role of public relations in the promotional mix

14. When a company receives bad publicity, public relations executives handle the effects of the bad publicity with _____ .

Check your answers to these questions before proceeding to the next section.

Mark the statement **T** if it is true and **F** if it is false.

1 Discuss the effect advertising has on market share and consumers

_____ 1. New brands tend to require higher advertising expenditures.

2 Identify the major types of advertising

_____ 2. A small high-tech company has just launched a new writing pen that has a memory, much like a small computer. The advertising campaign focuses on the innovativeness of the new product. This is an example of pioneering advertising.

_____ 3. The advertisements for Dippy Chips include the names of the major competitors in the potato chip market. The ads depict kids evaluating the crunchiness of three competing potato chips. This is an example of competitive advertising.

_____ 4. In the past, Toxic Waste, Inc. was blamed for dumping potentially dangerous chemicals into the local river. The company cleaned up its act and started to advertise the social responsibility demonstrated by its employees. This is an example of advocacy advertising.

_____ 5. "Gentler on your stomach, and stronger than our competitor's pain reliever" is an example of institutional advertising.

3 Discuss the creative decisions in developing an advertising campaign

_____ 6. A print ad depicts a picture of a frozen dessert accompanied by information about the dessert: "two servings, only 300 calories per serving, no cholesterol, and 100 percent of the Canadian RDA of vitamins and minerals." This is an example of an advertisement selling the product's benefits.

_____ 7. An advertisement for an energy-efficient light bulb tells viewers that they will save $10 per month on their utility bills. This is an example of a profit motive appeal.

_____ 8. An advertising campaign is the same as a TV commercial.

_____ 9. Roger recognizes the major way to differentiate his homes from competitors' houses is his emphasis on energy efficiency. This is his unique selling proposition.

4 Describe media evaluation and selection techniques

_____ 10. The Internet represents the largest share of advertising expenditures.

_____ 11. Magazines are very effective at targeting a specific demographic market.

_____ 12. Banner ads are a characteristic of Internet advertising.

_____ 13. A local greeting card store only runs newspaper advertisements the week before major card-sending holidays, such as Valentine's Day, Mother's Day, Halloween, and New Year's. This is an example of a pulsing schedule.

5 Define and state the objectives of sales promotion

_____ 14. The goal of sales promotion is generally long term.

_____ 15. Coupons, rebates, and point-of-purchase displays are examples of consumer sales promotion.

_____ 16. Trade sales promotion has become less important over the past decade.

7   Discuss the most common forms of consumer sales promotion

_____ 17. Crunchy-Worms cereal includes a free worm toy inside every box. Consumers can order the rest of the worm family by mailing the proofs-of-purchase from five boxes of cereal to the manufacturer for each additional worm. This is an example of a premium.

_____ 18. Fred has arranged a deal with local grocery stores to allow him to put up a display of his organic fruits at the end of the isles. Fred is using point-of-purchase displays to stimulate impulse buying.

8   List the most common forms of trade sales promotion

_____ 19. At the annual HAI event, helicopter manufacturers and vendors of helicopter-related products gather together in a convention centre and display their products in booths to customers and potential customers. This is an example of a trade show.

_____ 20. For its new product launch, a manufacturer offers a special introductory price to retailers and wholesalers who stock the product. This is an example of push money.

9   Discuss the role of public relations in the promotional mix

_____ 21. Publicity can help gain exposure for and position new products.

_____ 22. Companies receiving publicity cannot control the publicity at all.

Check your answers to these questions before proceeding to the next section.

AGREE/DISAGREE QUESTIONS

For the following statements, indicate reasons why you may agree and disagree with the statement.

1. It is difficult to prove whether or not advertising has an impact on sales.

   Reason(s) to agree:

   Reason(s) to disagree:

2. There is never truth in advertising; it is inherently biased.

   Reason(s) to agree:

   Reason(s) to disagree:

3. Sales promotion should be used only conjunction with advertising.

   Reason(s) to agree:

   Reason(s) to disagree:

4. Public relations is the least important of all the elements of the promotion mix.

   Reason(s) to agree:

   Reason(s) to disagree:

MULTIPLE CHOICE QUESTIONS

Select the response that best answers the question, and write the corresponding letter in the space provided.

1   Discuss the effect advertising has on market share and consumers

_____ 1. Peg used to work at a carpet store but now works at the Victory Toys Store. Peg is surprised at the high advertising-to-sales ratio at the store; advertising dollars are 11 percent of sales. This ratio is high because:
   a. certain industries traditionally spend a large amount of sales dollars on advertising, usually because of product-related factors
   b. Victory is outspending the rest of the industry in order to catch up in market share
   c. Victory is an inefficient advertiser
   d. all advertising work is done by agencies rather than by Victory
   e. Victory is the industry leader and has to stay ahead of other toy stores

2. The Mathis brand of televisions has a significant market share but spends proportionally less on advertising than competing brands. This is the case because:
   a. certain industries have a practice of spending a small amount of dollars, relative to sales, on advertising
   b. beyond a certain volume of promotion, diminishing returns set in
   c. there is no minimum level of exposure for advertising to have an effect on sales
   d. advertising will not stimulate economic growth for the industry
   e. the firms with large market share do not understand the advertising-to-sales relationship

3. The new advertisements for a beer marketer focus on humorous situations. This advertising is designed to influence:
   a. attitudes when consumers already have a positive image
   b. brand adversity
   c. perceptions of product attributes
   d. benefits
   e. needs of the target markets relative to the creative design of the campaign

2 Identify the major types of advertising

4. A large paper company runs advertisements that show how its employees are involved in the community. This is an example of _____ advertising.
   a. pioneering
   b. institutional
   c. comparative
   d. competitive
   e. product

5. Future Power, Inc. has begun an advertising campaign to manufacturers. The campaign promotes the advantages of using alternative battery technologies (such as the new GaAs battery) for toys, computers, and electric cars. This is _____ advertising.
   a. comparative
   b. innovative
   c. institutional
   d. competitive
   e. pioneering

6. A rental car company with the second largest market share runs advertisements showing how its customer service is superior to that of the largest competitor. This is an example of _____ advertising.
   a. comparative
   b. combat
   c. competitive
   d. institutional
   e. pioneering

3 Discuss the creative decisions in developing an advertising campaign

7. The first step in the advertising campaign decision process is to:
   a. make media decisions
   b. evaluate the campaign
   c. determine campaign objectives
   d. develop advertising copy
   e. make creative decisions

8. A financial services advertisement targets busy professional parents by showing them in a variety of situations during a typical frantic day. This is an example of a _____ execution.
   a. spokesperson
   b. demonstration
   c. fantasy
   d. lifestyle
   e. product symbol

9. In the advertisement for a bathroom cleaner, animated, talkative scrubbing bubbles are used to show how hard the bubbles work to clean. The lively scrubbing bubbles appear in all advertisements for this product and are depicted on the packaging. This is an example of a _____ executional style.
   a. fantasy
   b. lifestyle
   c. spokesperson
   d. product symbol
   e. scientific evidence

4 Describe media evaluation and selection techniques

10. A lawn and garden store has an arrangement with a lawn mower manufacturer that 50 percent of the cost of all radio and newspaper advertisements placed by the store will be paid for by the manufacturer. This is _____ advertising.
    a. comparative
    b. cooperative
    c. institutional
    d. corporate
    e. competitive

11. The Flow-Bee hair cutting vacuum cleaner attachment is shown during a half-hour television spot. The product is demonstrated on volunteer studio audience members, testimonials are given by Flow-Bee owners, and viewers are encouraged to order the product through an 800 telephone number. Flow-Bee is using the _____ form of direct-response advertising.
    a. megamercial
    b. ad expander
    c. extended sales pitch
    d. prolonged ad
    e. infomercial

12. Claire's Confections is currently deciding how much space or time will be placed in each medium that the company has selected. Claire's Confections is determining its:
    a. marketing mix
    b. promotional plan
    c. media mix
    d. advertising campaign
    e. reach objectives

13. The manufacturer of Furry's Ferret Food estimates that the product's new advertising campaign will reach 500,000 people and will cost $750,000 if the company uses newspaper ads and $1 million if it uses television. The company's decision seems to rest on:
    a. cost per contact
    b. flexibility
    c. noise level
    d. life span
    e. geographic selectivity

14. Because Calvin's Crystals wants to spend its promotional budget on advertisements that will have a long life span, it should use _____ advertising.
    a. magazine
    b. radio
    c. television
    d. newspaper
    e. outdoor

15. Kay's Catering has set up a seasonal plan for advertising, with dates selected in January, September, and December on three local radio stations, the city newspaper, and bus transit signs. This is a:
    a. message execution plan
    b. media profile
    c. media schedule
    d. reach program
    e. frequency timetable

16. Ricky's Rib Restaurant runs ads for one week, every other month, in the entertainment section of the newspaper. No other forms of advertising are used. This is a _____ scheduling plan.
    a. continuous
    b. flighted
    c. pulsing
    d. seasonal
    e. duplication

17. Craig is deciding which media to use. He knows there will be a need to make last minute changes to the advertising message, and adjustments once the campaign has started. Craig is concerned with medium:
    a flexibility
    b noise level
    c. life span
    d. fragmentation
    e. augmentation

5   Define and state the objectives of sales promotion

18. Sales promotion:
    a. inspires long-term brand loyalty
    b. is only directed to the ultimate consumer market
    c. is more difficult to measure than advertising
    d. is a smaller percentage of the promotion budget than advertising
    e. offers a short-term incentive to buy

19. The objectives of sales promotion include all of the following EXCEPT:
    a. support and increase the effectiveness of advertising
    b. boost consumer inventory
    c. increase trial
    d. reduce couponing
    e. encourage repurchase

6 Discuss the most common forms of consumer sales promotion

_____ 20. Campbell's Soup is offering a wooden recipe box with soup recipes to consumers who send in five proofs-of-purchase. This is an example of a:
  a. prize
  b. coupon
  c. premium
  d. contest
  e. free merchandise sample

_____ 21. The Dashing Dish Soap firm has decided to use free samples as a promotion technique because:
  a. its dish soap is similar to other dish soaps
  b. it is an inexpensive promotional tool
  c. this is an increasingly popular technique with manufacturers
  d. this allows the consumer to try the product risk-free
  e. trial-size containers are a form of advertising

_____ 22. One of the problems with coupons is:
  a. consumers do not trust them
  b. permanent decrease in price
  c. perception that they are too valuable
  d. only about two percent are redeemed
  e. all of these are problems with coupons

_____ 23. Manufacturers prefer rebates because of all the following EXCEPT:
  a. they allow manufacturers to offer price cuts directly to the consumer rather than through the retailer
  b. they reward frequent buyers
  c. they help manufacturers build customer databases
  d. many consumer forget or don't bother to redeem them
  e. manufacturers have more control over them versus other forms of promotion

7 List the most common forms of trade sales promotion

_____ 24. The Marble Manufacturing firm has offered a price reduction to the Fun-n-Games chain of toy stores as long as the stores take responsibility for sorting and bagging marbles by colour and size and for setting up special marble displays. The price reduction is also a:
  a. premium
  b. point-of-purchase discount
  c. merchandise guideline
  d. trade allowance
  e. form of push money

_____ 25. Free training programs allow manufacturers to:
  a. explain complex products to retailers
  b. build relationships with sales personnel
  c. entertain distribution channel members
  d. gain feedback regarding customer concerns and questions
  e. do all of these

_____ 26. Capital Finance has mailed its stockholders a brochure that included data from the firm on new customer services, management changes, and the firm's financial situation. This is an example of:
   a. lobbying
   b. corporate selling
   c. a sales promotion
   d. public relations
   e. stockholder marketing

_____ 27. The Clearly Can Corporation sponsored a citywide litter pickup contest and sent all the proceeds from recycling the collected cans to a local charity. The event was so popular that the local newspaper took pictures for the front page, and every local news station carried a story about Clearly Can's community activities. The newspaper pictures and the news stories exemplify:
   a. lobbying
   b. a sales promotion
   c. an attempt to build advertising credibility
   d. public relations aimed at the community at large
   e. publicity

_____ 28. Which of the following is NOT a major public relations tool?
   a. Issue sponsorship
   b. Event sponsorship
   c. Internet web sites
   d. Infomercials
   e. New product publicity

_____ 29. Plans to address snowstorms, product defects, rumours, and other emergencies are all part of:
   a. credit response teams
   b. consumer information services
   c. crisis management
   d. developmental deliberations
   e. emergency action plans

Check your answers to these questions before proceeding to the next section.

SCENARIO #1

Read the marketing scenario and answer the questions that follow.

Georgia is an assistant account executive at a large North York Street ad agency in Toronto. Her largest client is a beverage manufacturer that markets a well-known, old soft drink called "Pop Sizzle." Her ad agency has done the advertising for Pop Sizzle for many years. Most of the past advertising involved pitting Pop Sizzle against its largest competitor to communicate to consumers that most people prefer the taste of Pop Sizzle. Recently, however, the company has decided to change the brand's communication to be more image-based rather than product-based.

Georgia is meeting with her client tomorrow to determine the exact objective of the new advertising. She has worked all morning with the creative department to identify the product's benefit. So far, the best benefit statement is "Drink Pop Sizzle and be part of the cool crowd." The creative department envisions a TV commercial showing members of Generation Y having fun at a rock concert and drinking Pop Sizzle.

True/False:

_____ 1. Pop Sizzle should use pioneering advertising for its new positioning.

_____ 2. The ad agency has already come up with a slogan.

_____ 3. Pop Sizzle's new benefit statement is consistent with an image-driven campaign.

Multiple Choice:

_____ 4. Pop Sizzle's old advertising campaign is best described as:
   a. comparative advertising.
   b. competitive advertising.
   c. institutional advertising.
   d. pioneering advertising.
   e. advocacy advertising.

_____ 5. If the agency were to create a series of TV commercials and print ads that communicate the new positioning, it would be creating a(n):
   a. unique selling proposition.
   b. advertising campaign.
   c. media mix.
   d. series of slogans.
   e. infomercial

_____ 6. Which of the following executional styles best describes the upcoming TV commercial?
   a. Demonstration.
   b. Musical.
   c. Lifestyle.
   d. Product symbolism.
   e. Spokesperson.

_____ 7. The agency envisions using TV advertising for several reasons. Which of the following is NOT a reason to use TV advertising?
   a. It has wide reach for a mass market.
   b. It has a low cost per thousand people reached.
   c. It has a low total cost.
   d. It has both visual and audio capabilities.
   e. None of these are reasons not to use TV advertising

Short Answer:

8. Which creative decision has not been covered in the above scenario?

Read the marketing scenario and answer the questions that follow.

Sandra is a sales representative for Furry Friends Pet Food Company, a leading supplier of pet foods. She has been busy trying to get distribution on a new, low-fat and all natural dog food from grocery stores and pet supply stores. Furry Friends has provided some incentives for both consumers to buy the product and for retailers to stock the product. Promotions include a coupon for $2.00 off the first bag of dog food and a new nylon collar for dogs. The company is also offering dog lovers a chance to win a trip to Disneyland. The company is offering a special introductory price for six weeks and some extra monetary incentives for wholesalers to sell the products to grocery stores and pet supply stores.

In her seven years as a sales rep, Sandra has built strong relationships with her accounts. As a result, she has confidence that she'll meet her goal of getting authorization from 95 percent of her accounts. Sandra has responsibility for all the chain accounts in Vancouver.

True/False:

_____ 1. The above scenario involves all four types of promotion: advertising, sales promotion, publicity, and personal selling.

_____ 2. The $2.00 coupon and new nylon collar are types of consumer promotions.

_____ 3. Sandra's strong relationship with her accounts is most likely due to relationship selling.

Multiple Choice:

_____ 4. The free nylon dog collar is an example of what type of consumer promotion?
   a. Loyalty program.
   b. Premium.
   c. Trade allowance.
   d. Rebate.
   e. Sample

_____ 5. The chance for consumers to win a trip to Disneyland is an example of what type of promotion?
   a. Loyalty program.
   b. Premium.
   c. Contest.
   d. Sweepstakes.
   e. Bonus item.

_____ 6. The special introductory price given to wholesalers is an example of a(n):
   a. trade allowance.
   b. premium.
   c. slotting allowance.
   d. rebate.
   e. discount.

_____ 7. As evidenced by Sandra's area of account responsibility, Furry Friends uses which kind of sales force structure?
   a. Product line structure.
   b. Industry structure.
   c. Geographic structure.
   d. Individual account structure.
   e. None of these structures

8. What is the difference between consumer sales promotion and trade sales promotion? What other types of consumer sales promotions could Furry Friends offer? What other types of trade sales promotion could it offer?

ESSAY QUESTIONS

1. There are six major types of advertising. Name and define each of these six types, including special forms of each type.

2. List and describe four creative decisions in developing an advertising campaign.

3. Advertising media are channels that advertisers use in mass communication. Name and describe the five basic media vehicles. Cite at least two advantages and two disadvantages of each basic medium in your descriptions. Then name and describe three examples of new media forms.

4. What is the difference between consumer sales promotion and trade sales promotion?

5. List eight tools for consumer promotion.

6. You are the public relations manager for a chemical company. What are some common public relations tools you might use on a regular basis? What types of actions would you take if a crisis occurred (such as a chemical spill) and there was the possibility of unfavourable publicity?

APPLICATION #1

You are responsible for developing several advertisements for Less-U, a fat substitute product with no calories to be used in place of butter, margarine, or shortening in cooking. Name five common advertising appeals. For each appeal, give an example of a Less-U advertisement message using that appeal. Then name six common advertising executional styles. Briefly describe how you would design six different Less-U advertisements (one for each executional style).

You are the sales promotion manager for Steri-Flor, a new brand of floor disinfectant/cleanser. Your company uses a *pull* strategy, and you are responsible for recommending sales promotion tools to accomplish this strategy. Name and define the consumer promotional tools, and for each tool describe specific sales promotion activities you would recommend for Steri-Flor.

Now do the same for a push strategy.

CHAPTER 15: PRICING CONCEPTS

LEARNING OBJECTIVES

1 Discuss the importance of pricing decisions to the economy and to the individual firm

Pricing plays an integral role in the Canadian economy by allocating goods and services among consumers, governments, and businesses. Pricing is essential in business because it creates revenue, which is the basis of all business activity. In setting prices, marketing managers strive to find a level high enough to produce a satisfactory profit.

2 List and explain a variety of pricing objectives

Establishing realistic and measurable pricing objectives is a critical part of any firm's marketing strategy. Pricing objectives are commonly classified into three categories: profit oriented, sales oriented, and status quo. Profit-oriented pricing is based on profit maximization, a satisfactory level of profit, or a target return on investment. The goal of profit maximization is to generate as much revenue as possible in relation to cost. Often, a more practical approach than profit maximization is setting prices to produce profits that will satisfy management and stockholders. The most common profit-oriented strategy is pricing for a specific return on investment relative to a firm's assets. The second type of pricing objective is sales oriented, and it focuses on either maintaining a percentage share of the market or maximizing dollar or unit sales. The third type of pricing objective aims to maintain the status quo by matching competitors' prices.

3 Explain the role of demand in price determination

Demand is a key determinant of price. When establishing prices, a firm must first determine demand for its product. A typical demand schedule shows an inverse relationship between quantity demanded and price: When price is lowered, sales increase; and when price is increased, the quantity demanded falls. However, for prestige products, there may be a direct relationship between demand and price. The quantity demanded will increase as price increases.

Marketing managers must also consider demand elasticity when setting prices. Elasticity of demand is the degree to which the quantity demanded fluctuates with changes in price. If consumers are sensitive to changes in price, demand is elastic; if they are insensitive to price changes, demand is inelastic. Thus, an increase in price will result in lower sales for an elastic product and little or no loss in sales for an inelastic product.

4 Understand the concept of yield management systems

Yield management systems use complex mathematical software to profitably fill unused capacity. The software uses techniques such as discounting early purchases, limiting early sales at these discounted prices, and overbooking capacity. These systems are primarily used in services businesses and are substantially raising revenues.

5 Describe cost-oriented pricing strategies

The other major determinant of price is cost. Marketers use several cost-oriented pricing strategies. To cover their own expenses and obtain a profit, wholesalers and retailers commonly use markup pricing: They tack an extra amount onto the manufacturer's original price. Another pricing technique is to maximize profits by setting price where marginal revenue equals marginal cost. Still another pricing strategy determines how much a firm must sell to break even and uses this amount as a reference point for adjusting price.

6 Demonstrate how the product life cycle, competition, distribution and promotion strategies, customer demands, the Internet and extranets, and perceptions of quality can affect price

The price of a product normally changes as it moves through the life cycle and as demand for the product and competitive conditions change. Management often sets a high price at the introductory stage, and the high price tends to attract competition. The competition usually drives prices down, because individual competitors lower prices to gain market share.

Adequate distribution for a new product can sometimes be obtained by offering a larger-than-usual profit margin to wholesalers and retailers. The Internet enables consumers to compare products and prices quickly and efficiently. Extranets help control costs and lower prices. Price is also used as a promotional tool to attract customers. Special low prices often attract new customers and entice existing customers to buy more. Demands of large customers can squeeze the profit margins of suppliers.

Perceptions of quality also can influence pricing strategies. A firm trying to project a prestigious image often charges a premium price for a product. Consumers tend to equate high prices with high quality.

PRE-TEST

Answer the following questions to see how well you understand the material. Re-take it after you review to check yourself.

1. List and briefly describe three categories of pricing objectives.

2. Explain the difference between elastic demand, inelastic demand, and unitary elasticity. Describe their effect on pricing decisions.

3. List and briefly describe three pricing methods that use cost as a determinant.

4. List five alternative determinants of price.

CHAPTER OUTLINE

1 Discuss the importance of pricing decisions to the economy and to the individual firm

I. The Importance of Price

   A. What Is Price?

      1. **Price** is that which is given in an exchange to acquire a good or service.

      2. Price is related to the perceived value at the time of the transaction and is based on the amount of expected satisfaction to be received from the good or service, not the actual satisfaction.

   B. The Importance of Price to Marketing Managers

   Prices are the key to company revenues.

      1. Prices charged to customers multiplied by the number of units sold equal **revenue** for the firm. Revenue pays for every activity of the firm. Whatever is left over after paying for company activities is **profit**.

      2. If a price is too high in the minds of consumers, sales will be lost. If a price is too low, revenues may not meet the company's goals for return on investment.

      3. Trying to set the right price can be one of the most stressful and pressure-filled tasks for a marketing manager.

      4. In the business-to-business market, buyers are becoming more efficient and better informed.

2 List and explain a variety of pricing objectives

II. Pricing Objectives

   Companies set pricing objectives that are specific, attainable, and measurable. These goals require periodic monitoring to determine the effectiveness of the strategy.

   A. Profit-Oriented Pricing Objectives

      1. *Profit maximization* means setting prices so total revenue is as large as possible relative to total costs for a given item. Competitors' prices and the product's perceived value mediate profit-oriented pricing.

---

2. Another goal of profit-oriented pricing is satisfactory profits, a reasonable level of profits that is satisfactory to stockholders and management.

3. The most common of the profit objectives is **target return on investment (ROI)**, sometimes called the firm's return on total assets. ROI measures the effectiveness of management in generating profits with its available assets:

B. Sales-Oriented Pricing Objectives

1. **Market share** refers to a company's product sales as a percentage of total sales for that industry. Market share can be expressed in dollars of sales or units of product.

2. Rather than strive for market share, some companies try to maximize dollar or unit sales. A firm may use this strategy in an attempt to generate a maximum amount of cash in the short run or to sell off excess inventory, but this strategy may produce little or no profit.

C. Status Quo Pricing Objectives

1. **Status quo pricing** seeks to maintain existing prices or simply to meet the competition. This strategy requires little planning other than monitoring competitors' prices.

3   Explain the role of demand in price determination

III. The Demand Determinant of Price

The price that is set depends on not only pricing goals but also the demand for the good or service, the cost to the seller for that good or service, and other factors.

A. The Nature of Demand

1. **Demand** is the quantity of a product that will be sold in the market at various prices for a specified period. Ordinarily, the quantity demanded increases as the price decreases and decreases as the price increases.

    a. The *demand curve* graphs the demand for a product at various prices. The line usually curves down and to the right.
    b. The *demand schedule* is a chart that shows quantity demanded at selected prices.

2. **Supply** is the quantity of product that will be offered to the market by suppliers at various prices for a specified period. This is represented by the *supply curve*.

3. Competitive market prices are determined by a combination of supply and demand. The *supply schedule* shows the amount of product suppliers will produce at different prices.

4. When supply and demand are equal, a state called **equilibrium** is achieved. At equilibrium there is no inclination for prices to rise or fall.

B. Elasticity of Demand

Elasticity of demand refers to consumers' responsiveness or sensitivity to changes in price.

1. **Elastic demand** occurs when consumers are sensitive to price changes, whereas **inelastic demand** means that an increase or decrease in price will not significantly affect demand for a product.

    a.   If price goes down and revenue goes up, demand is elastic.

    b.   If prices goes down and revenue goes down, demand is inelastic.

    c.   If price goes up and revenue goes up, demand is inelastic.

    d.   If price goes up and revenue goes down, demand is elastic

    e.   If price goes up or down and revenue remains the same, the demand elasticity is unitary.

2.   **Unitary elasticity** means an increase in sales exactly offsets a decrease in price so that total revenue remains the same.

3.   Factors affecting elasticity are:

    a.   The availability of substitute goods and services

    b.   The price relative to a consumer's purchasing power

    c.   Product durability

    d.   The existence of other product uses

4   Understand the concept of yield management systems

IV. The Power of Yield Management Systems

A.   When competitive pressures are high a company must know when it can raise prices to maximize revenues.

B.   **Yield Management Systems** use complex mathematical software to profitably fill unused capacity by discounting early purchases, limiting early sales at these discounted prices, and overbooking capacity.

C.   Use of yield management systems is spreading from service industries such as hotels and airlines to other industries as they strive to manage capacity.

5   Describe cost-oriented pricing strategies

V.   The Cost Determinant of Price

Some companies price their products largely or solely on the basis of costs. This method can lead to overpricing and lost sales or to underpricing and lower returns on sales than necessary. Costs usually serve as a floor below which a good must not be priced.

A.   Types of Costs

1.   **Variable costs** are those that vary with changes in the level of output, for example, the cost of materials.

2.   **Fixed costs**, such as rent and executive salaries, do not change as output is increased or decreased.

3.   It is helpful to calculate costs per unit or average costs. **Average variable cost (AVC)** is total variable costs divided by quantity of output. **Average total cost (ATC)** is total costs divided by output.

4.   **Marginal cost** is the change in total costs associated with a one-unit change in output.

5.   All these costs have a definite relationship and can be represented by curves on a cost-quantity graph

B. **Markup pricing**, the most popular method used by wholesalers and retailers, is adding to the cost of buying the product from the producer an amount for profit and for expenses not previously accounted for. The total determines the selling price.

   1. Retailers tend to discuss markup in terms of its percentage of the retail price. For example, an item that costs $1 and is marked up to $2 is marked up 50 percent from the retailer's point of view.

   2. The maintained markup (or gross margin) is the difference between the cost and the final selling price.

   3. **Keystoning** refers to markups that are double the cost.

C. **Profit maximization pricing** occurs when marginal revenue equals marginal cost.

   1. **Marginal revenue (MR)** is the extra revenue associated with selling an additional unit of output.

   2. As long as the revenue of the last unit produced and sold is greater than the cost of the last unit produced and sold, the firm should continue manufacturing.

D. Break-Even Pricing

   1. **Break-even analysis** determines what sales volume must be reached for a product before the company breaks even and no profits are earned.

      Break-even = Total fixed costs / Fixed cost contributions

      Fixed cost contribution (per unit) = Price per unit - Average variable cost

   2. The advantage of break-even analysis is that a firm can quickly discover how much it must sell to cover costs and how much profit can be earned if higher sales volume is obtained. It is a simple formula requiring only cost information.

   3. The disadvantages of break-even analysis include the fact that it ignores demand and that some costs are difficult to categorize as fixed or variable.

6 Demonstrate how the product life cycle, competition, distribution and promotion strategies, customer demands, the Internet and Extranets and perceptions of quality can affect price

VI. Other Determinants of Price

A. Stages in the Product's Life Cycle

   As the product moves through its life cycle, the demand for the product and the competitive conditions usually change, affecting price.

   1. Prices are usually high during the *introductory stage* to recover development costs and take advantage of high demand originating in the core of the market.

   2. Prices generally begin to lower and stabilize as the product enters the *growth stage* and competitors enter the market. Economies of scale lead to lower prices.

   3. The *maturity stage* brings further price decreases, because competition is strong and weaker firms have been eliminated.

4. The *decline stage* may bring even more price decreases as firms attempt to salvage the last vestiges of demand. But when only one firm is left in the market, the prices may actually rise again as the product becomes a specialty good.

B. The Competition

1. High selling prices can attract other firms to enter a profitable market, usually at a slightly lower price.

2. When a firm enters a market, it has to decide whether to price at, below, or above market prices.

   a. A firm can price its product below the market price to gain quick market share.
   b. The new competitor can price above the market price if it has a distinct competitive advantage.
   c. The new competitor may choose to enter a market at the "going market price" and avoid crippling price wars, assuming it will succeed through nonprice competition.

C. Distribution Strategy

1. Adequate distribution depends on convincing distributors to carry the product. This can be accomplished by:

   a. Offering a larger-than-usual profit margin
   b. Giving dealers a large trade allowance

2. Manufacturers have been losing control of the distribution channel to wholesalers and retailers. Some distributors engage in **selling against the brand** where well-known brands are priced higher than the distributor's own private-label brand.

3. Purchasing goods through unauthorized channels allows wholesalers and retailers to obtain higher-than-normal margins.

4. Manufacturers try to maintain pricc control by using:

   a. Exclusive channels
   b. Pre-priced packaging

D. The Impact of the Internet and Extranets

1. The Internet connects buyers and sellers, allowing buyers to quickly and easily compare product and prices while sellers are able to tailor products and prices.

2. While the Internet helps drive down prices by making it easier for consumers to shop for the best bargain, it also makes it possible for on-line merchants to monitor each other's prices and to adjust their own without overly colluding.

3. Internet auctions continue to be big business. The future, however, belongs to B2B auctions, whereby consumers can trade directly with each other.

E. Promotion Strategy

1. Price is often used as a promotional tool. Sales and coupons can increase consumer interest.

F. Demands of Large Customers

Large customers of manufacturers often make specific pricing demands.

1. Guaranteed profit margins

2. Ticketing, packing, and shipping requirements

G. Relationship of Price to Quality

1. Consumers tend to rely on a high price as a predictor of good quality when they have great uncertainty about the purchase decision. This reliance on price as an indicator of quality seems to exist for all products, but exists more strongly for some items than for others.

2. Marketing managers can use high prices to enhance the image of their product in some cases. This is a **prestige pricing** strategy.

3. Consumers expect dealer or store brands to be cheaper than national brands. But if the savings are too great, consumers tend to believe that the dealer brand is inferior in quality.

VOCABULARY PRACTICE

Fill in the blank(s) with the appropriate term or phrase from the alphabetized list of chapter key terms.

average total cost (ATC)	markup pricing
average variable cost (AVC)	prestige pricing
break-even analysis	price
demand	price equilibrium
elastic demand	profit
elasticity of demand	profit maximization
extranet	return on investment (ROI)
fixed cost	revenue
inelastic demand	selling against the brand
keystoning	status quo pricing
marginal cost (MC)	supply
marginal revenue (MR)	unitary elasticity
market share	variable cost

1 Discuss the importance of pricing decisions to the economy and to the individual firm

1. The perceived value of a good or service that is exchanged for something else is _____.

2. Prices charged to customers multiplied by the number of units sold equals the _____ for the firm, which is the lifeblood of the organization. Whatever is left over of this (if anything) after paying for company operations is _____.

2 List and explain a variety of pricing objectives

3. The most common of the profit objectives is sometimes called the firm's return on total assets. The _____ measures the overall effectiveness of management in generating profits with its available assets. A sales-oriented pricing objective could be based on a company's product sales as a percentage of total sales for that industry, also known as _____. Another pricing objective seeks to maintain the existing prices or simply meet the competition; this is a(n) _____ objective.

3 Explain the role of demand in price determination

4. One determinant of price is the quantity of a product that will be sold in the market at various prices for a specified time period; this is _____, and the quantity of a product that people will buy depends on its price. Another determinant of price is the quantity of a product that will be offered to the market by suppliers at various prices for a specified time period; this is the concept of _____. When these two determinants of price are the same, a state called _____ is achieved.

5. Consumers' responsiveness to prices or sensitivity to changes in prices refers to _____. When consumers are sensitive to price changes, _____ occurs. Conversely, when an increase or a decrease in price does not significantly affect demand, _____ occurs. If an increase in sales exactly offsets the decrease in price so that total revenue remains the same, the situation is called _____, which is a rare phenomenon.

4 Understand the concept of yield management systems

6. Many industries, such as airlines and hospitality, use _____, a technique for adjusting prices that uses complex mathematical software to profitably fill unused capacity by discounting early purchases, limiting early sales at these discounted prices, and overbooking capacity

5 Describe cost-oriented pricing strategies

7. Economic costs are important determinants of price. A cost that deviates with changes in the level of output is a(n) _____. In contrast, a cost that does not change as output increases or decreases is a(n) _____. There are several useful calculated cost variables. Total variable costs divided by output is the _____. Total costs divided by output is the _____. The change in total costs associated with a one-unit change in output is the _____.

8. The most popular method used by wholesalers and retailers to establish a sales price is adding an amount to the cost for profit and expenses not previously accounted for; this is _____.
Retailers often double the cost of a product to arrive at its retail price, a tactic known as _____.

9. The additional revenue associated with selling an additional unit of output is called _____. When this is equal to marginal cost, _____ occurs, which is one type of pricing objective.

10. To determine what sales volume must be reached for a product before total costs equal total revenue, and no profits or losses are achieved, a marketer would use_____.

6 Demonstrate how the product life cycle, competition, distribution and promotion strategies, customer demands, the Internet and Extranets, and perceptions of quality can affect price

11. Stocking well-known brand items at high prices in order to sell store brands at discounted prices is known as _____.

12. Charging a high price to help promote a high-quality image is called _____.

13. Many manufacturers gave created a private network called a(n) _____ which links them to suppliers and customers. This network makes it possible for all channel members to reach pricing agreements more quickly.

Check your answers to these questions before proceeding to the next section.

TRUE/FALSE QUESTIONS

Mark the statement **T** if it is true and **F** if it is false.

1 Discuss the importance of pricing decisions to the economy and to the individual firm

_____ 1. Price is defined as what the customer pays for a good or service.

_____ 2. Profit is revenue minus all expenses.

_____ 3. Revenue is calculated as price times number of units sold minus expenses.

2 List and explain a variety of pricing objectives

_____ 4. Target return on investment (ROI) is the most common pricing objective used by firms.

_____ 5. PorterCo has a goal of cash maximization, which is an appropriate long-term pricing objective for most firms.

_____ 6. Status quo pricing objectives indicate that prices may change because prices are adjusted to meet the competition.

3 Explain the role of demand in price determination

_____ 7. The point at which demand and supply are equal is called unitary price.

_____ 8. When demand for a product has unitary elasticity, a firm will lose revenue if it decreases the price.

_____ 9. For a product like butter, the price is small relative to a consumer's purchasing power, and there are several alternate uses for the product. If this information is true, butter probably has elastic demand.

4 Describe cost-oriented pricing strategies

_____ 10. Markup pricing is one of the most common pricing methods used by intermediaries.

_____ 11. Break-even analysis determines what sales volume must be reached for a product before the company's total revenue equals total costs.

6 Demonstrate how the product life cycle, competition, distribution and promotion strategies, customer demands, the Internet and Extranets, and perceptions of quality can affect price

_____ 12. When a firm enters an industry in which products are in the maturity phase of the product life cycle, the firm generally faces a decision of whether to price at the market level or above the market.

_____ 13. Consumers use price as an indicator of the quality of a product, especially when consumers have a lot of knowledge about the product.

Check your answers to these questions before proceeding to the next section.

AGREE/DISAGREE QUESTIONS

For the following statements, indicate reasons why you may agree and disagree with the statement.

1. Of all the possible pricing objectives, profit maximization is the most important.

   Reason(s) to agree:

   Reason(s) to disagree:

2. Unitary elasticity is just theoretical; in practice, demand must either be elastic or inelastic.

   Reason(s) to agree:

   Reason(s) to disagree:

3. All pricing strategies should be somewhat cost-oriented.

Reason(s) to agree:

Reason(s) to disagree:

4. The higher a product or service is priced, the higher its quality perception.

Reason(s) to agree:

Reason(s) to disagree:

5. Pricing a product mostly involves quantitative analysis.

Reason(s) to agree:

Reason(s) to disagree:

MULTIPLE CHOICE QUESTIONS

Select the response that best answers the question, and write the corresponding letter in the space provided.

1 Discuss the importance of pricing decisions to the economy and to the individual firm

_____ 1. The Cool Shades Company prices its sunglasses at $30 per pair. This year, it has sold 10,000 pairs. Each pair of sunglasses costs the company $10 to produce, and the company has paid out $100,000 in marketing, R&D, and other expenses. All of the following statements about the company are true EXCEPT:
   a. The company's revenue is $300,000.
   b. The company is losing money on these sunglasses.
   c. The company's profit is $100,000.
   d. The company's cost of goods is $100,000.
   e. The company is pricing higher than the break-even price.

2 List and explain a variety of pricing objectives

_____ 2. The Foxy Furniture Firm has a pricing policy of setting prices so that the retail price is as high as the market will tolerate. However, the company constantly strives to keep costs at an industry low. The pricing policy is best described as:
   a. market share pricing
   b. status quo pricing
   c. demand oriented
   d. sales maximization
   e. profit maximization

_____ 3. Bartyl's Beer determines its prices based on maintaining revenues and expenses at acceptable levels. This would lead to pricing based on:
   a. satisfactory profits
   b. stable sales levels
   c. profit maximization
   d. market share
   e. consumer demand

_____ 4. The Kandy Korner managed to exceed its target ROI for the current fiscal year. The following results were found on its financial statements:

Gross revenues:	$250,000	Assets:	$500,000
Gross profits:	$100,000	Liabilities:	$200,000
Net profits:	$ 50,000	Equity:	$300,000

What was the actual ROI for The Kandy Korner?
   a. 20 percent
   b. 50 percent
   c. 33.33 percent
   d. 10 percent
   e. none of these

_____ 5. A Japanese electronics firm has launched a new CD player in the competitive U.S. market. The firm prices its products very low in order to gain a foothold in the market. This pricing objective is:
   a. increasing market share
   b. maximizing dollar sales
   c. satisfactory profits
   d. profit maximization
   e. target ROI

_____ 6. Kmart has lowered the price of a GE coffeemaker to $19.88. Target and Wal-Mart lower their prices on the coffeemaker to $19.97 and $19.85 the day after Kmart's price change. This is:
   a. cost-plus pricing
   b. target return pricing
   c. market share pricing
   d. predatory pricing
   e. status quo pricing

3 Explain the role of demand in price determination

_____ 7. Ben's Bagel Company used to price its bagels at 25¢ each. At this price, the company sold an average of 5,000 bagels per day. The company recently decided to double its price to 50¢, and the company watched its demand fall to 1,500 per day. The demand for bagels is most likely:
   a. inelastic
   b. unitary
   c. equilibrium
   d. elastic
   e. profitable

8. When Pinta-Painting Co. first started, it charged $750 per house and could not keep up with all the calls. Pinta-Painting raised the price to $1,000 per house, and now all eight painters are steadily busy but no longer forced to work fourteen-hour days. The $1,000 per house price is probably a(n):
   a. supply schedule
   b. price elasticity
   c. producer surplus
   d. equilibrium price
   e. inelastic price

9. When Unicorn Software lowered the price of its investment software package from $800 to $200, demand doubled from five units sold per month to ten units per month. However, total revenue dropped. This is an example of:
   a. substitute goods
   b. unitary elasticity
   c. inelastic demand
   d. consumer shortage
   e. elastic demand

10. Gwynn has lowered the price of his custom oven mitts from $6 to $5. He previously sold 300 oven mitts per month and now sells 360 per month. He is experiencing:
    a. unitary elasticity
    b. inelastic demand
    c. elastic demand
    d. consumer surplus
    e. producer shortage

5 Describe cost-oriented pricing strategies

11. When the PinkBall Company manufactures 1,000 pink balls, the cost of pink dye is $14. When output is raised to 2,500 balls, the cost of the dye is $35. The cost of the pink dye is a(n):
    a. inventory cost
    b. demand cost
    c. fixed cost
    d. marketing cost
    e. variable cost

12. The Custom-Natural Pizza store has daily sales that range from 50 to 250 pizzas. Which of the following is the BEST example of one of their fixed costs?
    a. payment on leased equipment
    b. flour and tomato sauce
    c. electricity and gas for baking
    d. paper products
    e. cash register tape

13. Output at the Pine Playhouse Company changed from fifteen to sixteen playhouses, and the total costs changed from $27,000 to $28,500. What was the marginal cost for the company?
    a. $1,800
    b. $1,781
    c. $1,500
    d. $27,000
    e. $28,500

14. The Glass 'n' Brass Lamp Shoppe figures the price of a lamp by doubling the cost of the lamp (or taking a 100% markup). Which pricing technique is the store using?
    a. turnover pricing
    b. keystoning
    c. marginal revenue pricing
    d. target ROI pricing
    e. maximum revenue pricing

15. R.J.'s Health Foods buys a brand of granola cereal for $1.50 and adds 49¢ to the cost to bring the retail price to $1.99. What pricing technique is the store using?
    a. marginal revenue pricing
    b. keystoning
    c. turnover pricing
    d. markup pricing
    e. break-even pricing

16. The Lollygag Lollipop Company has the following revenues and costs:

Sales price per lollipop:	$0.50
Variable costs per lollipop:	$0.30
Total fixed costs (annual):	$50,000

    What is the annual break-even quantity for the company?
    a. 50,000
    b. 250,000
    c. 100,000
    d. 166,667
    e. none of these are a break-even quantity

17. The manager of the Toothsome Toothbrush Company has calculated the sales volume at which the company's costs equal revenue. The manager announced at the quarterly sales meeting that 150,000 toothbrushes, at an average of $8 per brush, must be sold during next quarter to reach this point. Which important factor has been excluded from this analysis?
    a. fixed and variable cost determination
    b. break-even analysis
    c. target return pricing
    d. market share
    e. consumer demand

6 Demonstrate how the product life cycle, competition, distribution and promotion strategies, customer demands, the Internet and Extranets, and perceptions of quality can affect price

18. Klean Detergent is the market leader of clothes detergents and is in the maturity phase of its life cycle. There are many competitors in the market that challenge Klean's leadership. Which of the following statements is most likely true about Klean's pricing?
    a. As a market leader, Klean does not need to worry about price.
    b. Klean uses price promotion in order to maintain its market leadership.
    c. Klean must price lower than the other brands to maintain its leadership.
    d. Klean can increase its price since it is in the maturity stage.
    e. Klean should maintain a high price to maintain a high quality image.

19. HeartGood's Eggs decided to offer a much larger than customary profit margin to grocery wholesalers and retailers on their new low-cholesterol eggs. This pricing strategy is designed to facilitate all of the following EXCEPT:
    a. encouraging retailers to advertise this high-margin item
    b. giving dealers an incentive to promote the new product
    c. developing wide and convenient distribution
    d. maximizing profit margin for the producer
    e. encouraging trial by consumers if priced low by retailers

20. When an innovative new electronics product is introduced into the market, its initial pricing is usually high. This is most likely due to:
    a. The firm's distribution strategy
    b. The firm's promotion strategy
    c. The lack of relevant competition
    d. The product's quality image
    e. High product costs

21. Tommy knows little about computer diskettes and does not want to spend the time to learn about them. However, he needs to buy diskettes to use for a consulting project. Not wanting to make a poor choice, he is likely to:
    a. intuitively make the right choice
    b. buy an expensive brand of diskette, guessing that the price is related to quality
    c. avoid making a decision by not buying anything
    d. revise his goals and buy a CD instead
    e. buy the cheapest diskettes because most consumers feel that price is not directly related to quality

22. The advertisements for Ramarro Car claim that it is the most expensive car in the world. This is an example of a:
    a. target return pricing strategy
    b. market share pricing strategy
    c. prestige pricing strategy
    d. maintained markup pricing strategy
    e. profit maximization pricing strategy

23. The Goldstar Conveyor Corporation builds quality conveyor systems for warehouses, with innovative components and superior durability. The corporation has managed to keep its price lower than its competitors'. However, Goldstar's sales have been disappointing. For a fast and simple remedy, Goldstar should:
    a. reeducate the potential consumers about its products
    b. lower the quality of its products
    c. raise prices because of consumer expectations
    d. emphasize the low price in all the advertising
    e. look for a different product to manufacture

Check your answers to these questions before proceeding to the next section.

SCENARIO

Read the marketing scenario and answer the questions that follow. You will need a calculator to determine some of the answers.

Acme, Inc., markets the best-selling widget in the market called SuperDuper Widget. Last year, SuperDuper sold 5 million units in a 10 million-unit industry. The average price of a widget in the industry is $5.00. SuperDuper has been positioned as the low-cost widget with a price of $2.00 per unit. SuperDuper's chief competitor is Triple A Widget, which has a price point of $6.00. Triple A sold 3 million widgets last year with total revenues of $18 million.

This year, Acme's marketing managers would like to raise the price of SuperDuper to maximize profits. However, the managers understand that this is a big risk and decide to test market different prices to determine the elasticity of demand for these widgets. In the Detroit test market, managers raised SuperDuper's price to $2.50 per unit and ran with this price for three months. The result was a 40 percent decrease in the number of SuperDuper widgets sold.

True/False:

1. SuperDuper had the leading unit market share in the widget industry last year.

2. SuperDuper had the leading revenue market share in the widget industry last year.

3. According to the Detroit test market, Acme's marketing managers should raise the price of SuperDuper.

_____ 4. What was the total revenue in the widget industry last year?
   a. $5 million.
   b. $10 million.
   c. $50 million.
   d. $75 million.
   e. There is not enough information to determine this.

_____ 5. What was SuperDuper's revenue market share last year?
   a. 10%
   b. 20%.
   c. 30%
   d. 50%.
   e. There is not enough information to determine this.

_____ 6. Which of the following cannot be determined by the above scenario?
   a. SuperDuper had the leading unit market share in the industry last year.
   b. SuperDuper had a unit market share of 50%.
   c. SuperDuper did not make a profit last year.
   d. SuperDuper had a smaller revenue share than Triple A last year.
   e. All of these can be determined by the scenario.

_____ 7. According to the Detroit test market, the demand for SuperDuper widgets can be characterized as:
   a. elastic.
   b. inelastic.
   c. unitary.
   d. nonexistent.
   e. balanced.

Short Answer:

8. What would you do with SuperDuper's price? Why?

ESSAY QUESTIONS

1. List the three categories of pricing objectives and the specific objectives included in each category. Then describe disadvantages of using each type of pricing objective.

2. When a marketing manager sets a price to meet pricing goals, the price established depends on several factors. Name and describe these determinants of price.

3. As a product moves through its life cycle, the demand for the product and the competitive conditions tend to change. For each stage in the product life cycle, discuss pricing strategies appropriate for that stage. Then describe how price interacts with the other three Ps of the marketing mix.

APPLICATION #1

Last quarter the Xylo company sold 1,000 strapples for $1 each, the Yeti Company sold 600 strapples at $5 each, and the Zeta Company sold 400 strapples for $2.50 apiece. Assuming the three companies are the only firms competing in the strapple market, calculate unit and dollar market share for each company for last quarter.

APPLICATION #2

In the following scenarios, calculate answers related to the way retailers tend to calculate markups.

a) A coffeemaker is sold for $25. The retailer added $5 to the original cost. What is the markup percentage?

b) The cost of a calculator is $4 and the retailer applies a markup of $6. What is the markup percentage?

c) A bookstore retailer marks up all products by 25 percent. If a book costs the retailer $15, what will the final selling price be?

d) A gourmet food retailer marks up all products by 75 percent. If the selling price of a specialty cheese is $12, what was the cost to the retailer?

APPLICATION #3

Calculate the break-even quantity for TV-Terry.

TV-Terry Financial Information	
Salaries	$ 60,000
Promotion	80,000
Research and development	90,000
Equipment	20,000
Store lease	50,000
Total fixed costs	$300,000
TV-Terry selling price	$500
Variable cost	300

CHAPTER 16: SETTING THE RIGHT PRICE

LEARNING OBJECTIVES

1 Describe the procedure for setting the right price

Setting the right price on a product is a process consisting of (1) establishing pricing goals; (2) estimating demand, costs, and profits; (3) selecting a pricing policy to help determine a base price; and (4) fine-tuning the base price with pricing tactics.

A price strategy establishes a long-term pricing framework for a good or service. The three main types of price policies are price skimming, penetration pricing, and status quo pricing. A price-skimming policy charges a high introductory price, often followed by a gradual reduction. Penetration pricing offers a low introductory price to capture a large market share and attain economies of scale. Finally, status quo pricing strives to match competitors' price.

2 Identify the legal and ethical constraints on pricing decisions

Pricing decisions are subject to government regulation. Under the Competition Act there are laws that limit pricing decision-making, these include: resale price maintenance, price fixing, price discrimination, and predatory pricing.

The resale price maintenance is a law that prohibits manufacturers from controlling prices at the retail level. Price fixing prohibits the agreement between two or more firms on a particular price. It is also illegal for firms to discriminate between two or more buyers in terms of price. Lastly, predatory pricing, undercutting competitors with extremely low prices to drive them out of business is illegal pricing activity.

3 Explain how discounts, geographic pricing, and other special pricing tactics can be used to fine-tune the base price

Several techniques enable marketing managers to adjust prices within a general range in response to changes in competition, government regulation, consumer demand, and promotional and positioning goals. Techniques for fine-tuning a price can be divided into three main categories: discounts, allowances, rebates and value pricing; geographic pricing; and special pricing tactics.

The first type of tactic gives lower prices to those that pay promptly, order a large quantity, or perform some function for the manufacturer. Value-based pricing starts with the customer, considers the competition and costs, and then determines a price. Other tactics in this category include seasonal discounts, promotion allowances, and rebates (cash refunds).

Geographic pricing tactics—such as FOB origin pricing, uniform delivered pricing, zone pricing, freight absorption pricing, and basing-point pricing—are ways of moderating the impact of shipping costs on distant customers.

A variety of special pricing tactics stimulate demand for certain products, increase store patronage, and offer more merchandise at specific prices.

More and more customers are paying price penalties, which is an extra fee for violating the terms of a purchase contract. The perceived fairness of a penalty may affect some consumers' willingness to patronize a business in the future.

4 Discuss product line pricing

Product line pricing maximizes profits for an entire product line. When setting product line prices, marketing managers determine what type of relationship exists among the products in the line: complementary, substitute, or neutral. Managers also consider joint (shared) costs among products in the same line.

5   **Describe the role of pricing during periods of inflation and recession**

Marketing managers employ cost-oriented and demand-oriented tactics during periods of economic inflation. Cost-oriented tactics consist of dropping products with a low profit margin, delayed-quotation pricing, and escalator pricing. Demand-oriented pricing methods include price shading and increasing demand through the cultivation of selected customers, unique offerings, changing the package size, and systems selling.

      To stimulate demand during a recession, marketers use value pricing, bundling, and unbundling. Recessions are also a good time to prune unprofitable items from product lines. Managers strive to cut costs during recessions in order to maintain profits as revenues decline. Implementing new technology, cutting payrolls, and pressuring suppliers for reduced prices are common techniques used to cut costs.

PRE-TEST

Answer the following questions to see how well you understand the material. Re-take it after you review to check yourself.

1.   List the four steps in setting the right price.

2.   List and briefly describe four illegal issues regarding price.

3.   List five types of discounts, rebates, and allowances.

4.   List nine types of special pricing tactics.

1   Describe the procedure for setting the right price

I. How to Set a Price on a Product

    A.   Establish Pricing Goals

        The first step in setting a price is to establish pricing goals, which may be profit-oriented, sales-oriented, or status quo. These goals are derived from the firm's overall objectives.

    B.   Estimate Demand, Costs, and Profits

        1.   After establishing pricing goals, managers should estimate revenues at a variety of prices.

        2.   Next, corresponding costs should be determined and profit estimated. This information can help determine which price can best meet the firm's pricing goals.

    C.   Choose a Price Strategy

        1.   A **price strategy** defines the initial price and gives direction for price movements over the product life cycle. It is a basic long-term pricing framework, which establishes the initial price for a product and the intended direction for price movements over the product life cycle.

            The price policy is set for a specific market segment, based on a well-defined positioning strategy.

        2.   Three basic policies for setting a price on a new good or service are price skimming, penetration pricing, and status quo pricing.

            a.   **Price skimming** is a pricing policy whereby a firm charges a high introductory price, often coupled with heavy promotion. As the product progresses through its life cycle, the firm may lower the price to reach successively larger markets.

                1)   Price skimming is successful when demand is relatively inelastic, when a product is legally protected, when it represents a technological breakthrough, or when production is limited because of technological difficulties, shortages, or a lack of skilled craftspeople.

            b.   **Penetration pricing** sets a relatively low price for a product as a way to reach the mass market in the early stages of the product life cycle.

                1)   Penetration pricing is designed to capture a large market share, resulting in lower production costs.

                2)   Effective in price sensitive markets

                3)   A successful penetration pricing strategy can block entry into the market by competitors, because they cannot gain a large enough share of the market to be cost-effective.

            c.   Status quo pricing means maintaining existing prices or simply meeting the competition. Sometimes this policy can be the safest route to long-term survival if the firm is comparatively small.

---

2   Identify the legal and ethical constraints on pricing decisions

II.   The Legality and Ethics of Price Strategy

Under the Competition Act, there are laws that limit pricing decisions. These are:

A.   Resale Price Maintenance

This law prohibits manufacturers from controlling prices at the retail level.

B.   Price Fixing

Price fixing is an agreement between two or more firms on the price they will charge for a product.

C.   Price Discrimination

Price discrimination, the practice of charging different prices to different customers for the same product, is also prohibited under the Competition Act. Six elements are needed for price discrimination to occur:

1.   The seller must charge different prices to different customers for the same product.
2.   The two customers must be competitors.
3.   The seller must discriminate by price among two or more purchases, within a reasonably short time.
4.   The products sold must be commodities or other tangible goods.
5.   The products sold must be of like grade and quality (not identical but substitutable).
6.   The act of discrimination must be part of an ongoing practice of discrimination.

D.   Predatory Pricing

Predatory pricing is the practice of charging a very low price for a product with the intent of driving competitors out of business or out of a market. Once competitors have been driven out, the firm raises its prices.

1.   Under the Competition Act, pricing below cost to sell off excess inventory is not considered predatory, but pricing below cost to drive a competitor out of business is.

2.   Proving the use of this practice is difficult and expensive.

3   Explain how discounts, geographic pricing, and other special pricing tactics can be used to fine-tune the base price

III.   Tactics for Fine-Tuning the Base Price

The **base price** is the general price level at which the company expects to sell the good or service and is either above the market (price skimming), below the market (price penetration), or at the market (status quo).

A.   Discounts, Allowances, Rebates, and Value Pricing

1.   When buyers receive a lower price for purchasing in multiple units or above a specified dollar amount, they are receiving a **quantity discount**, the most common form of discount.

a.   A **cumulative quantity discount**, a deduction from list price that applies to the buyer's total purchases made during a specific period, is intended to encourage customer loyalty. The amount of the discount depends on the total amount purchased during the period, and the discount increases as the quantity purchased increases.

b. A deduction from list price that applies to a single order is a **noncumulative quantity discount**. This discount encourages larger orders.

2. A **cash discount** is a price reduction offered to a consumer, industrial user, or marketing intermediary in return for prompt payment of a bill. It saves the seller carrying costs and billing expenses, and it reduces the risk of bad debt.

3. A **functional discount** (or **trade discount**) is a discount to a wholesaler or retailer for performing channel functions.

4. A **seasonal discount** is a price reduction for buying merchandise out of season. It shifts the storage function forward to the purchaser.

5. A **promotional allowance** (**trade allowance**) is a payment to a dealer for promoting the manufacturer's products. It is both a pricing tool and a promotional device.

6. A **rebate** is a cash refund given for the purchase of a product during a specified period. A rebate is a temporary inducement that can be taken away without altering the basic price structure.

7. Zero-percent financing allows a purchaser to borrow money to pay for a product that would typically be financed (such as a new car) with no finance charge.

D. **Value-based pricing** is a pricing strategy that has grown out of the quality movement. Since the firm is customer driven, it starts with the customer, considers the competition, and then determines the appropriate price.

1. **Trade loading** occurs when a manufacturer temporarily lowers the price to induce wholesalers and retailers to buy more goods than can be sold in a reasonable time, thereby loading inventory with idle products.

2. In 1992, Procter and Gamble instituted a form a value pricing that coupled value prices with a reduction in coupons, product displays, and other forms of sales promotion and increases in advertising in an effort to reduce operating costs and strengthen brand loyalty.

3. Sometimes managers price their products too low in an attempt to either buy market share or to make decisions that can be justified objectively.

E. Geographic Pricing

1. **FOB origin pricing**, also called FOB factory or FOB shipping point pricing, is a pricing tactic that requires the purchaser to absorb the freight costs from the shipping point. FOB means the goods are placed "free on board" a carrier.

2. In **uniform delivered pricing**, the seller charges and bills every purchaser an identical, flat freight charge, regardless of the buyer's location. An example is UPS ground shipment.

3. **Zone pricing** is a modification of uniform delivered pricing that divides the market into segments or zones and charges a flat freight rate to all customers in a given zone. An example is a first-class postage stamp.

4. In **freight absorption pricing**, the seller pays all or part of the actual freight charges and does not pass them on to the purchaser.

5. A **basing-point price** requires the seller to designate a location as a basing point and charge all purchasers the freight cost from that point, regardless of the city from which the goods are shipped. Often multiple basing points are used.

F. Special Pricing Tactics

Special pricing tactics are used to stimulate demand for specific products, to increase store patronage, and to offer a wider variety of merchandise at a specific price point.

1. A merchant using a **single-price tactic** offers all goods and services at the same price (or perhaps two or three prices). Single-price selling removes price comparisons from the buyer's decision-making process.

2. **Flexible pricing** (or **variable pricing**) charges different customers different prices for essentially the same merchandise bought in equal quantities. It allows the seller to meet the price of the competition or to close a sale with a price-conscious customer.

3. **Professional services pricing**, used by lawyers, doctors, counsellors, etc - fees are based on the solution of a problem or performance of an act rather than on the actual time involved. For example, a doctor may have a set fee for a certain type of operation.

4. **Price lining** is the practice of offering a product line with several items placed in the line at specific price points. This series of prices for a type of merchandise creates a price line.

5. **Leader pricing** (or **loss-leader pricing**) is an attempt to attract customers by selling a product near cost or even below cost, hoping customers will buy other products while in the store.

6. **Bait pricing**, a deceptive and illegal practice, tries to get customers into a store through false or misleading price advertising and then uses high-pressure sales tactics to persuade customers to buy more expensive merchandise.

7. **Odd-even pricing** (or **psychological pricing**) means using odd-numbered prices to denote bargains and even-numbered prices to imply quality.

8. **Price bundling** is marketing two or more goods or services in a single package for a special price. The opposite approach, **unbundling**, reduces the add-ons that come with the basic product and charges for each separately.

9. **Two-part pricing** involves two separate charges to consume a single good or service. An annual membership fee supplemented by a court fee for each use of a tennis club is an example.

10. A **consumer penalty** is an extra fee paid by the consumer for violating terms of the purchase agreement.

4   Discuss product line pricing

IV. Product Line Pricing

Product line pricing is setting prices for an entire line of products, which is a broader concern than setting the right price on a single item.

A. Relationships among Products

One of several types of relationships may exist among the various products in a line:

1. The products may be *complementary*, meaning that an increase in the sale of one good causes an increase in demand for the complementary good.

2. Two products in a line may be *substitutes* for one another. If buyers purchase one item in the line, they are less likely to purchase a second item in the line.

3. A *neutral* relationship may exist between two products, with the demand for one product not related to demand for the other.

B. **Joint costs** are costs shared in the manufacturing and marketing of a product line. These costs can complicate the issue of product pricing, because the assignment of a portion of these costs to each product may be somewhat subjective

5   Describe the role of pricing during periods of inflation and recession

V.   Pricing During Difficult Times

A.   Inflation

When the economy is characterized by high inflation, special cost-oriented or demand-oriented pricing tactics are often necessary.

1.   Cost-Oriented Tactics

a.   One popular tactic is the removal of products with a low profit margin from the product line.

1)   This tactic can backfire if the product has been selling at high volume and contributing sizable profit, even at a very small margin.

2)   Even a product with a low profit margin may help the firm to gain certain economies of scale in production, or its removal may alter the price/quality image of the entire line.

b.   **Delayed-quotation pricing** is a popular pricing tactic for industrial installations.

1)   The price is not set on the product until the item is either finished or delivered.

2)   Long production lead times have forced this policy on many firms during periods of inflation.

c.   **Escalator pricing** is similar to delayed-quotation pricing in that the final selling price reflects cost increases incurred between the times when the order is placed and delivery is made. An escalator clause allows for price increases based on the cost-of-living index or some other formula.

2.   Demand-Oriented Tactics

a.   **Price shading** involves the use of discounts by salespeople to increase demand for one or more products in a line.

b.   Some firms cultivate selected demand from affluent organizations or consumers. Others concentrate on customers who favour performance over price.

c.   Buyers may tolerate higher prices if the seller has designed distinctive goods or services that uniquely fit the buyers' activities.

d.   Companies may pass on higher costs by shrinking product sizes and keeping prices the same.

e.   A buyer's dependence on the selling firm may be heightened by selling entire systems that include feasibility studies, installation, and training.

B.   Recession

Periods of reduced economic activity call for special marketing tactics.

1.   Value Pricing

a.   *Value pricing* stresses to customers that they are getting a good value for their limited funds.

b.   Although lower-priced products offer lower profit margins, volume increases can offset slimmer margins.

2.   Bundling or Unbundling

a.   If features are added to a *bundle*, consumers may perceive the offering as having greater value.

b.   Companies can *unbundle offerings* and lower base prices to stimulate demand.

3.   Strategies used with suppliers include renegotiating contracts, offering to help increase productivity, setting cost reduction targets, and reducing the number of suppliers.

VOCABULARY PRACTICE

Fill in the blank(s) with the appropriate term or phrase from the alphabetized list of chapter key terms.

bait pricing	price bundling
base price	price fixing
basing-point pricing	price lining
cash discount	price shading
consumer penalty	price skimming
cumulative quantity discount	price strategy
delayed-quotation pricing	product line pricing
escalator pricing	promotional allowance
flexible pricing (or variable pricing)	quantity discount
FOB origin pricing	rebate
freight absorption pricing	seasonal discount
functional discount (or trade discount)	single-price tactic
joint costs	trade loading
leader pricing (or loss-leader pricing)	two-part pricing
noncumulative quantity discount	unbundling
odd-even pricing (or psychological pricing)	unfair trade practice acts
penetration pricing	uniform delivered pricing
predatory pricing	value-based pricing
	zone pricing

1   Describe the procedure for setting the right price

1.   A definition of the initial price and the intended direction for price movements over the product life cycle is the

_____ .

2. There are three basic policies for setting a price on a new good or service. The policy that charges a high introductory price is _____. The policy that charges a relatively low price as a way to reach the mass market is _____. Finally, a firm may choose simply to meet the competition, which is a status-quo policy.

2 Identify the legal and ethical constraints on pricing decisions

3. Some pricing decisions are subject to government regulation. Laws that prohibit manufacturers from controlling prices at the retail level are _____. An agreement between two or more firms on the price they will charge for a product or service is _____ and violates the Competition Act. If a company charges a very low price for a product with the intent of driving competitors out of business or out of a market, the firm is practicing _____, which is illegal under the Competition Act.

3 Explain how discounts, geographic pricing, and other special pricing tactics can be used to fine-tune the base price

4. The general price level at which the company expects to sell the good or service is the _____. This price may be lowered through the use of discounts, allowances, and rebates.

5. There are several different ways to lower the base price. Merchants will often offer a discount to buyers that pay promptly, a pricing tactic known as a(n) _____. The most common form of discount is that which offers buyers a lower price for purchasing multiple units or above a specified dollar amount; this is a(n) _____ and can take two forms. The first form is a deduction from list price that applies to the buyer's total purchases made during a specific period; this is a(n) _____. In contrast, a deduction from list price that applies to a single order rather than to the total volume of orders is a(n) _____.

6. Another type of discount compensates intermediaries for performing a service within a distribution channel; this is called a(n) _____. A form of this type of price reduction occurs when a manufacturer temporarily lowers the functional discount to induce wholesalers and retailers to buy more goods than can be sold in a reasonable time; this is _____.

7. A price reduction for buying merchandise at an unpopular time is a(n) _____. A payment to a dealer for promoting the manufacturer's products is known as a(n) _____. A cash refund given for the purchase of a product during a specified period is called a(n) _____. Finally, setting the price at a level that seems to the customer to be a good price compared to the prices of other options is called _____.

8. Sellers have the option of using several different geographic pricing tactics. A price tactic that requires the purchaser to absorb the freight costs from the shipping point is _____. If the seller pays the actual freight charges and bills every purchaser an identical, flat freight charge, _____, or "postage stamp pricing" is being used. A modification of this pricing tactic divides the total market into geographic segments and charges a flat freight rate to all customers in a given segment; this is called _____. In another pricing tactic, the seller pays all or part of the actual freight charges and does not pass them on to the purchaser; this is _____. If a seller designates a specific location as a point from which freight costs are charged, regardless of the actual freight cost, _____ is being used.

9. There are a number of special pricing tactics. If a merchant offers all goods and services at the same price, a(n) _____ is being used. If different customers pay different prices for essentially the same merchandise bought in equal quantities, _____ is being practiced. If a seller offers a line of merchandise at specific price points, the tactic is called _____.

10. Another special pricing tactic is an attempt by the marketing manager to induce store patronage through selling a product near or below cost; this is _____. If store patronage is enhanced by misleading or false advertising, the illegal practice of _____ is being used. If the manager elects to end prices in an odd number or an even number, _____ is being used.

11. If two or more goods are marketed in a single package for a special price, the tactic is _____. Alternatively, if services that normally come with a product are charged for separately, _____ is taking place. If the pricing tactic involves two separate charges to consume a single product or service, _____ is being used. If buyers violate terms of a purchase agreement, the may be subject to a(n) _____ which is an extra fee paid.

4 Discuss product line pricing

12. Setting prices for an entire line of products is _____, which involves broader concerns than price tactics for individual products. One unique problem is that products in a product line may share marketing and manufacturing costs. These shared costs are _____, which must be assigned or allocated to the products.

5 Describe the role of pricing during periods of inflation and recession

13. During periods of inflation, several pricing tactics may be used. One tactic does not set the price on the product until the item is either finished or delivered; this is called _____. A similar form of this pricing tactic takes the form of a contractual clause stating that the final selling price will reflect cost increases incurred between the time an order is placed and delivery is made; this is _____. Another tactic involves the use of discounts by salespeople to increase demand for one or more products in a line; this is called _____.

Check your answers to these questions before proceeding to the next section.

Mark the statement **T** if it is true and **F** if it is false.

1 Describe the procedure for setting the right price

_____ 1. The first step to setting price is to estimate product demand and costs.

_____ 2. Penetration pricing is the opposite of price skimming.

_____ 3. It makes the most sense to use price skimming as a price policy when demand is relatively inelastic in the upper ranges of the demand curve.

_____ 4. Gary's Gas Station is located across the street from another competitive gas station. For weeks, the two have been in a price war. When Gary decreases his gas price by two cents per gallon, his competitor follows him. This is an example of status quo pricing.

2 Identify the legal and ethical constraints on pricing decisions

_____ 5. If the presidents of AT&T, Bell, and Sprint got together and decided what price they would all charge for their long-distance services, the presidents would be engaged in price discrimination.

3 Explain how discounts, geographic pricing, and other special pricing tactics can be used to fine-tune the base price

_____ 6. Promotional allowances given to retailers by manufacturers are usually passed down to consumers in the form of a temporary discounted price.

_____ 7. Functional discounts, noncumulative quantity discounts, and promotional allowances are examples of rebates given to the trade.

_____ 8. There's no such thing as pricing a product too low unless you're not covering costs.

_____ 9. Richard is an attorney who charges $250 per hour for legal consulting. This is an example of flexible pricing.

4 Discuss product line pricing

_____ 10. Rag fibres for paper and cotton seeds for cottonseed oil are two byproducts of the cotton textile industry. Because these products are produced together, they are complementary products.

5 Describe the role of pricing during periods of inflation and recession

_____ 11. PorterCo hand-manufactures reproduction Civil War cannons, which can take as long as two years to build. To protect itself and cover costs, PorterCo should use delayed-quotation pricing or escalator pricing.

Check your answers to these questions before proceeding to the next section.

For the following statements, indicate reasons why you may agree and disagree with the statement.

1. Firms would be better off to use EDLP (everyday low price) rather than to engage in a series of complex pricing discounts, rebates, and allowances.

    Reason(s) to agree:

    Reason(s) to disagree:

2. Leader pricing should not be practiced on a regular basis by supermarkets wishing to make a profit.

    Reason(s) to agree:

    Reason(s) to disagree:

3. Psychological pricing rarely works; consumers know what is going on!

    Reason(s) to agree:

    Reason(s) to disagree:

4. The only effective pricing strategy during a recession is to lower the price of the product.

    Reason(s) to agree:

    Reason(s) to disagree:

Select the response that best answers the question, and write the corresponding letter in the space provided.

1 Describe the procedure for setting the right price

_____ 1. The marketing manager of Techie-TV finds that the firm can gain market share and become the industry leader if it slashes prices by 50 percent. However, the vice-president of finance is committed to reporting a 25 percent return on investment at all times. This conflict illustrates:
   a. need for eliminating low-profit products
   b. a lack of concentration on the marketing concept
   c. pricing in a mature marketplace
   d. ignoring the target market
   e. trade-offs in pricing objectives

_____ 2. Mona Lisa toothpaste positions its product on its ability to whiten teeth after a few weeks of use. Its price is 30 percent higher than other toothpaste brands. Mona Lisa is using a:
   a. price-skimming strategy
   b. penetration pricing strategy
   c. status quo pricing strategy
   d. flexible pricing strategy
   e. leader pricing strategy

_____ 3. Southwest Airlines charges some of the lowest prices in the industry. As a result, the airline has been able to reach the mass market and to increase the incidence of air travel among those who might have chosen another means of travel. The company's current price policy would best be described as:
   a. skimming
   b. flexible
   c. penetration
   d. zone
   e. absorption

_____ 4. Two gas stations are located right across the street from each other. When one gas station drops its price per gallon by two cents, the other immediately follows with a two-cent drop. The second gas station is engaged in:
   a. leader pricing
   b. status quo pricing
   c. corporate espionage
   d. flexible pricing
   e. functional pricing

2 Identify the legal and ethical constraints on pricing decisions

_____ 5. The Specialty Surgical Practice has published a minimum fee schedule for services, and distributed this schedule throughout the medical profession. Specialty Surgical is guilty of:
   a. bait pricing
   b. price fixing
   c. unfair trade practices
   d. price discrimination
   e. predatory pricing

_____ 6. The Sharp Razor Company sells its disposable razors to several large discount retailers but gives special allowances only to one retailer. Sharp Razor is practicing:
   a. bait pricing
   b. price fixing
   c. unfair trade practices
   d. price discrimination
   e. predatory pricing

_____ 7. Price discrimination violates the:
   a.   Sherman Antitrust Act
   b.   Price Discrimination Act
   c.   Wheeler-Lea Amendment
   d.   Competition Act
   e.   Pricing Act

3 Explain how discounts, geographic pricing, and other special pricing tactics can be used to fine-tune the base price

_____ 8. When a customer of Cona Coffee Beans chooses to pay immediately on delivery rather than wait to be billed in thirty days, the salesperson is authorized to offer that customer a 5 percent discount. This 5 percent is an example of a:
   a.   quantity discount
   b.   rebate
   c.   cash discount
   d.   functional discount
   e.   promotional allowance

_____ 9. When the salesperson from Ample Appliances calls on retail appliance stores, she is authorized to offer the retailers a 25 percent discount from the list price in recognition of several retailer activities, including appliance unpacking, testing, and floor display setup. This 25 percent is called a:
   a.   functional discount
   b.   promotional allowance
   c.   quantity discount
   d.   seasonal discount
   e.   rebate

_____ 10. A sale on water skis and swimsuits at the Wisconsin-based Sunski Store during November is an example of which of the following pricing tactics?
   a.   seasonal discount
   b.   quantity discount
   c.   zone pricing
   d.   promotional allowance
   e.   functional discount

_____ 11. Walgreen's drug store receives a 15 percent allowance from a hair care colour brand for running an ad in its weekly circular on the brand. This is an example of a:
   a.   bundled pricing tactic
   b.   promotional allowance
   c.   functional discount
   d.   quantity discount
   e.   product rebate

_____ 12. A manufacturer of computer laser printers is offering $100 cash to consumers who buy one of its printers, produces a cash register receipt, a completed certificate, and proof of purchase. This is an example of a(n):
   a.   rebate
   b.   quantity discount
   c.   instant rebate
   d.   functional discount
   e.   promotional allowance

_____ 13. Shipping grain to international buyers can be risky because of price changes during the time for shipment, expense incurred over long distances, and quality of product delivered. To minimize exposure, a seller would likely employ:
   a.   freight absorption pricing
   b.   FOB origin pricing
   c.   zone pricing
   d.   basing-point pricing
   e.   uniform delivered pricing

_____ 14. Beacon's Books is an on-line retailer of books. Beacon's pays the freight charge on all books that it ships and bills the customer a flat charge on the shipping, no matter where it is shipped. The pricing tactic used is:
   a. quantity discounting
   b. uniform delivered pricing
   c. zone pricing
   d. freight absorption pricing
   e. FOB origin pricing

_____ 15. Buffington Bookcases sells specialty bookcases and office furniture accessories nationally through its catalogue. The company wants to simplify pricing and reduce its risk. Buffington also desires some type of difference in prices due to distance; therefore, the company uses:
   a. two-part pricing
   b. uniform delivered pricing
   c. freight absorption pricing
   d. zone pricing
   e. flexible pricing

_____ 16. Ben and Jerry's, Inc., would like to expand distribution of its frozen yoghurt to a new market area, but competition is intense. Ben and Jerry's should use the geographic pricing tactic of:
   a. freight absorption pricing
   b. zone pricing
   c. FOB origin pricing
   d. basing-point pricing
   e. multiple unit pricing

_____ 17. The Mirasha Car Parts Company has eight warehouses and has a pricing policy of charging freight from the closest warehouse to the customer, regardless of where parts are shipped. For instance, if the customer is in Houston, Texas, the closest warehouse to the customer is in Dallas. If the ordered car part actually comes from the California warehouse, the customer still pays freight from Dallas. This pricing policy is called:
   a. FOB origin pricing
   b. basing-point pricing
   c. zone pricing
   d. uniform delivered pricing
   e. freight absorption pricing

_____ 18. The Two-Bit Candy Store is a small retail establishment where all candies are sold for 25 cents per piece, regardless of the candy type or size. This pricing method is known as:
   a. price lining
   b. inflexible pricing
   c. single-price tactic
   d. price bundling
   e. leader pricing

_____ 19. Yolanda owns a yacht dealership and often will sell essentially the same type of yacht to different customers at very different prices. This policy is:
   a. two-part pricing
   b. flexible pricing
   c. illegal
   d. bait and switch
   e. price lining

_____ 20. At the Sports Stop, there are tennis rackets priced at $50, $75, $90, $125, and $250. The Sports Stop has chosen this price line structure because it will:
   a. reach several different target market segments
   b. maintain the product line at the same stage in the product life cycle
   c. result in customers determining a price-quality relationship, thus resulting in more sales of the expensive models
   d. enable the store to carry a larger total inventory
   e. force competitors out of the market

21. Bill's Supermarket is running a special on Kraft Macaroni and Cheese at ten for $2.00 and on corn on the cob at ten for $1.00. This is an example of:
   a. price bundling
   b. leader pricing
   c. price lining
   d. psychological pricing
   e. variable pricing

22. Microsoft offers spreadsheet software, word processing software, and graphics software as part of its "Microsoft Office" suite of products. This is an example of:
   a. price lining
   b. multi-part pricing
   c. psychological pricing
   d. basing-point pricing
   e. price bundling

23. The U-Storem facility charges a monthly warehouse fee of $25 for each ten-foot-square storage unit. In addition, each time a customer needs to enter the security-locked warehouse to add or remove products, the customer is charged $5. The U-Storem facility is using a pricing tactic known as:
   a. multiple unit pricing
   b. variable pricing
   c. price lining
   d. two-part pricing
   e. price bundling

4 Discuss product line pricing

24. When deciding on prices for an entire product line, the manager should consider all of the following EXCEPT whether the:
   a. products in the line could be substitutes for one another
   b. products will affect demand for the other product lines
   c. products share joint costs
   d. buyer considers the brand or the price first
   e. products in the line are complementary to one another

5 Describe the role of pricing during periods of inflation and recession

25. The government is requesting one dozen military tilt-rotor flying vehicles. It will take approximately four years for manufacturing and order filling by an aircraft company. Delayed-quotation pricing will be used because:
   a. the seller will place a later date on the product invoice to help accounts receivable in recording transactions
   b. flexible price-shading can then take place
   c. it will prevent a competitor from submitting an earlier bid
   d. submitting a bid after the closing date is possible
   e. it allows the final selling price to reflect cost increases incurred between the time the order is placed and the final delivery date

26. The Tempo Textile mill is writing up a contract with NASA for a heat-resistant space fabric that will take two years to design, test, and manufacture. Tempo has added an escalator clause to the contract, which is:
   a. similar to delayed-quotation pricing
   b. a demand-oriented pricing tactic
   c. similar to price shading
   d. a form of market penetration pricing
   e. also called "postage stamp" pricing

27. The salespeople at Piffle Printers routinely use discounts to increase demand for one or more products in a line, especially during times of inflation when customers are more price sensitive. This practice is called:
    a. escalator pricing
    b. price shading
    c. bid pricing
    d. delayed quotation
    e. proposition specification

Check your answers to these questions before proceeding to the next section.

SCENARIO

Read the marketing scenario and answer the questions that follow.

Toni is the product manager of a packaged gelato-style ice cream called "Diamante." Diamante competes in the same super-premium market segment as Ben & Jerry's, Haagen-Hazs, and Godiva. Diamante offers a variety of flavours, including espresso bean made with real espresso coffee and chocolate-covered espresso beans and zuppa made with cake and strawberry-flavoured gelato. All the ice cream flavours are sold in pint-size round containers for the same price.

Diamante is priced even higher than its competitors and is distributed in specialty markets, not in regular supermarkets. However, Toni offers a variety of pricing deals to the dealers who carry her ice cream. Retailers who pay bills within thirty days receive a two percent discount on the price. In addition, Toni provides a discount to retailers who promote her product during special seasons, such as the winter holidays.

True/False:

1. As the high-price leader in the ice cream segment, Diamante uses a penetration pricing strategy.

2. Diamante also uses a single-price tactic.

3. Toni's offering of a two percent discount to retailers who are able to pay their bills within thirty days is a form of illegal price discrimination.

Multiple Choice:

4. Diamante's high-price strategy will only work if:

    a. competitors do the same thing.
    b. retailers don't take a big mark-up.
    c. the market is willing to pay for the product.
    d. the product quality is significantly better.
    e. the company can keep its costs to a minimum

5. The two percent discount that Toni provides to retailers is called:

    a. a promotional allowance.
    b. a cash discount.
    c. a rebate.
    d. a seasonal discount.
    e. a trade discount.

6. The discount that Toni gives to retailers who promote her product during special holidays is called:

    a. a promotional allowance.
    b. a cash discount.
    c. a rebate.
    d. a seasonal discount.
    e. a trade allowance.

7. Which of the following actions would be considered illegal?

    a. Toni offers a discount to EJ's Fine Foods but not to Greg's Gourmet because EJ's buys a larger quantity.
    b. Toni checks a gourmet food chain for the retail price of her competitors and decides to price her products the same way.
    c. Toni undercuts her competitors' prices for a brief period of time to get higher market share.
    d. Toni meets with marketing managers from Ben & Jerry's to agree upon a price to charge for their products.
    e. None of these practices is illegal.

Short Answer:

8. What other types of pricing tactics could Toni use that will not damage the product's premium image?

ESSAY QUESTIONS

1. You are the marketing manager for a new athletic shoe company that offers trendy but functional shoes. You are in the process of deciding how to price your shoes. Using the four-step process of price setting, determine how you would achieve the right price.

2. List and define the three basic methods for setting a price on a new good or service. For each method, name advantages and disadvantages of using that method.

3. Many sellers sell their products to customers that are geographically dispersed, resulting in significant freight costs. Define four types of geographic pricing tactics that can be selected by a marketing manager to moderate the impact of freight costs on distant customers. For each tactic defined, specify the circumstances that would prompt the selection of that particular pricing method, and then give specific examples of products that are commonly priced in that manner.

4.   Marketing managers can use a wide variety of special pricing tactics to fine-tune prices. Name and define six of these special pricing tactics. For each tactic, give an example of a company, industry, or product that would use the tactic. Then give advantages and disadvantages of using each tactic.

5.   What conditions should exist when using product price lining as a strategy? What types of products are typically price lined?

6. You work for a luxury car manufacturer located in Canada. Unfortunately for your company, the country has just gone into a recession, and you fear that sales of the luxury vehicles will drop dramatically as consumer confidence in the economy decreases. Using the two possible tactics for pricing during a recession, what could you do?

APPLICATION

The FabLam Corporation manufactures three types of laminating machines: portable, vending, and desktop. The joint costs of land leasing, production equipment leases, insurance, and so on are allocated on an equal basis to the three types of machines sold. Last year's sales figures and allocated joint costs follow. Should FabLam stop selling its portable machine? Why or why not?

	Portable	Vending	Desktop
Sales	$40,000	$80,000	$90,000
Less: Cost of goods sold	50,000	50,000	50,000
Gross margin	($10,000)	$30,000	$40,000

LEARNING OBJECTIVES

1   Define one-to-one marketing and discuss its dependence on database technology

One-to-one marketing is an individualized marketing method that utilizes customer information to build long-term, personalized, and profitable relationships with each customer. Database technology makes it possible for companies to interact with customers on a personal, one-to-one basis. A database stores pertinent information about a company's customers and contacts and makes it readily available to the sales and marketing staff for assessing, analyzing, and anticipating customers' needs. Database technology allows marketers to sift through the millions of pieces of data to target the right customers, to develop the right communication based on these customer needs, and to monitor the ongoing relationship, making adjustments in message strategy as needed.

2   Discuss the forces that have influenced the emergence of one-to-one marketing

Many factors have influenced the emergence of one-to-one marketing. The desire for personalization of both product and communications has been addressed in the previous objective. Other factors include changes in demographic and behavioural characteristics that have produced a more fragmented, individualistic market.

3   Compare the one-to-one marketing communications process to the traditional marketing communications process

One-to-one marketing communications differs from the traditional marketing communications process because it addresses consumer informational needs on an individual basis. Therefore, there is less opportunity for environmental noise to interfere with the communication. In addition, the response to the message is measurable.

4   List eight common one-to-one marketing applications

Common marketing applications of customer databases include: 1) identifying profitable customers; 2) retaining loyal customers; 3) cross-selling other products or services; 4) designing targeted marketing communications; 5) reinforcing consumer decisions; 6) inducing product trial by new customers; 7) increasing the effectiveness of distribution channel marketing; and 8) improving customer service.

5   Discuss the basics of one-to-one marketing database technology

A database is a collection of data, especially one that can be accessed and manipulated by computer software. A marketing database is the compilation of names, addresses, and other pieces of pertinent information about individual customers and prospects that affects what and how marketers sell to them.

6   Describe the impact of the Internet on business practices

The Internet represents a new electronic channel to conduct a wide variety of marketing activities. Companies that embrace Internet technology can gain advantages associated with lower infrastructure, inventory, and transaction costs. The Internet also provides excellent opportunities for conducting marketing research. Tremendous amounts of secondary data are readily available, and the Internet allows for relatively easy collection of primary data in the form of e-mail surveys, Web-based surveys with graphics and multimedia, and on-line focus groups. Additional information related to the purchases of individual customers can be used to build profiles of customer preferences, and competitor information can be collected from direct observation or through shopping bots.

By using the Internet, consumers can access a greater variety of information before a purchase decision is made. For businesses, the Internet provides a tool for building better relationships with suppliers and customers. Every company must address the issue of whether or not it should have an Internet presence. For most companies, Internet marketing can be used to augment existing marketing programs. Planning the Internet marketing program involves analyzing the Internet marketing environment, articulating the company's on-line business strategy, and setting specific Internet marketing objectives and strategies.

---

7 Describe the current Internet marketing environment

Most Internet business activity can be distinguished as either business-to-consumer (B2C) electronic commerce or business-to-business (B2B) electronic commerce. In either case, knowing the on-line habits of the target market is essential. On-line buyers can be characterized as early adopters, the mainstream, and laggards.

One way to identify and target specific markets is through virtual communities, which include members who have a common interest, such as a hobby, sport, or other avocation. These virtual communities use bulletin boards, chat rooms, newsletters, or discussion lists to build social relationships and exchange information. By overcoming the physical distance that separates markets around the world, the Internet also facilitates targeting international markets. To be successful, organizations need to develop a global vision that recognizes social, cultural, economic, political, demographic, resource, infrastructural, and legal differences.

As communications and products become more digitized, diverse electronic technologies will converge and combine into a single high-speed communication and distribution channel that will carry broadband content to telephones, televisions, and computers. These technological advances will create new marketing opportunities.

8 Discuss on-line business strategies

To be successful, Web-based companies must develop sound business and marketing strategies. The Internet business strategy should start with a high-level goal and consider ways the Internet can be used to achieve that goal. This goal will determine the sophistication of the Internet presence and the desired level of interactivity, which can range from a purely informational corporate Web site to a fully interactive or transactional Web site.

Transactional Web sites are capable of implementing complex on-line business models. Three basic business models include direct selling models, Internet retailing models, and Internet marketplaces. Direct sellers can be product manufacturers such as Dell that use the Internet to sell directly to consumers. Producers of digital products including software, music, and information can use the Internet to both sell and distribute products directly to consumers.

Internet retailers and e-marketplaces provide the added convenience of a wide variety of products with easy access to price-comparison information. Despite these conveniences, however, drawbacks include lack of direct contact with the merchandise, reduced social interaction, and some difficulties resolving customer service complaints.

9 Discuss Internet marketing objectives and strategies

A company's Internet objectives can include improved communication, building traffic and establishing new market segments, promotion, personalized service, and distribution. Depending on the objective, Internet strategies will vary. The Internet can be used to improve communications with customers, providing access to inventory information, status of orders, new-product, recall, replacement or answering FAQs. On-line registration and transactions provide new sources of information and speed the buying-selling process.

On-line promotions include price specials, coupons, contests, newsletters, banner ads, and interstitial ads. Search engine registration builds on-line consumer awareness and recognition.

Clickstream data and cookie technology provide on-line businesses with valuable information about consumer behaviour but also raise concerns about consumer privacy.

10 Discuss one-to-one marketing using the Internet

The Internet offers the means by which marketers can interact with customers and potential customers on a one-to-one basis. The difficulty is in striking a balance between relationship development and intruding on the customer's privacy, a practice referred to as spamming.

11 Discuss privacy issues related to one-to-one and Internet marketing

Privacy concerns centre on the vast amounts of customer information collected and stored in marketing databases. Consumers are alarmed about the dissemination of this information without their knowledge or consent.

Answer the following questions to see how well you understand the material. Re-take it after you review to check yourself.

1. List six forces that have influenced the emergence of one-to-one marketing.

2. How is the communications process different in one-to-one marketing than in traditional marketing?

3. List eight common applications of marketing databases.

4. List the ways that the Internet affects business practices.

5. List three primary ways the Internet can be used to conduct marketing research.

6. List and briefly describe the three main on-line promotion alternatives.

---

1 Define one-to-one marketing and discuss its dependence on database technology

I. What is "One-To-One marketing?"

One-to-one marketing is an individualized marketing method that focuses on *share of customer* rather than *share of market*.

A. The Evolution of One-To-One Marketing

1. Prior to the Industrial Revolution, small merchants knew their customers and often customized goods to better suit their needs.

2. Mass production introduced the concept of "make and sell." All customers were perceived as having the same needs.

3. In the 1990's customers demanded the ability to buy precisely what met their individual needs and wants.

B. Why One-to-One Marketing Needs Database Technology

Database technology enables marketers to really communicate with their customers one at a time.

---

1. One-to-one marketing using *database technology* is preplanned and consciously executed.

2. Database technology allows marketers to get to know their customers on a personal one-to-one basis.

3. Developing databases for one-to-one marketing efforts can be expensive, but the return on investment can be huge.

2 Discuss the forces that have influenced the emergence of one-to-one marketing

II. Forces Influencing One-To-One Marketing

A. Increasing diversity of the family, and more importantly, the acceptance of diversity.

B. Consumers have less and less time to spend. Therefore they have become more demanding and more impatient.

1. Increased use of catalogues

2. Growth of Internet retailing

C. Decreasing brand loyalty can be attributed to excessive couponing and other "deals" proliferation of brands, and increased retailer power.

1. More emphasis on price and value

2. Relationship building with the retailer rather than brand

D. Emergence of new media alternatives.

E. The demand for advertising accountability as reflected by sales.

F. The impact of these trends is that today's consumer wants to be recognized as an individual requiring:

1. Satisfaction of unique needs and wants

2. More direct and personal marketing efforts

3. Loyalty to be rewarded

One-to-one marketing will increase in importance

3 Compare the one-to-one marketing communications process to the traditional marketing communications process

III. A Revised Marketing Communications Process

A. The revised **one-to-one marketing communications process** flows as follows:

1. The *sender* encodes individualized messages for customers and prospects identified from the database.

2. The message is then sent through a direct communications channel.

3. The customer or prospect, *receiver*, interprets the personalized message.

4. The customer or prospect responds to the communication.

5. The one-to-one marketer captures the response, feeding it back into the database.

B. Major differences between the traditional and revised communications process include:

1. Personalization of the message

2. Use of a direct channel

3. Near elimination of noise

4. Ability to capture the individual's response

4   List eight common one-to-one marketing applications

IV. One-To-One Database Marketing Applications

A marketing database is a *tool* that helps marketers reach customers and prospects with one-to-one marketing communications.

A. Identify the most profitable customers

Customers are most likely to purchase again because they have bought most recently, bought most frequently, or spent a specified amount of money.

B. Retain loyal customers

Loyalty programs reward loyal consumers for making multiple purchases.

C. Cross-sell other products or services

A database allows marketers to match product profiles and consumer profiles to cross-sell customers other products that match their demographic, lifestyle, or behavioural characteristics.

D. Design targeted marketing communications

Using transaction and purchase data in addition to personal or demographic information allows marketers to tailor a message.

E. Reinforce consumer purchase decisions

A database offers marketers an opportunity to reach out to customers to reinforce the purchase decision.

F. Induce product trial by new customers

Using the profile of its best customers, marketers can easily find new customers that look like its most profitable segment.

G. Increase the effectiveness of distribution channel marketing

Marketing databases enable manufacturers to advise retailers how to better meet customer needs, and make it possible to serve customers using direct channels instead of the traditional indirect channels.

H. Improve customer service

One-to-one marketing techniques are increasingly being used to improve the customer service.

5 Discuss the basics of one-to-one marketing database technology

V. The Basics of Marketing Database Technology

A. The **database development process** incorporates strategic planning as well as technical input.

1. One-to-one marketing using database technology is commonly referred to as **data driven marketing**.

2. A **database** is a collection of data, especially one that can be accessed and manipulated by computer software. A **marketing database** is the compilation of names, addresses, and other pieces of pertinent information about individual customers and prospects that affects what and how marketers sell to them. A data warehouse is a very large, corporate wide database culled from a number of separate systems.

B. Building a marketing database requires collecting the right data

1. *Internal data* is information a company captures and hopefully stores while it conducts business. Internal data consists of customer data, transaction information, product information, salesperson information, offer information, and response data.

   a. A **response list** includes the names and addresses of individuals who have responded to an offer of some kind.

   b. A **compiled list** generally includes names and addresses gleaned from telephone directories or membership rosters.

C. **Database enhancement** is the overlay of information to customer or prospect records for the purpose of better describing or better determining the responsiveness of customers or prospects.

1. Three reasons to use enhancements are to:

   a. Learn more about customers or prospects.
   b. Increase the effectiveness of customer marketing programs.
   c. Match profiles of best customers with those of prospects.

2. Sources of enhancement data are

   a. **Compiled data** includes names and addresses gleaned from telephone directories and membership rosters.
   b. **Modelled data** is information that has already been sorted into distinct groups or clusters of consumers or businesses based on census, household, or business-level data.
   c. **Customer data** could include such things as customer surveys, customer participation programs, product registration, warranty cards, or loyalty marketing programs.

D. One of the most important aspects of one-to-one marketing is the ability to analyze the data to profile the best customers or segments of customers, determine their lifetime value, and ultimately, to predict their purchasing behaviour through statistical modelling.

1. *Customer segmentation* is the process of breaking large groups of customers into smaller, more homogeneous groups.

2. **Recency, frequency, and monetary analysis (RFM)** is most commonly used to define a firm's best customers. Many marketers take RFM analysis one step further by introducing *profitability* into the equation.

---

3. **Lifetime value analysis (LTV)** projects the future value of the customer over a period of years.

4. Through **predictive modelling**, marketers try to determine what the odds are that some other occurrence will take place in the future. The occurrence the marketer is trying to predict is described by the *dependent variable*. The *independent variables* are the things that affect the dependent variable.

5. **Data mining** is the process of using statistical analysis to detect relevant purchasing behaviour patterns in a database.

6 Describe the Impact of the Internet on business practices

VI.

A. Electronic marketing channel

1. The Internet represents a new electronic channel for advertising, customer service, marketing research, transactions, and distribution.

2. The Internet provides opportunities to improve customer relationships.

B. Financial Implications of the Internet

1. On-line stores are challenging established brick-and-mortar stores

2. New technologies have resulted in creation of entirely new industries

3. Internet technology allow even small businesses to establish a presence in e-commerce

4. On-line purchasing is reducing costs for many businesses

C. Marketing Research through the Web

1. Easier access to secondary information from around the world

   a. Provides more current information
   b. Allows complex searches
   c. Incorporates multimedia
   d. Lower publication costs

2. Revolutionizes primary data collection

   a. Web-based surveys
   b. Cyber focus groups

3. Valuable competitive intelligence tool

4. Allows opportunities for on-line price comparisons with competitors

D. Integrating Conventional and Internet Marketing Strategies
Integrating conventional and Internet marketing strategies should include consideration of:

1. analysis of the Internet marketing environment

2. statement of the company's on-line business strategy

3. specific Internet marketing objectives and strategies

7 Describe the current Internet marketing environment

VII. The Internet is still a new frontier attracting many kinds of explorers.
   A. Basic Forms of Virtual Business

1. Business-to-consumer (B2C) electronic commerce

2. Business-to-business (B2B) electronic commerce

   B. Internet Demographics and Trends

1. Almost two-thirds of Canadians users have access to the internet.

2. The "digital divide" between upper-income, educated Internet users and non-users is narrowing.

3. In Canada, internet usage is about equal between men and women, but the growth potential is higher among women.

4. Internet buyers are divided into early adopters, mainstream, and laggards depending on how quickly they embraced Internet commerce. Marketing strategies differ among the groups.

5. Marketers must use both push and pull strategies to get people to their web sites.

   C. The Global Village

1. The Internet is helping to overcome physical distance separating people around the world.

2. Marketers need to be sensitive to cultural, economic, political, demographic, legal, resource, and infrastructure differences among members of the global village.

8 Discuss on-line business strategies

VIII. On-line Business Strategies

You do not have to start big to be successful on the Internet, but with a rapidly changing business climate, on-line marketers need to constantly evaluate and adjust their strategies.

To survive and prosper on the Internet requires companies to:

1. Offer products that fulfill customer needs, wants, or desires

2. Sell your products at a fair price to customers

3. Use promotion to make potential customers aware of your products.

4. Make your products available to customers when and where they want them.

   A. Internet Goals include any of the following and more:

1. Increase or enhance company exposure.

2. Improve customer service

3. Provide new products or services

4. Add value to existing products or services

---

5.   Lower overall costs for the company

6.   Create one-to-one relationships with customers

Goals should be refined along the SMART model discussed in Chapter 2.

B.   Internet Presence

Well-executed web sites position a company relative to the company's target markets.

The most common type of Web site is a corporate Web site—providing consumers with information about the organization.

The interactive or transactional Web site permits two-way communication, facilitates transactions and delivery of electronic products, and collection of information about customers.

C.   Direct Selling Model

1.   The direct selling model eliminates intermediaries between the buyer and seller.

2.   The direct selling model is best suited for selling and distribution of digital products, however some hard-goods companies, like Dell, have excelled at direct selling over the Internet.

D.   Internet Retailing

Internet retailing or e-tailing, is one of the most widely studied areas of Internet marketing. From a buyer's perspective the three differences between Internet shopping and real store purchasing are:

1.   For many people on-line shopping is more convenient.

2.   Consumers cannot touch or feel products

3.   Atmospherics of a store are not present, nor sales staff

E.   Internet Marketplaces

1.   E-marketplaces bring together buyers and sellers, consolidating ordering, bidding, and delivery.

2.   E-marketplaces based on a common interest are called **virtual communities**

a.   Chat rooms, bulletin boards, newsletters or discussion lists all are being used to bring together people with similar interests. Virtual community members develop trust among their members. Opinions, both positive and negative, about a company's products are quickly distributed among virtual communities and strongly influence consumers.

b.   On-line magazines, e-zines, are focused on a particular subject. Advertising on e-zines is a way to target highly interested consumers.

9   Discuss Internet marketing objectives and strategies

IX.   A company's Internet efforts should be consistent with their overall business strategy. On-line objectives, like traditional marketing objectives should be well defined and quantifiable.

A.	Product Strategies on the Web

Certain products, ones which consumers do not feel the need to touch or smell to evaluate, sell better on the Internet. Products consumers consider commodities such as books, golf balls, or tickets are better suited than perfumes, houses, and automobiles. On-line marketers are using virtual tours to overcome consumers' resistance to purchase some products electronically.

Branding is an important tool companies can use to reassure customers and distinguish their products from competitors' offerings. Two-way communication allows on-line marketers to explain and sell their products to consumers.

B.	On-line Distribution Options

Internet-based businesses can use traditional or alternative distribution systems. Digital products can be delivered directly to customers. Electronically connected warehouse systems can expedite distribution. Most Internet retailers arrange for customer orders to be fulfilled from a central warehouse and shipped directly.

C.	On-line Promotion

On-line promotion allows for information-rich content and enables two-way communication.

On-line promotion includes:

1.	Advertisements

   a.	**Banner advertisements** – typically a rectangular ad that runs the full width of the top of a Web page.
   b.	**Button advertisements** – smaller versions of banner ads, but in various sizes and appearing anywhere on the Web page
   c.	**Interstitial advertisements (or pop-up)** – ads that appear in a separate browser while a Web page is loading

2.	E-mail marketing
   a.	**Untargeted (spamming)** – mass electronic junk mailing
   b.	**Targeted e-mail marketing** – mailing to prequalified recipients who are interested in receiving the message

3.	**E-zines** – special interest newsletters that are distributed electronically

D.	Pricing on the Internet

1.	With shopping bots, it is easier for most consumers to do price comparisons on the Internet.

2.	Auctions facilitate the price setting for sellers.

3.	Companies that offer products both on-line and off-line must decide whether to use different prices. Many times on-line purchasing is less expensive for sellers either through reducing labour costs or eliminating middlemen margins. This encourages firms to lower their prices on-line.

E.	Evaluating the Outcome

Evaluating on-line efforts is most commonly captured by measuring **hits** and **page views** and by following visitors' **clickstream**. This can be accomplished through **cookie** technology that allows marketers to track the behaviour of consumers on Web sites.

10 Describe one-to-one marketing using the Internet

X. One-To-One Marketing and the Internet

   A. Internet companies are learning more about their customers and using this information to fine-tune their marketing efforts and build relationships with each customer on a more individual level.
      1. One advantage of on-line one-to-one marketing is the ability to deliver personalized promotional messages to each customer visiting a company's Web site.

      2. When used in conjunction with on-line ad-serving technology, one-to-one marketing has the power to make the Internet an effective and cost-efficient advertising vehicle.

      3. Increasingly, more and more companies are realizing that e-mail is the ideal one-to-one medium, capable of establishing and building enduring customer relationships with a highly targeted lists of prospects.

11 Discuss privacy issues related to one-to-one marketing

XI. Privacy Concerns With One-To-One Marketing

   A. One-to-one marketing concerns many Canadians because of the potential for invasion of privacy. It is critical that marketers remember that these relationships should be built on trust.

   B. The popularity of the Internet for direct marketing, consumer data collection, and as a repository of sensitive consumer data has also alarmed privacy-minded consumers.

   C. Canadian firms must deal with federal legislation in the form of the Personal Information Protection and Electronic Documents Act (PIPED Act), provincial privacy legislation, as well as foreign privacy laws.

VOCABULARY PRACTICE

Fill in the blank(s) with the appropriate term or phrase from the alphabetized list of chapter key terms.

banner advertisements	hit
business-to-business electronic commerce (B2B)	interactive Web site
business-to-consumer electronic commerce (B2C)	interstitial advertisement
button advertisements	lifetime value (LTV) analysis
clickstream	marketing database
compiled list	modeled data
cookie	one-to-one marketing
corporate Web site	one-to-one marketing communication process
custom data	page view
database	predictive modeling
database enhancement	recency, frequency, and monetary (RFM) analysis
data-driven marketing	response list
data mining	targeted e-mail marketing
e-marketplace	untargeted e-mail marketing
e-tailing	virtual community
e-zine	

1 Define one-to-one marketing and discuss its dependence on database technology

1. A customer-based, information-intensive, and long-term-oriented, individualized marketing method that focuses on share of customer rather than share of product is called _____.

2 Discuss the forces that have influenced the emergence of one-to-one marketing

2. The _____ is a revised marketing communications process that is characterized by the use of personalized communication, the lack of interfering noise, and the ability to capture the response of the customer.

5 Discuss the basics of one-to-one marketing database technology

3. The process of gathering, maintaining, and analyzing information about customers and prospects to implement more efficient and effective marketing communications is known as _____. At the core of this is a _____, which is a collection of data, especially one that can be assessed and manipulated by computer software. A _____ is a compilation of names, addresses, and other pieces of pertinent information about individual customers and prospects that affects what and how marketers sell to them.

4. Databases can be created from a _____ which includes the names and addresses of individuals who have responded to an offer of some kind, such as by mail or through product rebates. Other firms create a database from a _____, a customer list that is developed by gathering names and addresses from telephone directories and membership rosters.

5. _____ is the overlay of information on customer or prospect records for the purpose of better describing or better determining the responsiveness of customers of prospects. One form of this data is called _____ _____, or information that has been sorted into distinct groups or clusters of consumers or businesses based on census, household, or business level data. Another type of data that could be used to build a database is _____, which is acquired by the marketer through customer surveys, customer participation programs, product registration, warranty cards, or loyalty marketing programs.

6. By manipulating data, marketers can find answers to decision points. One manipulation technique that can be used is called _____, which determines the firm's best customers by identifying those customers who have purchased most recently, most frequently, and who have spent the most money. Another manipulation technique is _____, which projects the future value of the customer over a period of years. Yet another technique, called _____, helps marketers determine, based on some set of past occurrences, what the odds are that some other occurrence will take place in the future. A final data manipulation technique is _____, or the process of using statistical analysis to detect relevant purchasing behaviour patterns in a database.

6 Describe the Impact of the Internet on business practices

7. Using the Internet to conduct business between an organization and individual consumers is called _____, while use of the Internet to conduct business between two or more organizations is _____.

7 Discuss on-line business strategies

8. A _____ is a special type of e-marketplace, or a group of people with a common interest who interact on and contribute content to a communal Web site. Similarly, electronic magazines or _____ focus on a particular topic and provide advertising opportunities for marketers of relevant products.

9. A_____ provides information about the company but provides little opportunity to communicate with the organization. _____ permits two-way electronic communication between an organization and its customers.

10. Internet retailing has been shortened to _____, and a group of retailers on a Web site is called an _____.

9 Discuss Internet marketing objectives and strategies

11. The sequence in which a person visited a Web site provides _____ data.

12. Paid advertisements usually on the bottom or top of a Web page are _____, while smaller ads placed on the side or in the text are called _____.

13. Advertisements that appear on a separate browser are called pop-ups or _____.

14. E-mail to "unqualified" e-mail addresses is called spam or _____, while e-mail to qualified addresses is called _____.

15. A_____ is a record that a file was requested form a Web site, while a _____ records which single page was requested. A _____passes electronic information from a user's hard drive to the server.

TRUE/FALSE QUESTIONS

Mark the statement **T** if it is true and **F** if it is false.

1 Define one-to-one marketing and discuss its dependence on database technology

_____ 1. The key to successful one-to-one marketing is the effective use of database technology.

2 Discuss the forces that have influenced the emergence of one-to-one marketing

_____ 2. An increase in brand loyalty has helped the emergence of one-to-one marketing.

_____ 3. Marketers must work harder to get consumers' attention because of the diversity of needs and competition for their attention.

3 Compare the one-to-one marketing communications process to the traditional mass marketing communications process

___ 4. One of the key differences in the communications process of one-to-one marketing is that it generally involves less noise.

___ 5. One-to-one marketing does not use mass media to reach customers.

4 List eight common one-to-one marketing applications

___ 6. When consumers log onto the Web site of Amazon.com, they are greeted by name and provided a list of books that they might be interested in purchasing based on past purchases. This is an example of retaining loyal customers.

___ 7. An Internet marketer of fresh flowers sends a message to all new customers that they will have the satisfaction of knowing that the flowers will arrive to the recipient's house on time and that they recipient will be pleased. This is an example of reinforcing consumer purchase decisions.

5 Discuss the basics of one-to-one marketing database technology

___ 8. Ed's Electronics store has gathered the names and addressed of individuals who responded to the store's latest advertisement through the purchase of an electronics product. The store plans to use this list in subsequent promotions. This list is an example of a response list.

___ 9. An e-business collects customer data each time a customer purchases an item on-line. The business uses this data to project the future value of each customer over a period of years. The e-business is conducting recency-frequency-monetary analysis.

6 Describe the Impact of the Internet on business practices

___ 10. The Internet is just another way to advertise.

___ 11. The Internet provides financial advantages almost exclusively to large corporations.

___ 12. It is usually easier, faster, and less expensive to conduct an e-mail survey than a mail survey.

7 Describe the current Internet marketing environment

___ 13. The "digital divide" refers to the differences in technological expertise among Internet users.

___ 14. Attitudes toward Internet usage are influenced by attitudes toward technology, income, and motivation to use technology.

___ 15. Universal electronic translators overcome the problem of different languages around the world.

___ 16. The Internet can eliminate disadvantages of doing business in developing countries.

___ 17. One of the winners in Internet commerce have been firms providing just-in-time delivery to customers.

8 Discuss on-line business strategies

___ 18. One advantage of small Internet companies is they tend to be more agile, able to respond quickly to the changing market conditions of the electronic marketplace.

___ 19. Web marketers have found that if they build a good Web site people will find out about it and visit the site.

_____ 20. The advantage of a corporate Web site is you do not have to listen to consumers.

_____ 21. Interactive Web sites are more expensive to create and maintain than corporate sites.

_____ 22. The Internet is particularly well suited for direct selling and distribution of digital products.

_____ 23. E-tailing is the sale of electronic and digital products over the Internet.

9 Discuss Internet marketing objectives and strategies

_____ 24. Clickstream data allow Internet marketers to analyze which pages were viewed, in which order and for how long.

_____ 25. The Internet is better suited to sell customized products than commodities.

_____ 26. Branding is not important to Internet marketers because people can see the product on the Web site.

_____ 27. Internet marketing often reduces the length of distribution channels.

_____ 28. The Internet allows marketers to provide greater content in their advertising compared to most traditional media.

_____ 29. Buttons are better than banners because they bigger.

_____ 30. Spam is sending e-mail to "unqualified" e-mail addresses.

_____ 31. Because it is easy to do price comparisons on the Internet, Web marketers should always offer lower prices on their Web sites than in their stores.

_____ 32. A hit is a better measure of Web site visitors because it records when a file has been requested.

_____ 33. Bulletin boards, chat rooms, and electronic newsletters are all examples of coordinated clickstreams.

11 Discuss privacy issues related to one-to-one marketing

_____ 34. Privacy issues are not a primary concern of customers who are targeted through one-on-one marketing.

Check your answers to these questions before proceeding to the next section.

AGREE/DISAGREE QUESTIONS

For the following statements, indicate reasons why you may agree and disagree with the statement.

1. One-to-one marketing will eventually take over mass marketing.

Reason(s) to agree:

Reason(s) to disagree:

2. One-to-one marketing is more conducive to business marketing than to consumer marketing.

   Reason(s) to agree:

   Reason(s) to disagree:

3. Without database technology, one-to-one marketing would not be possible.

   Reason(s) to agree:

   Reason(s) to disagree:

4. Consumer concerns over privacy will make one-to-one marketing more difficult in the future.

   Reason(s) to agree:

   Reason(s) to disagree:

5. The Internet has made marketing much easier.

   Reason(s) to agree:

   Reason(s) to disagree:

6. Marketing research conducted on-line can be biased and unscientific.

Reason(s) to agree:

Reason(s) to disagree:

7. The Internet has changed how marketers work with the four Ps.

Reason(s) to agree:

Reason(s) to disagree:

MULTIPLE CHOICE QUESTIONS

Select the response that best answers the question, and write the corresponding letter in the space provided.

1 Define one-to-one marketing and discuss its dependence on database technology

_____ 1. Which of the following is NOT a characteristic of one-to-one marketing?
a. it is long-term-oriented
b. it focuses on market share
c. it is individualized
d. it is customer-based
e. it is information-intensive

2 Discuss the forces that have influenced the emergence of one-to-one marketing

_____ 2. All of the following have influenced the emergence of one-to-one marketing EXCEPT:
a. new technology to lower production costs
b. the increasing diversity of the Canadian population
c. the demand for accountability
d. decreasing brand loyalty
e. new media alternatives

_____ 3. The decline in brand loyalty can be attributed to:
a. excessive sales promotions
b. the increasing power of retailers
c. the proliferation of brands available
d. none of these
e. all of these

3 Compare the one-to-one marketing communications process to the traditional mass marketing communications process

_____ 4. The communications process for one-to-one marketing differs from that of traditional marketing in that the former:
   a. does not involve message encoding
   b. contains less "noise"
   c. utilizes the Internet
   d. has not require translation of the message
   e. requires no marketing research

_____ 5. Andrea's favourite Web site is a music retailer that offers the largest variety of music in the world. Each time she logs onto the Web site, she receives a personalized message that suggests that she consider buying CDs by new jazz artists, based on her past jazz purchases. Andrea reads and interprets the message before deciding what to do. Andrea is in the act of:
   a. encoding
   b. providing feedback
   c. decoding
   d. channelling
   e. receiving

4 List eight common one-to-one marketing applications

_____ 6. Which of the following is NOT a common application of one-to-one marketing?
   a. retaining loyal customers
   b. identifying the best customers
   c. maintaining control over brand equity
   d. providing sales leads to telemarketers
   e. inducing product trial by new customers

_____ 7. Many high-end hotel chains award "points" for every dollar spent in one of their hotels. Customers who earn a high number of points are given special privileges that may include upgraded hotel rooms or several free nights. This application of one-to-one marketing is an example of:
   a. retaining loyal customers
   b. reinforcing customer purchase decisions
   c. maintaining control over brand equity
   d. designing targeted marketing communications
   e. inducing product trial by new customers

_____ 8. When a customer buys one of its cars, a Neptune Motor Company dealership sends out the entire team that was responsible for handling the customer's business. The team congratulates the customer for his/her purchase in a small celebration. This is an example of:
   a. increasing the effectiveness of distribution channel marketing
   b. reinforcing customer purchase decisions
   c. identifying the best customers
   d. designing targeted marketing communications
   e. inducing product trial by new customers

_____ 9. An Internet music seller has noticed through your past purchases that you are interested in alternative rock. As a result, each time you log into the music seller's Web site, you are greeted with a list of suggested best sellers in the area of alternative rock. This is done in an attempt to:
   a. increase the effectiveness of distribution channel marketing
   b. reinforce customer purchase decisions
   c. cross-sell other products
   d. maintain control over brand equity
   e. induce product trial by new customers

_____ 10. The compilation of names, addresses, and other pieces of pertinent information about individual customers and prospects that affects what and how marketers sell to them is called a:
   a. marketing intelligence system
   b. marketing database
   c. predictive model
   d. data mart
   e. data mine

_____ 11. Evan recently purchased a new CD player with a $100 rebate offer. He completed the rebate certificate and sent it to the manufacturer. The rebate certificate contained Evan's full name, his phone number, his address, and some purchase information. Evan has most likely become part of the manufacturer's:
   a. data mine
   b. demographic list
   c. compiled list
   d. data mart
   e. response list

_____ 12. As a member of a professional women's association, Sarah receives special offers from women's clothing catalogue companies that specialize in business clothing. Sarah is most likely part of a:
   a. data mine
   b. demographic list
   c. compiled list
   d. data mart
   e. response list

_____ 13. The PSYTE database breaks down Canadian neighbourhoods into 60 distinct clusters based on over 250 demographic and consumer behaviour variables. This form of data enhancement is an example of:
   a. predictive modeling
   b. custom data
   c. lifetime value analysis
   d. modelled data
   e. recency-frequency-monetary analysis

_____ 14. A greeting card company gave away a free card to any customer who purchased two cards and completed a small questionnaire on the back of the coupon. The coupon captured the customer's name, address, phone number, birthday, and several pieces of information about purchasing behaviour. The data received by the card company is an example of:
   a. predictive modelling
   b. custom data
   c. lifetime value analysis
   d. modelled data
   e. recency-frequency-monetary analysis

_____ 15. An Internet travel agency would like to build a database of customers who spent over $5,000 in airline ticket purchases. The company should consider conducting:
   a. predictive modelling
   b. a custom data analysis
   c. a lifetime value analysis
   d. a modelled data analysis
   e. a recency-frequency-monetary analysis

_____ 16. A luxury car company has enjoyed repeat purchases from its most loyal customers and calculates the "value" of its most loyal customers at over $300,000. The car company has conducted:
   a. predictive modelling
   b. a custom data analysis
   c. a lifetime value analysis
   d. a modelled data analysis
   e. a recency-frequency-monetary analysis

6   Describe the Impact of the Internet on business practices

_____ 17. The Internet is a means of :
    a. advertising
    b. providing customer service
    c. conducting marketing research
    d. distribution of goods and services
    e. all of the above and more

_____ 18. Teresa has developed a system to keep track of all the information she has collected about her customers. Whenever a customer calls, e-mails, or makes an appointment to visit anyone in her company, they can access this information and use it to better serve customer needs. This is an example of using electronic technology to:
    a. build and improve relationships with customers
    b. advertise directly to customers
    c. adjust pricing strategies
    d. spam
    e. shop on-line

_____ 19. Lower start-up costs for Internet-based businesses:
    a. justify greater government supervision
    b. reduce barriers to entry increasing competition
    c. are a myth
    d. increase the importance of data gathering
    e. do all of these

_____ 20. Web-based surveys have the advantage over mail surveys of:
    a. costing less to design
    b. allowing respondents to alter the survey instrument
    c. allowing the use of graphics and multi-media in the survey
    d. reaching more people in the population
    e. all of these are advantages of Web-based surveys

7   Describe the current Internet marketing environment

_____ 21. The "digital divide" refers to:
    a. male engineers between 18 and 35 years of age
    b. college students
    c. professional versus non-professionals
    d. professionals with post graduate degrees
    e. those who have and do not have access to the Internet

_____ 22. The manager at Sandpiper Assisted Living Home has just purchased computers for the use of residents in the complex. She would like to help residents use the Internet to shop for things they are no longer able to go to stores and purchase, but she knows on-line buying behavior is influenced by:
    a. peoples' attitudes toward technology
    b. income
    c. motivation to use technology
    d. familiarity with technology
    e. all of the influence on-line buying behaviours

_____ 23. Which of the following is NOT a factor creating conflict in expansion of the global Internet village?
    a. cultural differences
    b. economic differences
    c. demographic differences
    d. mortality differences
    e. legal differences

24. The Internet can help developing countries in all of these ways EXCEPT:
    a. it is relatively cheap
    b. versatile
    c. technically efficient
    d. allow access to global markets
    e. it overcomes language barriers

25. Moving from atoms to bits refers to:
    a. nuclear energy
    b. growth of the global village from the large countries to all parts of the universe
    c. the transition from physical to information resources
    d. sub-atomic analysis of market conditions
    e. all of these are issues related to moving from atoms to bits

8 Discuss on-line business strategies

26. Abby knows it will be equally difficult to survive as an Internet business or a bricks and mortar business. To better her chances as an Internet business she know she will need to:
    a. offer products the fulfill customer needs, wants, and desires
    b. sell her products at a competitive price
    c. use promotion to make people aware of her business and products
    d. develop a distribution system to provide products when and where people want them
    e. do all of these

27. Fred is a sole proprietor with customers living primarily in the 200 km radius around his small town in Winnipeg. He receives calls from so many customers that it often takes him days to get back to each customer. Fred could use the Internet primarily to meet which goal?
    a. provide new products and services
    b. lower overall costs
    c. increase company exposure
    d. improve customer service
    e. mass-customization

28. Which of the following products is best suited for selling over the Internet?
    a. Canadian Business Street Journal
    b. laser eye surgery
    c. herbs
    d. home construction
    e. all are equally suited for selling over the Internet

9 Discuss Internet marketing objectives and strategies

29. Bill puts a counter on his new business Web site and within a week has 1,000 hits. This means:
    a. the demographics of Internet users is consistent with his forecast
    b. 1,000 of the files on his Web site have been requested.
    c. 1,000 people have visited his Web site
    d. 1,000 people will be ordering his product.
    e. nothing; you cannot tell anything from hits.

30. Branding is important for Internet marketers because it:
    a. allows sellers to increase their price
    b. shows people where to look on the Internet
    c. helps overcome consumer reluctance in on-line sales.
    d. provides an implicit warranty to consumers
    e. allow businesses to reduce overhead costs

31. Many airlines use the Internet to offer last-minute price discounts. The airlines probably recognize:
    a. on-line consumers are last-minute buyers
    b. on-line consumers are more price-sensitive than traditional consumers
    c. Internet costs are lower so they pass along the savings to consumers
    d. Federal regulations require them to lower on-line prices
    e. Their pricing structure needs to be fixed.

10 Describe one-to-one marketing using the Internet

_____ 32. All of the following are advantages to using the Internet for one-to-one marketing EXCEPT:
   a. it is less costly than non-Internet one-to-one marketing
   b. e-mail makes one-to-one marketing more convenient
   c. it is easier to create a customer database using the Internet
   d. the Internet reaches virtually everybody
   e. it allows the one-to-one marketer to cross-sell effectively

11 Discuss privacy issues related to one-to-one marketing

_____ 33. Which of the following is NOT true regarding privacy issues with Internet-based marketing?
   a. There is widespread misunderstanding among consumers about existing privacy laws and regulations.
   b. Currently, only financial institutions, doctors, and insurance companies are prohibited from revealing certain information to third-party organizations.
   c. "Spamming" is considered to be a violation of privacy by most consumers.
   d. The government routinely sells huge amounts of personal information to compilers.
   e. It is illegal for marketers and educational institutions to sell information about their customers or students to outside vendors.

_____ 34. The only federal regulation to date that governs privacy issues protects which type of consumer?
   a. Children
   b. Mentally disabled consumers
   c. Senior citizens
   d. College students
   e. Professionals

Check your answers to these questions before proceeding to the next section.

SCENARIO #1

Read the marketing scenario and answer the questions that follow.

E-College is a fictional college that offers several academic programs on-line. A fully accredited educational institution, E-College grants associate degrees, bachelor's degrees, and master's degrees in business, liberal arts, communications, and counselling. E-College was started to meet the needs of adults who work full-time and could not attend a traditional university but who wanted to earn a college degree. Students who participate in the program are assigned a student services professional who provides academic advising, counselling, and other services that are related to non-instructional issues at the college. Students have different instructors for each course and receive personalized attention through e-mail. Research analysts at the college constantly run analyses to determine geographic, demographic, psychographic, and behavioural characteristics of their students. They also try to determine how much impact their students have on the college's future enrolment.

True/False:

_____ 1. E-College uses a mass marketing approach.

_____ 2. The assignment of a single student services professional to each student is an example of how the college is trying to retain a loyal customer.

_____ 3. E-College will most likely be a trendy idea that will disappear within five years.

_____ 4. Which of the following forces probably had the greatest effect on E-College being created?

    a. Increasing diversity.
    b. More demanding, time-poor consumers.
    c. Decreasing brand loyalty.
    d. Demand for accountability.
    e. Decreasing number of traditional institutions.

_____ 5. The analyses that researchers run on demographic, psychographic, and other characteristics of the student body involve what type of analysis?

    a. Customer segmentation analysis.
    b. Recency-frequency-monetary analysis.
    c. Lifetime value analysis.
    d. Predictive modelling.
    e. Analytic modelling.

_____ 6. The analysis that researchers conduct to determine what type of impact current students have on future enrolment is probably best described as:

    a. Customer segmentation analysis.
    b. Recency-frequency-monetary analysis.
    c. Data mining.
    d. Predictive modelling.
    e. Analytic modelling.

_____ 7. E-College uses a variety of one-to-one marketing applications. Which of the following is not mentioned in the above scenario?

    a. Identifying the best customers.
    b. Retaining loyal customers.
    c. Inducing product trial by new customers.
    d. Improving customer service.
    e. All of these are mentioned.

Short Answer:

8. What else could E-College do to enhance its one-to-one marketing effort?

Read the marketing scenario and answer the questions that follow.

Jeff is a marketing manager at E-point, an Internet company that has created an on-line appointment reservation interface. The system can be used by a number of people: medical offices, hair salons, car repair shops, and anywhere else where people tend to make regular appointments. The software enables people to log onto the Internet, connect through E-point with their service provider, say the doctor's office, and view an on-line schedule that shows available appointment times. E-point is a unique offering on the market.

In order to get his company off the ground, Jeff has arranged with portals like Yahoo! and MSN to carry an E-point icon at the bottom of their toolbars. In addition, he has visited many of the large employers to encourage them to require the inclusion of E-point as an option in corporate health insurance packages. Jeff knows that workers who can schedule their appointments on-line will spend less time away from their desk taking care of this personal business.

Service providers would pay E-point a small monthly subscription and a nominal fee for every appointment someone books with them using E-point. There is no cost to the person making the appointment.

True/False:

_____   1.   E-point will not be able to fully leverage the capabilities of the Internet because it is a small company.

_____   2.   The arrangements with Yahoo! and MSN constitute affiliate marketing.

_____   3.   Jeff is engaging in business-to-consumer e-commerce.

Multiple Choice:

_____   4.   The aspects of the Internet marketing environment most likely to affect E-point are:

    a.   competitors do the same thing.
    b.   the elimination of intermediaries.
    c.   the manipulation of multimedia features.
    d.   the development of customer-centric marketing.
    e.   the demographics of Internet users.

_____   5.   Jeff has considered transforming E-point's Web site into a portal where people could exchange information about good service providers, subscribe to a virtual newsletter on time management, and purchase software that allows them to download their full appointment schedules from E-point to their PDAs. Jeff is thinking about making E-point a(n):

    a.   promotional tool.
    b.   virtual community.
    c.   e-tailer.
    d.   cyber marketplace.
    e.   transactional advertiser.

_____   6.   E-point wants to send information about healthcare products to those people who have scheduled appointments with physicians who treat related problems. E-point could avoid potential privacy problems by:

    a.   allowing people to opt-in.
    b.   sending untargeted e-mail message.
    c.   using a group e-mail address.
    d.   sending information e-mails only at certain times of the year.
    e.   only sending information about benign health issues.

7.   Which of the elements of E-point's marketing mix are affected by the Internet?

   a.   product, place, promotion
   b.   place, price, promotion
   c.   product, promotion, price
   d.   product, place, price.
   e.   product, place, promotion, price

<u>Short Answer</u>:

8.   How could Jeff improve his promotional efforts?

ESSAY QUESTIONS

1.   You are a marketing consultant. One of your major clients is a retailer of rugged clothing for hiking, camping, and other sports. Lately, your client has felt that it has lost sales due to its rather unfocused marketing efforts and is intrigued by one-to-one marketing. As the consultant, list some advantages that your client might enjoy from conducting one-to-one marketing.

2.   You are a marketing manager for a vacation resort in Jamaica called "Island Breeze." You have been asked by the vice president of marketing to look into building a marketing database to conduct one-to-one marketing. List eight common uses for this database, and indicate one specific example as it applies to your company.

3. As the general manager for a luxury car dealership, you have built a database that includes all kinds of information about past and current customers. List five data manipulation techniques and indicate by example how each one could be used.

4. You are about to launch your own business and would like to build your own home page on the World Wide Web. What are three elements your Internet marketing plan should include?

5. You are going to give a lecture to marketing students about how new technologies have influenced the four Ps of the marketing mix. What topics should you cover?

Select your favourite on-line shopping Web site. If you have purchased products on the Web site before, simply login and see what kinds of communication you receive from the vendor. If you haven't shopped on-line before, register as a user and potential buyer (you don't have to actually buy the products). Note the following as you review the Web site:

1) Are you personally greeted once you enter the Web site or log on?

2) What other types of communication do you receive as a user?

3) What kinds of information does the Web site request of you? Do you have information that is totally optional?

4) How does the Web site make you "feel?"

5) Other observations:

CHAPTER 18: CUSTOMER RELATIONSHIP MANAGEMENT

1   Define customer relationship management

Customer relationship management (CRM) is a company-wide business strategy designed to optimize revenue, profitability, and customer satisfaction by focusing on highly defined and precise customer groups. This is accomplished by organizing the company around customer segments, encouraging and tracking customer interaction with the company, fostering customer satisfying behaviour, and linking all processes of a company from customers through suppliers.

2   Explain how to establish customer relationships within the organization

Companies that implement a CRM system adhere to a customer-centric focus or model. A customer-centric company builds its system on what satisfies and retains valuable customers, while learning those factors that build long lasting relationships with those customers. Building relationships through CRM is a strategic process that focuses on learning, managing customer knowledge, and empowerment.

3   Explain how to establish and manage interactions with your current customer base

The interaction between the customer and the organization is considered to be the foundation upon which a CRM system is built. Only through effective interactions can organizations learn about the expectations of their customers, generate and manage knowledge about them, negotiate mutually satisfying commitments and build long-term relationships. Effective management of customer interactions recognizes that customers provide information to organizations across a wide variety of touch points. Consumer-centric organizations are implementing new and unique approaches for establishing interactions specifically for this purpose. They include Web-based interactions, point-of-sale interactions and transaction-based interactions.

4   Outline the process of acquiring and capturing customer data

Based on the interaction between the organization and its customers, vast amounts of information can be obtained. In the CRM system, the issue is not how much data that can be obtained, but rather what type of data is acquired and how to use the data effectively for relationship enhancement. The channel, transaction, and the product or service consumed, all constitute touch points between a customer and organization. These touch points represent possible areas within a business where customer interactions can take place and, hence, the opportunity for acquiring data from the customer.

5   Describe the use of technology to store and integrate customer data

Customer data gathering is complicated because information needed by one unit of the organization (e.g., sales and marketing) is often generated by another area of the business or even a third party supplier (e.g., independent marketing research firm). Because of the lack of standard structure and interface, organizations are relying on technology to capture, store, and integrate strategically important customer information. The process of centralizing data in a CRM system is referred to as data warehousing. A data warehouse is a central repository of customer information collected by an organization.

6   Describe how to analyze data for profitable and unprofitable segments

Customer relationship management, as a process strategy, attempts to manage the interactions between a company and its customers. To be successful, organizations must identify customers that yield high profitability or potential profitability. In order to accomplish this task, significant amounts of information must be gathered from customers, stored and integrated into the data warehouse, then analyzed for commonalities that can produce segments that are highly similar, yet different from other customer segments. Data mining tools operate to identify significant relationships among several customer dimensions within vast data warehouses.

7 **Explain the process of leveraging and disseminating customer information throughout the organization**

One of the benefits of a CRM system is the capacity to share information throughout the organization. This allows an organization to interact with all functional areas to best develop programs targeted for its customers. This process is commonly referred to as campaign management. Campaign management involves developing customized product/service offerings for the appropriate customer segment and pricing and communicating these offerings for the purpose of enhancing customer relationships.

PRETEST

Answer the following questions to see how well you understand the material. Re-take it after you review to check yourself.

1. What is customer relationship management?

2. What are three important concepts in establishing customer relationships within an organization?

3. Briefly explain how to acquire and capture customer data.

4. What is a data warehouse?

5. What is data mining? Why is it important for customer relationship management?

1   Define customer relationship management

I.   What is Customer Relationship Management?

Customer relationship management (CRM) is a company-wide business strategy designed to optimize profitability, revenue, and customer satisfaction by focusing on highly defined and precise customer groups.

While customer service is critical to CRM, it is only one of many components of a CRM system.

A.   To initiate the CRM cycle, a company must:

1.   Establish customer relationships within the organization
2.   Determine the level of interaction that the customer has with the company
3.   Acquire and capture all relevant information about the customer
4.   Use the appropriate technology to store and integrate customer data
5.   Analyze customer data to determine profitable and unprofitable customer segments
6.   Disseminate the data throughout the entire organization.

B.   Implementing a Customer Relationship Management System

In a successful CRM system:

1.   Customers take centre stage in the organization.

2.   The business must focus on the day-to-day management of the customer relationship across all points of customer contact throughout the entire organization.

2   Explain how to establish customer relationships within the organization

II.   Establishing Customer Relationships Within the Organization

A.   Companies that use a CRM system must adhere to a **customer-centric focus,** an internal management philosophy in which the company customizes its product offering based on data generated through interactions between the customer and the company.

A customer-centric focus requires learning, knowledge management, and empowerment.

B.   Learning

1.   **Learning** in a CRM system is an informal process of collecting customer information through customer comments and feedback on product or service performance.

C.   Knowledge Management

1.   **Knowledge management** is a process by which learned information from customers is centralized and shared in order to enhance the relationship between customers and the organization.

D.   Empowerment

1.   Empowerment involves delegating authority to solve customers' problems. Organizational representatives make commitments at the **customer interaction,** which is the point at which the customer and the representative exchange information and develop learning relationships.

2. During the interaction, the organizational representative must focus on each individual customer, what each customer's requests are, what negotiations will result in a mutually satisfying relationship, and how to learn from each interaction.

3 Explain how to establish and manage interactions with your current customer base

III. Establishing and Managing Interactions with Current Customer Base

A. The interaction between the customer and the organization is the foundation upon which a CRM system is built. Following a customer-centric approach, interactions occur as follows:

1. Customer and organization interact through a formal communication channel, through a previous relationship, or by some current transaction by the customer.

2. The data that customers provide to organizations impact a wide variety of **touch points**, which are areas of a business where customer data is gathered and sued to guide and direct the decision making within that business unit.

3. A common touch point is the **knowledge centre,** the organization's internal operational component that manages and fulfills the customer request.

4. Information from the knowledge centre then leads to the requested activity or service.

B. Web-Based Interactions

1. Web-based interactions are increasing because many customers prefer to communicate on their own terms.

2. When customers purchase products on-line, the data is captured at the knowledge centre, compiled, and used to segment customers, refine marketing efforts, develop new products, and deliver a degree of individual customization to improve customer relationships.

C. Point-of-Sale Interactions

1. Customer data is now collected at the point-of-sale at stores. The information is then used for marketing and merchandising purposes, for determining who are the store's best customers, and for determining what types of inventory they buy.

D. Transaction-Based Interactions

1. Transaction-based interactions focus on the exchange of information at the point of the actual transaction.

2. Once a credit card is swiped (or a check is processed), two major streams of information are produced: information about what the customer purchased and how much they purchased; and information about the customer's profile.

4 Outline the process of acquiring and capturing customer data

IV. Acquiring and Capturing Customer Data

A. Acquiring and capturing customer data requires three external touch points: the channel, the transaction, and the product/service.

B. Channel

    1. The channel is the traditional approach for acquiring data from customers. It includes store visits, conversations with salespeople, PC interaction on the Web, traditional phone conversations, or wireless communication.

    2. The important issue is the method of communication used by the customer.

C. Transaction

    1. The transaction presents the opportunity to collect vast amounts of data about customers. This data can include anything from simple contact information (name, phone number) to behavioural data (customer life cycle, product preferences).

    2. The transaction can also provide data on profitability, risk, desirability, and customer loyalty.

D. Product and Service

    1. The physical and psychological consumption of a firm's product or service provides data on consumption patterns of an individual customer.

    2. The most important customer data is the customer's report of the performance of the product or service. This information can be disseminated to the entire organization to improve product performance, etc.

5 Describe the use of technology to store and integrate customer data

V. Use of Technology to Store and Integrate Customer Data

A. What Is Data Warehousing?

    1. A **data warehouse** (or **information warehouse**) is a central repository of customer data collected by an organization.

    2. The data warehouse allows different departments or functions within an organization share data about customers.

    3. Data warehouses enable companies to better customize their products and services according to their customers' needs and wants. They also allow organizations to monitor important financial aspects of the relationship.

6 Describe how to analyze data for profitable and unprofitable segments

VI. Analyzing Data for Profitable and Unprofitable Segments

A. Given the 80/20 principle (20 percent of customers represent 80 percent of the revenue), companies following CRM must determine who the profitable and unprofitable customers are. The 20 percent is identified through data mining.

B. Data Mining

    1. **Data mining** is the process of finding hidden patterns and relationships among variables and characteristics from customer data stored in the data warehouse.

    2. Data mining is used to recognize significant patterns of variables and characteristics as they pertain to particular customers or customer groups.

3. Data mining is capable of automatically predicting trends and behaviours and discovering previously unknown patterns.

C. The Data Mining Process

    1. Data mining involves **modelling**, the act of building a model in one situation where you know the answer and then applying it to another situation where the answer is unknown.

    2. The data mining process can model any customer activity as long as the information exists in the data warehouse.

    3. The two critical factors for success with data mining are:

        a. A large, well integrated data warehouse
        b. A well-defined understanding of how the end result of the mining activities will be used and leveraged throughout the organization.

7 Explain the process of leveraging and disseminating customer information throughout the organization

VII. Leveraging and Disseminating Customer Information throughout the Organization

A. Companies practicing CRM must be able to leverage and disseminate the information they analyze throughout their organizations. Managers can then tailor marketing strategies to best penetrate the identified segments.

B. When all functional areas in an organization participate in the development of programs targeted for their customers, this is known as **campaign management**. Campaign management involves outbound communications to customers designed to sell a company's product or service.

C. Campaign management also achieves personalization by developing customized product and service offerings for the appropriate segment; pricing these offerings attractively; and communicating these offerings in a manner that enhances customer relationships.

D. Product and Service Customization

    1. Using information contained in the data warehouse, highly customized or personalized products and services can be developed for customers.

E. Pricing

    1. Shared information from customer interactions is also used to develop individualized pricing plans for each customer.

F. Communication

    1. Communication means interacting in a manner that is most effective and non-intrusive for the customer.

    2. Campaign management facilitates effective planning of marketing campaigns and improves the relationship between the company and the customer.

Fill in the blank(s) with the appropriate term or phrase from the alphabetized list of chapter key terms.

campaign management	knowledge management
channel	learning
customer-centric	modelling
customer relationship management (CRM)	point-of-sale interactions
data mining	score
data warehouse	touch point
empowerment	transaction
interaction	transaction-based interactions
knowledge centre	Web-based interactions

1 Define customer relationship management

1. A company-wide business strategy designed to optimize profitability, revenue, and customer satisfaction by focusing on highly defined and precise customer groups is called _____.

2 Explain how to establish customer relationships within the organization

2. Under the _____ philosophy, the company customizes its product and service offering based on data generated through interactions between the customer and the company. Therefore, the company engages in _____, an informal process of collecting customer data through customer comments and feedback on product or service performance. Then the company takes this learned information from customer and centralizes and shares it with others in the organization. This process is called _____.

3. In a customer-centric organization, there is a delegation of authority to all organizational representatives who can solve customer problems; this delegation of authority is known as _____. Organizational representatives make commitments during a(n) _____ with the customer.

3 Explain how to establish and manage interactions with your current customer base

4. In a customer relationship management (CRM) system, a(n) _____ is all possible areas of a business where customers communicate with that business. An extremely common area is the _____, an organization's internal operational component that manages and fulfills customer requests.

5. Other types of interactions that company representatives can have with customers are _____, which uses the Internet, and _____, which happen at the point of sale. A final type of interaction is _____which occurs between and customer and the company at the point of transaction.

4   Outline the process of acquiring and capturing customer data

6. The process of acquiring and capturing customer data begins with the _____, a medium of communication through which the customer interacts with a business at an external touch point. Once this has occurred, a(n) _____ occurs; this is the interaction that involves an exchange of information and product or service.

5   Describe the use of technology to store and integrate customer data

7. Technology is used to store and integrate customer data. The data is stored in a(n) _____, which is a central repository for data from various functional areas of the organization. This information can then be accessed by anyone in the organization that needs information about the customer.

6   Describe how to analyze data for profitable and unprofitable segments

8. _____ is the process of finding hidden patterns and relationships in the customer data stored in the data warehouse. This works best through a process called _____, which builds upon a situation where the answer is known and then applies the scenario to another situation where the answer in unknown. Each prediction is assigned a(n) _____, or a numerical value that is assigned to each record in a data warehouse that indicates the likelihood that the customer whose record has been scored will exhibit the behaviour in question.

7   Explain the process of leveraging and disseminating customer information throughout the organization

9. Through _____, all functional areas of an organization participate in the development of programs targeted to its customers.

Check your answers to these questions before proceeding to the next section.

TRUE/FALSE QUESTIONS

Mark the statement **T** if it is true and **F** if it is false.

1   Define customer relationship management

_____ 1. Customer relationship management focuses mainly on building a relationship only with external customers.

2   Explain how to establish customer relationships within the organization

_____ 2. The customer-centric philosophy is very similar to the marketing concept.

_____ 3. As a customer service representative for an electronics store, George has the authority to solve customer problems without going through his boss or the salesperson. George has empowerment.

3   **Explain how to establish and manage interactions with your current customer base**

_____   4.   By definition, touch points must occur face-to-face between the customer and a company representative.

4   **Outline the process of acquiring and capturing customer data**

_____   5.   Tina just ordered a book from Amazon.com and immediately received an email confirming her order. Amazon has just used a valid communication channel with its customer.

5   **Describe the use of technology to store and integrate customer data**

_____   6.   Angela works as a receptionist in a doctor's office. When patients come to visit, she goes into a special room where printed medical files are located and pulls the appropriate files from the room. The room represents a kind of data warehouse.

6   **Describe how to analyze data for profitable and unprofitable segments**

_____   7.   When Tina logs back onto Amazon.com, she receives a message from the company that greets her and recommends some books that she might like to read. It is very likely that Amazon.com has engaged in data mining.

_____   8.   Data mining can be used by retailers to determine what kinds of products to stock in their stores.

7   **Explain the process of leveraging and disseminating customer information throughout the organization**

_____   9.   Campaign management requires all functional areas of the organization to be involved in the development of programs targeted to its customers.

_____   10.   European companies were the first to embrace customer relationship management

Check your answers to these questions before proceeding to the next section.

AGREE/DISAGREE QUESTIONS

For the following statements, indicate reasons why you may agree and disagree with the statement.

1.   Customer relationship management is basically the same as the marketing concept.

    Reason(s) to agree:

    Reason(s) to disagree:

---

2. Knowledge is empowerment.

   Reason(s) to agree:

   Reason(s) to disagree:

3. Without database technology, customer relationship management would not be possible.

   Reason(s) to agree:

   Reason(s) to disagree:

4. It is easier for on-line businesses to engage in customer relationship management than businesses that don't operate on-line.

   Reason(s) to agree:

   Reason(s) to disagree:

MULTIPLE CHOICE QUESTIONS

Select the response that best answers the question, and write the corresponding letter in the space provided.

1   Define customer relationship management

_____ 1. The first stage of the customer relationship management (CRM) cycle is to:
   a. acquire and capture data based on customer interactions
   b. establish and manage interactions with the current customer base
   c. analyze data for profitable or unprofitable segments
   d. leverage and disseminate customer information throughout the enterprise
   e. establish customer relationships within the organization

_____ 2. Loretta works in a large consumer packaged goods company. Her job is to manage the customer database and make it available to anyone in the organization who needs information on customers. Loretta in engaged in which phase of the CRM cycle?
   a. acquire and capture data based on customer interactions
   b. establish and manage interactions with the current customer base
   c. analyze data for profitable or unprofitable segments
   d. leverage and disseminate customer information throughout the enterprise
   e. establish customer relationships within the organization

2   Explain how to establish customer relationships within the organization

_____ 3. Whirl-Whiz Appliance Company has collected information through surveys given to consumers who bought its washing machines. The company found out through these surveys that customers who bought a certain type of washer didn't always buy the matching dryer. Through these surveys, company has engaged in:
   a. empowerment
   b. learning
   c. knowledge management
   d. touch points
   e. database management

_____ 4. Gloria is a front desk check-in professional at a posh resort. When a long-time visitor comes to check into her room, Gloria has found that her room type – a small suite – is all booked. To provide the ultimate customer service to her guest, Gloria decides to upgrade the visitor to the Empress Suite for the same price as the small suite. Gloria was able to make this decision because of:
   a. knowledge management
   b. data mining
   c. empowerment
   d. data warehousing
   e. database management

3   Explain how to establish and manage interactions with your current customer base

_____ 5. All possible areas of a business where customers communicate with that business are called:
   a. interactions
   b. communication channels
   c. knowledge centres
   d. touch points
   e. data warehouses

_____ 6. Nathan works over seventy hours per week as a stock broker on Wall Street and has little time to go to retail stores to shop for clothing and household items. Thus, he tends to sit at his computer and shop. His interactions with the seller can be best described as:
   a. Web-based interactions
   b. point-of-sale interactions
   c. transaction-based interactions
   d. mail-based interactions
   e. face-to-face interactions

4   Outline the process of acquiring and capturing customer data

_____ 7. Which of the following would NOT be considered as a channel for customer interactions?
   a. the Internet
   b. store visits
   c. wireless communications
   d. television
   e. salesperson at a store

_____ 8. Noah has just finished shopping at his favourite Web site for music. He types in his credit card number, verifies the information that he input, and clicks the "submit" button. Noah has just completed:
   a. a channel
   b. a touch point
   c. a transaction
   d. a point-of-sale interaction
   e. the customer relationship management cycle

_____ 9. Which of the following is NOT a "ground rule" regarding customer data for a CRM system?
   a. Information is retained beyond the initial contact with the customer and accumulated over the customer's entire life span with the organization.
   b. Customer data is sold to outside sources for additional income.
   c. The customer takes centre stage in the organization.
   d. Customer information must be centralized so that a single definitive source is established, typically within the knowledge centre.
   e. Information must define the product or service that the customer desires, the customer's preferences for future products and services, and contact methods for future interactions.

5   Describe the use of technology to store and integrate customer data

_____ 10. Customer data is stored in a(n) _____, where various functional areas of the organization can share customer information.
   a. data mine
   b. data warehouse
   c. on-line database
   d. communication channel
   e. vault

_____ 11. Data warehouses can do all of the following except:
   a. enable companies to better customize products and services according to their customers' preferences
   b. generate customer profiles that categorize customers as either profitable or unprofitable
   c. help companies monitor important financial aspects of the customer relationship
   d. help companies target highly specific customer groups with special services
   e. create superior customer service

6   Describe how to analyze data for profitable and unprofitable segments

_____ 12. Ethan works at a credit card company which tracks purchases by its credit card holders. Through his company's database system, Ethan analyzes the purchase behaviour of the company's customers and tries to draw patterns in their behaviour. This information will be used later to target specific market segments with special services. Ethan is engaged in:
   a. data mining
   b. data warehousing
   c. customer interactions
   d. learning
   e. empowerment

_____ 13. In its data mining process, the Great Outdoors on-line retailer analyzes the purchase pattern of its highest spenders to try to predict the expenditures for the upcoming season. Analyzing a situation that is known and then applying it to a situation that is unknown as called:
   a. data mining
   b. learning
   c. scoring
   d. modelling
   e. data warehousing

_____ 14. The Ashwood Furniture Company engages all its functional areas – from the salespeople to the delivery people to the financing group – in the development of its product and services in an effort to enhance customer relationships. This is known as:
   a.   customer relationship management
   b.   campaign involvement
   c.   campaign management
   d.   service marketing
   e.   empowerment

_____ 15. Campaign management:
   a.   applies the customer relationship management philosophy to the marketing mix
   b.   helps analyze the needs of customers
   c.   involves all functional areas of the organization
   d.   involves customer feedback at all levels
   e.   includes all these elements

Check your answers to these questions before proceeding to the next section

SCENARIO

Read the marketing scenario and answer the questions that follow.

Tronica is a fictional electronics retail chain that sells a wide variety of electronics products, including computers and software, home entertainment systems, telecommunications equipment, music, videos, and DVDs. Tronica implemented a customer relationship management system last year. First, the company conducted research among its past customers to determine what product lines and service the stores should carry and promptly adapted the offerings at the stores based on this research. Store management gives authority to lower-level employees to make decisions about customer service issues – such as delivery, returns, or warranty – without having to go through "the boss." The chain also invested in a sophisticated database to track customer purchase information, preferences, and other customer issues. Researchers at the corporate headquarters can use the customer data to identify significant purchase patterns and segment the market.

True/False:

_____ 1.   Tronica is a customer-centric organization.

_____ 2.   Tronica empowers its employees.

_____ 3.   Tronica has a sales orientation.

Multiple Choice:

_____ 4.   The database in which Tronica invested is probably housed in a:
   a.   data warehouse.
   b.   data mine.
   c.   databank.
   d.   knowledge centre.
   e.   file storehouse.

_____ 5.   When researchers use customer data to identify significant purchase patterns or to segment the market, they are probably engaged in:
     a.   learning.
     b.   focus groups.
     c.   data mining.
     d.   secondary research.
     e.   targeting strategy.

_____ 6.   Which of the following would most likely NOT be an external touch point for Tronica?
     a.   A customer completing a product registration card.
     b.   A customer telephoning the store's customer service department.
     c.   A customer talking to Tronica's delivery personnel at the customer's home.
     d.   A customer's information being passed onto the marketing department.
     e.   All of these are external touch points for Tronica.

_____ 7.   The last step in customer relationship management in which Tronica most likely engages is:
     a.   Establishing and managing interactions with the current customer base.
     b.   Leveraging and disseminating customer information throughout the enterprise.
     c.   Using technology to store and integrate customer data.
     d.   Analyzing data for profitable/unprofitable segments.
     e.   Campaign management.

Short Answer:

7.   What else would Tronica have to do to engage in campaign management?

ESSAY QUESTIONS

1.   Describe the customer relationship cycle from the viewpoint of a college or university.

2. Why is technology so crucial in customer relationship management?

3. What is the difference between a data warehouse and data mining? How are they related?

APPLICATION

Think of the last large purchase that you recently made, such as a car, a stereo, a TV, a house, or a large household appliance. From the shopper's point of view, discuss: 1) whether the company from which you purchased the product was "customer-centric" and why; 2) the various "touch points" where the company representatives communicated with you; 3) what kinds of information the company collected about you; 4) how you think this information will be used in the future to target you as a consumer. What did you think of your overall experience? How could the company improve its customer relationship management?

Solutions

PRETEST SOLUTIONS

1. The process of planning and executing the conception, pricing, promotion, and distribution of ideas, goods, and services to create exchanges that satisfy individual and organizational goals.
   (text p. 4)

2. The five conditions are:
   - There must be at least two parties
   - Each party has something that might be of value to the other party
   - Each party is capable of communication and delivery
   - Each party is free to accept or reject the exchange offer
   - Each party believes it is appropriate or desirable to deal with the other party
   (text p. 4)

3. Product, price, promotion, and distribution

4. The production orientation, the sales orientation, the marketing orientation, and the societal marketing orientation.
   (text pp. 4-7)

5. **Sales orientation**:
   - Inward focus based on organization's needs
   - Focus on selling goods and services
   - Product targeted at everyone
   - Profit is gained through maximum sales volume
   - Goals achieved through intensive promotion

   Marketing orientation:
   - Outward focus, based on wants and preferences of customers
   - Focus on satisfying customer wants and needs and delivering superior value
   - Product targeted at specific groups of people
   - Profit is gained through customer satisfaction
   - Goals achieved through coordinated marketing and interfunctional activities
   (text pp. 7-13)

6. The seven steps in the marketing process are: (1) Understanding the organization's mission and the role marketing plays in fulfilling that mission; (2) Setting marketing objectives; (3) Gathering, analyzing, and interpreting information about the organization's situation; (4) Developing a marketing strategy by deciding exactly which wants and whose wants the organization will try to satisfy and by developing appropriate marketing activities to satisfy these wants; (5) Implementing the marketing strategies; (6) Designing performance measures; and (7) Evaluating marketing efforts and making changes, if needed.
   (text p. 13)

7. Four reasons for studying marketing are: (1) Marketing plays an important role in society; (2) Marketing is important to business; (3) Marketing offers outstanding career opportunities; and (4) Marketing affects your life every day.
   (text pp. 13-15)

VOCABULARY PRACTICE SOLUTIONS

1. marketing
2. exchange
3. production orientation, sales orientation, marketing orientation, societal marketing orientation
4. marketing concept
5. customer value
6. customer satisfaction
7. relationship marketing
8. teamwork
9. empowerment

TRUE/FALSE SOLUTIONS

(question number / correct answer / text page reference / answer rationale)

1. T 6
2. T 7 In a typical marketing exchange, one party offers goods and services in exchange for a price.
3. F 7 A sales orientation would be a more appropriate description for a firm that does not research consumer needs and wants but rather relies on a strong sales effort.
4. F 7 A sales orientation is based on "pushing products" to customers, while a market orientation is based on satisfying customer needs while meeting organizational objectives.
5. F 10 The customer needs to determine the benefits and the sacrifices; these perceptions cannot be defined by the marketer.
6. T 16 The marketing mix will be studied more in future chapters.
7. F 16 The marketing process DOES include a thorough analysis of the organization's situation which will impact marketing strategies.
8. T 18 Most marketing activities should support the general objectives of the firm.
9. F 18 About one-fourth to one-third of the workforce is engaged in marketing activities, one of the most common types of activities in Canadian business.

AGREE/DISAGREE SOLUTIONS

(question number / sample answers)

1. Reason(s) to agree: In order for a firm to be marketing oriented, it must operate efficiently (production orientation) and use aggressive selling techniques to push products through distribution channels.
   Reason(s) to disagree: Maintaining a production orientation or a sales orientation can actually hurt the firm's marketing efforts. If too much focus is given to production or sales, the firm will lose focus on customer satisfaction, the ultimate goal of marketing.
2. Reason(s) to agree: An organization with a marketing orientation must ensure that all employees—and especially those who are in direct contact with customers—understand that the firm's goal is to satisfy customer needs. Organizations such as Nordstrom's, Disney, and Southwest Airlines understand this concept well, and all employees are trained in delivering good customer service.
   Reason(s) to disagree: Though this concept sounds good, it is not practical. By making marketing "everyone's job," no one in the organization has accountability for marketing. While customer service can be delivered by everyone, there are many other aspects of marketing – such as promotion, planning, and marketing research – that require the expertise of a trained marketing department.
3. Reason(s) to agree: Just as engineering majors or journalism majors do not need to take marketing, neither should finance, management, accounting, or other majors. Marketing is a separate field that requires a level of expertise that should be reserved for those who plan to make a career out of it.
   Reason(s) to disagree: Any student majoring in a business area—and even those in related non-business areas, such as communications or public relations—should be required to take at least one marketing course. A business professional needs to know marketing in order to accept and work toward the organization's long-term goals, which are likely to be marketing-driven.

MULTIPLE-CHOICE SOLUTIONS

(question number / correct answer / text page reference / answer rationale)

1. c 4 Marketing must involve at least two parties in order for an exchange to occur.
2. b 4 Exchange involves the trade of items of value but does not necessarily involve formal organizations, profit, or money/legal tender.
3. e 4 As long as there is an organization and a client/user/customer/consumer group willing to engage in the exchange act, then marketing activities are relevant.
4. d 4 Marketing and exchange are not limited to profit seeking transactions, and there can be many types of costs other than direct costs and monetary payment.
5. d 4 The production orientation is a philosophy that focuses on the internal capabilities of the firm rather than on the desires and needs of the of the marketplace.
6. e 4 The production orientation guides a company to build whatever it builds best; that is, whatever it has the experience and expertise in doing.
7. a 5 Only the sales orientation assumes that aggressive sales techniques will sell more products, regardless of customer desires and needs.
8. d 5 Beth is concerned with meeting the needs and wants of the marketplace and, therefore, has a marketing orientation.
9. d 5 Family Shelter is exemplifying the marketing concept by concentrating on the needs of a specific group of customers.

10. e   7   Organizations with a societal marketing orientation seek the long-term best interests of society. The donation of earnings to an environmental cause is illustrative of this orientation.

11. e   7   A sales orientation has the short-term goal of increasing sales, which can be easily done through intensive sales promotions, such as discount pricing. A marketing orientation involves coordination among many organizational functions, such as production, research and development, finance, and marketing.

12. b   13   Appraising marketing personnel is generally a human resources activity (management) rather than a marketing activity.

13. e   13   Developing a new advertising campaign is part of promotion, or communicating with the target market.

14. e   13   Marketing is an important conceptual base that will help assess the needs and wants of the various business contacts and customers. Marketing is a key component of every business.

15. d   13   The marketing concept stresses the commitment to satisfying customer needs and wants with an entire range of marketing tools, not just selling or advertising.

SCENARIO SOLUTIONS

1. False.   Because the sales agents aggressively pursue business with discounts and promotions, the company seemed to have more of a sales orientation before 2002.

2. True   The creation of the customer database, the focus on keeping existing customers satisfied, and the feedback process are all signs of a marketing orientation.

3. False   Sales agents still pursue new business, but existing policyholders have become important new sources of additional income. An old saying in marketing is "it' s cheaper to keep a current customer than to gain a new one."

4. c   By keeping customer profiles updated and sending information about coverage needed for life changes, the company is engaging in relationship marketing.

5. a   Before 2002, the company held a sales orientation, which targets the mass market (everybody) without taking into account different needs. Everybody would include people with high incomes, people who already have insurance, etc.

6. d   All the choices reflect a marketing orientation.

7.   Seven common marketing activities are: 1) Understanding the mission statement and the role that you play within that mission; 2) setting marketing objectives; 3) gathering and analyzing the organization's situation; 4) developing marketing strategies; 5) implementing strategies; 6) designing performance measures; and 7) evaluating marketing efforts and making needed changes.

ESSAY QUESTION SOLUTIONS

1. The five conditions of exchange are:
   - There must be at least two parties.
   - Each party has something that might be of value to the other party
   - Each party is capable of communication and delivery
   - Each party is free to accept or reject the exchange offer
   - Each party believes it is appropriate or desirable to deal with the other party

   Marketing can occur even if an exchange does not take place. Many of the activities of marketing (distribution, promotion, pricing, product development, and so on) can take place without a final exchange. (text p. 3)

2. The **production orientation** focuses firms on their internal production capabilities rather than the desires and needs of the marketplace.

   The **sales orientation** assumes that buyers resist purchasing items that are not essential, and that buyers will purchase more of any item if aggressive selling techniques are used. Again, this orientation does not address the needs and wants of the marketplace.

   The **marketing orientation** is dependent on the customer's decision to purchase a product and provides increased responsiveness to customer needs and wants.

   The **societal marketing orientation** refines the marketing orientation by stating that the social and economic justification for an organization's existence is the satisfaction of customer wants and needs while meeting the organization's objectives and preserving or enhancing both the individual's and society's long-term best interests. (text pp. 3-7)

3. Five key areas in which a market orientation differs from a sales orientation are as follows:
    -   **The organization's focus**: A market orientation has an "outward" focus based on the wants and preferences of customers, while a sales orientation has an "inward" focus based on the organization's needs.
    -   **The firm's business**: A market orientation defines business as satisfying customer needs and delivering value, while a sales orientation defines business as selling goods and services.
    -   **Those to whom the product is directed**: A market orientation targets specific groups of people who have needs for products, while a sales orientation targets everybody in order to maximize short-term sales.
    -   **The firm's primary goal**: A market orientation has the goal of gaining profit through customer satisfaction, while a sales orientation has the goal of gaining profit through maximum sales volume.
    -   **Tools the organization uses to achieve goals**: A market orientation achieves goals through coordinated marketing and interfunctional activities, while a sales orientation achieves goals through intensive promotion.

    (text pp. 7-10)

4. Marketing process activities include:
    -   Understanding the organization's mission
    -   Setting marketing objectives
    -   Performing a situation analysis, including strengths, weaknesses, opportunities, and threats
    -   Developing a marketing strategy, including a target market specification, and marketing mix, including product, place, promotion, and price
    -   Implementing the marketing strategy
    -   Designing performance measures
    -   Periodically evaluating marketing efforts, and making changes if needed

    (text p. 13)

APPLICATION SOLUTIONS

2-3. Elements that would make a Web site seem marketing-oriented include: 1) an assumption that most Web site viewers are seen as potential customers or the target market; 2) the Web site seems more focused on the wants, needs and preferences of customers rather than on selling product; 3) the Web site is not targeted at everyone; it's targeted at specific groups of people (you may not even be part of the target market); 4) the Web sites features promotions that appeal to the target market; and 5) the Web site uses colourful graphics that are appealing to the target market. There may be other elements that make the Web site seem more marketing-oriented.

4-5. Elements that may make the Web site appear NOT to be marketing-oriented are: 1) a focus on investors, not on consumers; 2) a focus on the internal elements of the company, such as employment or general company information; 3) a strong focus on the product features but not the product benefits; etc.

CHAPTER 2: STRATEGIC PLANNING FOR COMPETITIVE ADVANTAGE

PRETEST SOLUTIONS

1. The six major elements of a marketing plan are:
    -   **Business mission**: The firm's long-term vision.
    -   **Objectives**: Statements of what is to be accomplished through marketing activities.
    -   **Situation analysis**: An analysis of the firm's or product's strengths, weaknesses, opportunities, and threats
    -   **Target market selection**: Selection of the group of people to whom marketing efforts will be targeted
    -   **Marketing mix**: Strategies for the 4 Ps (product, place, promotion, and price)
    -   **Implementation**: Action plan for marketing activities

    (text p. 26)

2. Four strategic alternatives are:
    -   **Market penetration**: Sell more products to the present market
    -   **Product development**: Sell new products to the present market
    -   **Market development**: Sell the present products to a new market
    -   **Diversification**: Sell new products to new markets

    (text p. 32)

3. A tool that can be used to select a strategic alternative is a **portfolio matrix**, which allocates resources between product or SBUs on the basis of relative market share and market growth rate. Categories are:
   - Stars: High growth, high share products that need high investment to continue firm's growth;
   - Cash cows: Low growth, high share products that are "mi lked" for their excess profits;
   - Problem children: High growth, low share products that either need investment or they will turn into dogs;
   - Dogs: Low growth, low share products that should not receive many resources.

   (text pp. 34-35)
4. A marketing strategy is the activity of selecting and describing one or more target markets and developing and maintaining a marketing mix that will produce mutually satisfying exchanges with target markets.

   (text p. 36)
5. The four Ps are:
   - **Product**: The product offering, its packaging, warranty, brand name, company image, etc.
   - **Place (distribution)**: Making product available when and where customers want them.
   - **Promotion**: Communication of the product to the target market; includes personal selling, advertising, public relations, and sales promotion.
   - **Price**: What a buyer must give up to obtain a product.

   (text pp. 37-38)

VOCABULARY PRACTICE SOLUTIONS

1. strategic planning
2. planning, marketing planning
3. marketing plan
4. mission statement
5. marketing myopia
6. strategic business unit (SBU)
7. marketing objective
8. SWOT analysis
9. environmental scanning
10. competitive advantage
11. cost competitive advantage, experience curves
12. product/service differentiation, niche competitive advantage
13. market penetration, market development, product development, diversification
14. portfolio matrix, star, cash cow, problem children (or question marks), dog
15. sustainable competitive advantage
16. marketing strategy
17. market opportunity analysis
18. marketing mix, 4 Ps
19. implementation, evaluation, control
20. marketing audit

TRUE/FALSE SOLUTIONS

(question number / correct answer / text page reference / answer rationale)

1. T 24
2. F 25 The first step is to create, or to review, the business mission statement.
3. F 26 Because Mike's Motos defines its business in terms of the benefits customers seek rather than in terms of specific goods or services, it does not suffer from marketing myopia.
4. F 28 This objective is neither measurable nor time specific.
5. T 28
6. T 29
7. F 29 This represents a weakness.
8. T 32
9. T 32
10. T 36
11. F 37 The use of theatres to communicate a motion picture release is an example of promotion. Using theatres to show the film would be an example of place.
12. T 38
13. F 38 A marketing audit is not preoccupied with past performance but instead looks to the future allocation of marketing resources. Additionally, both small and large firms use marketing audits.

AGREE/DISAGREE SOLUTIONS

(question number / sample answers)

1. Reason(s) to agree: The basic outline for a marketing plan takes into account a variety of organizational types, including non-profit organizations. All organizations should have a mission statement, objectives, a situation analysis, a target market, a marketing mix, and implementation and evaluation and control.
    Reason(s) to disagree: Some small firms may not find it necessary to go through all the steps of a basic marketing plan. Doing a complete analysis of a small firm's situation may be too tedious, as the owners probably already know what the situation is. Also, non-profit organizations cannot put together strategies for the "4 Ps" since there may not be a product or a price.

2. Reason(s) to agree: Once a situation analysis is complete, the situation can change immediately. Though a firm's strengths and weaknesses do not change quickly, opportunities and threats can change in a matter of minutes. Documenting the analysis seems silly when the business environment is so fluid.
    Reason(s) to disagree: It is never a waste of time to thoroughly analyze a firm's situation. Though the environment can change quickly, it is important for a firm to understand what its current resources are, what its weaknesses are, and to be responsive to both threats and opportunities. Unless these are stated explicitly, there may not be acceptance from all managerial levels.

3. Reason(s) to agree: The tools assume that an organization has either separate strategic business units (SBUs) or many different products. If a small firm had only one product to sell, it is simple to decide what resources the product should get: all of them!
    Reason(s) to disagree: Even small firms can benefit from these tools. By understanding where the firm's product(s) fit in the marketplace, it can find a positioning strategy that will help it compete.

4. Reason(s) to agree: If a strategy is sound, then the implementation should follow naturally. It is more important to do the right thing than to do something right.
    Reason(s) to disagree: A strategy will fall apart if it is not implemented well. If a new product is launched with a sound strategy (good positioning, good advertising, etc.), and the sales force has structural problems that prevent it from selling the product to the customer, then the new product may fail. The failure will be due to the poor implementation, not strategy. Implementation is at least as important as strategy.

MULTIPLE-CHOICE SOLUTIONS

(question number / correct answer / text page reference / answer rationale)

1. d   26   Only designing a marketing information system is not part of the six-step process in strategic planning.
2. c   26   All the listed activities are part of the strategic planning process.
3. b   26   A mission statement answers the question, "What business are we in and where are we going?"
4. e   26   The mission statement dictates the firm's business based on a careful analysis of benefits sought by current and potential customers, as well as existing and anticipated environmental conditions.
5. b   26   The concept of running department stores is a much narrower focus than the broad range of opportunities found in "providing a range of products and services."
6. b   26   This mission statement is too broad and does not state the business that the firm is in.
7. d   26   A broad mission statement for a telephone company would recognize that the firm's business is total communications service.
8. c   28   An SBU usually has its own mission statement, target markets, and separate functional departments.
9. a   28   Marketing objectives should consistent with organization objectives, should be measurable, should be realistic, and should specify a timeframe. The first objective fits these criteria the best.
10. d   28   A situation analysis attempts to ascertain the present situation and forecast trends.
11. d   28   Corporate culture is the pattern of basic assumptions held by an organization's members in order to cope with its environments. This negative culture represents a weakness of the firm's internal organization.
12. c   28   A firm's strengths and weaknesses are internal; its opportunities and threats come from the outside.
13. b   32   Market development involves finding new uses for a product to stimulate sales among new and existing customers.
14. d   32   Product development involves selling a new product to existing markets.
15. e   33   Diversification is defined as selling a new product to a new market.
16. a   34   The portfolio matrix designates the SBUs as dogs, cash cows, stars, or problem children.
17. b   35   Cash cows generate cash, have dominant market share, and are in low-growth industries.

---

18. c 35 Problem children are SBUs with large cash demands because of their rapid growth and poor profit margins.

19. c 35 This program is a cash cow. Though enrolment has been declining, the program is still large and "pays the bills." The best strategy is to hold or preserve the program.

20. a 35 Rising "stars" should be built to further capitalize on their success.

21. b 35 Cash cows are profit-generators that need little resources, so the strategy should be to "hold."

22. c 36 Target markets are the chosen market segments that have a need for the firm's product offerings.

23. d 37 The product is the starting point for any marketing mix. Without it, pricing, distribution, and promotion are irrelevant. The production capacity can be changed to fit the proposed product.

24. e 37 Distribution strategies are concerned with making products available when and where customers want them.

25. c 37 Promotion covers a wide range of communication vehicles. Publicity is generally a nonpaid form of communication and is a subset of promotion.

26. c 38 The only element that is often subject to quick and easy change is price.

27. d 38 Implementation involves all of the steps listed.

28. a 38 Control involves that mechanism for correcting actions in the planning and implementation phases.

29. c 38 A marketing audit is a thorough, systematic, periodic evaluation of the goals, strategies, organization, and performance of the marketing organization. A marketing audit will evaluate the past, present, and future performance of all aspects of the marketing department.

30. d 39 Planners need to stretch their imaginations and search for creative solutions to problems. Planning is a constant process and should include top management.

31. e 39 Creating a special department where none has been before may make management feel as though something has been accomplished, but it may also alienate other employees and even slow down the progress toward a marketing orientation unless the other four steps are taken.

SCENARIO SOLUTIONS

1. False. As the fastest growing and most successful product lines, subnotebook and hand-held computers represent stars.

2. False As long as the line remains profitable and does not require vast resources, the company should keep the line. There are still some loyal customers.

3. True As the stars of the portfolio, the subnotebooks and hand-helds need a disproportionately large share of the company's resources as they represent the company's "future."

4. b Cash cows are established lines of business that are not growing very much but that generate large amount of cash, which are often reinvested in other growth businesses.

5. c Question marks are products that have not yet proven themselves and represent low share, high growth businesses.

6. d The best strategy is hold, since the products are cash cows. This will allow the company to maintain market share and get as much profit as possible while the technology is still current.

7. b The best strategy for a star is to build the business as it is still growing to maximize sales and profit.

8. Two advantages are: 1) It allows a company to spend resources more efficiently, especially cash resources, and 2) It allows a company to see if it has "holes" in its SBUs or product offerings. For instance, a company with too many question marks may be drained financially. Two disadvantages are: 1) It is difficult to manage marketing managers who are in charge of dogs since they will never get many resources; and 2) It often does not work for certain industries – especially high-tech ones – since technology cannot always be predicted. Today's stars may become tomorrow's dogs much more quickly than non-tech products.

ESSAY QUESTION SOLUTIONS

1. The elements of the marketing plan are:
   1. Define the business mission
   2. Set marketing objectives
   3. Conduct a situation analysis (SWOT)
   4. Select target market(s)
   5. Establish the marketing mix (product, place, promotion, price)
   6. Implement, evaluate, and control the plan
   (text p. 26)

2. A marketing objective is a statement of goals—of what is to be achieved—through marketing activities. The criteria for a good objective are to be: (1) realistic; (2) measurable; (3) time specific, and (4) consistent. A good example of an objective is given in the textbook (for a retail pet food company): "To achieve 10 percent dollar market share in the specialty pet food market within 12 months of product introduction." (text, pp. 28)

3. A target market is a group of individuals or organizations toward whom marketing activities are focused. The three general strategies for selecting target markets are:
    *   Appealing to the entire market with one marketing mix; an example is Coca-Cola targeting the mass market for its Coke Classic;
    *   Concentrating on one segment; an example is Topol toothpaste targeting smokers who are concerned about white teeth; and
    *   Using multiple marketing mixes; an example is the Gap clothing store targeting a young adult market for its casual clothing outlets and the children's market with an even younger clothing line.
    (text, p. 36)

4.

Market Growth Rate	Star	Problem Child, or Question Mark	**High**
(In constant dollars)	Cash Cow	Dog	**Low**
	High	**Low**	

Market Share Dominance
(Share relative to largest competitor)

Stars: Stars are market leaders that are growing quickly. Star SBUs often have large profits but require much cash to finance the rate of growth. The tactic for marketing management is to protect existing market share and to obtain a majority of new users entering the market.

Cash cows: These SBUs usually generate more cash than is required to maintain market share. The basic strategy is to maintain market dominance with price leadership and technological product improvements. Excess cash can be allocated to other areas where growth prospects are the greatest.

Problem children: Rapid growth coupled with poor profit margins causes cash demands for this class of SBUs. Three alternative strategies can be enacted: (1) invest heavily to obtain better market share, (2) acquire competitors to get the necessary market share, or (3) drop the SBU. If cash is not provided, these SBUs will become dogs.

Dogs: Because dogs have low-growth potential and a small market share, they usually end up leaving the marketplace. Mature markets, no new users, stiff competition, and market leader dominance characterize SBUs in this category. Tactics include resegmenting markets, harvesting, or dropping the SBU.
(text, pp. 34-35)

---

5. **Product:** This includes development of the new cereal, production assistance, packaging and labelling, branding, and other components.

Place (or distribution): The cereal must move through a channel of distribution to get from the manufacturer to the final consumer. This channel will probably involve wholesalers and retailers (grocery stores). Physical distribution (stocking and transportation logistics) is also part of the place or distribution component.

Promotion: Promotion of the cereal might include any or all of the following to inform, educate, persuade, and remind target markets about the cereal's benefits: personal selling, advertising (TV, radio, magazines, billboards, and so on), sales promotion (such as coupons and rebates), and public relations.

Price: Pricing is an important component of the marketing mix because it is flexible and therefore can be used as a powerful strategic tool against competitive cereals.

(text pp. 37-38)

APPLICATION SOLUTIONS

Application #1:

Be careful to understand what a strength, a weakness, an opportunity, and a threat really are. Strengths and weaknesses are part of the internal analysis of a company. Strengths for an airline may include strong customer service or best on-time arrivals. Weaknesses may include high fixed costs or relatively new managers. Opportunities and threats are part of the external analysis of a company. Opportunities are positive external environmental factors, such as increasing population growth. Threats are negative external factors such as upcoming legislation that restricts the way you do business.

Application #2:

Airline industry: 1) Cost competitive advantage: Southwest Airlines with its no-frills, low-cost service is a good example; 2) Product/service differentiation: Singapore Airlines is a good example because it has won several customer service awards throughout the years for its excellent passenger service; 3) Niche competitive advantage: specialized airlines such as Aloha Air (flies passengers to Hawaii) or a charter service that flies passengers to Las Vegas.

Discount stores: 1) Cost competitive advantage: Wal-Mart with its everyday low prices; 2) Product differentiation: Zellers with its trendy, high-style products at slightly higher prices; 3) Niche competitive advantage: Any number of local deep discounters, such as Dollarama.

CHAPTER 3: THE MARKETING ENVIRONMENT AND MARKETING ETHICS

PRETEST SOLUTIONS

1. A target market is a defined group of people most likely to buy a firm's product.
   (text, p. 54)
2. Social factors that affect marketing are: the values held by various consumers (such as "self-sufficienc y" or "wor k ethic"); dual-career families and their "po verty of time;" the growth of component lifestyles; the changing role of families; and the growth of women in the workplace.
   (text pp. 55-57)
3. Demography is the study of people's vital statistics, such as their age, race and ethnicity, and location.
   (text, p. 57)
4. Four generations that are often used as target markets are:
   - Generation Y: Born between 1979 and 1994, Generation Y is composed of children of younger Baby Boomers. They are "b orn to shop" and have become savvy consumers at a young age. This generation is culturally, ethnically, and economically diverse.
   - Generation X: Born between 1965 and 1978, Generation X is composed of children of older Baby Boomers. Many Generation X-ers were latchkey children who were left to fend for themselves as their dual-career parents worked. Members of this generation do not mind indulging themselves and are cynical, savvy, and technology-driven.
   - Baby Boomers: Born between 1945 and 1964, Baby Boomers are the largest generation in Canadian history, and represent Canada's mass market. Baby Boomers are entering their 50s but still cling to their youth. They were taught to think for themselves and were more independent than their own children, the Generations X and Y.
   - Older Consumers: Today, many older consumers, who are the parents of the Baby Boomers, are healthy and robust compared to the older people of past generations. They have driven marketers to develop innovations in order to help them in advancing years—such as snap-on lids for detergent. Older consumers spend on their grandchildren, creating Grandparents Clubs that offer discounts on toy purchases for grandchildren.
   (text pp. 59-62)

5.   Legislation that impacts marketing include:
- Federal Legislation: The Competition Bureau is the federal department charged with administering most marketplace laws.
- Provincial Laws: Provincial legislation poses difficulties because the laws vary from province to province. For example, Bill 101 in Quebec requires French to be the primary language in all promotional activities.
- Self-Regulation: Some business organizations make voluntary efforts to regulate the activities of their members.
- NAFTA: The North American Free Trade Agreement is an agreement among Canada, the United States and Mexico that has created the world's lar gest free trade zone.

(text p. 68-70)

VOCABULARY PRACTICE SOLUTIONS

1.   target market
2.   environmental management
3.   poverty of time, component lifestyle
4.   demography
5.   Generation X, baby boomers, personalized economy, Generation Y
6.   multiculturalism
7.   inflation, recession
8.   basic research, applied research
9.   Competition Bureau
10. ethics, morals
11. code of ethics
12. corporate social responsibility
13. pyramid of corporate social responsibility

TRUE/FALSE SOLUTIONS

(question number / correct answer / text page reference / answer rationale)

1.	T	54	
2.	F	54	Marketers can control the four P's, but they have no direct control over external environmental elements.
3.	F	56	Most Canadians define themselves by a variety of different measures, which make up the component lifestyle, which may include a profession but may also include hobbies and other descriptors.
4.	T	57	
5.	F	60	Generation X followed the Baby Boomers.
6.	F	61	Baby boomers are defined by their year of birth. Marital status, employment, and number of children are not factors.
7.	T	59	
8.	F	62	Ethnic market segmentation is on the rise due to different values and needs of these segments.
9.	T	65	
10.	F	70	A purely competitive market does not exist in the real world.
11.	F	72	Business ethics are actually a subset of the values held by society.
12.	T	75	

AGREE/DISAGREE SOLUTIONS

(question number / sample answers)

1.   Reason(s) to agree: Generation X—composed of people ages eighteen to thirty—are rebellious, distrustful of authority, and cynical. This is directly a function of age, not necessarily of the times. When Baby Boomers were younger, they had some of the same characteristics. Marketing to Generation X, then, should be similar to the way firms marketed to Baby Boomers when they were ages eighteen to thirty.
Reason(s) to disagree: Despite the fact that Baby Boomers were also once young, rebellious, and distrustful of authority, Generation X is different because they grew up under different circumstances. They were bombarded even more with media messages, and many were latchkey children. They came into the workforce during tough economic times and were unable to find jobs as easily. Marketers cannot treat the two generations the same way because they have different values.

2.   Reason(s) to agree: Canada is composed of many different cultures, and these cultures blend together to become what is known as "Canadia n" culture. It is to this collective group that firms should market their products.

    Reason(s) to disagree: Canada is not a melting pot; rather, it is a "m osaic" of cultures, each being distinct and separate from the others but working together to form what is known as "Canadia n" culture. Because they are distinct and separate, firms should adapt their marketing programs to each culture.

3.   Reason(s) to agree: Though the demographic, technological, political, legal, and ethical environments are important, it is the economic environment that has the greatest impact on marketing efforts. It does not matter what demographic trend is occurring; consumer spending habits are directly influenced by what is happening in the economy. When the economy is in prosperity, consumers spend more; when the economy slows, consumers' confidence decreases and they spend less. This has the most significant impact on business.

    Reason(s) to disagree: The demographic, technological, political, legal, ethical, and economic environments all have equal importance to most firms. Though the economic environment may have the most significant short-term impact, the other factors can have a significant long-term impact.

4.   Reason(s) to agree: Let's face it: the for-profit firm is in business in make profits. Anything that is done—philanthropic actions, social responsibility—has the ultimate goal of making money in the long run. The upside is that society can benefit from the actions, regardless of the ulterior motive.

    Reason(s) to disagree: Organizations are made up of people, and people have a conscience. They make decisions based on many levels of morality—preconventional, conventional, or postconventional—but the person who makes decisions based on postconventional morality is doing what he or she thinks is the right thing to do, regardless of the profit or other impact on the firm.

MULTIPLE-CHOICE SOLUTIONS
(question number / correct answer / text page reference / answer rationale)

1.	c	54	The Baby Boomers would be considered the firm's target market: the group of people to whom its marketing efforts are targeted.
2.	d	55	The factors of the other choices are demographic, economic, and technological; not social.
3.	a	55	Managers have the least amount of information available about social trends, which are the most important factor for estimating the success of clothing styles in the future.
4.	a	55	A trend to view anything disposable as wasteful and harmful to the environment is a threat for this firm.
5.	b	56	A component lifestyle pieces together products and services that fit a variety of interests and needs and does not conform to a certain stereotype.
6.	b	59	Generation Y is the cause of the increase of children's p roduct offerings in the 1990s.
7.	d	60	Generation X is most likely to be unemployed or underemployed.
8.	d	61	The number one trait was "to think for themselves." This created a need for marketers to target the individualistic characteristics of this important but large target group.
9.	e	62	About 3 in 10 Canadians are not of French or British descent.
10.	b	65	In times of inflation, consumers are more price conscious and less brand-loyal.
11.	a	66	Reduced income, production, and employment result in reduced demand. These conditions define a recession.
12.	e	66	Applied research attempts to develop new or improved products.
13.	c	68	The Competition Bureau of Industry Canada is responsible for enforcing laws covering trade practices, competition, credit, labelling and packaging, copyright, hazardous products, patents, trademarks, and much more.
14.	b	70	The nature of the competitive environment dictates the amount of flexibility a firm will have with its pricing.
15.	b	72	Preconventional morality is described as calculating, self-centred, and even selfish, and based on what will be immediately punished or rewarded. The firm will be immediately rewarded by higher profits if it sells the potentially harmful meat.
16.	b	72	Conventional morality moves from an egocentric viewpoint toward the expectations of society. The beer company is trying to operate by the standards set by society.
17.	c	73	Postconventional morality represents the morality of the mature adult. People are less concerned about how others might see them and more concerned about how they judge themselves over the long run. The chemical company is concerned with the long-term good of society.

18.	e	75	Social responsibility is the obligation that business feels for the welfare of society. By hiring the blind, the firm is helping to meet the needs of society.
19.	e	75	Social responsibility is a long-term commitment that business makes to the betterment of society.
20.	b	75	Economic responsibility is the basis of the other levels of corporate social responsibility.

SCENARIO SOLUTIONS

1. **False.** The requirement to be a joint venture is part of the political environment, as Hong Kong (as part of China) is communist.

2. **True** Ocean Park is a competitor, but it will most likely benefit from the attendance that Disneyland draw to Hong Kong.

3. **False** As described, Disneyland Hong Kong's m arket is based on geography, not demographics.

4. **b** Social change is not mentioned in the scenario at all.

5. **a** The Chinese government is the entity that can restrict or open the flow of residents from mainland China. This is an example of the political environment (government).

6. **d** Ocean Park is technically a competitor, though it probably won't have a huge impact on Disneyland.

7. **c** The pool of investors is an example of the economic environment. The willingness of the investors to buy equity shares, should they be offered, will highly depend on the economic conditions in the country.

8. The factors not mentioned in the scenario are demographics, social change, and technology. How demographics can impact the company: China has a negative birthrate, partially due to the strict population control policy of the government. Thus, the population of children is lower than that of most countries. Disneyland may have to adjust to this by building more adult-oriented attractions. How social change can impact the company: since China has allowed its residents more and more exposure to Western culture, more and more Chinese may have positive attitudes toward all things Western, even commercialism. How technology can impact the company: the technology that exists for new rides and attractions, such as the newer "simulation" rides or 3D shows, will impact the types of attractions Disney has to offer.

ESSAY QUESTION SOLUTIONS

1. There are six environmental factors discussed in the text. Here are some possibilities of how these factors might affect movie marketing to children:

    Social Change: Values, attitudes, beliefs, changing role of women, component lifestyles.

    Demographics: The size and growth rates of different generation groups (Gen Y, Gen X, Baby Boomers, older consumers), changing ethnic groups.

    Economic Conditions: The economic cycle (recession, recovery, prosperity), inflation, interest rates.

    Technology: The Internet, manufacturing technology, communications technology.

    Competition: Structure of an industry, size and strength of competitors, degree of interdependence in the industry.

    Political and Legal Factors: Federal legislation, provincial laws, self-regulation, and NAFTA.

    (text pp. 55-71)

2. Several trends are apparent in the 1990s:

    Canada is growing older, or approaching middle-age. The longer life span of Canadians suggests a growing market for products and services targeted toward the elderly: easy-open packages, insurance, easy-to-read labels, items designed for those with arthritic hands, food products for people with dentures, and health-care programs.

    Canada is growing at a slower rate. The annual growth rate is less than 1 percent, and populations of younger Canadian citizens are shrinking. Marketers should shift their emphasis to groups with a higher growth rate, such as the elderly, or focus on the specialized needs of market niches.

    The greatest degree of multiculturalism is found in the largest census metropolitan areas across the nation (Toronto, Vancouver, Calgary, Edmonton, and Montreal). These areas are of key importance for regional marketing efforts.

    Many ethnic markets are not homogeneous. There is not an Asian market or an Indian market but instead there are many niches within ethnic markets, which signals the need for micromarketing strategies.

    (text pp. 58-64)

3.　　**Preconventional morality** is childlike in nature. It is calculating, self-centered, and even selfish, and based on what will be immediately punished or rewarded. The Bolt salesperson might say, "It does not matter to whom I sell my products or how the products are used in the long run. That is not my problem. All that matters is the great profit I can get from every sale."

　　Conventional morality moves from an egocentric viewpoint toward the expectations of society. Loyalty and obedience to the organization (or society) become paramount. The Bolt salesperson might say, "I need to make sure that I sell my products in such a way that the company remains profitable, but I should only sell to carefully screened, responsible, adult customers."

　　Postconventional morality represents the morality of the mature adult. At this level people are less concerned about how others might see them and more concerned about how they see and judge themselves over the long run. The Bolt salesperson might say, "Even though the sale of my product is legal and will increase company profits, is it right in the long run? Might it do more harm than good in the end? Maybe I should quit this job and go back to school."

　　(text, pp. 72-73)

4.　　Information technology and the Internet have been responsible for many of the productivity gains experienced by Canadian businesses in the past decade. The role of the Internet in improving productivity has largely revolved around innovation, collaboration (improving and accelerating communication), design, purchasing, manufacturing, logistics (e.g., facilitating expanded sales and distribution networks), marketing, and service.

　　(text, pp. 66-67)

5.　　The pyramid of corporate social responsibility portrays four kinds of responsibility: economic, legal, ethical, and philanthropic. Economic performance is the foundation for the structure, because if the company does not make a profit, then the other three responsibilities are moot. While maintaining a profit, business is expected to obey the law, do what is ethically right, and be a good corporate citizen.

- Philanthropic responsibilities are to be a good corporate citizen, contribute resources to the community, and improve the quality of life.
- Ethical responsibilities are to be ethical, do what is right, just, and fair, and to avoid harm
- Legal responsibilities are to obey the law, which is society's codification of right and wrong, and play by the rules of the game.
- Economic responsibilities are to be profitable, because profit is the foundation on which all other responsibilities rest.

　　(text, pp. 75-76)

APPLICATION SOLUTIONS

There are six environmental factors discussed in the text. Here are some possibilities of how these factors might affect movie marketing to children:

Social Change: Values and held by this age group will change over time. The movie should pay attention to what's "cool" in fashion, music, and attitudes, as well as to what parents are saying about kids' fashions, music, and attitudes.

Demographics: After ten years of exploding birth rates (Generation Y), the birth rate will continue to decline. Though your demographic is still large, the teen demographic is becoming larger at this point.

Economic Conditions: Right now, Canada is in a slight recession. Though children will still go to movies during a recession, this will affect your pricing.

Technology: New technology will affect the special effects that your movie is expected to have – children in this age group have high expectations of technology and what it can do.

Competition: Competition is always a factor in the movie-making business. Movies studios like Disney, Warner Brothers, and DreamWorks always fight for market share.

Political and Legal Factors: The rating system used by the movie industry is a legal issue used to warn parents about the movie content.

(text pp. 35-70)

PRETEST SOLUTIONS

1. The five steps of the consumer decision-making process are:
   - Need recognition: An imbalance between actual and desired states.
   - Information search: Consumer seeks information about various alternatives to satisfy the need.
   - Evaluation of alternatives: Consumer evaluates the different products that will satisfy the need.
   - Purchase: Consumer purchases the product(s).
   - Postpurchase behaviour: Consumer evaluates the purchase decision and may be satisfied or unhappy with the decision.
   (text p. 91)

2. Five factors that could influence the level of consumer involvement in decision-making are previous experience with the purchase or product, interest in the purchase, perceived risk of negative consequences, the situation around the purchase, and social visibility of the product.
   (text pp. 97)

3. Three cultural factors influencing consumer decision-making are:
   - Culture and values: A consumer's ow n culture and the values that it holds will influence decisions.
   - Subculture: A homogeneous group of people who share values with the overall culture but also have values unique to its own smaller group.
   - Social class: A group of people who are considered nearly equal in status or community esteem, who socialize among themselves, and who share behavioural norms.
   (text 99-106)

4. Three social factors influencing consumer decision-making are:
   - Reference groups: All the formal and informal groups that influence a consumer's decis ion-making.
   - Opinion leaders: People within specific reference groups who influence others.
   - Family: Has a large influence on consumer decision-making.
   (text pp. 106-111)

5. Three individual factors influencing consumer decision-making are:
   - Gender: Men and women make purchase decisions differently.
   - Age and family life cycle: Consumers may make decisions based on either their age or their stage in the family life cycle (such as being "mar ried with children" or "single ").
   - Personality, self-concept, and lifestyle: An individual's personality traits, self-concept (how he or she sees themselves), and lifestyle (a mode of living) influence decision-making.
   (text pp. 111-114)

6. Four psychological factors influencing consumer decision-making are:
   - Perception: The process by which we select, organize, and interpret stimuli into meaningful and coherent pictures.
   - Motivation: The driving force that causes a person to take action.
   - Learning: The process that creates changes in behaviour through experience and practice.
   - Beliefs and attitudes: Beliefs are an organized pattern of knowledge that an individual holds as true about his or her world. Attitudes are learned tendencies to respond consistently toward a given object.
   (text pp. 115-121)

VOCABULARY PRACTICE SOLUTIONS

1. consumer behaviour
2. consumer decision-making process, stimulus, need recognition
3. want
4. evoked set, internal information search, external information search, marketing-controlled information source, nonmarketing-controlled information source
5. cognitive dissonance
6. involvement
7. routine response behaviour, limited decision making, extensive decision making
8. culture, subculture
9. reference groups, primary membership group, secondary membership group, aspirational group, nonaspirational reference group, norms, opinion leaders
10. socialization process
11. social class

12. personality, self concept, ideal self image, real self-image
13. lifestyle
14. perception, selective exposure, selective distortion, selective retention
15. motive, Maslow's hie rarchy of needs, learning, stimulus generation, stimulus discrimination
16. value, belief, attitude

TRUE/FALSE SOLUTIONS
(question number / correct answer / text page reference / answer rationale)

1.	T	90	
2.	T	93	
3.	F	96	This describes an extensive buying decision.
4.	F	96	Acquiring information about an unfamiliar brand in a familiar product category is called limited decision-making.
5.	T	96	
6.	F	100	The entire nation of Canada is probably a culture. Canada can, however, be divided into a number of subcultures, such as age, region, or ethnicity.
7.	F	105	Canada's social class system may not be similar to those in other countries. Additionally, the class delineations are not clearly defined.
8.	T	107	
9.	F	113	Affordability has nothing to do with personality.
10.	F	115	This describes selective retention because the information was not remembered. If selective distortion had occurred, Jon would have changed or distorted the information he read.
11.	T	117	
12.	F	120	Attitudes are formed toward brands, while beliefs are formed about specific attributes.

AGREE/DISAGREE SOLUTIONS
(question number / sample answers)

1. Reason(s) to agree: Even in making trivial decisions, such as deciding which restaurant to go to, consumers go through every step of the decision making process. Consumers recognize a need ("we're hungry"), search for information ("whic h restaurant is near us?"), evaluate alternatives ("there are t hree restaurants, which one sounds the best to you?"), purchase (go to the restaurant and buy lunch), and engage in postpurchase behaviour (evaluate the food).
    Reason(s) to disagree: Certain types of purchases, such as impulse purchases, do not require all the steps in the decision making process. Consumers may not even think about the purchase until they are at the checkout counter of a grocery store, for instance.

2. Reason(s) to agree: Culture is beliefs, values, and lifestyles that are shared and learned by members of a society. As such, cultural values cut across all social groups that belong to that culture.
    Reason(s) to disagree: Different social classes are different subcultures. While some basic values are shared, subcultures have distinctions that set them apart from each other. For example, the higher classes may place a high value on higher education, while lower social classes may place a higher value on economic independence.

3. Reason(s) to agree: Manufacturers of cosmetics, clothing, and even sports cars portray aspirational reference groups in their advertisements in order to appeal to a specific target market. Cosmetics companies show beautiful women with flawless skin, while sports car manufacturers may show a savvy man who "has everything." Marketers want to show specific target markets what they could become if they bought the product.
    Reason(s) to disagree: Some of the most effective advertisements show "real people," not beautiful people. By showing real people, marketers are trying to get target markets to identify more directly with the product as "somet hing for me."

4. Reason(s) to agree: In marketing, it does not matter which product is better, it only matters what the consumer perceives is the better product.
    Reason(s) to disagree: Reality (scientific studies) can influence how consumers perceive things.

MULTIPLE-CHOICE SOLUTIONS
(question number / correct answer / text page reference / answer rationale)

1.   c   90   The TV commercial is an external stimulus.
2.   d   91   A want is often brand specific, whereas a need is something an individual depends on in order to function efficiently. A person may need clothing but want specific brands.
3.   b   92   Public sources of information such as magazines, consumer rating organizations, or even professionals not associated with the marketing company are known as nonmarketing-controlled information sources.
4.   e   95   Each option offered would help to reduce the postpurchase anxiety a consumer might experience.
5.   a   96   The buying of frequently purchased, low-cost goods is typically routine response behaviour.
6.   e   97   Because of the situational factors, this low-cost item is a high-involvement product in this case.
7.   d   98   This is a low-involvement purchase that requires little search. The best strategy is to put the candy at the point-of-purchase, where impulse decisions are often made.
8.   e   103   This is the definition of a subculture.
9.   b   105   As a college-educated professional, Joe is part of the upper middle class.
10.   e   107   Aspirational groups are those groups that someone would like to join but currently is not a member.
11.   b   107   A nonaspirational or dissociative group is one that the consumer attempts to maintain distance from and does not want to imitate in purchase behaviour.
12.   c   107   Frozen corn is a low-cost, low-involvement good. Reference group influence is more strongly felt on high-risk (beer or cigarettes), socially visible (clothing, beer, or cigarettes), or high-cost (car) products.
13.   a   110   The family is the most important social institution for many consumers.
14.   b   111   Consumer is used to denote the user of the good or service. This question emphasizes how wide a difference there can be between consumer and purchaser.
15.   d   113   Ideal self-image represents the way an individual would like to be.
16.   a   114   Lifestyle is defined by one's activities, interests, and opinions.
17.   c   115   Selective retention is the process whereby a consumer remembers only that information which supports personal feelings or beliefs.
18.   b   117   Safety needs are one of the first needs that individuals seek to satisfy, and the alarm system's selling point is the safety and security it provides.
19.   b   119   Lever Brothers' intention is to encourage trial of the product in order to engage learning (process that creates a change in behaviour).
20.   e   119   Stimulus generalization occurs when one response (positive attitude for a product) is extended to a second, similar stimulus (new product, same brand).
21.   c   120   A belief is often developed about the attributes of a product. Attitudes, however, are more complex and encompass values.
22.   d   121   The text offers these three choices as methods to employ when attempting an attitude change.

SCENARIO SOLUTIONS

1.   True
2.   True
3.   False   The vendor Web sites represent marketing-controlled sources.
4.   c   C-Net and Consumer Reports are objective sources that are not heavily influenced by product vendors.
5.   b   Information search is often done on the Internet today.
6.   b   Cognitive dissonance is the inner tension a consumer feels after recognizing an inconsistency between behaviour and values or opinions – in this case, some of the other photographers made her feel as though she could have gotten a better camera.
7.   a   Extensive decision-making reflects high involvement from the consumer for a generally high cost product, much more external information searches, and many different alternatives.
8.   There is no right or wrong answer.

ESSAY QUESTION SOLUTIONS

1.   Consumer behaviour is a series of processes a consumer uses to make purchase decisions, as well as to use and dispose of purchased goods and services. Consumer behaviour also includes factors that influence decisions and product use. Consumer marketing managers must understand consumer behaviour in order to develop a marketing mix that meets those needs.
     (text p. 90)

2.   The three levels of buying decisions are routine response behaviour, limited decision-making, and extensive decision-making.
     Routine response behaviour is used for frequently purchased, low-cost goods and services. Little search and decision time are needed for these products. Examples include regular grocery items (milk, bread, eggs).
     Limited decision-making requires a moderate amount of time for gathering information and deliberative about an unfamiliar brand in a familiar product category. Examples include selecting another brand of cereal when your favourite brand is out.
     Extensive decision-making is used when buying an unfamiliar, expensive product or an infrequently bought item. This requires the use of several criteria for evaluating options and much time for seeking information. Examples include purchasing a house, a car, a stereo, or a TV.
     (text pp. 96-97)

3.   There are five levels in Maslow's hierarchy of needs:
     Physiological needs are the most basic level of human needs and include food, water, and shelter.
     Safety needs include security and freedom from pain and discomfort.
     Social needs involve a sense of belonging and love.
     Self-esteem needs include self-respect, feelings of accomplishment, prestige, fame, and recognition.
     Self-actualization is the highest human need. It refers to self-fulfillment and self-expression.
     (text pp. 117-118)

4.   A reference group is a formal or informal group of people that influence the buying behaviour of an individual. Four reference groups are:
     Primary membership groups are all people with whom an individual interacts regularly, such as family, friends, and coworkers. Friends and coworkers probably have the greatest influence on your wardrobe.
     Secondary membership groups are people with whom an individual interacts more formally, such as clubs, professional groups, and religious groups. A church group may influence how an individual dresses at church functions.
     Aspirational reference groups are those that a person would like to join. An individual may see an attractive model in a magazine advertisement and want to dress like that model.
     Nonaspirational reference group are those from whom an individual tries to dissociate him- or herself. The individual may avoid dressing like others at school in order to present a more professional image.
     (text pp. 106-107)

5.   The three methods are listed with some possible examples.
     Changing beliefs about attributes: The company could work to promote the image of a family brand by changing consumers' beliefs about adult versus children's toothpastes. Any negative beliefs or misconceptions should also be changed. For example, consumers may believe the toothpaste wears enamel or stains teeth when in fact it does not.
     Changing the importance of beliefs: The company could start emphasizing certain attributes that already exist. These might include environmental concerns (a package made of 100 percent recycled materials) or consumer preferences (the favourite choice of all consumers).
     Adding new beliefs: The company could try to expand the consumption habits of consumers by encouraging them to brush more than three times a day. The company could also emphasize additional attributes to the ones already in use such as more cavity fighting ingredients, enamel builders, or patriotism (a red, white package with a Canadian flag on it).
     (text pp. 120-122)

APPLICATION SOLUTIONS
Application #1:
For this high-involvement decision process, you would go through these steps:

1. **Need recognition:** You want to go to graduate business school.
2. **Information search:** You check both internal and external sources of information. Internal sources can include your own skills, knowledge, and feelings about geographic location of the schools. External sources can include college catalogues, college visits and interviews, and college guides that rank and describe various business programs.
3. **Evaluation of alternatives:** You consider attributes of various schools in an evoked set. These attributes might include overall reputation of the school, tuition rates, availability of scholarships or other financial aid, and geographic location.
4. **Purchase:** You apply to the schools you select. Upon hearing which schools will accept you, you decide which school you'll enter a nd accept the offer. You start your studies at the school.
5. **Postpurchase behaviour:** You are satisfied with your purchase, which was the result of extensive decision-making. Alternatively, you are dissatisfied with your purchase, leave the school, and begin the process again.

(text pp. 90-95)

Application #2:
The factors that affect involvement level are previous experience, interest, perceived risk of negative consequences, situation, and social visibility.

Previous experience. Because there may be no previous experience or familiarity with the product, level of involvement will be high.

Interest. Areas of interest vary by individual. You may or may not be interested in athletic shoes. However, purchasing the shoes indicates an interest in the social group and probably a high level of involvement.

Perceived risk of negative consequences. Several types of risks are involved in the purchase. With expensive shoes, loss of purchasing power and opportunity costs result in financial risk. A social risk is taken, because wearing these shoes may cause a positive or negative reaction from other peer groups. For example, some might view the purchase as frivolous. Finally, there is a psychological risk involved in the form of anxiety or concern about whether the "right" shoes have been purchased and are acceptable to other members of the social club.

Situation. The circumstances of the social club make the shoes a high-involvement purchase.

Social visibility. Because these shoes are on social and public display, wearing the shoes makes a statement about the individual. This would also make the purchase a high-involvement one.

(text p. 97)

CHAPTER 5: BUSINESS MARKETING

PRETEST SOLUTIONS

1. Business marketing is the marketing of goods and services to individuals and organizations for purposes other than personal consumption.
   (text p. 132)
2. A strategic alliance is a cooperative arrangement between business firms.
   (text p. 134)
3. Four major categories of business market customers are:
   - **Producers:** organizations that produce finished goods or services.
   - **Resellers:** retailers and wholesalers that buy finished goods and resell them for a profit.
   - **Governments:** national, provincial, or local governments.
   - **Institutions:** organizations that seek to achieve goals other than the standard business goals of profit, market share, and return on investment. These could include churches, labour union, or charities.

   (text pp. 137-139)
4. Seven types of business goods and services are:
   - **Major equipment:** capital goods such as large or expensive machines, mainframe computers, furnaces, generators, airplanes, and buildings.
   - **Accessory equipment:** such as portable tools and office equipment that are less expensive and shorter-lived than major equipment.
   - **Raw materials:** unprocessed products such as mineral, ore, lumber, wheat, corn, fruit, vegetables, and fish.

- **Component parts**: either finished items for assembly or products that need very little processing before becoming part of some other product.
- **Processed materials**: products used directly in manufacturing other products.
- **Supplies**: consumable items that do not become part of the final product.
- **Business services**: expense items that do not become part of a final product.

(text pp. 144-145)

5. Five important aspects of business buying behaviour are:
   - **Buying centre**: all those persons who become involved in the purchase decision.
   - **Evaluative criteria**: criteria that are used to evaluate a purchase decision, such as price, service, and quality.
   - **Buying situations**: whether the product being considered is a "new buy," a "modi fied rebuy," or a "straight re buy."
   - **Purchasing ethics**: ethical decisions involved in purchasing.
   - **Customer service**: service given by potential suppliers.

(text pp. 146-150)

VOCABULARY PRACTICE SOLUTIONS

1. business marketing
2. strategic alliance (strategic partnership)
3. keiretsu
4. North American Industry Classification System (NAICS)
5. derived demand, joint demand, multiplier effect (or accelerator principle)
6. reciprocity
7. major equipment, accessory equipment, raw materials, component parts, OEM, processed materials, supplies, business services
8. buying centre
9. new buy, modified rebuy, straight rebuy

TRUE/FALSE SOLUTIONS

(question number / correct answer / text page reference / answer rationale)

1.	F	132	Since the end user of the product is the consumer, Hitsui is engaged in consumer marketing, not business marketing. Just because a manufacturer uses retailers in its distribution does not mean that it is engaged in business marketing.
2.	F	132	Because of the Internet, GE' s business market sales are larger than its consumer sales.
3.	T	134	
4.	F	137	Firms can "pr oduce" services as well as goods.
5.	T	137	
6.	F	139	Institutions generally have goals other than standard business goals. For instance, churches don't ge nerally make a profit but depend on donations to offset costs.
7.	F	139	As its name indicates, NAICS (North American Industry Classification System) has been adopted only by Mexico, Canada, and the United States.
8.	F	141	This represents inelastic demand.
9.	F	143	It is business marketing channels that are more direct and shorter than consumer channels.
10.	T	143	
11.	T	144	
12.	F	149	Adding features is an example of a modified rebuy.

AGREE/DISAGREE SOLUTIONS

(question number / sample answers)

1. Reason(s) to agree: Because business customers are fewer and far more important on an individual basis, it is more important for firms to develop strategic alliances in order to provide strong products and services to important business customers.

   Reason(s) to disagree: Strategic alliances are no more important to business marketers than to consumer marketers. Each type of organization can use alliances in any aspect of their business: from R&D to distribution.

2. Reason(s) to agree: Because business customers are fewer, marketers can get to know them well. Products can be targeted—and even tailored—to these customers to increase the chance for a sale.
   Reason(s) to disagree: Business customers are much more sophisticated buyers than consumers. Business marketing requires a thorough understanding of the buying situation, the people involved in the buying decision, and the customer's ove rall goals. Business buying can be highly complex and even political.

3. Reason(s) to agree: Just like consumers, business customers start with need recognition, seek information, evaluate alternative solutions, purchase, and engage in postpurchase behaviour.
   Reason(s) to disagree: Business buying behaviour is much more complex and includes several other steps in the process, such as establishing evaluative criteria, setting up buying situations, and establishing purchasing ethical guidelines.

4. Reason(s) to agree: A lot of hard work would go into a single sale to a business market, but the sale would be a big one.
   Reason(s) to disagree: There are rewards to selling to consumers markets as well. Since consumer goods tend to be better known than most business goods, the salesperson could enjoy the prestige of a well-known product.

5. Reason(s) to agree: The more prevalent e-commerce becomes, the greater efficiencies companies will experience. This will result in lower prices, greater purchasing power, and a higher standard of living for everyone.
   Reason(s) to disagree: E-commerce only benefits those who can really take advantage of the opportunities it provides. Not all industries and companies are a good fit for e-commerce, so not everyone benefits from it.

MULTIPLE-CHOICE SOLUTIONS

(question number / correct answer / text page reference / answer rationale)

1.	e	132	All the offered transaction types define business exchanges.
2.	d	132	Business markets will continue to be larger and more powerful than consumers markets with the use of the Internet.
3.	c	134	Strategic alliances are difficult to maintain over time.
4.	e	137	All of these businesses are producers.
5.	d	138	Reseller is the best answer because Sysco purchases finished goods and resells them. Sysco does not produce the goods or change their form and is not an institution. Because it actually purchases the goods, it is not just a transportation company. Inventory carrier is an unrelated term that does not explain why Sysco would break down quantities into cases.
6.	b	138	The most common process involves sealed bids, with selection going to the lowest price.
7.	a	139	The only example of a for-profit organization in the list is convenience stores, and they would not be customers of an institutional-only supplier.
8.	a	139	NAICS is only used to classify firms within North America.
9.	c	140	NAICS currently uses a six-digit classification system.
10.	a	141	Joint demand is the demand for two or more items used together in the final product.
11.	a	141	A product is price inelastic if a change in price leads to a small change in quantity demanded or does not significantly affect demand for the product. This often happens with utilities or other services that are highly demanded.
12.	e	141	When two or more items are used in combination in the final product, they have a joint demand.
13.	d	143	Businesses tend to be more formal in purchasing procedures and perform more paperwork and more analysis.
14.	a	143	Reciprocity is the normal business practice of using customers as suppliers of goods or services.
15.	e	144	Fishing is an extractive industry, and the fish are sent with little or no alteration to Star-Kist. This fits the definition of raw materials.
16.	b	145	The engines are finished items, ready for assembly into another item.
17.	e	145	As the manufacturer of the finished software that gets stored on the CDs, Microsoft is a good example of an OEM (original equipment manufacturer) market.
18.	a	147	A gatekeeper is anyone who regulates the flow of information in a purchasing decision situation.
19.	c	148	Because this is a new and complicated purchase, it will require a thorough analysis by the industrial buyer.
20.	a	149	When a previously purchased item needs to be reordered, but with changes or additions, it is a modified rebuy.
21.	c	149	Ordering the product again without consideration of competitive products represents a straight rebuy.

SCENARIO SOLUTIONS

1. True
2. False   The hospital is an institution which prescribes the pharmaceuticals but doesn't sell t hem to users.
3. True   As a sales representative, Ryan is part of marketing's pr omotional activities.
4. b   Drugstores purchase pharmaceuticals from producers and resell them to people with prescriptions.
5. a   Since there is a patent on the product and since it has the leading share, the product most likely enjoyed inelastic demand. If the price were to increase, the demand probably wouldn't change very much.
6. c   The purchasing manager actually negotiates the purchase of pharmaceuticals.
7. a   As the resident experts on pharmaceuticals and their impact on health, doctors are the influencers in the buying centre.
8.   **New Buy:** A new buy is a situation requiring the purchase of a product for the first time. When Burke's ulcer medicine first hit the market, Ryan would have forced a "new buy" situation because the medicine has a patent and is a strong performer.

       Modified Rebuy: A modified rebuy is a situation where the purchaser wants some change in the original good or service. Since it is unlikely that the hospital would force a change in a drug, the change would probably occur with a service issue, such as speeding up the delivery of the product.

       Straight Rebuy: A straight rebuy is a situation in which the purchaser reorders the same goods or services without looking for new information or investigating other suppliers. If the ulcer medicine is that much stronger than competitor's medicines, it is likely that the hospital will use this situation the most.

ESSAY QUESTION SOLUTIONS

1. A strategic alliance is a cooperative arrangement between business firms. Strategic alliances may include licensing agreements, joint ventures, distribution agreements, research and development consortia, and other general forms of partnership. Strategic alliances are becoming very important in business marketing because firms are realizing that they can become more competitive by taking on a partner that may have more expertise in a certain area or that has access to certain markets. Successful strategic alliances allow all partners to gain substantial benefits from the alliance.
(text pp. 134-135)

2. **Producers** include individuals and organizations that purchase goods and services for the purpose of making a profit by using them to produce other goods, to become part of other goods, or to facilitate the daily operations of a firm. Text examples include General Motors, Bombardier, and Alcan.

       Resellers include those wholesale and retail businesses that buy finished goods and resell them for a profit. Examples could include any grocery store or retail-clothing store.

       Government organizations include a large number of buying units that purchase goods and services. The federal, provincial, and municipal (MASH) governments are all examples.

       Institutions are nonprofit organizations that have different primary goals from ordinary businesses. This category includes churches, civic clubs, foundations, and labour unions.
(text pp. 137-139)

3. Eleven differences are:

       Demand: There are several differences between organizational and consumer demand. Organizational demand is derived from the demand of consumer products, tends to be price inelastic, has joint demand with related products used in combination with the final product, and tends to fluctuate more than consumer demand.

       Purchase volume: Business customers buy in much larger quantities (both in single orders and in total annual volume) than do consumers.

       Number of customers: Business marketers tend to have far fewer customers than consumer marketers.

       Location of buyers: Unlike consumer markets, business customers tend to be geographically concentrated.

       Distribution structure: Channels of distribution tend to be much shorter in business marketing. Direct channels are also more common.

       Nature of buying: Business buying is usually more formalized with responsibility assigned to buying centres or purchasing agents.

       Nature of buying influence: More people are involved in business purchasing decisions than in consumer purchases because many levels and departments of the firm are involved in the purchase.

Type of negotiations: Bargaining and price negotiation are more common in business marketing, including lengthy stipulations of final contracts.

Use of reciprocity: Business purchasers often buy from their customers, and vice versa.

Use of leasing: Businesses often lease equipment, unlike consumers who more often purchase products.

Primary promotional method: Personal selling is often emphasized in business marketing, while advertising is emphasized in consumer marketing.

There are several similarities between business and consumer buying behaviour. First, both types of buyers use a decision process to make choices, although the steps can be different. Additionally, the personal makeup of individual buyers in a business purchasing situation continues to influence the purchase. Finally, both types of buyers react to environmental and situational factors when making a purchasing decision, including the influences of other role players (household members versus other organization members), influence of culture (either subcultures or organizational culture), or other environmental conditions (lifestyle or work style).
(text pp. 141-144)

4.　　The seven types of business goods and services are:

Major equipment such as large or expensive machines, computer systems, or generators.

Accessory equipment, or shorter-lived and less expensive equipment, such as fax machines, power tools or microcomputers.

Raw materials, or unprocessed extractive or agricultural products, such as mineral ore, lumber, and wheat.

Component parts such as spark plugs, tires, or electric motors for cars.

Processed materials, or materials used in manufacturing other products, such as sheet metal, chemicals, and plastics.

Supplies such as business stationery, cleansers, or paper towels.

Business services such as advertising, marketing research, or air freight.
(text pp. 144-146)

5.　　The benefits of Internet marketing can be great for business marketers. Some benefits include increased efficiency, cost reduction, improved customer service, one-to-one relationships, new product introduction, and expanded markets.
(text p. 132)

6.　　The North American Industry Classification System (NAICS) is a detailed numbering system developed by the United States, Canada, and Mexico to classify North American business establishments by their main production processes. This will allows businesses in all three countries to immediately identify type of business markets when they do business in the other two countries.
(text pp. 139-140)

7.　　**New buy:** A new buy is a situation requiring the purchase of a product or service for the first time. In this case, Pike's would have no experience buying colour copiers or has not established any relationship with a vendor of colour copiers. Pike's may be a new or small company that currently does not have any colour copiers at all. Alternatively, Pike's may be involved in value engineering and searching for less expensive alternatives than buying colour copiers. These could include photography or hand reproduction of colour materials.

Modified rebuy: In this case Pike's would have experience with copiers in general and an established relationship with office equipment vendors. The focus would be on the new need of added colour capabilities.

Straight rebuy: In this case the purchase of colour copiers would be a routine purchasing decision or a reorder of previously ordered colour copiers from the same vendor. Perhaps Pike's is a reseller of colour copiers.
(text p. 203-204)

The **initiator** of the buying decision could be identified as the salesperson who identified the need but more likely would be the sales force manager who suggested the purchase be made.

Influencers/evaluators might include the finance office (which would control the amount of money available for the purchase), members of the sales force (who might provide information about phones that competitors are using), and the purchasing department (which would have a good knowledge of alternative suppliers).

Gatekeepers could include management (which would only approve of certain phone models that are compatible with existing phone systems), the finance office (which may only approve a limited budget), and the purchasing department (which would recommend matches with likely vendors).

The **decider** might be the president of the company, the president of marketing, or the sales force manager; the decider is the person with the power to approve the brand of phone.

The **purchaser** will be the purchasing agent in the purchasing department who will negotiate the terms of the sale.
Users will include all sales force members who will use the cellular phone.
(text pp. 146-147)

CHAPTER 6: SEGMENTING AND TARGETING MARKETS

PRETEST SOLUTIONS

1. A market is people or organizations with needs or wants and with the ability and the willingness to buy. A market segment is a subgroup of the market who share one or more characteristics that cause them to have similar product needs.
(text p. 160)

2. The four basic criteria for segmenting consumer markets are: 1) substantiality; 2) identifiability and measurability; 3) accessibility; and 4) responsiveness.
(text p. 161-162)

3. Five bases for segmenting consumer markets are:
   - Geographic segmentation: Segmenting by region of the country or world, market size, market density, or climate.
   - Demographic segmentation: Segmenting by age, gender, income, ethnicity, or family life cycle.
   - Psychographic segmentation: Segmenting by personality, motives, lifestyles, or geodemographics (neighbourhood lifestyle characteristics such as segmenting by postal codes).
   - Benefit segmentation: Segmenting by benefits that consumers seek from products.
   - Usage-rate segmentation: Segmenting by the amount of product bought or consumed.
   (text pp. 162-172)

4. Two bases for segmenting business markets are:
   - Company Characteristics: Segmenting according to location, customer type, customer size, or product use.
   - Buying Processes: Segmenting according to key purchasing criteria, purchasing strategies, importance of purchase, or personal characteristics.
   (text p. 172-174)

5. The six steps in segmenting a market are:
   - Select a market or category for study.
   - Choose a basis or bases for segmenting the market.
   - Select segmentation descriptors.
   - Profile and evaluate segments.
   - Select target markets.
   - Design, implement, and maintain appropriate marketing mixes for each segment.
   (text pp. 174-175)

6. Three strategies for selecting target markets are:
   - Undifferentiated targeting: targeting the entire mass market.
   - Concentrated targeting: focusing on a market niche, or a single segment.
   - Multisegment targeting: targeting two or more well-defined segments.
   (text pp. 175-178)

6. Positioning is developing a specific marketing mix to influence potential customers' overall perception of a brand, product line, or organization in general.
(text p. 178)

VOCABULARY PRACTICE SOLUTIONS

1. market
2. market segment, market segmentation
3. segmentation bases (variables)
4. geographic segmentation
5. demographic segmentation, family life cycle (FLC)
6. psychographic segmentation, geodemographic segmentation
7. benefit segmentation, usage rate segmentation, 80/20 principle
8. satisficer, optimizer
9. target market
10. undifferentiated targeting strategy, concentrated targeting strategy, niche, multisegment targeting, cannibalization
11. positioning, position, product differentiation, perceptual mapping, repositioning

TRUE/FALSE SOLUTIONS

(question number / correct answer / text page reference / answer rationale)

1. F 160 Animals are not able to make purchases, nor do they have the authority to buy, and, therefore, they cannot be called a market.
2. F 160 Even large companies like Coca-Cola practice market segmentation, as evidenced by the large variety of products that are offered at specific market segments.
3. T 160
4. T 161
5. F 168 Targeting baby boomers indicates age as a segmentation variable; no reference is made to marital status and parental status, which are considered in the family life cycle.
6. F 169 Psychographic segmentation specifically using variables of personality and lifestyle would better suit the Sharper Image.
7. T 221
8. F 175 Directing one marketing mix at the entire market is an undifferentiated strategy.
9. F 177 By targeting three distinct age groups, the Gap stores are using a multisegment strategy.
10. F 179 Perceptual maps tell marketers how various brands are perceived by consumers.
11. T 179

AGREE/DISAGREE SOLUTIONS

(question number / sample answers)

1. Reason(s) to agree: Market segmentation helps firms to define customer needs and wants more precisely. By doing this, firms can allocate resources more efficiently and more accurately define marketing objectives.
   Reason(s) to disagree: Market segmentation does not necessarily have to happen. It could be argued that undifferentiated targeting is actually the absence of market segmentation in that it views the market as one mass market with no individual segments. Some firms use this strategy very effectively.
2. Reason(s) to agree: Substantiality indicates whether a market is large enough to sustain sales and profit over the long term. The other criteria—identifiability and measurability, accessibility, and responsiveness—are secondary after determining the market size.
   Reason(s) to disagree: All the criteria are equally important. If any of the criteria is lacking, the market segmentation will not be successful.
3. Reason(s) to agree: All firms decide where to distribute their products. Retail outlets practice geographic segmentation by locating themselves near their geographic segments. Manufacturers practice geographic segmentation by selecting which distribution channels and retail outlets will offer their product.
   Reason(s) to disagree: Global markets are, by definition, not geographically segmented. A firm can sell products through the Internet with no intention to target one geographic market versus another.
4. Reason(s) to agree: Psychographic segmentation is very difficult and requires a lot of primary research into consumer personalities, lifestyles, and motives. Firms cannot pick up secondary sources of research and "find" their psychographic segments easily. Besides, the psychographic elements of consumers (personalities, etc.) are self-reported and may not be as accurate as pure demographic or geographic data.
   Reason(s) to disagree: Regardless of the inaccuracy of psychographic data, elements of consumer personalities, lifestyles, or motives are very real to the consumer. Though most firms choose demographic and geographic segmentation because of the ease of finding accurate data, psychographic segmentation may allow a firm to differentiate itself in the minds of consumers.

5. Reason(s) to agree: Repositioning rarely works. Once a brand is established and well known (whether for good or bad reasons), it is very difficult and expensive to change the image that the consumer has of the brand. One example is Oldsmobile's failed attempt to change its image to be a young adult's car. Another example is Coke's attempt to target a younger market with a sweeter product ("New Coke"). It is better to launch a new product with a clean slate than to change old attitudes and views about a product.

Reason(s) to disagree: It is more expensive to launch a new product than to reposition an old one. A new product must build awareness before it builds a large consumer franchise. An old product can be repositioned, as long as the repositioning is believable.

MULTIPLE-CHOICE SOLUTIONS
(question number / correct answer / text page reference / answer rationale)

1. c 160 A market is a group of people or organizations that has wants and needs that can be satisfied by particular product categories, has the ability to purchase these products, is willing to exchange resources for the products, and has the authority to do so.

2. d 160 Dividing one large market into groups is called market segmentation.

3. c 160 The purpose of segmentation is to group similar consumers and to serve their needs with a specialized marketing mix.

4. a 160 The rapidly changing nature of most markets (business and consumer) dictates a frequent and regular re-examination of the segmentation process.

5. e 161 Like any marketing institution, each of the factors mentioned is an important criterion to consider when employing a segmentation strategy.

6. e 161 Complexity is not a criterion; simplicity would be preferred.

7. d 161 Substantiality means that the selected segment will be large enough to warrant developing and maintaining a special marketing mix.

8. a 161 Serving the specific needs of a segment must be commercially viable, even if the number of potential customers is small.

9. a 161 Identifiability and measurability is the first problem: How does one know who is shy and timid and how many shy and timid people are out there? The company would have to know that before it can gauge if there are enough of them. If there were enough timid people, they would probably be responsive to a special product and accessible because of mass media.

10. b 162 Accessibility is the ability to communicate information about the product offering to the segment.

11. c 162 Responsiveness is in force when a target segment responds differently (hopefully more positively) to the marketing mix than other segments.

12. c 162 A segmentation base is the characteristic used to segment the market.

13. b 162 Targeting by terrain is an example of geographic segmentation.

14. d 164 Generation X is an age variable and is therefore demographic.

15. a 164 The only demographic variable is age.

16. b 168 By targeting marital status and the number of children in a household, the minivan is using family life cycle as its segmentation base.

17. d 169 Adventurous and fun-loving describe personality, which is a psychographic base.

18. e 172 By targeting heavy smokers, Wrigley's is using usage-rate segmentation (targeting "heavy users of cigarettes).

19. a 171 The pens are designed to offer different benefits and uses to different target groups.

20. c 172 The 80/20 principle proposes that a minority of a firm's customers will purchase a majority of the volume of the product.

21. b 174 Satisficers use a simple, quick purchasing strategy of looking for the first available adequate supplier.

22. a 172 Company characteristics include geographic location, type of company, company size, and product use.

23. d 175 An undifferentiated strategy would put Industry-Quip up against entrenched competitors, and the firm would have no product advantage.

24. a 176 Because it is the only outlet in this small community and is likely to serve a variety of needs, it would have a substantial marketing cost savings if it employed an undifferentiated segmentation strategy.

25. a 177 Left-Out is concentrating on one specific target market, which is a concentrated (or niche) targeting strategy.

26.	e	178	Cannibalization occurs when sales of a new product cause a decline in sales of a firm's existing products.
27.	d	179	The graphical display shows a perceptual map of consumers' percepti on of tea brands.
28.	e	181	Oldsmobile tried to reposition itself toward a younger target market, which may or may not have perceived the car as being for them.
29.	e	181	All the choices could be used in segmenting markets in other countries.

SCENARIO SOLUTIONS

1. True
2. False   Claire is using a concentrated strategy by focusing on one market segment.
3. False   Active and health-conscious people are examples of psychographic segmentation.
4. a   Geography doesn't ap pear to be a factor in Claire's tar get market.
5. b   Demographics include age and gender as well as ethnic origin, income, and family life cycle.
6. a   Claire has not considered if this target market is large enough to warrant her product development and marketing.
7. b   Claire has developed the product but has not developed the rest of the market mix: price, promotion, and distribution.
8. **Undifferentiated strategy:** This approach views the market as one big market with no individual segments and thus requires a single marketing mix. This probably doesn't make sense for VeggieChip which would not have strong appeal to the mass market.

    Concentrated strategy: This approach focuses on a single market segment. This is the approach that VeggieChip is taking, and it makes sense because fewer people with specific needs would buy such a health product.

    Multisegment strategy: This approach chooses two or more well defined market segments and develops a distinct marketing mix for each. This strategy could work if Claire could find another distinct segment that would buy the chips. An example would be mothers of young children who want to feed their children only the healthiest snacks in addition to the current target market.

ESSAY QUESTION SOLUTIONS

1. A market is a group of people or organizations with needs or wants and the ability and willingness to buy. A market segment is a subgroup of the market who shares one or more characteristics that cause them to have similar product needs. Market segmentation is important because it helps marketers define customer needs and wants more precisely.
   (text p. 160)

2. **Substantiality:** A selected segment must be large enough to warrant developing and maintaining a special marketing mix. (This means that the segment is commercially viable.) One could assume that many people have a dry scalp problem, especially in dry climates, after a sunburn, or when participating in outdoor activities with high winds (skiing, sailing, and so on).

   Identifiability and Measurability: The segments must be identifiable and their size measurable. Descriptive data regarding demographic, geographic, and other relevant characteristics of segment members must be available. It may be difficult to identify people who have dry scalps and describe them in terms of relevant characteristics. People may not realize that they have dry scalps and therefore may not respond to marketing research probes.

   Accessibility: The firm must be able to reach members of targeted segments with customized marketing mixes. If the segment is not measurable and cannot be described, it may be difficult to precisely know how to reach the dry scalp segment. Where do people with dry scalps shop? What media do they watch or read? What are their buying habits?

   Responsiveness: The market segment must respond differently from other segments to a marketing mix; otherwise, there is no need to treat that segment separately. People with dry scalps may not consider their problem to be important enough to respond differently and may continue to buy their current shampoo, which seems to meet needs.
   (text p. 161-162)

3. [Many different examples can be used. Make sure that each variable was used correctly.]
   Geographic variables: Target neighbourhoods near college campuses.
   Demographics variables: Target young women (aged 15-30).
   Psychographics variables: Target "New Ag e" followers.
   Benefits-sought variables: Target people who need a way to relax.
   Rate of product usage: Target people who are heavy users of aromatherapy products, such as shampoo or cologne.
   (text pp. 162-172)

4.   Possible benefits for toothpaste could include:
        Cavity/decay prevention--Crest
        White/bright teeth--Ultra Brite, Gleem, MacLeans, Plus White, Rembrandt
        Fresh breath--Close-Up, Pepsodent
        Tartar control--Tartar Control Crest, Tartar Control Colgate
        Plaque reduction--Dental Care, Viadent, Dentagard, Peak
        Stain remover--Pearl Drops, Topol, Caffree, Zact, Clinomyn, Rembrandt
        Gingivitis/gum disease prevention--Crest, Colgate, Metadent
        Flavour/great taste--Aim, Colgate, Stripe
        Fun for kids--Crest Sparkle, Oral-B Sesame Street, Colgate Jr.
        No mess--any pump or squeeze bottle toothpaste
        Sensitive teeth--Sensodyne, Denquel, Promise
        All-in-one--Aquafresh
        Denture cleaning--Dentu-Creme, Dentu-Gel, Complete
        Baking soda--Arm & Hammer, Metadent
        Low price--Arm & Hammer, store brands, brands on sale
        (text p. 171-172)

5.   Undifferentiated strategy: Target everyone within a five-mile radius of the store. (Your thinking is that everyone should eat organic foods!)
        Concentrated strategy: Target higher income families that are extremely health conscious.
        Multisegment strategy: Target higher income professional women who are health conscious and elderly people who are health conscious.
        (text pp. 175-178)

6.   A perceptual map is a means of displaying or graphing, in two or more dimensions, the location of products, brands, or groups of products in customers' minds. Marketers use perceptual maps to determine many things, such as how their own brands are perceived, how competitive brands are perceived, and where market gaps may exist.
        (text p. 179)

7.   5, 4, 1, 3, 6, 2 is the proper order of steps. See Exhibit 6.6.

APPLICATION SOLUTIONS
Application #1:
There are five possible ways to segment this market:
- One homogeneous market consisting of ten people (one segment)
- A market consisting of ten individual segments
- A market composed of two segments based upon age group (five adults and five children)
- A market composed of three segments based upon region (four South, two Northeast, four West)
- A market composed of five segments based on age group and region (one Adult/South, two Adult/Northeast, two Adult/West, three Child/South, two Child/West)

(text pp. 162-167)

Application #2:
The map should be as follows:
Upper left quadrant: Coca-Cola, Pepsi-cola
Upper right quadrant: Gatorade, Powerade
Lower left quadrant: Dasani, Evian, Aquafina
Lower right quadrant: Propel
(text p. 180)

PRETEST SOLUTIONS

1. Marketing research is the process of planning, collecting, and analyzing data relevant to a marketing decision. Three roles are:
    *   Descriptive: Gathering and presenting factual statements.
    *   Diagnostic: Explaining data.
    *   Predictive: Addressing "what if" questions.
    (text pp. 190-191)

2. Steps in the marketing research process are: 1) Identifying and formulating the problem or opportunity; 2) Planning the research design and gathering primary data; 3) Specifying the sampling procedures; 4) Collecting data; 5) Analyzing the data; 6) Preparing and presenting the report; and 7) Following up on recommendations.
    (text p. 194)

3. Advantages to Internet-based research are: 1) rapid development, real-time reporting; 2) dramatically reduced costs; 3) personalized questions and data; 4) improved respondent participation; and 5) contact with the hard-to reach.
    (text pp. 213-214)

4. Scanner-based research is a system for gathering information from a single group of respondents by continuously monitoring the advertising, promotion and pricing they are exposed to and the things they buy. An example is BehaviorScan research, which tracks purchases of households through store scanners.
    (text p. 215-216)

5. The purpose of competitive intelligence is to help managers assess their competition in order to become more efficient and effective competitors.
    (text p. 216)

VOCABULARY PRACTICE SOLUTIONS

1. marketing information, decision support system (DSS)
2. database marketing
3. marketing research
4. marketing research problem, marketing research objectives, management decision problem
5. secondary data, newsgroups
6. primary data, research design
7. survey research, mall intercept interview
8. computer-assisted personal interviewing, computer-assisted self-interviewing
9. central-location telephone (CLT) facility
10. executive interviews
11. focus group, group dynamics
12. open-ended question, closed-ended question, scaled-response question
13. observation research, mystery shoppers
14. experiment
15. sample, universe
16. probability sample, random sample, nonprobability sample, convenience sample
17. measurement error, sampling error, frame error, random error
18. field service firms, cross-tabulation
19. unrestricted Internet sample, screened Internet sample, recruited Internet sample
20. scanner-based research, BehaviorScan, InfoScan
21. competitive intelligence

TRUE/FALSE SOLUTIONS

(question number / correct answer / text page reference / answer rationale)

1.	F	190	Marketing information is everyday information about the marketing environment.
2.	T	190	
3.	F	190	Marketing research focuses on a specific problem or opportunity that has arisen, not on general environmental information.
4.	F	194	The next step in the process is to determine marketing research objectives.

5.	F	195	Because the results from this survey were collected at another time, for another (although similar) purpose, the survey would represent secondary research data.
6.	T	202	
7.	T	203	
8.	T	209	
9.	F	210	This describes a convenience sample.

AGREE/DISAGREE SOLUTIONS
(question number / sample answers)

1. Reason(s) to agree: Since secondary data are not designed for specific marketing problems faced by a specific firm, they will most likely not help the firm solve its own specific problem.
   Reason(s) to disagree: Some secondary data may provide enough information for general problems or opportunities, such as discovering how many people comprise a demographic target market.

2. Reason(s) to agree: Because focus groups are derived from small sample sizes and because data coming from these groups are qualitative, they should only be used as a first step to any important decisions made by a firm.
   Reason(s) to disagree: Focus groups can be used to gauge certain situations, such as consumer feelings about new product ideas. By conducting focus groups across different geographic markets, a firm can "unbias" the information coming from the groups.

3. Reason(s) to agree: Information gathered from marketing research will always be flawed because of many different issues, such as sampling errors or the inaccuracy of attitudinal data (consumers' self reports may not be accurate).
   Reason(s) to disagree: Whether information is perfect or not is in the eyes of the marketer. If research uncovers information that is good enough for certain decision-making, then it can be deemed to be perfect.

4. Reason(s) to agree: As long as competitive intelligence is collected in an ethical manner – by researching public secondary sources such as periodicals, annual reports of publicly-traded firms, Web sites, etc. – competitive intelligence is totally ethical.
   Reason(s) to disagree: Since firms are in business to make money, there is always motivation for a manager to conduct use any and all methods for conducting competitive intelligence. Managers have been known to use their sales force to get information from buyers about competitors, to pose as innocents (such as college students) who are gathering information for a term paper, and to use insider information. There is a fine line between competitive intelligence and industrial espionage.

MULTIPLE-CHOICE SOLUTIONS
(question number / correct answer / text page reference / answer rationale)

1.	d	190	Decision support systems are easy to learn and use, even by people with little computer knowledge.
2.	b	190	Managers' ability to give instructions and see results illustrates the interactivity of a DSS.
3.	c	190	Definition of database marketing.
4.	e	191	One of the roles of market research is to be diagnostic and to explain what happened.
5.	a	191	Researching consumer attitudes without researching why they have these attitudes is considered to be descriptive research.
6.	e	191	Predictive research tells managers the impact (decrease in sales) of a marketing decision (pricing).
7.	d	194	The first step must be to recognize the marketing problem.
8.	e	194	The key to conducting marketing research is systematically conducting research activities by first defining the problem.
9.	c	194	A marketing research objective should identify the specific information that the research will find out.
10.	c	196	Secondary data have been previously collected for some other purpose and may not fit the current research problem.
11.	b	196	Accessibility is not a quality issue.
12	b	197	By typing the competitor's URL, you can often find annual reports that contain sales information available to the public.
13.	c	205	Focus groups consist of a few people and, therefore, cannot be used to generalize about an entire universe.
14.	a	202	Collecting primary data is more expensive than collecting secondary data.
15.	a	202	Piggyback studies gather data on two different projects using one questionnaire to save money.

16.	a	202	A mall intercept allows demonstration of the product, and the others do not. A laboratory experiment is not a survey.
17.	a	203	Telephone interviews are of moderate cost, when compared to in-home or mall interviews, yet are more expensive than mail surveys. Telephone interviews are also a fast survey method.
18.	c	214	The major disadvantage to using the Internet is that the sample will be biased; Internet users are heavily skewed toward well-educated, technically-oriented males.
19.	c	208	A type of research that does not rely on direct interaction with people is observation research.
20.	a	208	Observation research is the only data collection process in which there is no interaction and no possibility of influencing the behaviour of the subjects. Response rates are a factor of survey research only.
21.	b	210	A probability sample is characterized by every element in the population having a known nonzero probability of being selected, allowing an estimate of the accuracy of the sample.
22.	b	210	A random probability sample occurs when every population member has an equal chance of being selected.
23.	a	210	A convenience sample is based on the use of respondents who are readily accessible.
24.	a	214	By calling potential respondents and asking them to participate in a survey, the company is using a recruited Internet sample.
25.	e	215	The Internet has done all these things.
26.	b	215	Scanner-based research systems gather information over time from a single panel of respondents. This attempts to develop an accurate picture of the direct causal relationship between marketing efforts and actual sales.

SCENARIO SOLUTIONS

1. False   Michael has only completed a few of the steps: problem formulation, planning the research design, and collecting the data.

2. True   The problem/opportunity is to determine what services the company can provide and how to increase business.

3. True   Primary data is collected for the first time and not available in secondary sources.

4. c   The scenario ends before any analysis is done on the data.

5. d   Only primary data was collected.

6. c   The selection of the company's best customers was not highly scientific and, thus, represents more of a convenience sample.

7. a   The telephone survey of dog owners who work full-time is the best since this represents the target market. There is no reason to conduct any of the other options since they won't answer the research question.

8.   Michael must still: 1) Analyze the data that he collected from focus groups and the pet store intercept surveys; 2) Prepare and present the reports to the owners; and 3) Follow-up with the owners on whether their questions were answered.

ESSAY QUESTION SOLUTIONS

1.   Marketing research entails planning, collecting, and analyzing data relevant to marketing decision making, and communicating results of this analysis to management. Marketing research provides decision makers with data on the effectiveness of current marketing strategies. Marketing research is the primary data source for the DSS. The three functional roles of marketing research are descriptive, diagnostic, and predictive.

Marketing research improves the quality of marketing decision making by shedding light on the desirability of various marketing alternatives. It can also help managers trace problems. Managers might use research to find out why something did not work out as planned. Marketing research can identify incorrect decisions, changes in the external environment, and strategic errors. Finally, marketing research provides insight into questions about the marketplace. Marketing research can help managers develop the marketing mix by providing insights into lifestyles, preferences, and purchasing habits of target consumers. Finally, marketing research can help foster customer value and quality.
(text pp. 190-191)

The descriptive role of marketing research includes gathering and presenting factual statements. The diagnostic role of research explains and assigns meaning to data. The predictive role allows the researcher to use the descriptive and diagnostic research to predict the results of a planned marketing decision.

2.   1.   Identify and formulate the problem or opportunity
      2.   Plan the research design and gather primary data
      3.   Specify the sampling procedures
      4.   Collect the data
      5.   Analyze the data
      6.   Prepare and present the report
      7.   Follow up
      (text p. 194)

3.   Your memo should include the following six advantages to conducting surveys on the Internet are:
      • The speed with which a survey can be created, distributed to respondents, and received back from respondents
      • Low cost
      • The ability to track attitudes, behaviour, and perceptions over time
      • The convenience of asking two or three "q uick" questions
      • The ability to reach large numbers of people
      • The ability to create visually pleasing surveys

      Your memo should include the following three disadvantages to conducting surveys on the Internet are:
      • The biased sampling of the Internet (Internet users are not representative of the population as a whole)
      • Problems with security on the Internet
      • Unrestricted Internet samples (anyone who desires can complete a survey; this results in biased sampling)

      Researchers can avoid getting unrestricted Internet samples two ways: by using screened Internet samples (whereby respondents are selected based on certain criteria, such as age or income or geographic region) and by suing recruited Internet samples (whereby respondents are recruited by telephone or other methods before the administration of the Internet survey).
      (text pp. 213-215)

4.   Competitive intelligence is a system that helps managers assess their competition and vendors in order to become more efficient and effective competitors. Advantages of competitive intelligence are that it helps managers assess their competition and their vendors, which results in fewer surprises. It also allows managers to predict changes in business relationships, identify marketplace opportunities, guard against threats, forecast a competitor's strategies, discover new or potential competitors, learn from the success or failure of others, learn about new technology, and learn about the impact of government regulations on the competition.
      (text p. 216-217)

APPLICATION SOLUTIONS
      C   Closed-ended multiple choice
      B   Closed-ended dichotomous
      A   Open-ended
      F   Two questions in one (Nikes? Reeboks? Both at once?)
      G   Biased/leading (Excellence is assumed.)
      D   Scaled-response
      E   Ambiguous (What does "soon" mean?)
      (text pp. 206-207)

CHAPTER 8: PRODUCT CONCEPTS

PRETEST SOLUTIONS
1.   A product is everything, both favourable and unfavourable, that a person receives in an exchange. Four types of consumer products are:
      • Convenience products: A relatively inexpensive item that merits little shopping effort.
      • Shopping products: A more expensive product that is found in fewer stores.
      • Specialty products: A product for which consumers shop extensively.
      • Unsought products: A product unknown to the buyer or a known product that the buyer does not actively seek.
      (text pp. 232-234)

2.   Product item: A specific version of a product that can be designated as a distinct offering among an organization's pr oducts. Example: Gillette's MACH 3 razor.

Product line: A group of closely related products. Example: Gillette's entire offering of blades and razors.

Product mix: All the products an organization sells. Example: Gillette sells blades, razors, toiletries, writing instruments, and lighters.

(text p. 234)

3.   A brand is a name, term, symbol, design, or combination thereof that identifies a seller's products and differentiates them from competitors' p roducts. Three branding strategies are:
- Generic products versus branded products: Whether or not to brand your product.
- Manufacturer's brands versus private brands: Whether a retailer should use manufacturer's brand name or its own private label name.
- Individual brands versus family brands: Whether to use individual brands names (such as Tide detergent) or family brand names (such as Sony's e ntire line of electronics products).

(text pp. 237-242)

4.   Three different branding strategies for entering international markets are:
- To use one brand name everywhere (such as Coca-Cola using the same brand name everywhere);
- To adapt or modify the brand to the local market;
- To use different brand names in different markets (such as Gillette changing its Silkience hair care name to "S oyance" in France and "Sientel " in Italy.

(text pp. 246)

5.   The three most important functions of packaging are to contain and protect the product; to promote products; and to facilitate the storage, use, and convenience of products.

(text pp. 247)

6.   Warranties not only protect the buyer from defective products but also give essential information about a product.

(text p. 248)

VOCABULARY PRACTICE SOLUTIONS

1.   product
2.   business (industrial) product, consumer product
3.   convenience product, shopping product, specialty product, unsought product
4.   product item, product line, product mix
5.   product mix width, product line depth
6.   product modification, planned obsolescence
7.   product line extension
8.   brand, brand name, brand mark
9.   brand equity, global brand, brand loyalty
10.   generic product, manufacturer's brand, private brand, individual branding, family brand, co-branding
11.   trademark, service mark, generic product name
12.   persuasive labelling, informational labelling, universal product code (UPC)
13.   warranty, express warranty, implied warranty

TRUE/FALSE SOLUTIONS

(question number / correct answer / text page reference / answer rationale)

1.   F   232   Consumers do not buy products based on features; they buy products based on the *benefits* they deliver.
2.   F   232   Because Tammy puts so much effort into an information search, makeup is better classified as a shopping product.
3.   T   233
4.   F   234   What is described is actually part of Sony's product mix, not its product line. A product line is a group of related products.
5.   F   235   Sometimes adding too many products to the product line weakens the brand equity.
6.   T   235
7.   T   237
8.   T   242
9.   T   244

AGREE/DISAGREE SOLUTIONS
(question number / sample answers)

1.　Reason(s) to agree: For most products, price is the number one feature for consumers. When buying a car, for instance, consumers select cars based on a price range first, then on other features. In some industries, brand names almost do not matter any more (such as long distance service, which has become heavily price driven).

　　Reason(s) to disagree: Branding is still very important. A brand name distinguishes one company's product from that of its competitors and is associated with certain features and imagery. One good example is Coca-Cola, the best-known brand in the world. The equity that has been developed throughout the decades on Coke is more important than the actual taste of the product, as Coca-Cola saw when it tried to introduce New Coke in 1985.

2.　Reason(s) to agree: Private brands—or brands that are owned by retailers or wholesalers (rather than manufacturers)—are usually always priced lower than the manufacturers' bran ds. People cannot afford to pay the prices of major brands will naturally go to the private brands, which may be perceived as "go od enough" since it has the same ingredients.

　　Reason(s) to disagree: It is not only lower income consumers who purchase private brands. Many higher income people, who do not see the merit of paying a premium for manufacturers' brands, also purchase private brands. Whether a higher income consumer chooses to purchase a manufacturer's brand or a private brand has more to do with the value impression that he/she has rather than the income.

3.　Reason(s) to agree: By adapting products, including brands, to local markets, the global marketer has a better chance of acceptance from the local market. Brand names often do not translate well into other languages, and products may not sell if some adaptations are not made.

　　Reason(s) to disagree: Products and brands do not have to be adapted to local markets. Sometimes the image of the product's home country is just as important as the product itself. Levi's is an exa mple of a U.S.-based company that markets "Ame ricana" to other cultures and does not adapt the product on purpose. McDonald's is another example of a successful global brand that does not adapt its products (it adapts some of its product offerings, however) and markets American culture. It does adapt its promotions and its environment to match that of its market, however.

4.　Reason(s) to agree: Family branding helps to develop overall brand equity and to tie together products that otherwise would not be related. Using a strong brand name developed on a strong product on other products that are related will help boost sales of the newer products. Gillette has been very successful at family branding, as well as Sony, because they use strong company brand names to communicate certain quality features across their entire product line or product mix.

　　Reason(s) to disagree: Family branding is not necessary for strong brand equity development. Products such as Tide detergent have existed on their own for many years and may target very different markets versus other detergents made by the same company, Procter & Gamble. When targeting different market segments, individual branding may be more appropriate.

MULTIPLE-CHOICE SOLUTIONS
(question number / correct answer / text page reference / answer rationale)

1.	e	232	The product is the first decision around which the others are based.
2.	a	233	The fact that David did not consider another brand shows that the car was a specialty product.
3.	b	232	Shopping products are usually more expensive than convenience products and are found in fewer stores. Consumers usually compare items across brands or stores.
4.	c	232	The lack of forethought that went into this purchase made it a convenience product.
5.	a	234	An organization's product mix includes all of the products that it sells.
6.	e	235	Product line depth is the number of product items in a product line.
7.	a	235	Quality modifications entail changing a product's dependability or durability.
8.	b	236	Functional modifications are changes in a product's versatility, effectiveness, convenience, or safety.
9.	d	236	Planned obsolescence should not be done at the expense of safety or quality.
10.	c	236	Adding products to a product line entails line extension.
11.	e	237	Coca-Cola is enjoying a strong brand equity: the value of the brand name to the company.
12.	c	237	A global brand is a brand where at least 20 percent of its sales occurs outside its home country.
13.	e	241	A private brand is one owned by the retailer.

14.	b	241	The dealer will get a higher margin on a private brand.
15.	b	242	Individual branding is the policy of using different brand names for different products. Individual brands are used when products differ greatly in use, performance, quality, or targeted segment.
16.	e	242	When two separate brands (in this case, from two separate companies) use their brands on a product or package, this is known as co-branding.
17.	d	243	A generic product name identifies a product by class of type and cannot be trademarked.
18.	a	244	Guarantees are not a function of packaging; they are a function of warranties.
19.	d	246	Currency and pricing considerations are not the prime considerations when considering branding and packaging strategies.
20.	b	248	An express warranty is any written guarantee.
21.	e	248	This is the definition of a warranty.
22.	a	248	An implied warranty is an unwritten guarantee that the good or service is fit for the purpose for which it was sold.

SCENARIO SOLUTIONS

1. False   Dune is a manufacturer's brand.
2. True   As evidenced by the brand loyalty the brand enjoys.
3. False   They are an example of a product line.
4. d   The product mix is all the products that a company offers.
5. a   The product line is a group of closely related products, in this case, bar soaps.
6. b   A line extension is an additional product added to an existing line in order to compete more broadly in the industry. In this case, Liquid Dune helps the company compete in the liquid hand soap category.
7. c   A private label brand is owned by a wholesaler or retailer, in this case, by Wal-Mart. It doesn't matter who actually manufacturers the brand.
8.   Brand equity is the value of the company and its brand names. Dune has a loyal following and large market share, and the company probably highly depends on the brand to carry most of its sales and profits. Therefore, the protection of Dune as a brand is very important to the company. The company should protect the brand legally (through active protection of the trademark) and should extend its line to other items without watering the brand name down.

ESSAY QUESTION SOLUTIONS

1.   **Convenience products** are relatively inexpensive items that require little shopping effort. The products are bought regularly, usually without significant planning. Convenience products may include candy, soft drinks, combs, aspirin, small hardware items, dry cleaning, car wash services, and so on.

Shopping products are more expensive than convenience products and found in fewer stores. Consumers spend some effort comparing brands and stores. Shopping products may include washers, dryers, refrigerators, televisions, furniture, clothing, housing, choice of university, and so on. Shopping products can be homogeneous (consumers perceive the products as being essentially the same) or heterogeneous (consumers perceive the products to differ in features, style, quality, and so on).

Specialty products are those items for which consumers are willing to search extensively. Consumers are extremely reluctant to accept substitutes for specialty products. Brand names and service quality are important. Fine watches, luxury cars, expensive stereo equipment, gourmet restaurants, and specialized medical services could all be considered specialty products.

Unsought products are those that the buyer does not know about or does not actively seek to buy. These products include insurance, burial plots, encyclopaedias, and so on.
(text pp. 232-234)

2.   A product item is a specific version of a product that can be designated as a distinct offering among an organization's products. A product mix width refers to the number of product lines that an organization offers. A product line is a group of closely related product items.
(text p. 234)

3.   Strategies could include:
- Generic branding
  - Advantages: low pricing and high volume
  - Disadvantages: no brand equity for a well-known company.
- Branded product
  - Advantages: to build brand equity over time and to gain higher profit
  - Disadvantages: none.
- Individual branding
  - Advantages: can target other market segments that other Gillette products do not currently target
  - Disadvantages: does not build on company's good name
- Family branding
  - Advantages: build on company's positive image and name
  - Disadvantages: may cannibalize other products

Note: In this case, it does not make sense to co-brand.
(text, pp. 240-242)

4.   Four ways to adjust a product line are:
- Product modification: changing one or more of a product's characteristics. The infamous "New Coke" was a change in the basic Coke formula to make it taste sweeter. New Coke was later deleted from the product line, and Coke Classic was brought back.
- Repositioning: changing consumers' perceptions of a brand. Sprite was repositioned from being a "lemon-li me" drink toward a younger (mostly male) market.
- Product line extensions: adding additional products to an existing product line. The addition of Cherry Coke, Decaffeinated Coke, Diet Coke, and Vanilla Coke to the basic Coca-Cola franchise are examples of line extensions.
- Product line contraction: the opposite of line extensions, this strategy actually decreases the number of products in a product line. The deletion of New Coke from the Coke product line in the 1980s is a good example.
(text, pp. 235-237)

APPLICATION SOLUTIONS

Application #1:

Product mix width refers to the number of product lines that an organization offers. In this case the width of the product mix is three: coffees, appliances, and desserts. Product line depth is the number of product items in a product line. There are five items in the coffee line, three items in the appliance line, and two items in the dessert line.

The company could adjust its portfolio with modifications (quality, functional, or style), additions, repositioning of products, or extending or contracting product lines.
(text pp. 234-235)

Application #2:

Your proposal should include:
- **One Brand Name Everywhere.** This strategy is useful when the company markets mainly one product and the brand name does not have negative connotations in any local market. Advantages of a one-brand strategy are greater identification of the product from market to market and ease of coordinating promotion from market to market. This strategy may be difficult for Q-T-Pie because a variety of products are sold. Additionally, it is not likely that "Q-T-Pie" carries the same meaning in all languages or communicates the benefits of the product.

- **Adaptations and Modifications.** If the brand name is not pronounceable in the local language, the brand name is owned by someone else, or the brand has a negative connotation in the local language, minor modifications can make the brand name more suitable. This could be a viable alternative for Q-T-Pie.
- **Different Brand Names in Different Markets.** Local brand names are often used when translation or pronunciation problems occur, when the marketer wants the brand to appear to be a local brand, or when regulations require localization. This could also be a viable alternative for Q-T-Pie.

(text pp. 246-247)

CHAPTER 9: DEVELOPING AND MANAGING PRODUCTS

PRETEST SOLUTIONS

1. The six categories of new products are:
    - New-to-the-world products
    - New product lines
    - Additions to existing product lines
    - Improvements or revisions of existing products
    - Repositioned products
    - Lower priced products

    (text pp. 256-257)

2. The seven stages of new product development are:
    - Develop a new product strategy
    - Generate new product ideas
    - Screen ideas for best ones
    - Conduct a business analysis
    - Develop the product prototypes
    - Test the product in laboratory and test markets
    - Commercialize (introduce) the product to the market

    (text p. 259)

3. Reasons why new products may fail are:
    - No discernible benefit versus existing products
    - Poor match between product features and customer desires
    - Overestimation of the market size
    - Incorrect positioning
    - Price is too high or too low
    - Inadequate distribution
    - Poor promotion
    - Inferior compared to competitors

    (text p. 265)

4. Diffusion is the process by which the adoption of an innovation spreads. Five categories of adopters are:
    - **Innovators:** The first 2.5 percent of all those who adopt the product. They are risk-taking and like to try new ideas.
    - **Early adopters:** The next 13.5 percent of all those who adopt the product. They are opinion leaders.
    - **Early majority:** The next 34 percent of all those who adopt the product. They are more likely to weigh pros and cons before adopting a product and rely on the group for information.
    - **Late majority:** The next 34 percent of all those who adopt the product. They are conservative and tend to adopt the product because most of their friends already have it.
    - **Laggards:** The last 16 percent of all those who adopt the product. They are very conservative and are tied to tradition.

    (text pp. 266-267)

5. The four stages of the product life cycle are:
    - **Introductory stage:** Full scale launch of the product. Sales grow slowly, and marketing costs are high.
    - **Growth stage:** Sales grow at an increasing rate as awareness of the product grows. Advertising and other promotional costs are high, and competitors enter the market.
    - **Maturity stage:** Sales start to flatten out. The market approaches saturation as new users are more difficult to identify. Profits and sales are at an all-time high.
    - **Decline stage:** A long-run drop in sales occurs. Product may eventually die or be pulled before it does.

    (text pp. 269-272)

VOCABULARY PRACTICE SOLUTIONS

1.   new product
2.   new product strategy
3.   product development
4.   brainstorming
5.   screening, concept test
6.   business analysis, development
7.   test marketing, simulated (laboratory) test marketing, commercialization
8.   simultaneous product development
9.   adopter, innovation, diffusion
10.   product life cycle, product category, introductory stage, growth stage, maturity stage, decline stage

TRUE/FALSE SOLUTIONS

(question number / correct answer / text page reference / answer rationale)

1.	F	256	Line extensions, such as new ice cream flavours, are considered to be a type of new product.
2.	T	258	
3.	F	260	Brainstorming does not involve evaluation of the ideas as they are generated; criticism of any kind is avoided.
4.	F	260	Concept tests are typically completed during the idea screening stage of the process.
5.	T	262	
6.	T	262	
7.	T	264	
8.	F	266	This is known as the diffusion process.
9.	T	266	
10.	F	266	Carol would be considered an innovator since she is among the first to see the new movies.
11.	F	269	Sales of any product do not follow precise bell-shaped curves over a set period of time. The length of time a product spends in any one stage of the product life cycle may vary dramatically.

AGREE/DISAGREE SOLUTIONS

(question number / sample answers)

1.   Reason(s) to agree: In today's competitive marketplace, too much testing and too much time spent on generating ideas can cause a product failure. Another company may be thinking about the same idea and may launch the product before you. Also, when a product is tested—especially in the market—competitors can find out about the new product.
Reason(s) to disagree: Following each step methodically will help increase the success rate of the new product. Each step is necessary, though each step should be accomplished efficiently. Too much time should not be spent on idea generation, for instance, while enough time should be given to product testing to ensure that all strategies are sound.

2.   Reason(s) to agree: The most important quality of a new product idea is the positioning that it holds. If the positioning is good—that is, if the new product delivers unique benefits that the target market wants—then it will certainly succeed.
Reason(s) to disagree: Even products with a sound, unique, and desirable positioning can fail in their execution. If the advertising is incorrect or inadequate, if the price is too high or too low, or if distribution does not occur quickly enough, the product can fail, despite its original strategy.

3.   Reason(s) to agree: A new products committee can only generate a limited number of ideas. Employees from around the organization should be encouraged to join in the new products idea generation, as the volume of ideas is necessary.
Reason(s) to disagree: While getting ideas from all employees is good, the lack of a new products committee will de-emphasize the necessity of new-product development. If no committee is called upon to be the leader of new-product development, no one will have accountability for the effort.

4.   Reason(s) to agree: Products such as fads, fashions, styles, or even some high-tech products do not follow the traditional product life cycle theory. Fads go from introduction to decline very quickly and jump over some stages. Styles (a recurring product) come and go every several years and can be "reborn" at any time. High-tech products become obsolete very quickly, and new technology takes their place before the old products even die.
Reason(s) to disagree: Regardless of the type of product, every product undergoes some kind of life cycle. The product may not go through a traditional life cycle, but it does grow, mature, and eventually decline.

(question number / correct answer / text page reference / answer rationale)

1. b   256   New-to-the-world products, where the product category itself is new, are also called discontinuous innovations.
2. a   256   An addition to the existing product line is considered a new product by marketers.
3. c   257   Repositioning an existing product and targeting it toward new market segments (microwave users) is another type of new product because it is new to that segment.
4. a   256   Klean's "new an d improved" is an example of revising an old product.
5. c   258   The least likely invitee would be the lawyers, who may not understand the market as well as all the other team members.
6. d   258   The first step in the process is the development of a new products strategy that will set the stage for the other steps (even idea generation).
7. c   260   Brainstorming is a process in which a group thinks of as many ways to vary a product or solve a problem as possible--without considering the practicality of the idea.
8. a   260   Screening is the first filter stage of the new product development process and is used to eliminate inappropriate product ideas.
9. c   260   Concept testing allows consumers to express opinions about a product before a prototype is developed.
10. e   260   In the business analysis stage of new product development, preliminary demand, cost, sales, and profitability estimates are made.
11. b   262   Many products that test well in the laboratory are next subjected to use tests; they are placed in consumers' homes or businesses for trial.
12. d   262   Test marketing is a limited introduction of a product and a marketing program to determine the reactions of potential customers in a market situation.
13. a   262   A good test market does not have to be large.
14. b   263   Simulated (laboratory) market tests usually entail showing members of the target market advertising for a variety of products; then purchase behaviour, in a mock or real store, is monitored.
15. b   264   During commercialization, production materials and equipment are ordered.
16. e   265   A poor match to customer needs is a violation of the marketing concept.
17. b   266   There are five categories: innovator, early adopter, early majority, late majority, and laggard.
18. d   268   It is the product characteristics that affect the adoption rate most heavily. The "buy Canadian" movement is external to the acceptance of the product.
19. d   271   The growth stage is characterized by high sales and heavy promotion.
20. a   271   The maturity stage is characterized by market saturation and heavy promotion to battle the fierce competition.
21. b   272   Declining sales are characteristics of the decline stage.
22. a   272   Sales usually peak during the maturity stage, so line extensions are often used to "breathe li fe" into the brand before it's to o late.

SCENARIO SOLUTIONS

1. True   A discontinuous innovation is a product that is new to the world.
2. False   As of the printing of this study guide, Game Boy Advance is still in the growth stage; technology doesn't c hange that fast!
3. True   Even though later generations of Game Boy were simply technological improvements of the original Game Boy, they are considered types of new products.
4. c   All three are new generations of the original Game Boy.
5. b   Additions to existing product lines include new products that supplement a firm's established line.
6. c   As with most technological products, the new generations of products are generally launched during the maturity stage of the previous generation's life cycle. This is because the market for the previous generation has been saturated and sales and profits are not expected to grow much more, paving the way for a new product.
7. a   Once Game Boy Advance was introduced, the price dropped on Game Boy Colour to force out distribution.

8.	Innovators would be the first to adopt the product. They were probably waiting in line a few hours before the stores opened and sold the product for the first time! Early adopters probably purchased the product within the first few weeks after the launch. Early majority collect information before they adopted the product, most likely hearing reviews from the early adopters. Late majority may just now be getting around to purchasing the product. Laggards will probably purchase the product just as the next generation of Game Boy is being launched.

ESSAY QUESTION SOLUTIONS

1.	**New-to-the-world products (discontinuous innovations)** are products that are introduced in an original form. Text examples include computers and facsimile machines.
	New product lines are products that the firm has not offered in the past but will introduce into an established market. The text examples include the Ski-Doo and Sea-Doo from Bombardier.
	Additions to existing product lines are new products that supplement a firm's established line. Complementary products can also supplement a firm's offerings. Text examples are Tide detergent in tablet form and Downy Wrinkle Releaser.
	Improvements or revisions of existing products are usually minor changes that may entail the addition or deletion of ingredients. Many of these products are labelled "new and improved." Text examples include Breyers Soft'n Creamy! Ice cream and Heinz EZ Squirt ketchup.
	Repositioning means that existing products are targeted at new markets or market segments. The text example is Dippity-do marketed to adults since 1965 was repositioned to target teen buyers.
	Lower-cost products are those that provide similar performance to competing brands at a lower cost. Lower cost may result from technological advantages, economies of scale in production, or lower marketing costs. The text example includes Hewlett-Packard Laser Jet 3100 is a combined scanner copier, printer and fax machine that is priced lower than many conventional printers.
	(text pp. 256-257)

2.	The seven steps of the new product development process are:
	- New product strategy
	- Idea generation
	- Screening
	- Business analysis
	- Development
	- Testing
	- Commercialization
	(text p. 259)

3.	Criteria for choosing a test market include:
	- Demographics and purchasing habits that mirror the overall market
	- Good distribution in test cities
	- Media isolation
	- Similarity to planned distribution outlets
	- Relative isolation from other cities
	- Availability of advertising media that will cooperate
	- Diversified cross section of ages, religion, cultural-societal preferences, etc.
	- No atypical purchasing habits
	- Representative as to population size
	- Typical per capita income
	- Good record as a test city, but not overly used
	- Not easily "jammed" by competitors
	- Stability of year-round sales
	- No dominant television station; multiple newspapers, magazines, and radio stations
	- Availability of retailers that will cooperate
	- Availability of research and audit services
	- Free from unusual influences

An advantage of test marketing is that it gives management an opportunity to evaluate alternative strategies and to see how well the various aspects of the marketing mix fit together. Test marketing may reduce risk by allowing modification of a marketing mix before national introduction or withdrawal of a product with failure characteristics. However, test markets have several disadvantages: costs of test markets are high, and a product's success in a test market does not guarantee it will be a nationwide hit.
	(text p. 263)

4.

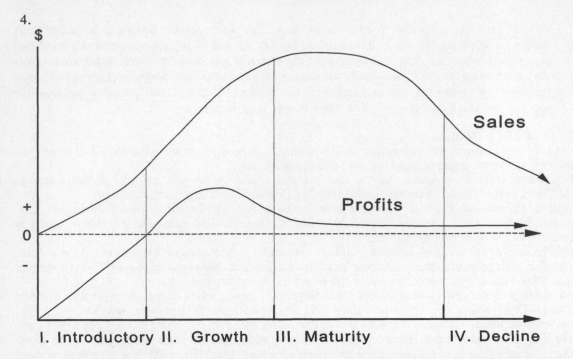

I. Introductory II. Growth III. Maturity IV. Decline

The sales line should start at zero sales at the beginning of the introductory stage, accelerate during the growth stage, peak in the maturity stage, and decrease during the decline stage.

The profit line should start in the negative range during the introductory stage, break even at the start of the growth stage, peak during the growth stage, fall during the maturity stage, and reach a near-zero asymptote during the decline stage. At no point should the profit line be above the sales line.

The introductory stage is characterized by a high failure rate, little competition, frequent product modification, limited distribution, slow sales, high marketing and production costs, negative profits, and promotion that stimulates primary demand.

The growth stage is characterized by increased sales, new competitors, healthy profits that peak, aggressive brand promotion, expanded distribution, price reductions, and possible acquisitions.

The maturity stage is characterized by a peak in sales, lengthened product lines, style modifications, price reductions, falling profits, competitor turnover, heavy promotion, and brand "wars."

The decline stage is characterized by a long-run drop in sales and profits, less demand, widespread competitor failure, reduction of advertising costs, and possible elimination of the product.
(text pp. 269-272)

5.   **Innovators** represent the first 2.5 percent of adopters. They are venturesome and eager to try new products. They have higher incomes, better education, self-confidence, and less reliance on group norms than noninnovators. Moreover, they are active outside of their community. Innovators obtain information from scientific sources and experts. They may see a new movie in a special preview showing.

Early adopters represent the next 13.5 percent of adopters. They are reliant on group norms and values, oriented to the local community, and likely to be opinion leaders. They may see a new movie during the first week after it is launched

The early majority is the next 34 percent to adopt. They are deliberate in their information collection and are likely to be the friends and neighbours of opinion leaders. They may see a new movie during the season (summer or holidays) that it is launched.

The late majority is the next 34 percent to adopt. They adopt with skepticism to conform to social pressure. They tend to be older and below average in income and education. They rely on word-of-mouth communication rather than the mass media. They will see the movie after half the population sees it (maybe after it wins some awards, such as an Academy Award).

Laggards are the final 16 percent to adopt. They are tradition-bound and do not rely on group norms. Laggards have the lowest socioeconomic status, are suspicious of new products, and are alienated from a rapidly advancing society. Marketers typically ignore laggards. They may wait until the movie is in video form.
(text pp. 266-268)

Solutions to this exercise will vary greatly, and many cities may fit the criteria well. A hint: Use the Google search engine and type in "Test Marketin g". http://www.google.ca

---

CHAPTER 10: SERVICES AND NONPROFIT ORGANIZATION MARKETING

PRETEST SOLUTIONS

1. Four characteristics of service products are:
    - Services are intangible performances.
    - Services are produced and consumed simultaneously.
    - Services have greater variability.
    - Services are perishable.

    (text pp. 282-283)

2. Five components of service quality are:
    - **Reliability**: ability to perform the service dependably, accurately, and consistently.
    - **Responsiveness**: ability to provide prompt service.
    - **Assurance**: knowledge and courtesy of employees and their ability to convey trust.
    - **Empathy**: caring, individualized attention to customers.
    - **Tangibles**: the physical evidence of the service.

    (text p. 284-285)

3. Five "gaps " that can occur in service quality are:
    - **Gap 1**: gap between what customers want and what management thinks customers want.
    - **Gap 2**: gap between what management thinks customers want and the quality specifications that management develops to provide the service.
    - **Gap 3**: gap between the service quality specifications and the service that is actually provided.
    - **Gap 4**: gap between what the company provides and what the customer is told it provides.
    - **Gap 5**: gap between the service that customers receive and the service they want.

    (text pp. 285-286)

4. Internal marketing is treating employees like customers and developing systems and benefits that satisfy their needs.

    (text p. 292)

5. Unique aspects of nonprofit organizations for the following:
    - **Objectives**: focus not on profit but on generating enough funds to cover expenses and to provide certain services to its constituencies.
    - **Target markets**: are not "buyin g" the product and may be apathetic or strongly opposed to the organization. Organizations may feel pressured to maximize their limited funding and to go after undifferentiated segments and may complement the positioning of for-profit organizations.
    - **Products**: offer benefits that are often complex, indirect, or weak. Many products elicit very low involvement ("do n't litter") .
    - **Distribution**: can be difficult, but determining where the target market is located and how to deliver the services to the market is critical.
    - **Promotion**: may be prohibited, or funding for promotion may be limited. Nonprofit organizations must rely on volunteers for promotion. They must also make use of existing services for sales promotion and rely on public service announcements (PSAs). Nonprofit organizations often license their names and/or images to communicate to a larger audience.

    (text pp. 294-296)

VOCABULARY PRACTICE SOLUTIONS

1. service
2. intangibility
3. search quality, experience quality, credence quality
4. reliability, responsiveness, assurance, empathy, tangibles
5. gap model
6. core service, supplementary service
7. mass customization
8. internal marketing
9. nonprofit organization, nonprofit organization marketing
10. public service advertisement (PSA)

TRUE/FALSE SOLUTIONS

(question number / correct answer / text page reference / answer rationale)

1.	F	282	Services represent nearly 70 percent of the Canadian GDP.
2.	F	284	This is an example of responsiveness, not reliability.
3.	T	288	
4.	F	292	IBM is practicing internal marketing. Relationship marketing is focused on customers, not employees.
5.	F	293	Services can be exported. Examples of "ex ported" services include accounting or legal consulting.
6.	F	293	Target markets are often more difficult to persuade because the benefits are less direct.
7.	T	295	
8.	F	296	Advertisements are PSAs only if there is no charge to the sponsor of the message.
9.	T	296	

AGREE/DISAGREE SOLUTIONS

(question number / sample answers)

1. Reason(s) to agree: The main objective of service providers is to deliver services to customers, and much more direct human contact is needed to accomplish this. In service organizations, almost all employees are trained well in customer service.

   Reason(s) to disagree: Whether a firm is selling a service or whether it is selling a good, good customer service is needed. Even when customers buy goods (such computers), they expect representatives from the manufacturer to answer questions and to provide assistance in operating the product.

2. Reason(s) to agree: All the gaps that can occur with services can also occur with goods. Gaps can occur when goods are not designed to fulfill the needs of customers, when management does not understand what customers want, or when the goods are not promoted effectively.

   Reason(s) to disagree: The gap model does not exist for goods as it does for services. The reason is that service quality is much more intangible and difficult to assess; every time a service is delivered, it is different. A good is tangible and more easily evaluated to determine if gaps can be fixed.

3. Reason(s) to agree: A strong organizational image will give customers confidence in the firm and its people—its most important resource for providing service.

   Reason(s) to disagree: In service marketing, it is difficult to divide products (services) from their providers. Thus, it is important to focus on promoting both the products and the organization.

4. Reason(s) to agree: Many nonprofit organizations exist to serve the needs of a specific target market, such as the non-smoking campaign (targeted at smokers) or psychological counselling (targeted at people with specific types of psychological problems). Though the target markets may be apathetic or hostile toward the organization, they are easily identified.

   Reason(s) to disagree: Some nonprofit organizations do not have clear target markets. Political campaigns could target many different constituencies by focusing on different issues.

MULTIPLE-CHOICE SOLUTIONS

(question number / correct answer / text page reference / answer rationale)

1.	a	282	Services are described as intangible.
2.	c	283	Services can be evaluated just like any other business, through customer surveys.
3.	d	283	Search quality is a characteristic that can be easily assessed before purchase.
4.	c	283	Experience quality is a characteristic that can be assessed only after use.
5.	a	283	Credence quality if a characteristic of services that consumers may have difficulty assessing even after purchase because they do not have the necessary knowledge or experience.
6.	d	286	This illustrates a gap between what management thinks customers want (freshly cooked chicken) and the quality specifications that management develops to provide the service (to minimize chicken waste).
7.	a	286	This illustrates a gap between what customers want (low teacher to child ratio) and what management thinks customers want (lower tuition).
8.	c	286	This illustrates a gap between what the company provides (no respect for passengers) and what the customer is told it provides (respect for passengers).
9.	e	286	Gateway is likely providing services to accomplish all the above.
10.	d	288	These are examples of a supplementary service to the core service: airline transportation.
11.	e	289	Convenience via location is the key issue in the distribution decision for services.

12.	c	290	The note is an example of something tangible to an otherwise intangible product.
13.	b	291	A focus on matching supply and demand by varying prices to ensure maximum use of productive capacity at any specific point in time is an operations-oriented pricing objective for service firms.
14.	c	292	Building social bonds includes staying in though with customers, learning about their needs, and designing the service to meet those needs.
15.	c	293	Computer microchip manufacturing is product-, rather than service-oriented. Additionally, this industry is at a disadvantage compared to Asian products.
16.	e	293	An understanding and use of marketing offers a framework for decision making, tools for effective communication, and increased support from customers and interested groups.
17.	c	294	Success in a nonprofit organization is measured by how well service goals are met and how well it serves the community.
18.	d	295	Sources of donations are likely to be apathetic or opposed.
19.	b	295	The organization could not clearly explain the content of its services and, therefore, had inadequately defined the product.

SCENARIO SOLUTIONS

1. True
2. False — Services are perishable, which means that they cannot be stored, warehoused, or inventoried. Once Leilani provides service to a guest, it ceases to exist.
3. True
4. d — The rooms are the resort's most basic benefit that guests buy.
5. b — Supplementary activities are the group of services that support or enhance the core service.
6. b — Responsiveness is the ability to provide prompt service.
7. a — People processing takes place when the service is directed at a customer, not at the customer's assets, physical possessions, or minds.
8. — Yes, she is engaged in relationship marketing. By being responsive, reliable, trustworthy, and pleasant to deal with, Leilani is hoping that guests will continue to come back to the resort for their vacations.

ESSAY QUESTION SOLUTIONS

1. The four characteristics are as follows:
   - Services are intangible performances. Though restaurants sell tangible goods – such as the food – the intangible characteristics include the quality of service from the server and the host or maitre d' and the atmosphere.
   - Services are produced and consumed simultaneously. For instance, when a server performs a service, the guest enjoys the service. This is done at the same time.
   - Services have greater variability. Every guest is treated somewhat differently since everyone has a different personality, has different tastes, and asks different questions.
   - Services are perishable. When a server performs a service, it is completed. The guest cannot "take it home" with him/her.

   (text pp. 282-284)

2. **Product:** Four important issues regarding the service process are (1) what is being processed, (2) core and supplementary services, (3) customization versus standardization, and (4) the service mix. Three types of service processing occur: people, possession, and information processing. The service product consists of the basic, or core service, and additional supplementary service. Customized services are more flexible and responsive, and also can command a higher price. Standardized services are more efficient and may have lower costs. Firms must also consider their service mix--the portfolio of services they offer.
   Place: Convenience is the key factor influencing the selection of a service provider by a customer. The first step in developing a service distribution strategy is setting objectives, including intensity of distribution. Next, management must decide whether to distribute services directly to end users or indirectly through other firms. Management must select locations, and this choice most clearly reveals the relationship between a firm's target market strategy and distribution strategy. Scheduling of service provision must also be determined.
   Promotion: Four promotional strategies for services include (1) stressing tangible cues, (2) using personal information sources such as celebrity endorsements, (3) creating a strong organizational image by managing the physical environment, and (4) using postpurchase communication with customers.

Price: Intensive price competition in the service industry indicates that close scrutiny should be paid to the pricing of each service offered. Three categories of pricing objectives have been suggested for services, including (1) revenue-oriented pricing, (2) operations-oriented pricing, and (3) patronage-oriented pricing. Service firms often use a combination of these objectives.
(text, pp. 287-291)

3.   Internal marketing is treating employees as customers and developing systems and benefits that satisfy their needs. Because most service businesses have a lot of face-to-face contact with customers, it is important for employees to be happy in their service jobs. When they are happy, it is reflected in the service that they provide to customers. Also, internal marketing allows management to "practice what they preach."
(text, p. 292)

APPLICATION SOLUTIONS
Product:
- The benefits of quitting smoking may be complex, long-term and intangible. Teen-agers see themselves as "invincible" and may not react to fear tactics.
- The benefits of quitting smoking may also be weak. Many teen-agers live for today, and the addiction to tobacco and the need to boost self-image may be more important in the short-run.
- Involvement is very high in this cause ("stop smoking") and requires very effective promotional messages in order to persuade the target audience to take action. Resistance to the persuasive attempts will be strong.

Place (distribution): Unless the non-smoking campaign has facilities that help the target market to quit smoking, distribution will probably not be relevant.

Promotion:
- Professional volunteers may be needed to "spread the word" and to start and operate a grass-roots campaign aimed at stopping smoking among teen-agers.
- Sales promotion techniques can be used to provide incentives to those who stop smoking for a certain period of time.
- Public service announcements can be used since you are representing a nonprofit organization. This will be especially important, given that budgets will likely be very limited.
- Licensing of clever logos or slogans can be used to promote the cause.

Price: Price will be less relevant to the non-smoking campaign than for other non-profit causes. Your organization will likely be funded by the state or by other organizations, and you will be operating a cost centre and managing budgets.
(text pp. 287-291)

CHAPTER 11: MARKETING CHANNELS AND SUPPLY CHAIN MANAGEMENT

PRETEST SOLUTIONS
1.   A marketing channel is a set of interdependent organizations that ease the transfer of ownership as products move from producer to business user or consumer.
(text p. 308)
2.   Three intensities of distribution are:
- **Intensive:** Achieve mass market selling by distributing the good everywhere possible.
- **Selective:** Work closely with selected intermediaries who meet certain criteria.
- **Exclusive:** Work with a single intermediary for products that require special resources.
(text pp. 317-318)
3.   Channel conflict is a clash of goals or methods to achieve goals among channel members.
Channel leadership occurs when one member of a marketing channel exercises authority and power over other members.
Channel partnering is the joint effort of all channel members to create a supply chain that serves customers and creates a competitive advantage.
(text pp. 318-320)

4.   Six major functions of the supply chain are:
- Procuring supplies and raw materials;
- Scheduling production;
- Processing orders;
- Managing inventories of raw materials and finished goods;
- Warehousing and materials-handling; and
- Selecting modes of transportation.

(text pp. 321-325)

VOCABULARY PRACTICE SOLUTIONS

1.   marketing channel (channel of distribution), channel members
2.   discrepancy of quantity, discrepancy of assortment, temporal discrepancy, spatial discrepancy
3.   direct channel
4.   dual distribution (multiple distribution), strategic channel alliance
5.   intensive distribution, selective distribution, exclusive distribution
6.   channel power, channel control, channel leader
7.   channel conflict, horizontal conflict, vertical conflict
8.   channel partnering
9.   logistics, supply chain, supply chain management
10.   logistics information system, supply chain team
11.   mass customization, just-in-time production
12.   order processing system, electronic data interchange (EDI)
13.   inventory control system, materials requirement planning (MRP), distribution resource planning (DRP), materials-handling system
14.   electronic distribution, outsourcing

TRUE/FALSE SOLUTIONS

(question number / correct answer / text page reference / answer rationale)

1.	F	308	The marketing channel is the set of organizations that ease the transfer of ownership as products move from manufacturer to the consumer. The supply chain is the chain of all business entities that perform or support the logistics function.
2.	T	308	
3.	T	309	
4.	T	310	
5.	F	310	Agents are brokers are used in markets with many small manufacturers and many small retailers who need to be "ma tched up."
6.	T	313	
7.	F	314	One of the benefits of supply chain management is increased revenues.
8.	T	314	
9.	F	317	This is the objective of intensive distribution.
10.	F	317	This is an example of exclusive distribution.
11.	T	317	
12.	T	318	
13.	T	319	
14.	F	320	The supply chain team is responsible for transportation.
15.	T	321	
16.	T	322	
17.	F	323	This is an example of electronic data interchange (EDI).
18.	T	326	
19.	F	328	Uncertainty regarding shipping usually tops the list of reasons why smaller companies resist international markets.

AGREE/DISAGREE SOLUTIONS

(question number / sample answers)

1.   Reason(s) to agree: By going directly from manufacturer to retailer, products may be less costly, will take less time to get to the retailer, and will be in transit less time. Savings can be passed on to consumers.

Reason(s) to disagree: The direct route is not always the best route. Sometimes wholesalers can actually save costs by purchasing in bulk quantities (something small retailers may not be able to do) and sending out assortments of goods tailored to specific retailer's requests. Wholesalers can add value to the marketing channel by providing marketing services and transportation services.

2.	Reason(s) to agree: Channel leaders exert power and influence over other channel members, and many channel members might not react well to this.

Reason(s) to disagree: If the channel leader manages the relationships well among the channel members, it can have a positive influence that will avoid conflict.

3.	Reason(s) to agree: Intensive distribution allows manufacturers or wholesalers to distribute their products through the largest number of outlets possible. Their products will gain more exposure, and consumers are more likely to buy them. Even computer companies are going from selective distribution to a slightly more intensive distribution by selling computers in deep discount stores.

Reason(s) to disagree: Quantity does not mean quality. Selling a prestige product through intensive distribution will NOT necessarily increase revenue; it may even decrease revenue because it could destroy the mystique and image of the product.

4.	Reason(s) to agree: Services are intangible, so distribution through marketing channels is impossible. Many of the functions of logistics—materials handling, inventory management, warehousing—are not appropriate for intangible products.

Reason(s) to disagree: All services have tangible aspects. Banking services are "distributed" in a bank, a retail location where customers are served. Airlines companies have ticketing agencies and counters at airports. Even electrical companies have distribution—through electrical lines right to consumers' homes.

MULTIPLE-CHOICE SOLUTIONS

(question number / correct answer / text page reference / answer rationale)

1.	b	308	Economies of scale are not one of the responsibilities of marketing channels; it is a responsibility of a manufacturer.

2.	a	308	A manufacturer may only produce one product, yet consumers may need a variety of products to be satisfied. This is a discrepancy of assortment.

3.	b	309	A temporal discrepancy is created when a product is produced, but a consumer is not ready to purchase it.

4.	e	310	For customized and highly technical business products, the most common channel structure is the direct channel because of the amount of interaction and direct communication that is required.

5.	e	312	Some producers select two or more different channels to distribute the same products to target markets, a practice called dual or multiple distribution.

6.	d	317	Intensive distribution is distribution aimed at maximum market coverage. This distribution is used for many convenience goods and attempts to make the product available in every outlet where the potential customer might want to buy it.

7.	a	317	Selective distribution is achieved by screening dealers to eliminate all but a few in any single geographic area. With fewer retailers, the product must be one that consumers are willing to search for, such as shopping goods and some specialty products.

8.	e	318	The most restrictive form of distribution, exclusive distribution, entails establishing one or a very few dealers within a given geographic area. Because buyers are willing to search or travel to acquire the product, this form of distribution is limited to consumer specialty or luxury goods and major industrial equipment.

9.	c	318	Because of its influence and dominance in the channel, Wal-Mart is a channel leader.

10.	a	319	Since all the parties are retailers, the conflict is horizontal.

11.	d	320	Definition.

12.	c	321	Stages of the product life cycle may affect the size of the warehouse but should not affect the location. The other four items clearly affect the location decision.

13.	d	321	Tailor-made, or built-to-order, computers is an example of mass customization.

14.	d	322	Just-in-time is based on a reduction of inventory by receiving the parts from suppliers to the assembly line at the time of installation. This reduces capital tied up in inventory.

15.	b	323	Electronic data interchange is the direct electronic transmission, from computer to computer, of standard business forms between two organizations. When this technique is used orders can become virtually paperless and information about the order is available to both firms.

16.	d	323	The materials-handling system moves and handles inventory into and out of the warehousing subsystem.

17.	a	325	Rail transportation often involves rough handling and lack of speed, making raw materials more suitable for rail transport.
18.	c	325	Motor carriers are not as fast as airplanes, but they are much less expensive, particularly when dealing with a bulky product like meat.
19.	b	325	Limited handling and speed, available with airway transportation, mean less risk because there is diminished opportunity for damage and spoilage.
20.	a	325	Water carriers are the only type of carrier that can cross the ocean from Europe, carry heavy products, and perform product services while in transit.
21.	e	325	By reducing the time for the total transaction, ExxonMobil improved service delivery. Installing overhead televisions to broadcast news and sports while cars waited for a pump would have been a function of minimizing wait times.
22.	e	326	In contract logistics, a manufacturer or supplier turns over the entire function of buying and managing transportation to a third party. Contract warehousing is a growing trend in the area of contract logistics.
23.	c	328	If a product is fairly standardized, does not require much service, and is being distributed in a culturally dissimilar country, independent foreign intermediaries are typical, It is unlikely that the domestic firm could act as a channel captain in a VMS.

SCENARIO SOLUTIONS

1. False   Selling sunglasses directly to consumers through the Internet is an example of a direct channel.
2. False   The scenario does involve a distribution issue, but Ralph's business could also use some promotion.
3. True
4. b   Companies that use the retailer channel normally have their own sophisticated distribution and transportation system. Ralph's business is to o small for that.
5. c   Agents and brokers are independent salespeople who help manufacturers sell their products by matching them to retailers.
6. e   Selective distribution is achieved by screening dealers to eliminate all but a few in any single area.
7. b   The branding strategy should have absolutely no impact on channel selection.
8.   Ralph should probably choose option #3 since he has no sales force. The agent/broker channel is best used when both the manufacturer is small and the number of retailers is small. He can still go through a wholesaler, but the agent/broker can help match him up to customers.

ESSAY QUESTION SOLUTIONS

1. **Specialization and division of labour:** Specialization and division of labour maintains that breaking down a complex task into smaller, simpler ones and allocating them to specialists will result in much greater efficiency. Marketing channels achieve economies of scale through specialization and division of labour. Some producers do not have the interest, financing, or expertise to market directly to end users or consumers. These producers hire channel members to perform functions and activities that the producers are not equipped to perform or that these intermediaries are better prepared to perform. Channel members can perform some functions and activities more efficiently than producers, and they enhance the overall performance of the channel because of their specialized expertise.

   Overcoming discrepancies: Channel members help bridge the gap that several discrepancies create:
   - **Discrepancy of quantity:** Large quantities produced to achieve low unit costs create quantity discrepancies (the amount of product produced compared to the amount an end user wants to buy). Marketing channels overcome quantity discrepancies by making products available in the quantities that buyers desire.
   - **Discrepancy of assortment:** This discrepancy occurs when mass production does not allow a firm to produce all the items necessary for buyers to receive full satisfaction from products. Marketing channels overcome discrepancies of assortment by assembling in one place assortments of products that buyers want.
   - **Temporal discrepancy:** This is created when a product is produced, but the consumer is not ready to purchase it. Marketing channels overcome temporal discrepancies by maintaining inventories in anticipation of demand.

- **Spatial discrepancy:** Mass production requires a large number of potential purchasers, so markets are usually scattered over large geographic regions. Marketing channels overcome spatial discrepancies by making products available in locations convenient to consumers and business buyers.

Contact efficiency: Channels simplify distribution by reducing the number of transactions required to get products from manufacturers to consumers.
(text, pp. 308-309)

2. **Intensive distribution** is aimed at maximum market coverage. The manufacturer tries to have the product available in every outlet where the potential customer might want to buy it. If a buyer is unwilling to search for a product, the product must be placed closer to the buyer. Assuming that the product is of low value and is frequently purchased, a lengthy channel may be required. Candy, gum, cigarettes, soft drinks, and any other type of convenience good or operating supply would be distributed intensively.

Selective distribution is achieved by screening dealers to eliminate all but a few in any single geographic area. Since only a few retailers are selected, the consumer must be willing to seek out the product. Shopping goods such as electronic equipment and appliances and some specialty products are distributed selectively. Accessory equipment manufacturers in the business-to-business market usually follow a selective distribution strategy.

Exclusive distribution entails establishing one or a few dealers within a given geographic area. This is the most restrictive form of market coverage. Since buyers may have to search or travel extensively to purchase the product, exclusive distribution is usually limited to consumer specialty goods, a few shopping goods, and major industrial equipment. Some products distributed exclusively include Rolls Royce automobiles, Chris Craft boats, Pettibone tower cranes, and Coors beer.
(text, pp. 317-318)

3. Channel conflict occurs when channel members have a clash of goals or methods of achieving goals. Two types of channel conflict are:
- **Horizontal conflict:** occurs among channel members at the same level, such as two or more wholesalers, two or more retailers, or two or more manufacturers. An example is two merchant wholesalers that blame each other for predatory pricing in order to get business from retailers.
- **Vertical conflict:** occurs among channel members at different levels, such as between a retailer and a wholesaler, a wholesaler and a manufacturer, or a retailer and a manufacturer. An example is a retailer that becomes angry when a manufacturer decides to expand its so-called "exclusive" line of products to other retail outlets.
(text, pp. 318-319)

4. **Sourcing and procurement:** The goals of sourcing and procurement are to reduce the costs of raw materials and supplies. Companies that purchase will strategically manage suppliers in order to reduce the total cost of raw materials and services. Purchasers and suppliers often form a cooperative relationship to ensure that both entities are receiving benefits.

Production scheduling: Production begins when product forecasts are given to the production plant. The manufacturer must then schedule the production to meet forecasts and special large orders. Two considerations must be taken in production scheduling. Manufacturers might be asked to engage in mass customization, or to build products to specifications requested by a large customer. Another consideration is that some customers are demanding just-in-time (JIT) delivery, requiring manufacturers to schedule JIT production and to require their own suppliers to deliver raw materials literally just-in-time for production. This has the benefit of lowering inventory costs.

Order processing: Order processing is a subsystem of physical distribution that begins with order entry, continues with order handling, and ends with a filled order. As the order enters the system, management must monitor two flows: the flow of goods and the flow of information. Order processing has been affected by computer systems that allow automated order entry, customer information systems, delivery instructions, and other tasks. Without human intervention, fewer errors are made and customer service is improved.

Inventory control: An inventory control system develops and maintains an adequate assortment of products to meet customers' demands. The objective of inventory management is to balance minimum inventory levels (to reduce costs) while maintaining an adequate supply of goods to meet customer demand. Two major decisions managers must make regarding inventory are when to buy (order timing) and how much to buy (order quantity).

Warehousing and materials-handling: The final user may not need or want the good at the same time the manufacturer produces and wants to sell it. Warehousing allows manufacturers to hold these products until shipment to the final consumer is demanded. Key warehousing decisions include location, number and size, and type of warehouse. Alternative types include private warehouses, public warehouses, and distribution centres.

A materials-handling system moves inventory into, within, and out of the warehousing subsystem. Activities include receiving goods into the warehouse or distribution centre; identifying, sorting, and labelling the goods; dispatching the goods into a temporary storage area; and recalling, selecting, or picking the goods for shipment. Packaging and bar coding are also possible functions. The goal of an effective materials-handling system is to move items quickly with minimal handling.

Transportation: The transportation subsystem allows physical distribution managers to select from a variety of different transportation modes that best fit their criteria. The subsystem is responsible for the actual movement of goods through the channel of distribution to the final consumer.
(text, pp. 321-325)

5.   *Transportation modes include*:
        Railroad: coal, farm products, minerals, sand, and chemicals
        Motor carriers: clothing, food, computers, and paper goods
        Pipelines: oil, coal, chemicals, and water
        Water: oil, grain, sand, ores, coal, and cars
        Airways: technical instruments, perishable products, and documents
        Transportation criteria include:
        Cost: The total amount it will cost to use a specific carrier to move the product from the point of origin to the destination. Airways have the highest cost, while water is the cheapest mode.
        Transit time: The total time a carrier has possession of goods. Water has the highest transit time, and air is the fastest mode.
        Reliability: The consistency of the service provided by the carrier to deliver goods on time and in an acceptable condition. Pipelines are the most reliable, while water transport is the least reliable.
        Capability: Ability of the carrier to provide the appropriate equipment and conditions for moving specific kinds of goods. Water has the most capability, while pipelines have the least.
        Accessibility: The carrier's ability to move goods over a specific route or network. Trucks have the best accessibility, and pipelines have the most limited accessibility.
        Traceability: Relative ease with which a shipment can be located and transferred. Air is the best mode, and pipeline is the worst.
        (text, p. 325)

APPLICATION SOLUTIONS

Coffee beans are grown in small trees called *coffea* in the moist mountains of Colombia. The green beans are harvested are often blended to achieve a certain flavour. Coffee beans are shipped to Canada to a coffee roaster, which may be a wholesaler or a retailer. Then the coffee is sold to a gourmet coffee retailer. The distribution channel is generally: 1) farmer, who sells to 2) coffee wholesaler, who sells to 3) coffee retailer. The roasting process may occur with either the wholesaler or the retailer. Many gourmet coffee retailers roast the beans right on the spot for the freshest flavour.

CHAPTER 12: RETAILING

PRETEST SOLUTIONS
1.   Retailing is all the activities directly related to the sale of goods and services to the ultimate consumer for personal, nonbusiness use.
        (text p. 342)
2.   Ten types of stores are:
        • Department stores
        • Specialty stores
        • Supermarkets
        • Convenience stores
        • Drugstores
        • Full-line discount stores
        • Discount specialty stores
        • Warehouse clubs
        • Off-price retailers
        • Restaurants
        (text p. 344)

---

3.   Four types of nonstore retailing are:
     - Automatic vending: the use of machines to offer goods for sale.
     - Direct retailing: selling products door-to-door, office-to-office, or at home sales parties.
     - Direct marketing: getting consumers to make a purchase from their home, office, or other non-retail setting.
     - Electronic retailing: use of TV networks and on-line retailing.
     (text pp. 352-356)
4.   The six Ps of retailing are:
     - Product: product offering.
     - Place: proper location.
     - Promotion: positions the store in consumers' minds.
     - Price: the appropriate price.
     - Presentation: atmosphere and other qualities of store.
     - Personnel: people that work in the store who offer customer service.
     (text p. 361)

VOCABULARY PRACTICE SOLUTIONS
1.   retailing
2.   independent retailers, chain stores
3.   gross margin
4.   department store, buyer
5.   specialty store
6.   supermarket, scrambled merchandising, convenience store, drugstore
7.   discount store, full-line discount store, mass merchandising
8.   hypermarket, supercentre
9.   specialty discount store, category killer
10.   warehouse membership clubs
11.   off-price retailer, factory outlet
12.   nonstore retailing, automatic vending
13.   direct retailing, direct marketing, direct-response marketing, telemarketing, on-line retailing
14.   franchise, franchiser, franchisee
15.   retailing mix, product offering, private brands
16.   atmosphere
17.   agents and brokers, merchant wholesalers

TRUE/FALSE SOLUTIONS
(question number / correct answer / text page reference / answer rationale)

1.	F	342	Because L.L. Bean sells directly to consumers who buy the products for nonbusiness use, L. L. Bean is considered a retailer.
2.	T	343	Revenue minus cost of goods sold will result in gross margin, not net income.
3.	F	348	Mass-merchandising shopping chains have greater sales volume and number of stores than department stores.
4.	T	345	
5.	F	347	This would be an example of scrambled merchandising because it involves offering nontraditional goods for a pharmacy.
6.	F	349	Discount specialty stores have earned this nickname.
7.	T	353	
8.	F	354	This is known as direct retailing.
9.	T	358	
10.	F	361	The six Ps of retailing are product, price, place, promotion, presentation, and personnel.
11.	F	365	Freestanding stores require customers to actively seek them out and so must work to attract customers.
12	T	373	

(question number / sample answers)

1. Reason(s) to agree: Millions of consumers already have access to anything they want to buy—food, clothing, house wares, toys, flowers—through nonstore retailing. Even high-involvement purchases, such as expensive antiques, are available on-line. As computer technology becomes even more sophisticated, and as retailers become more savvy in providing customer service without face-to-face contact, customers will have little reason to leave their homes and can spend more leisure time without having to shop.

   Reason(s) to disagree: There will always be a need for retail stores. Customers cannot simply order everything on-line or through the telephone. Many customers enjoy the "human" side of store retail shopping: shopping with friends, socializing with store personnel, and enjoying the atmosphere that only a store retail environment can provide. Technology can have a "dehumanizing" effect on retailing.

2. Reason(s) to agree: Large retail chains—from Starbucks Coffee to Chapters bookstores to discount stores such as Wal-Mart—are taking over the world. These chains are able to buy in huge quantity and to offer merchandise at lower costs to consumers, thus putting the small independents out of business. They have even entered small towns, where independent retailers have always thrived.

   Reason(s) to disagree: Small retailers will always have a purpose. As their large counterparts are offering homogenized merchandise throughout the country or even throughout the world, small retailers can tailor their merchandise to the local market more easily. They can differentiate themselves with unique merchandise and outstanding customer service, because these elements are more easily controlled by smaller business.

3. Reason(s) to agree: By adapting their merchandise offerings to foreign markets, Canadian retailers can ensure that they are meeting customer demand.

   Reason(s) to disagree: Adaptation is not always the correct strategy. Adaptation may not be required (such as in electronics, where customer preferences are similar throughout the world) and may not even be preferred (some foreign markets want to purchase the Canadian image).

MULTIPLE-CHOICE SOLUTIONS
(question number / correct answer / text page reference / answer rationale)

1. b 342 Large retail operations represent about 50 percent of the nation's retail sales.
2. b 343 Gross margin is the percentage of sales after cost of goods has been subtracted from net sales.
3. b 342 Definition.
4. e 342 Definition.
5. c 346 In many cases supermarkets offer a wide variety of nontraditional goods and services under one roof, a strategy called scrambled merchandising.
6. a 348 These strategies are used by mass merchandisers.
7. c 348 A hypermarket combines both a supermarket and discount department store and is huge in size. Hypermarkets require enormous sales volume.
8. d 349 Discount specialty stores are single-line stores offering merchandise such as sporting goods, electronics, auto parts, office supplies, or toys. These stores offer a nearly complete selection of one line of merchandise and use self-service, discount prices, high volume, and high-turnover merchandise to their advantage.
9. c 350 Warehouse membership clubs sell a limited selection of brand name appliances, household items, and groceries, usually in bulk on a cash-and-carry basis to members only.
10. a 350 Off-price discount retailers purchase goods at cost or less from manufacturers' overruns, bankruptcies, irregular stock supplies, and unsold end-of-season output. The other four categories may be current customers and would not have a use for the overruns and out-of-season stock.
11. d 350 A factory outlet is a type of off-price retailer that is owned and operated by a manufacturer and carries one line of merchandise--its own.
12. c 352 By selling sauce in a restaurant, the chef is conducting store retailing.
13. b 353 Direct marketing refers to a variety of techniques such as telephone selling, direct mail, and catalogues.
14. d 355 Use of a cable television channel to display goods that are then sold over the phone is the shop-at-home network format.
15. c 358 The ties to the franchiser's policies may be very restrictive for an innovative businessperson because certain products and procedures must be adhered to.
16. a 361 The six Ps of retailing are product, price, place, promotion, personnel, and presentation, not packaging.

17. b 365 A freestanding store has the advantage of low site costs and will be a benefit if consumers are willing to seek it out.

18. d 365 Malls have unified images, convenient parking, and expensive leases. It is unlikely that a small, specialty store would be an anchor. The mall atmosphere and other stores will attract shoppers.

19. a 365 Anchors are the large stores at the ends of shopping malls and may sell a variety of products, not just expensive ones.

20. d 366 The predominant aspect of the store's presentation is the atmosphere--how the store's physical layout, decor, and surroundings convey an overall impression.

21. d 368 Suggestion selling seeks to broaden customers' origi nal purchases with related items.

22. d 369 Retail operations have not shown a large trend toward merging with retailers in other countries.

23. a 369 Franchises are well-received internationally, and governments are making franchising more attractive.

24. c 371 Entertainment is one of the most popular strategies in retailing in recent years.

25. d 373 By taking title to goods and reselling them to retailers (drugstores), McKesson is a merchant wholesaler.

26. e 374 An agent is a professional sales person or groups of sales people who represent a manufacturer, a wholesaler, or a retailer.

SCENARIO SOLUTIONS

1. False The catalogue and on-line business are also part of retailing, which is defined as the activities directly related to the sale of goods and services to the ultimate consumer for personal, nonbusiness use.

2. True Product width refers to the assortment of products offered, in this case a wide variety of home furnishings.

3. True

4. c A specialty store specializes in a given type of merchandise, in this case, home furnishings.

5. b A private label brand is one that is designed and developed using the retailer's name .

6. a Atmosphere is the overall impression conveyed by a store's physical layout, décor, and surroundings.

7. d Chain stores are owned and operated as a group by a single organization.

8. Pottery Barn has many competitors. The most direct competitors are other specialty chain stores such as Pier I Imports, which sell furniture and other home furnishings and are often located in shopping malls like Pottery Barn. Other retailers such as IKEA offer a more modern, Scandinavian design. Still other local and national furniture stores like Leons and The Brick, and department stores like Sears and The Bay sell furniture.

ESSAY QUESTION SOLUTIONS

1.

Type of Retailer	Service Level	Assortment	Price Level
Department store	high	broad	moderately high
Specialty store	high	narrow	high
Supermarket	low	broad	moderate
Convenience store	low	medium/narrow	moderately high
Discount store	moderate/low	medium/broad	moderately low
Warehouse club	low	broad	low/very low
Off-price retailer	low	medium/narrow	low

(text, p. 344)

2. **Product:** The product offering, or merchandising mix, must satisfy the target customers' desires. This level of satisfaction is often determined as a level of width and depth of the product assortment. Inventory management and physical distribution are also key issues when dealing with products at the retail level.

Place: This involves selecting a proper site or location for the store. Managers must decide on a community, a specific site, and store type, including whether to be a freestanding store or part of a shopping centre or mall.

Promotion: Retail promotional strategy includes advertising, public relations, publicity, and sales promotion. The objective of the promotional strategy is to help position the store relative to competitors in consumers' minds. Retail promotion is often done on a local basis.

Price: The right price is a critical element in retailing strategy. Price is a key element in a retail store's positioning strategy and classification.

Presentation: The presentation of a retail store to its customers helps determine the store's image. The predominant aspect of this is atmosphere, which includes employee type and density, merchandise type and density, fixture type and density, sound, odours, and visual factors.

Personnel: People are a unique aspect of retailing because most retail sales involve a customer-salesperson relationship. Personal selling issues and setting the quality level of customer service are two important personnel issues.

(text, pp. 361-368)

3.   The retail mix consists of product, place, promotion, price, presentation, and personnel.

- **Product:** The Gap offers both a large width of products, mostly under a private label brand (The Gap brand).
- **Place:** The Gap is usually located in large shopping malls and have traditional retail hours of 10:00 AM to 9:00 PM.
- **Promotion:** The Gap uses many different types of promotion, from discounts on purchases when you open a store credit card, to television and print advertisements using trendy models to attract a younger market.
- **Price:** Price is middle range. The Gap also owns Old Navy, its price-value chain, and Banana Republic, its high-end chain.
- **Presentation:** The layout and atmosphere is casual and friendly. Music reflects a younger generation.
- **Personnel:** Personnel is usually young (from late teens to late twenties). Sales associates are trained to greet customers and to provide good customer service.

(text, pp. 361-368)

APPLICATION SOLUTIONS

You could compete by using the following three trends:

- **Entertainment:** Though providing entertainment is not new to gourmet coffee retailers, you could differentiate yourself by providing unique entertainment. These could include magicians, comedy poetry readings, stand-up comics, or unusual music.
- **Convenience and efficiency:** Most gourmet coffee shops do not have drive-through windows. By incorporating one, you could provide a fast-food approach to an otherwise upscale product. In addition, you could gain much business by opening the drive-through early for early morning commuters.
- **Customer management:** Most coffee shops already offer frequency cards (whereby a customer can get a free coffee after the purchase of a certain number). You could go one step beyond and take vital information about a customer (such as birthdays, typical orders, etc.) and sent direct mailings, offering the customer a special coupon for their favourite latte on their birthday or telling the customer about a favourite entertainer who will make an appearance. This one-on-one marketing approach will turn your customer into a loyal one, a strategy that will be hard to match by the large coffee chains.

CHAPTER 13: MARKETING COMMUNICATION AND PERSONAL SELLING

PRETEST SOLUTIONS

1.   The four elements of the promotion mix are:
- **Advertising:** any form of paid communication in which the sponsor or company is identified.
- **Public relations:** evaluates public attitudes, identifies areas within the organization that the public may be interested in, and executes a program of action to earn public acceptance.
- **Sales promotion:** consists of all marketing activities that stimulate consumer purchasing and deal effectiveness.
- **Personal selling:** a situation in which two people communication in an attempt to influence each other in a purchase situation.

(text pp. 391-393)

---

2. The four steps of the communication process are:
   - **Sender and encoding**: the sender, or originator of the message, encodes the message to a second party. Encoding is the conversion of the sender's ideas a nd thoughts into a message.
   - **Message transmission**: sender transmits the message through a channel, such as through a medium (radio, TV, etc.) or by his/her own voice.
   - **Receiver and decoding**: the receiver of the message decodes, or interprets, the message.
   - **Feedback**: the receiver sends a response to the original message.

   (text p. 395)

3. AIDA is a model used by advertisers to get the target market to buy a product. AIDA stands for:
   - **Attention**: the advertiser must gain the attention of the target market with the message.
   - **Interest**: the advertiser must create interest in the product through the message.
   - **Desire**: the advertiser must make the target market want the product.
   - **Action**: the advertisement should be effective enough to entice the target market to actually purchase the product.

   (text pp. 399-400)

4. A push strategy uses aggressive personal selling and trade advertising to convince a wholesaler or retailer to carry and sell particular merchandise. A pull strategy stimulates consumer demand to obtain product distribution.

   (text pp. 404-405)

5. Advantages of personal selling as promotional tool are:
   - It provides a detailed explanation or demonstration of the product.
   - The sales message can be varied according to the motivations and interests of each prospective client.
   - It can be directed only to qualified people.
   - Costs can be controlled by adjusting the size of the sales force in one-person increments.
   - It is considerably more effective than other forms of promotion.

   (text p. 407)

6. The steps in the selling process are:
   - Generating leads.
   - Qualifying leads
   - Approaching the customer and probing needs
   - Developing and proposing solutions.
   - Handling objections.
   - Closing the sale
   - Following up

   (text p. 409)

VOCABULARY PRACTICE SOLUTIONS

1. promotion, promotional strategy, differential advantage
2. promotional mix, advertising, public relations, publicity, sales promotion, personal selling
3. communication, interpersonal communication, mass communication
4. sender, encoding, channel, receiver, decoding, feedback, noise
5. AIDA concept
6. push strategy, pull strategy
7. integrated marketing communications
8. relationship selling
9. sales process (sales cycle)
10. lead generation, cold calling, referral, networking
11. lead qualification
12. preapproach, needs assessment
13. sales proposal, sales presentation
14. negotiation
15. follow-up
16. quota
17. straight commission, straight salary

TRUE/FALSE SOLUTIONS

(question number / correct answer / text page reference / answer rationale)

1. T 390
2. T 390
3. T 390
4. F 391 This describes the role of public relations.
5. T 393
6. T 395
7. F 396 Even though a message is received, it will not necessarily be properly decoded; receivers interpret messages based on idiosyncratic frames of reference. Noise may also be a problem
8. F 395 Encoding is the conversion of a sender's ideas and thoughts into a message, usually in the form of words or signs.
9. T 395
10. F 395 Noise is anything that interferes with, distorts, or slows down the transmission of information.
11. T 397
12. T 398
13. T 398
14. F 399 AIDA stands for attention, interest, desire, and action.
15. F 400 Personal selling is the most effective at converting interest into a purchase.
16. T 402
17. T 404 This describes a push strategy.
18. T 406
19. F 407 Personal selling is generally one-on-one and does not reach masses. Advertising is the promotion tool used to reach a mass audience.
20. T 407
21. F 407 Personal selling is more important for high priced and high-involvement products.
22. F 408 The key difference is the process of building a long-term, value-added relationship.
23. T 408
24. F 409 The first step in the selling process is generating sales leads.
25. T 411
26. F 414 A good salesperson always follows up.
27. F 418 This is a combination of salary and commission.

AGREE/DISAGREE SOLUTIONS

(question number / sample answers)

1.   Reason(s) to agree: It is advertising that is most effective at attracting attention of a product. Without attention, the other elements (interest, desire, action) will not take place.

   Reason(s) to disagree: Advertising may be the most important promotional tool in some situations, such as selling many consumer products, but it is not as effective in selling business products. In this selling situation, tools such as personal selling may be much more important.

2.   Reason(s) to agree: While advertising may be effective at the first two steps in AIDA (gaining attention and interest in the product), it is not as effective at generating desire and action (purchase). It takes other promotional elements, such as personal selling or sales promotion, to achieve these.

   Reason(s) to disagree: An effective advertisement can make potential customers go through all the steps. A good advertisement will create desire for the product and in some cases even action. Without advertising, the target market could never buy the product because it would not be aware of it.

3.   Reason(s) to agree: Personal selling involves pushing a product to a target market. Not very many salespeople will walk away from a potential customer, even if the customer does not appear to have a "need" for the product at first. A good example is a tenacious telemarketer who does not take "n o" for a first answer and persists on speaking to the lead.

   Reason(s) to disagree: Personal selling is a part of true marketing. A savvy salesperson will always conduct a needs assessment to determine if the prospect is a good one, and what the prospect truly needs.

4.   Reason(s) to agree: The selling process does not apply to certain situations, such as fund raising for a nonprofit organization.

   Reason(s) to disagree: Even some nonprofit organizations could use the seven-step process. Fund raisers can (1) generate leads (potential donors); (2) qualify leads (determine who is likely to give); (3) approach the donor and ask questions; (4) develop and propose solutions (present how the donors can contribute by allowing deductions from payroll); (5) handle objections (why the donor cannot or will not give); (6) close the sale (get the commitment from the donor); and (7) follow-up (a thank you letter).

MULTIPLE-CHOICE SOLUTIONS
(question number / correct answer / text page reference / answer rationale)

1. d 390 A differential advantage is a set of unique features of a company and its products that are perceived by the target market as significant and superior to the competition.
2. b 391 Advertising is a form of impersonal, sponsor-paid, one-way mass communication.
3. e 392 Publicity is public information about a company or service appearing in the mass media as a news item.
4. d 393 Oral, face-to-face presentation in a conversation with one or more prospective purchasers for the purpose of making sales constitutes personal selling.
5. c 393 Sales promotion includes marketing activities that stimulate consumer purchasing such as coupons, contests, free samples, and trade shows.
6. c 394 Communication to large audiences, usually through a medium such as television or a newspaper, is called mass communication.
7. d 395 Noise is anything that interferes with, distorts, or slows down the transmission of information.
8. e 396 Receivers are the people who decode the message.
9. d 395 Noise is anything that interferes with, distorts, or slows down the transmission; it is not a channel of communication.
10. b 395 See Exhibit 13.2
11. e 396 All are types of feedback.
12. d 397 Personal selling allows the marketer to control not only the message being communicated but to persuade an otherwise reluctant buyer.
13. b 397 The publicity from the media is not controllable by the marketer.
14. a 398 Informative promotion is a necessary ingredient for a highly technical product or service.
15. b 398 Persuasive promotion is designed to stimulate purchase or action.
16. b 399 Since Coca-Cola is already well-known, the company uses reminder advertising constantly.
17. a 399 Reminder advertising is used for mature products.
18. a 399
19. b 400 Public relations is used to attract attention in the first place.
20. c 399 Sales incentives are used to induce purchase, which requires consumer desire.
21. d 401 The size of the marketer should have no impact on the promotional mix.
22. b 406 Definition.
23. e 406 There are no Federal requirements for adding diversity in advertising messages.
24. a 407 Personal selling is difficult to achieve when customers are geographically dispersed; this is where advertising is more effective.
25. c 407 The product is technical, complex, and industrial and could use good personal selling efforts.
26. c 407 An expensive product can benefit from personal selling as the main promotional tool.
27. c 408 Traditional personal selling focuses more on getting the sale rather than building relationships.
28. a 408 Relationship selling uses all these approaches.
29. e 410 Lead generation is the identification of potential customers who are most likely to buy the seller's offerings.
30. a 410 Networking is the process of finding out about potential clients from acquaintances.
31. d 413 In the approach stage, sales people will often demonstrate the product in an effort to close the sale.
32. e 415 Salespeople often offer concessions during negotiations to get the prospect to buy the product.
33. a 418 Straight commission plans offer no base salary.

SCENARIO SOLUTIONS

1. False   The two-month free subscription is a sales promotion tactic.
2. False   The use of a sales agency is a push strategy.
3. True
4. b   Advertising was done on network TV, the Internet, and local newspapers; sales promotion included the two-month free subscription; and sales agents represent the personal selling process. Only public relation is not mentioned.
5. d   The magazine should first inform consumers of the magazine's existence .
6. a   The use of a sales agency is a push strategy.
7. b   Integrated marketing communication (IMC) is the coordination of all promotional messages to assure the consistency of the message at every contact point where a company meets the consumer.

8.   The major element missing from the promotional mix is the lack of public relations. If the magazine is unique enough (i.e., targeted to Asian men), the publicity for this magazine should be very good. Juan should create an entire public relations campaign to gain further awareness of his magazine. In many cases, this may go even farther than his advertising would.

ESSAY QUESTION SOLUTIONS

1. **Advertising** is a form of impersonal, one-way mass communication paid for by the sponsor. Advertising is transmitted by different media, including television, radio, newspapers, magazines, books, direct mail, billboards, and transit cards.

    Public relations is the marketing function that evaluates public attitudes, identifies areas within the organization that the public may be interested in, and executes programs to earn public understanding and acceptance. A solid public relations program can generate favourable publicity. A firm can generate publicity in the form of news items, feature articles, or sporting event sponsorship.

    Sales promotion includes a wide variety of activities for stimulating consumer purchasing and dealer effectiveness. Examples include free samples, contests, bonuses, trade shows, and coupons.

    Personal selling involves a planned face-to-face presentation to one or more prospective purchasers for the purpose of making sales. Personal selling is more prevalent in the industrial goods field because of the complex, technical nature of many industrial products. Personal selling can also be used to encourage wholesalers and retailers to carry and resell a product. One form of personal selling is telemarketing. (text, pp. 391-393)

2.

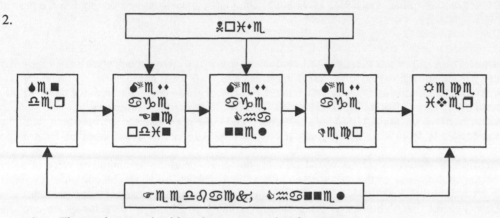

1. The sender encodes ideas into a promotional message.
2. The message is transmitted through a channel, or communication medium.
3. The message may or may not be received.
4. The receiver decodes the message. Messages may or may not be properly decoded.
5. The receiver's response to a message is feedback to the source. In promotions, feedback is indirect rather than direct.
6. Any phase of this process may be hindered by noise.
(text, pp. 394-396)

3. The AIDA model steps are Attention-Interest-Desire-Action.
    Attention: A salesperson would attract a potential customer's attention by a greeting and approach.
    Interest: A good sales presentation, demonstration, or promotional literature handed out during the sales presentation would create interest in the product.
    Desire: The salesperson could create desire by illustrating how the product's features will satisfy the consumer's needs.
    Action: The salesperson could make a special offer or a strong closing sales pitch to obtain purchase action. (text, pp. 397-401)

4. **Nature of the product:** Industrial products are usually promoted with more personal selling than advertising. Consumer products are promoted primarily through advertising. Sales promotion, branding, and packaging are more important for consumer goods than industrial goods. When the costs or risks of a product's use increases, personal selling becomes more important.
    Stage in product life cycle: During the introduction stage, emphasis is placed on advertising and public relations as well as some sales promotion and personal selling. During growth, sales promotion efforts are reduced, while advertising and public relations continue. At maturity, sales promotion and advertising become the focus. All promotion is reduced during the decline stage.

Target market characteristics: Widely scattered customers, highly informed buyers, and brand-loyal repeat purchasers generally require a blend of more advertising and sales promotion and less personal selling. Personal selling is required for industrial installations, even if buyers are extremely competent. Print advertising can be used when potential customers are difficult to locate.

Type of buying decision: A routine, low-involvement buying decision requires sales promotion and reminder advertising. Advertising and public relations can be used for a new purchase situation, while personal selling is most effective for complex buying decisions.

Available funds: A firm with limited funds can rely heavily on free publicity if the product is unique. If personal selling is necessary, the firm may use manufacturers' agents who work on a commission basis. Some sales promotions can also be inexpensive. Although advertising is very expensive, it has low cost per contact, which may be necessary for a large potential market. There is usually a trade-off among the funds available, the number of people in the target market, the quality of communication needed, and the relative of the promotional elements.

Push and pull strategies: A push strategy is a situation in which manufacturers use aggressive personal selling and trade advertising to convince a wholesaler or a retailer to carry and sell their merchandise. The wholesaler, in turn, must push the merchandise forward by persuading the retailer to handle the goods. The retailer then uses advertising, displays, and so on to convince the consumer to buy the pushed products. A pull strategy stimulates consumer demand to obtain product distribution. In this case, the manufacturer focuses its promotional efforts on end consumers. As consumers demand the product, the retailer orders the merchandise from the wholesaler. As the wholesaler is confronted with rising demand, it places orders for the pulled merchandise from the manufacturer. Stimulating consumer demand pulls the product through the distribution channel. Heavy sampling, consumer advertising, cents-off campaigns, and couponing are part of a pull strategy.
(text, pp. 401-405)

5. **Sales lead generation:** You can get sales leads to sell computers from your own organization's data base, by networking at industry trade shows, or by doing research on firms in your local area.

    Sales lead qualification: From your sales leads, you should screen out those firms that are not likely to buy from those who are likely to buy. This can be determined by initial interest in the computers.

    Doing a needs assessment: You should find out customers and their needs, the competition, and the industry. Are customers ready to make a decision about buying new computers? What kinds of features do they seek?

    Developing and proposing solutions: Once you determine customer needs, you should develop a sales proposal that is relevant to the needs of the customer and make the presentation about the computer products that you have. The presentation should include the types of computers, the service contract, and pricing.

    Handling objections: During the presentation, the customer is likely to object to certain elements of the proposal. Know in advance what the customer might object to, and know how to handle these objections during the presentation.

    Closing the sale: At the end of a sales presentation, you can attempt to close the sale if the prospect's objections are handled properly. Whenever the customer makes a commitment to buy, sale closing and order processing should begin. However, if the commitment to buy is not forthcoming, a number of techniques can be used to attempt to close the sale, including negotiation on the computers.

    Following up: Once the customer has purchased the computers, you should follow up. This should including calling or visiting the customer to determine if there were any problems with the computers and service.
    (text, pp. 407-415)

5. You can use any type of compensation but should have strong rationale for the type you are recommending. The advantage of straight commission is that it puts pressure on sales people to perform; the disadvantage is that it causes a lot of stress and does not allow for a poor sales period. Straight salary has the advantage of giving sales people some financial security and would be appropriate for an established product where account management is important. A combination of the two seems ideal.
    (text, pp. 418-419)

APPLICATION SOLUTION

AIDA stands for:

* Attention: How did the commercial capture your attention (think of music, visuals, copy)
* Interest: How did it capture your interest?
* Desire: Did the commercial make you want to buy the product?
* Action: Did you, in fact, purchase the product?

PRETEST SOLUTIONS

1. Three types of product advertising are:
   - **Pioneering advertising**: stimulates primary demand for a new product or product category.
   - **Competitive advertising**: influences demand for a specific brand.
   - **Comparative advertising**: directly or indirectly compares two or more competing brands on one or more specific attributes.

   (text, p. 433)

2. The steps to creating an advertising campaign are:
   - Determine advertising objectives
   - Make creative decisions
   - Make media decisions
   - Evaluate the campaign

   (text pp. 435-439)

3. Seven types of media are:
   - Newspapers
   - Magazines
   - Radio
   - Television
   - Outdoor media
   - The Internet and World Wide Web
   - Alternative media, such as computer screen savers, interactive kiosks, and video shopping carts

   (text pp. 439-444)

4. Six types of consumer sales promotion tools are:
   - Coupons and rebates
   - Premiums
   - Loyalty marketing programs
   - Contests and sweepstakes
   - Sampling
   - Point-of-purchase promotion

   Six types of trade sales promotion tools are:
   - Trade allowances
   - Push money
   - Training
   - Free merchandise
   - Store demonstrations
   - Business meetings, conventions, and trade shows

   (text pp. 449-456)

5. Six public relations tools include:
   - New product publicity
   - Product placement
   - Consumer education
   - Event sponsorship
   - Issue sponsorship
   - Internet Websites

   (text pp. 457-459)

VOCABULARY PRACTICE SOLUTIONS

1. advertising response function
2. institutional advertising, advocacy advertising, product advertising, pioneering advertising, competitive advertising, comparative advertising
3. advertising campaign, advertising objectives
4. medium, media planning
5. advertising appeal, unique selling proposition
6. cooperative advertising
7. infomercial
8. cost per contact, media mix, reach, frequency, audience selectivity

9. media schedule, continuous media schedule, flighted media schedule, pulsing media schedule, seasonal media schedule
10. media schedule
11. consumer sales promotion, trade sales promotion
12. coupon, rebate, premium, loyalty marketing program, frequent buyer program, sampling, point-of-purchase display
13. trade allowance, push money
14. crisis management

TRUE/FALSE SOLUTIONS
(question number / correct answer / text page reference / answer rationale)

1. T 430
2. T 434
3. F 434 This is *comparative* advertising.
4. T 433
5. T 433 This ad sells the product's attributes.
6. F 436 This represents the product's attrib utes, not its benefits.
7. T 436
8. F 436 An advertising campaign is a series of related advertisements focusing on a common theme, slogan, and set of adverting appeals.
9. T 437
10. F 443 Television still represents the largest share of advertising expenditures.
11. T 445
12. T 443
13. F 447 This is a seasonal media schedule since ads are used only before periods when people would tend to buy cards.
14. F 448 Sales promotion is generally short-term, whereas advertising is long-term.
15. T 448 Consumer sales promotions are targeted at the ultimate consumer.
16. F 448 Trade sales promotion has become even more important over the past decade.
17. T 449
18. T 453
19. T 455
20. F 455 This is an example of a trade allowance.
21. T 457
22. F 457 It is difficult to control the actual publicity, but marketers can influence what the media says about them through an effective public relations campaign.

AGREE/DISAGREE SOLUTIONS
(question number / sample answers)

1. Reason(s) to agree: Many other variables may affect a product's sales—such as sales promotions, selling efforts, or a change in price—so that advertising efforts cannot be isolated. Sometimes a product's sales will even decrease, even when advertising is in place.

    Reason(s) to disagree: An advertiser could prove the effect of its advertising by isolating advertising efforts somehow. If the advertiser, for instance, decides to stop advertising for a while without changing anything else in the marketing mix, it can determine what impact this will have on sales.

2. Reason(s) to agree: Advertising has the ultimate goal of selling a product or of creating a perception of an institution in the minds of consumers. As such, advertising messages may not necessarily lie but may withhold certain information known to the advertiser that may be negative about the product or company.

    Reason(s) to disagree: Advertising can be quite truthful, especially when product claims are backed by reputable and scientific research. There are a number of antitrust laws that protect the consumer against false and misleading advertising.

3. Reason(s) to agree: Sales promotion cannot stand alone in a promotion mix. Coupons, rebates, discounts, sweepstakes, etc., are only effective when there is awareness of the product, which can only be accomplished through advertising.

    Reason(s) to disagree: As a communication tool, sales promotion can actually work in the place of advertising when limited spending is required.

4. Reason(s) to agree: After advertising, personal selling, and sales promotion, public relations is simply an addition to the entire promotion mix. Advertising generally covers much of what public relations wants to achieve—shifting of attitudes and perceptions about a company or its products.

Reason(s) to disagree: Public relations—and its product, publicity—is a key component of the promotion mix. Whereas consumers recognize advertising as "biase d," journalists who are deemed to be objective in their writing generate publicity. Some businesses rely heavily on publicity when advertising budgets are tight—such as local restaurants, whose success may be based on a single food critic's positive review.

MULTIPLE-CHOICE SOLUTIONS
(question number / correct answer / text page reference / answer rationale)

1. a 430 In general, toy sellers have a large advertising-to-sales ratio. This is common for this industry and is not a sign of inefficiency.
2. b 431 There is a saturation point for advertising.
3. a 431 Humorous ads have been shown to be most effective at reinforcing already positive attitudes.
4. b 433 The company is trying to enhance its image to the public in the form of institutional advertising.
5. e 434 Pioneering advertising is intended to stimulate primary demand for a new product or product category and is heavily used g the introductory stage of the product life cycle.
6. a 434 By comparing its customer service to that of its competitor, the company is conducting comparative advertising.
7. c 435 The first step in the process is to decide what you want to accomplish in by determining objectives.
8. d 438 By showing the typical busy life of professional parents, this company is using a lifestyle execution.
9. d 438 A product symbol (such as the animated scrubbing bubbles) is one executional style that uses a character to represent the product.
10. b 440 Cooperative advertising is an arrangement under which a manufacturer pays a percentage of the advertising cost that a retailer places for the manufacturer's brand.
11. e 442 A relatively new form of direct-response advertising, the infomercial, is in the form of a 30-minute advertisement that resembles a TV talk show.
12. c 444 The media mix is the combination of advertising that will be conducted among the various media vehicles.
13. a 444 Cost per contact is the cost of reaching one member of the market. Comparing the cost of contacting the same amount of people using different media mixes is a common aid in selecting media.
14. a 445 Some media, such as magazines, have a long life span with the consumer, and advertisements may be seen repeatedly. Ads in other media such as radio and television are gone instantly.
15. c 447 The media schedule designates when and where advertising will appear.
16. b 447 The flighted media scheduling strategy schedules ads heavily for a period, then drops them for a period, and then repeats them.
17. a 445 A medium's fle xibility refers to how easily something can be changed at the last minute.
18. e 448 Sales promotion generally has a short-term objective.
19. d 449 Sales promotion does NOT reduce couponing; it probably increases it.
20. c 450 A premium is an extra item offered to consumers, usually in exchange for some proof that the promoted product has been purchased.
21. d 452 By trying the product, consumers are more likely to buy the product.
22. e 450 Couponing has lost its appeal over the years, but manufacturers continue to offer them because retailers demand it.
23. b 450 Since rebates are a one-time offer, they do not build customer loyalty.
24. d 455 A trade allowance is a temporary price reduction offered by manufacturers to retailers.
25. e 455 Training programs have multiple objectives.
26. d 457 Public relations seeks to achieve these goals.
27. e 457 Publicity is what is received in the form of news as a result of an effective public relations campaign.
20. d 457 Infomercials are a type of TV commercial that is paid for.
21. c 460 Crisis management is a coordinated effort to handle the effects of unfavourable publicity or of another unexpected, unfavourable event.

SCENARIO #1 SOLUTIONS

1. False   As an established brand with large share, Pop Sizzle does not need to use pioneering advertising.
2. False   The agency has come up with a benefits statement, not a slogan.
3. True   Since the benefits statement focuses on lifestyle and "cool ness" instead of product attributes, it is clearly more image-driven.
4. a   Comparative advertising compares two or more specifically named brands on an attribute, in this case, taste.
5. b   Definition of an advertising campaign.
6. c   Lifestyle is the best description since the advertisement will show Gen Y-ers having fun at a concert.
7. c   TV is one of the most expensive of all media, though it has a low cost per thousand because of the immense audience that it reaches.
8.   The scenario does not cover the campaign evaluation.

SCENARIO #2 SOLUTIONS

1. False   The scenario involves only two types of promotion: sales promotion and personal selling.
2. True
3. True
4. b   A premium is an extra item offered to the consumer.
5. d   A sweepstakes is a type of sales promotion that allows consumers to win something by chance, not by performance (which would be a contest).
6. a   A trade allowance is a price reduction offered by manufacturers to intermediaries, such as wholesalers and retailers.
7. c   Sandra's territ ory is Vancouver, which is an example of a geographic structure.
8.   Consumer sales promotion targets the ultimate user – or consumer – of the product. In this case, it would be dog owners. Trade sales promotion targets a channel member. In this case it would be wholesaler or distributors, grocery stores, and pet supply stores. Other types of consumer promotions that the company could offer are: 1) rebates (e.g., $5.00 off the first bag of dog food, rebate by mail with proof of purchase); 2) loyalty program (e.g., buy ten bags of food and get one free); 3) contest (e.g., send in photos of your dog, and the best photo wins a year's sup ply of dog food); 4) sampling (e.g., giving out free samples at pet supply shops); 5) point-of-purchase promotion (e.g., set up special displays of the dog food at retailers). Other trade promotions that the company could offer are: 1) training programs; 2) free merchandise; 3) store demonstrations; 4) trade show participation.

ESSAY QUESTION SOLUTIONS

1. **Institutional advertising** is used when the goal of the campaign is to establish, change, or maintain the image of a product or service, the company, or the industry. Institutional advertising has four important audiences: (1) the public, which includes legislators, businesspeople and opinion leaders; (2) the investment community, which is mainly comprised of stockholders; (3) customers; and (4) the company's employees.

   Advocacy advertising is a special form of institutional advertising that allows a corporation to express its views on controversial issues. Most advocacy campaigns react to unfair criticism or media attacks. Other campaigns may attempt to ward off impending regulatory threats.

   Product advertising touts the benefits of a specific product or service. It is used if the advertiser wishes to enhance the sales of a specific product, brand, or service. Product advertising can take three forms: pioneering advertising, competitive advertising, and comparative advertising.

   Pioneering advertising is intended to stimulate primary demand for a new product or product category. It is used during the introductory stage of the product life cycle to offer information about product class benefits.

   Competitive advertising is used to influence demand for a specific brand of a good or service. This advertising emphasizes the building of brand name recall and favourable brand attitudes. This type of advertising is often necessary during the growth stage of the product life cycle, when competitive entry eliminates the need to stimulate product category demand. This type of advertising stresses subtle differences between brands such as target market or price.

   Comparative advertising compares two or more specifically named or shown competitive brands on one or more specific product attributes. Advertisers may make taste, price, and preference claims often at the expense of the competing brand. The federal Competition Act prohibits advertisers from falsely describing competitors' products.
   (text, pp. 433-435)

2. Four creative decisions are:
   - Identifying product benefits: Advertisers must understand the difference between product features and benefits. The benefits should be stressed in advertising.
   - Developing and evaluating advertising appeals: An advertising appeal is a reason for a person to buy a product. The advertisement should have a unique selling proposition.
   - Executing the message: This involves the way an advertisement portrays its information. AIDA should be used as a blueprint for executing an advertising message.
   - Postcampaign evaluation: Advertisers must evaluate the effectiveness of the advertising campaign in achieving its goals.

   (text, pp. 435-439)

3. **TRADITIONAL**

   Newspapers are generally a mass-market medium. The largest source of newspaper ad revenue stems from the local retail sector through cooperative advertising between retailers and manufacturers. Advantages include (1) geographic selectivity and flexibility, (2) short-term advertiser commitments, (3) news value and immediacy, (4) advertising permanence, (5) stable readership, (6) high individual market coverage, (7) co-op and local tie-in availability, and (8) short lead-time. Disadvantages include (1) little demographic selectivity, (2) limited colour capabilities, (3) different local and national rates, (4) low pass-along rate, (5) may be expensive, and (6) noise from competing ads and news stories.

   Magazine advertising has increased in recent years because of segmented niche marketing. Advantages include (1) good colour reproduction, (2) message longevity, (3) demographic selectivity, (4) regional and local market selectivity, (5) long life, and (6) high pass-along rate. Disadvantages include (1) long-term advertiser commitments, (2) slow audience build-up, (3) limited demonstration capacity, (4) lack of urgency, (5) long lead times, and (6) high total cost.

   Radio is another medium that lends itself well to cooperative advertising. Local advertising accounts for 77 percent of radio ad volume. Advantages include (1) low cost, (2) high frequency, (3) immediate message, (4) short-notice rescheduling, (5) stable audience, (6) portable medium, (7) negotiable costs, (8) short-term advertiser commitments, (9) entertainment carryover (10) audience selectivity, (11) geographical selectivity, and (12) low production costs. Disadvantages include (1) no visuals, (2) short message life, (3) background sound, and (4) commercial clutter.

   Television can be divided into four basic types: network television (CBC and CTV which are national networks), independent stations, cable television and direct broadcast satellite television. Advantages include (1) wide reach, (2) creative demonstration opportunities, (3) immediate messages, and (4) entertainment carryover. Disadvantages include (1) little demographic selectivity, (2) short message life, (3) consumer skepticism toward claims, and (4) high cost.

   Outdoor advertising is a flexible, low-cost medium that may take a variety of forms. Examples include billboards, skywriting, bus shelters, taxicabs, giant inflatables, construction site fences, minibillboards in malls, lighted moving signs in bus terminals and airports, and ads painted on the sides of cars and trucks. Outdoor advertising reaches a broad and diverse market. Therefore, it is normally limited to promoting convenience products and select shopping products. Advertisers usually base billboard use on census tract data. Advantages include (1) repetition, (2) moderate cost, and (3) flexibility. Disadvantages include (1) short message, (2) lack of demographic selectivity, and (3) high noise.

   NEW FORMS

   Fax machines can be used to electronically deliver direct mail, advertisements, menus, and other solicitations.

   Video shopping carts can provide shoppers with product information and advertisements triggered by the cart's location in the store.

   Electronic place-based media include video monitors placed throughout stores that broadcast appropriate (often custom) programming and advertisements.

   Interactive advertising uses personal computers to transmit immediate, personalized advertisements to consumers.

   Minibillboards are used in high schools and college campuses with ads personalized to each school.

   Cinema/video: Advertisements are now being placed at the beginning of movies in theatres and on rented videocassettes.

   Infomercials are a relatively new form of direct-response advertising that take the form of 30-minute talk-show format commercials.

   Computer: screen savers, CD-ROMs, on-line ads on the web, home pages, etc.

   (text, pp. 440-444)

4. Consumer sales promotion involves activities targeted at the ultimate user – or consumer – of a product. Trade sales promotion is targeted to a channel member, such as a distributor or retailer. (text, p. 448)

5. Consumer sales promotion tools include coupons, rebates, premiums, loyalty marketing programs, contests and sweepstakes, sampling, point-of-purchase promotion, and on-line sales promotion. (text, pp. 449-453)

6. Public relations tools include:
    Press relations. Placing newsworthy information in the news media to attract attention to a person, product, or service.
    Product publicity. Publicizing specific products.
    Corporate communications. Creating internal and external communications to promote understanding of the firm or institution.
    Public Affairs. Building and maintaining national or local community relations.
    Lobbying. Dealing with legislators and government officials to promote or defeat legislation and regulation.
    Employee and investor relations. Maintaining positive relationships with employees, shareholders, and others in the financial community.
    Counselling. Advising management about public issues and company positions and image.
    Crisis management. Responding to unfavourable publicity or a negative event.
    During a crisis, the public relations team should:
    ▪   Get professional public relations help for handling news media relations.
    ▪   React quickly and start early. The worst damage to a company or product's reputation tends to occur immediately after the problem becomes public knowledge.
    ▪   Avoid the "no comment" response and do not ignore the situation.
    ▪   Make a team effort. Rely on senior management, public relations professionals, attorneys, quality control experts, manufacturing employees, and marketing personnel.
    ▪   Provide lots of communication and squelch incorrect rumours.
    ▪   Do not try to shift the blame away from the company. Take responsibility for the results of the problem.
    (text, pp. 455-460)

APPLICATION SOLUTIONS
1. Advertising appeals include:
   Profit motive: The low price of Less-U will save consumers money.
   Concern for health: Less-U will give body-conscious consumers the trim, healthy body necessary for a long, healthy life.
   Love/romance: Less-U will create a new, sexy body that is necessary for attracting romantic partners.
   Fear: Overweight consumers should be embarrassed at their present state; without Less-U, these consumers will be unattractive and die early.
   Admiration: An attractive celebrity spokesperson could promote Less-U.
   Convenience: Less-U will save food preparation time and is available at all convenient outlets.
   Fun and pleasure: While slender, the consumer can enjoy fun sports.
   Vanity and egotism: Consumers can be shown admiring their new, shapely figures.
   Environmental consciousness/considerate of others: Less-U could be promoted as having environmentally-friendly packaging, or showing how slender consumers take up less room and is more considerate of others.
   Advertising executional styles include:
   Slice-of-life: Family members in a normal household setting such as a dinner table or living room could discuss the merits of Less-U.
   Lifestyle: The ad could not only show how important a healthy body is for family members, but also show how much the family members enjoy baked desserts and how Less-U fits into this lifestyle.
   Spokesperson/testimonial: A typical family member or celebrity could make a testimonial or endorse Less-U.
   Fantasy: This ad could build a fantasy for a family member who cooks and after using Less-U the person wins baking contests, accolades from friends and relatives, and other recognition.
   Humour: Famous comedians could make light fun of "fat" and "skinny" cookies.
   Real or animated product symbols: This ad could show an animated Less-U character being baked into cakes and cookies.

Mood or image: This ad would build a mood or image around Less-U--perhaps one of rewards and pleasure because people could eat more desserts prepared with Less-U.

Demonstration: Chefs from cooking shows could demonstrate the use of Less-U and its benefits in an ad.

Musical: The benefits of Less-U could be demonstrated through an MTV-style music video.

Scientific: Research or scientific evidence could be used to demonstrate Less-U's superiority over butter, margarine, and shortening.

(text, p. 438)

2. For a "pull" strategy:

- **Coupons** are certificates given to consumers entitling them to an immediate price reduction when they purchase the item. Coupons for Steri-Flor could be mailed to households or placed in home magazines.
- **Premiums** are items offered to the consumer, usually requiring proof of purchase. The premium should be related to the product in some way. Premiums could be offered to purchasers of Steri-Flor, with proof of purchase required. Related premiums might be floor mops, sponges, buckets, or other items related to floor cleaning.
- **Frequent-buyer programs** reward brand-loyal customers for repeat purchases of products or services.
- **Contests** are promotions in which participants compete for prizes based on some skill or ability. Entrants could write an essay or poem about Steri-Flor or complete a puzzle about Steri-Flor's attributes.
- **Sweepstakes** allow anyone to participate and are characterized by chance drawings for prizes. Steri-Flor could offer a sweepstakes for people to win free housecleaning services, trips, cash prizes, or a year's supply of Steri-Flor.
- **Sampling** refers to free samples and trial sizes. Sampling allows consumers to try products with minimal risk. Trial sizes reduce the risk of trying new products. They also eliminate the problem of being stuck with a large quantity of a disliked product. Steri-Flor could be sent in small samples to households with instructions for use or comparison against the consumer's regular floor cleaner. Trial sizes could also be sold at a minimal price at grocery stores.
- **Point-of-purchase displays** are special displays set up at retail locations to build traffic, advertise the product, or induce impulse buying. Displays could be designed in the shape of the Steri-Flor packaging, or a display could show comparison floor samples. The displays would encourage consumers to stock up on Steri-Flor.

(text, pp. 449-453)

For a "push" strategy:

- **Trade allowances** are price reductions offered by manufacturers to intermediaries. The price reduction or rebate is in exchange for performance of specified functions or purchasing during special periods. Trade allowances could be offered to wholesalers in the form of price reductions or rebates. In exchange, wholesalers would promise to purchase during the holiday season or perform marketing functions for Steri-Flor.
- **Push money** is a bonus that intermediaries receive for pushing the manufacturer's brand. The push money is often directed toward the retailer's salespeople. Money or trips could be offered as a bonus to the wholesaler's sales force for pushing the Steri-Flor brand.
- **Training** programs may be provided for an intermediary's personnel if the product is complex. Because Steri-Flor may not be very complex, training may be in the form of teaching sales techniques or effective communications and demonstrations.
- **Free merchandise** may be offered in lieu of quantity discounts. It may also be used as payment for trade allowances provided though other sales promotions. Steri-Flor could offer one free case of the product for every ten cases purchased, or free cases could be offered in exchange for promotional functions performed by the intermediary.
- **Store demonstrations** can be performed at the retail establishment for customers. Customers can then sample products or see how they are used. Demonstrators could set up booths in stores to show comparisons of Steri-Flor cleaned floors versus floors cleaned by competing products.
- **Business meetings, conventions, and trade shows** are all ways to meet other vendors and potential customers of floor-cleaning products.

(text, pp. 455-456)

PRETEST SOLUTIONS

1. Three categories of pricing objectives include:
   - Profit-oriented objectives: Profit maximization, satisfactory profits, target return on investment
   - Sales-oriented objectives: Market share, sales maximization.
   - Status quo pricing objectives
   (text pp. 477-479)

2. **Elastic demand**: is a situation in which consumer demand is sensitive to changes in price. When demand is elastic, marketers must be very careful about changing price or the demand will be affected significantly.
   Inelastic demand: is a situation in which an increase or a decrease in price will not significantly affect demand for the product. When demand is inelastic, the marketer has more leeway in increasing prices to maximize profit.
   Unitary elasticity: means that an increase in sales exactly offsets a decrease in prices so that total revenue remains the same.
   (text pp. 481-483)

3. Three pricing methods using cost as a determinant are:
   - **Markup pricing**: cost of buying the product from the producer plus amounts for profit and for expenses not otherwise accounted for.
   - **Profit maximization pricing**: occurs when marginal revenue equals cost.
   - **Break-even pricing**: pricing based on determining what sales volume must be reached before total revenue equals total costs.
   (text pp. 486-488)

4. Five alternative pricing determinants are:
   - Stage in the product life cycle
   - Competitors' p rices
   - Distribution strategy
   - Promotion strategy
   - Relationship of price to quality
   (text pp. 490-495)

VOCABULARY PRACTICE SOLUTIONS

1. price
2. revenue, profit
3. return on investment (ROI), market share, status quo pricing
4. demand, supply, price equilibrium
5. elasticity of demand, elastic demand, inelastic demand, unitary elasticity
6. yield management systems
7. variable cost, fixed cost, average variable cost (AVC), average total cost (ATC), marginal cost (MC)
8. markup pricing, keystoning
9. marginal revenue (MR), profit maximization
10. break-even analysis
11. selling against the brand
12. prestige pricing
13. extranet

TRUE/FALSE SOLUTIONS

(question number / correct answer / text page reference / answer rationale)

1. F 476 Price is not just monetary; it is what the customer gives up in exchange for a product or service, such as time or energy.
2. T 476
3. F 476 Revenue is simply price times the number of units sold.
4. T 478
5. F 479 Maximization of cash should never be a long-run objective.
6. F 479 Status quo pricing maintains existing prices or prices that meet competition.
7. F 483 The point at which demand and supply are equal is called equilibrium price.
8. F 483 Total revenue will remain the same, even if prices change, in unitary elasticity.
9. T 484
10. T 486

11. T 488
12. F 491 Firms in such situations must usually choose between pricing below the market or at the market level.
13. F 495 Consumers use price as a quality indicator when there is a substantial degree of uncertainty involved in the purchase decision.

AGREE/DISAGREE SOLUTIONS
(question number / sample answers)

1. Reason(s) to agree: Most firms have both a short- and long-term goals of maximizing profit. Therefore, pricing objectives must be consistent with this goal.
    Reason(s) to disagree: Some firms may have a short-term goal of maximizing market share, which may be done at the expense of profit. To maximize share, a firm may have to price low in order to gain quick sales volume. This practice has been used by many Japanese firms entering a foreign market.

2. Reason(s) to agree: It would be a real coincidence if an increase (or decrease) in price directly offset a decrease (or increase) in sales.
    Reason(s) to disagree: Theoretical or not, unitary elasticity could occur. Products that are discounted for a short period of time during a sales promotion may experience unitary elasticity, whereby the decrease in price is offset in the short-term by an increase in sales volume. The objective in this case is to get more products into the hands of consumers, who try the product and may repurchase even when the price is raised to its normal level.

3. Reason(s) to agree: Since most firms have a profit goal, pricing must at least cover costs.
    Reason(s) to disagree: Sometimes pricing is not based on costs directly. When competition is fierce, pricing may actually fall below costs. Supermarkets follow a strategy called "loss leadership," whereby they price an item below their cost in order to bring customers into their stores to purchase other, more profitable products.

4. Reason(s) to agree: Prestige products, such as Rolex or Rolls Royce, enjoy a high quality perception, partially due to the high price that these products command.
    Reason(s) to disagree: In many product categories, price is not the only determinant of quality. If a product's q uality does not deserve its high price, the high pricing strategy will not work in the long run.

5. Reason(s) to agree: Pricing involves much quantitative analysis, including the elasticity of demand, fixed and variables costs, and break-even analysis.
    Reason(s) to disagree: Though many quantitative analyses must be used to determine pricing, much of it is driven by how competitors price their products and what kind of positioning or imagery the marketing manager is trying achieve with its brand.

MULTIPLE-CHOICE SOLUTIONS
(question number / correct answer / text page reference / answer rationale)

1. b 476 The company is not losing money; in fact, it is making $100,000 in profit.
2. e 477 Profit maximization means setting prices so that total revenue is as large as possible relative to total costs.
3. a 477 The objective of satisfactory profits is characterized by seeking a level of profits that is satisfactory to management and shareholders.
4. d 478 ROI is net profits after taxes divided by total assets: $50,000/500,000 = 10 percent.
5. a 478 By pricing low to gain short-term unit sales volume, the firm is trying to gain market share.
6. e 479 Status quo pricing is best described as meeting the competition.
7. d 481 Since the total revenue dropped when the price was doubled, the demand is elastic.
8. d 481 When demand and supply are approximately equal, price equilibrium is reached.
9. c 481 Inelastic demand is characterized by a decrease in price that leads to an increase in demand, but the increase in demand does not offset the decrease in revenue caused by the price decrease.
10. a 483 Under unitary elasticity the increase in demand exactly offsets the decrease in price. In this case, $6 \times 300 = 1800$ and $5 \times 360 = 1800$.
11. e 486 Variable costs vary with the level of output.
12. a 486 The payment on leased equipment remains the same, no matter how many pizzas are produced, and therefore is a fixed cost.
13. c 486 Marginal cost is the change in total costs associated with a one-unit change in output.
14. b 487 Keystoning doubles costs to set prices.
15. d 486 Markup pricing is adding profit to the base cost of a product.
16. b 489 Break-even quantity is the total fixed costs ($50,000) divided by fixed cost contribution per unit ($.20).

17. e 486 The analysis only includes company costs but does not consider consumer demand.
18. b 491 In the maturity stage of the product life cycle, price promotion often occurs to maintain market share.
19. d 492 The egg producer is passing a large portion of its profit margin on to the wholesalers and retailers, not maximizing profit margin for itself.
20. c 490 Since the product is new and innovative, it has no direct competition.
21. b 495 Most consumers equate price and quality.
22. c 496 Prestige pricing strategy sets high prices to connote high product quality and exclusiveness.
23. c 496 The price needs to fit the product quality for a more cohesive image.

SCENARIO SOLUTIONS

1. True SuperDuper has a 50 percent unit market share (5 million divided by 10 million).
2. False SuperDuper has a 30 percent revenue market share (10 million divided by 50 million), while Triple A has a 36 percent market share (18 million divided by 50 million).
3. False The increase in price resulted in an even larger decrease in volume in Detroit.
4. c 10 million widgets sold times $5 average price = $50 million.
5. b SuperDuper's revenues were $10 million ($2.00 times 5 million units); the total revenue for the widget industry was $50 million ($5 average price times 10 million); so, SuperDuper's revenue market share was 20 percent ($10 million divided by $50 million).
6. c There is no information about profit in the entire scenario.
7. a Since unit sales dropped 40 percent when price raised only 25 percent (from $2.00 to $2.50), demand seems to be elastic. Consumer demand is very sensitive to price changes.
8. It would be best to leave SuperDuper's price as is, as long as competitors don't drop or lower prices. The test market indicates that consumer demand for SuperDuper is very sensitive since the volume dropped dramatically when the price was raised. You could also test another price point that is less dramatic – say, $2.25 – to see what happens to demand.

ESSAY QUESTION SOLUTIONS

1. **Profit-oriented pricing objectives include:**
   - Profit maximization
   - Satisfactory profits
   - Target return on investment

Profit-oriented pricing objectives have several disadvantages. In particular, profit maximization has two problems. First, many firms do not have adequate accounting data for setting profit maximization goals. Additionally, this goal does not provide a basis for planning because it is vague and lacks focus. Target ROI may be difficult to evaluate because it should be viewed against the competitive environment, risks in the industry, and economic conditions.

Sales-oriented pricing objectives include:
   - Market share (dollars or units)
   - Sales maximization (dollars or units)

These demand-oriented objectives can also have disadvantages. In particular, dollar/unit sales maximization objectives ignore profits, competition, and the marketing environment as long as sales are rising. This type of sales maximization should be used on a short-term basis only.

Status quo pricing objectives include:
   - Maintaining the existing price
   - Meeting the competition

While these passive policies are simple, they may not be responsive to price changes required by consumers. (text, pp. 477-480)

2. The price established depends primarily on demand for the good or service and the cost to the seller for that good or service. Other factors that would influence price include stage in the product life cycle, the competition, distribution strategies, promotion strategies, and perceived quality.

- **Demand:** The quantity of a product that people demand to buy depends on its price. The higher the price, the fewer goods consumers will demand. Conversely, lower prices increase demand levels. Elasticity of demand is also an important factor. Elastic demand occurs when consumers are sensitive to price changes. Inelastic demand means that an increase or a decrease in price will not significantly affect demand for the product. Unitary elasticity exists when the increase in sales exactly offsets the decrease in price so that total revenue remains the same. Factors that affect elasticity of demand include (1) the availability of substitute goods and services, (2) price relative to a consumer's purchasing power, (3) product durability, and (4) other uses for the product.
- **Cost:** Setting prices based solely on costs ignores demand and other important factors such as marketing mix components or consumer needs and wants. Prices determined strictly on the basis of cost may be too high for the target market, thereby reducing or eliminating sales. Cost-based prices may also be too low, causing the firm to earn a lower return than it should. Costs play an important role in price setting, however. Costs serve as a threshold guideline or a floor below which a good or service must not be priced in the long run. Cost-based pricing methods include (1) markup pricing, (2) formula pricing, (3) break-even analysis, and (4) target return pricing.
- **Stage in the product life cycle:** Management usually sets prices high during the introduction stage, and prices begin to decline throughout the life cycle as demand for the product and competitive conditions change.
- **Competition:** If a firm faces no competition, it may set high prices. These high prices, however, serve to attract competitors. If a firm is in a competitive industry, the firm faces a decision of whether to price below the market or at the market level.
- **Distribution strategy:** Adequate distribution for a new product can often be attained by offering a larger than usual profit margin to intermediaries. A variation is to give dealers large trade allowances to stimulate demand at the retail level. Finally, consumers may purchase a higher-priced item if it is located at a convenient outlet.
- **Promotion strategy:** Reduced prices are often used as a promotional tool to induce consumers to shop in a particular store. Price promotions can also take the form of discount coupons and rebates.
- **Relationship of price to quality:** Consumers tend to rely on price as an indicator of product quality; that is, a higher price indicates higher quality in the form of better materials, more careful workmanship, or higher service levels. Conversely, lower price indicates lower quality as illustrated by the adage, "you get what you pay for." Marketers can take advantage of the price-quality phenomenon by increasing the price of the product to enhance the image of their product. This is known as a prestige pricing strategy.

(text, pp. 480-485)

3. **Introduction:** Generally, prices are set high in the introduction stage to recover development costs. However, pricing strategies followed in this stage depend on demand elasticity. If demand is inelastic, a high introductory price is warranted. If demand is elastic and consumers are price-sensitive, price should be set at the market level or lower.

Growth: Price may stabilize at this level as competitors enter the marketplace. Price may fall somewhat as economies of scale allow lower costs to be passed on to the consumer in the form of a lower price.

Maturity: This stage brings on further price declines as competition increases and inefficient, high-cost firms are eliminated. Remaining competitors typically offer similar prices. Price increases are cost-initiated rather than demand-initiated.

Decline: In the final stage of the product life cycle, prices may decline even further as the few remaining competitors attempt to salvage the last vestiges of demand. If only one firm is left in the market, prices will stabilize or even rise as the product becomes a specialty good.

Product: Price levels must be set according to the cost of the product, demand for the product, elasticity of demand for the product, and the perceived relationship of price to quality of the product.

Place/distribution: Adequate distribution for a new product can often be attained by offering a large profit margin to wholesalers and retailers. Price can be set higher than normal if the product is distributed to outlets that are convenient to the consumer.

Promotion: Price is often used as a promotional tool to increase consumer interest. Special low prices are often advertised as an inducement. Discount coupons, cents-off campaigns, price rebates, and other discounts are all price-promotion marketing tools.

(text, pp. 490-495)

Application #1

The following calculation table shows the resultant unit and dollar shares. Market share should be expressed in percentage points.

Company	Units Sold	Unit Price	Total Dollars	Unit Share	Dollar Share
Xylo	1,000	$1.00	$1,000	1,000/2,000 = 50%	$1,000/5,000 = 20%
Yeti	600	$5.00	$3,000	600/2,000 = 30%	$3,000/5,000 = 60%
Zeta	400	$2.50	$1,000	400/2,000 = 20%	$1,000/5,000 = 20%
	2,000		$5,000		

(text, pp. 478-479)

Application #2

Markup percentages for the retailer are stated in terms of the final selling price. The dollar markup is calculated as selling price minus cost, and percentage markup can be calculated by dividing dollar markup by selling price.

  a) Dollar markup ÷ selling price = percent markup
      $5 ÷ $25 = 20%
  b) Selling price = (dollar markup + cost)
      Dollar markup ÷ selling price = percent markup
      $6 ÷ ($6 + $4) = 60%
  c) Dollar markup = (selling price - cost)
      (Selling price - cost) ÷ selling price = percent markup
      (S - $15) ÷ S = .25
      (S - $15) = .25S
      $15 = .75S
      Selling price = $20
  d) (Selling price - cost) ÷ selling price = percent markup
      ($12 - C) ÷ $12 = .75
      ($12 - C) = (.75 × $12)
      C = $12 - $9 = $3

(text, pp. 486-487)

Application #3

Using the break-even formula indicates that TV-Terry must sell 1,500 televisions to break even.

  Fixed cost contribution = selling price - variable cost
  FCC = $500 - $300 = $200
  Break-even quantity = total fixed costs ÷ fixed cost contribution
  BEQ = $300,000 ÷ $200 = 1,500 units

(text, pp. 488-490)

CHAPTER 16: SETTING THE RIGHT PRICE

PRETEST SOLUTIONS

1. The four steps in setting the right price are:
    * Establish pricing goals
    * Estimate demand cost and profits
    * Choose a price strategy to help determine a base price
    * Fine tune the base with pricing tactics
    Following these steps can lead to the right price
    (text p. 506)
2. Four illegal issues regarding price are:
    * **Unfair trade practices:** Selling a product below cost.
    * **Price fixing:** An agreement between two or more firms on the price they will charge for a product.
    * **Price discrimination:** Charging different customers different prices for no reason.
    * **Predatory pricing:** Charging a very low price for a product with the intent of driving competitors out of business or out of a market.
    (text pp. 509-511)

3. Types of discounts, rebates, and allowances that can be used are:
   - Quantity discounts
   - Cash discounts
   - Functional discounts
   - Seasonal discounts
   - Promotional allowances
   - Rebates
   - Zero-percent financing

   (text pp. 511-512)

4. Nine types of special pricing tactics are:
   - Single-pricing
   - Flexible pricing
   - Professional services pricing
   - Price lining
   - Leader, or loss leader, pricing
   - Bait pricing
   - Odd-even pricing
   - Price bundling
   - Two-part pricing

   (text pp. 514-518)

VOCABULARY PRACTICE SOLUTIONS

1. price strategy
2. price skimming, penetration pricing
3. unfair trade practice acts, price fixing, predatory pricing
4. base price
5. cash discount, quantity discount, cumulative quantity discount, noncumulative quantity discount
6. functional discount (or trade discount), trade loading
7. seasonal discount, promotional allowance, rebate, value-based pricing
8. FOB origin pricing, uniform delivered pricing, zone pricing, freight absorption pricing, basing-point pricing
9. single-price tactic, flexible pricing (or variable pricing), price lining
10. leader pricing (or loss-leader pricing), bait pricing, odd-even pricing (or psychological pricing)
11. price bundling, unbundling, two-part pricing, consumer penalty
12. product line pricing, joint costs
13. delayed-quotation pricing, escalator pricing, price shading

TRUE/FALSE SOLUTIONS

(question number / correct answer / text page reference / answer rationale)

1. F 506 The first step in setting price is to establish pricing goals.
2. T 508
3. T 507
4. T 509
5. F 509 The presidents are engaging in price fixing, which is also illegal.
6. T 511
7. F 512 Rebates involve a cash refund for the purchase of a product during a specific period.
8. F 513 Pricing a product too low may result in decreased sales, especially if consumers believe the quality or other product attributes are being compromised.
9. F 515 This is an example of professional services pricing.
10. F 519 Complementary products are those that are consumed together, not produced together. The sale of one complement causes an increase in the sale of the related complement.
11. T 521

AGREE/DISAGREE SOLUTIONS
(question number / sample answers)

1.   Reason(s) to agree: Some firms, such as Procter & Gamble and Wal-Mart, have greatly reduced the number of discounts given to customers and have simplified their pricing strategies altogether. By using EDLP, manufacturers can eliminate "tra de loading" (which happens when retail or wholesale customers buy products in bulk when discounted). In addition, retailers can advertise less and maintain a consistent pricing strategy.

Reason(s) to disagree: In some industries, discounted pricing and "specials" may be too ingrained to eliminate without losing business. Products that are discounted for sales promotion and that are advertised as such can bring customer traffic into a store, which can produce more profits in the long run.

2.   Reason(s) to agree: Leader pricing indicates that retailers are pricing certain items at or below cost in order to bring traffic into the store. If customers buy nothing else at the store, the store can lose money very quickly.

Reason(s) to disagree: Supermarkets have been successful at leader pricing because customers will rarely go to the supermarket to buy just one item (the promoted item) but will pick up other, more profitable products.

3.   Reason(s) to agree: Pricing at product at $9.99 instead of $10.00 is an insult to consumers. They realize that there is only a one cent difference. Retailers should just round up their pricing to make it easier for customers to pay at the cash register.

Reason(s) to disagree: Many consumers perceive that odd-numbered prices (such as $9.99) indicates that a product is discounted. Because of this, they may be more likely to pick up the product.

4.   Reason(s) to agree: Since price is the single most important criteria for the purchase of most products, prices should be reduced during tough economic times.

Reason(s) to disagree: Customers do not buy just on price; they purchase value. By bundling product together or by introducing new "value-p riced" product to complement a more expensive line, marketers can hold their market share during a recession.

MULTIPLE-CHOICE SOLUTIONS
(question number / correct answer / text page reference / answer rationale)

1. e   506 Different individuals in an organization may have pricing objectives that are not mutually compatible and will involve trade-offs.
2. a   507 Price skimming is pricing high to capitalize on a product's uni queness.
3. c   508 Penetration pricing is pricing low in order to gain volume market share.
4. b   509 Status quo pricing is simply meeting the competition.
5. b   509 Publishing and circulating minimum fee schedules is an example of price fixing.
6. d   510 Price discrimination is illegally offering two or more customers different prices which can cause unfair competition.
7. d   510 Price discrimination violates the Competition Act.
8. c   512 A cash discount is offered to those who make immediate payment upon delivery.
9. a   512 A functional discount is the customary discount from list price that is offered to intermediaries in recognition of their functions that are performed in the selling of the product.
10. a   512 A seasonal discount is a price reduction for buying merchandise out of season.
11. b   512 A promotional allowance may be used to offer free goods or displays to a retailer in return for promoting a manufacturer's products, or it may pay for some or all of the advertising costs.
12. a   512 A rebate is a cash refund given for the purchase of a product during a specific period of time.
13. b   513 Because title will pass to the purchaser at the time of shipment with FOB origin pricing, the risks and costs will also pass to the purchaser at that point.
14. b   514 With uniform delivered pricing, all customers will pay the same price regardless of their location.
15. d   514 With zone pricing, the freight prices are set according to geographic areas.
16. a   514 With freight absorption pricing, the seller pays all or part of the freight costs and does not pass them on to the purchaser, keeping the purchase price low.
17. b   514 With basing-point pricing, customers pay freight from a set base point, regardless of the location from which the goods are shipped.
18. c   515 The single price tactic offers all goods and services at the same price.
19. b   515 Flexible pricing is defined as selling essentially the same product to different customers for different prices.
20. a   515 Price lines allow a retailer to appeal to several different target markets. It is not an uncommon strategy, and The Sports Stop's competitors probably use it also. It should not affect inventory overall and will not force a price-quality comparison.

21. b 516 Leader pricing involves selling a product near or even below cost to attract business.
22. e 517 Marketing two or more products in a single package for a special price is called price bundling.
23. d 518 Two-part pricing involves two separate charges to consume a single product or service.
24. d 519 The manager is trying to determine the relationships between the various products in the line and is looking at the products, not the buyer.
25. e 521 Delayed-quotation pricing delays the setting of the final price.
26. a 521 Like delayed-quotation pricing, escalator pricing allows for price increases and delays the setting of the final price.
27. b 521 These activities fit the description of price shading.

SCENARIO SOLUTIONS

1. False Diamante is using a price skimming strategy as the high-price leader.
2. True
3. False As long as the discount is offered to anyone who can pay within thirty days, it is not a form of price discrimination.
4. c The market must be willing to pay the higher price – and this may be due to a number of factors, including anticipation for the product – which is not necessarily related to higher quality.
5. b A cash discount is generally given for the prompt payment of a bill.
6. a A promotional allowance is given to retailers who promote the product; seasonal discounts are given when retailers buy products out of season.
7. d Meeting with competitors to agree upon a price is called price fixing, which is illegal.
8. Toni already uses promotional allowances and cash discounts. Other pricing tactics include: quantity discounts, functional discounts, seasonal discounts, and rebates. She could also use single-pricing, price-lining, odd-even pricing, and price bundling. Other tactics are probably not appropriate since they may harm the brand's ima ge.

ESSAY QUESTION SOLUTIONS

1. The four-step process is:
   Establish price goals: You must first decide what you want to achieve through pricing. An example would be to gain quick market share and to position the shoes as a complement to other athletic shoes (not as a replacement to the pricier sport-oriented shoes).
   Estimate demand, costs, and profit: You must conduct market research to get an idea of what kind of demand exists for these trendy shoes. If the demand is elastic, for example, this will dictate lower pricing. Working with your manufacturing facilities, you should get an idea of all costs involved in producing and marketing the shoes, as well as determine what profit is acceptable to your company.
   Choose a price strategy: You should then determine a long-term strategy that will be used for the introduction of the shoes and for the other phases of the product life cycle. For example, you could use a penetration pricing policy that would price products lower than other name brand athletic shoes so that consumers would buy your shoes in addition to more sports-oriented shoes.
   Fine tune the base with pricing tactics: You should plan other pricing tactics for the introduction of the shoes. This could include providing introductory promotional allowances to entice retailers to feature the new shoes, functional discounts to wholesalers and retailers who stock the shoes, quantity discounts to those that purchase several cases at once, and geographic pricing.
   (text pp. 506-513)

2. There are three basic methods for setting a price on a new good or service: price skimming, price penetration, and status quo pricing.
   Price skimming: With this method a high introductory price is charged that skims the top off a market in which there is inelastic demand. The high introductory price attracts a smaller market share but recoups costs quickly. Price-skimming advantages include (1) quick recovery of product development or educational costs, (2) pricing flexibility that allows subsequent lowering of price, and (3) the ability to market prestige products successfully. Disadvantages include encouragement of competitive entry into the market.
   Penetration pricing: With this method a firm introduces a product at a relatively low price, hoping to reach the mass market in the early stages of the product life cycle. The low price allows the product to penetrate a large portion of the market, resulting in large market share and lower production costs. Penetration pricing advantages include (1) a tendency to discourage competitive entry, (2) large market share due to high volume sold, and (3) lower production costs resulting from economies of scale. Disadvantages include (1) lower profits per unit, (2) higher volume required to reach the break-even point, (3) slow recovery of development costs, and (4) inability to later raise prices.

Status quo pricing: With this method the price charged is identical or close to that of the competition. This strategy may be used more often by small firms for survival. Status quo policies have the advantage of simplicity. Disadvantages include ignoring demand or cost.
(text, pp. 507-509)

3. **FOB origin pricing:** This price tactic requires the purchaser to pay for the cost of transportation from the shipping point. A manager would choose to use FOB origin pricing if he or she is not concerned about total costs varying among the firm's clients or if freight charges are not a significant pricing variable. Industrial products such as hydraulic cranes and power plants are shipped FOB factory.
Uniform delivered pricing: With this price tactic, the seller pays the actual freight charges, but bills every buyer with an identical, flat freight charge. This equalizes the total cost of the product for all buyers, regardless of location. A manager would select this policy if the firm is trying to maintain a nationally advertised price or when transportation charges are a minor part of total costs. The tactic also reduces price competition among buyers. This pricing method could be used for most consumer food and drug items or small industrial parts.
Zone pricing: This price tactic is a modification of uniform delivered pricing in which the geographic selling area is divided into zones. A flat freight rate is charged to all customers in a given zone, but different rates will apply to each zone. A marketing manager would use this strategy to equalize total costs among purchasers within large geographic areas. Canada Post uses this structure. This structure may also be used by building suppliers.
Freight absorption pricing: With this price tactic, the seller pays all or part of the actual freight charges and does not pass these charges along to the customer. A manager would choose this tactic if competition is extremely intense, if the firm is trying to break into new market areas, or if greater economies of scale are a company goal. Media direct marketers often use this tactic for records, tapes, kitchenware, and other consumer items.
Basing-point pricing: This method requires the seller to designate a location as a basing point and charge all purchasers with the freight cost from that point (regardless of the point from which the goods are actually shipped). This tactic might be used for firms that sell relatively homogeneous products and for which transportation costs are an important component of total costs. Basing-point pricing has been prevalent in the steel, cement, lead, corn oil, wood pulp, sugar, gypsum board, and plywood industries.
(text, p. 513-514)

4. **Single-price tactic:** In this case, all goods and services are offered at the same price (or perhaps two or three prices). Examples of retailers employing this tactic include One Price Clothing Stores, Dre$$ to the Nine$, Your $10 Store, and Fashions $9.99. Advantages include (1) removal of price comparisons from the buyer's decision-making process, (2) a simplified pricing system, and (3) minimization of clerical errors. Disadvantages include (1) continually rising costs and (2) necessity for frequent revisions of the selling price.
Flexible pricing: With this pricing tactic, different customers pay different prices for essentially the same merchandise bought in equal quantities. This policy is often found in the sale of shopping goods, specialty merchandise, and industrial goods (except for supply items). Automobile dealers and appliance retailers commonly follow this practice. Advantages include (1) allowance for competitive adjustments for meeting or beating another seller's price, (2) ability for the seller to close a sale with price-conscious consumers, and (3) the ability to procure business from a potential high-volume shopper. Disadvantages include (1) the lack of consistent profit margins, (2) the potential ill will of high-paying purchasers, (3) the tendency for salespeople to automatically lower the price to make a sale, and (4) the possibility of a price war among sellers.
Professional services pricing: This is used by people who have lengthy experience, training, and are certified by a licensing board. Fees may be based on the solution of a problem or performance of an act. Flat rate pricing may also be used. Examples include lawyers, physicians, or family counsellors. Advantages include (1) prices justified according to the education and experience of the service provider, and (2) the simplicity of flat-rate pricing. Disadvantages include (2) difficulty in attaching dollar amounts to experience, education, or certifications, and (2) a temptation to charge "all the traffic will bear" in an inelastic demand situation.
Price lining: When a seller establishes a series of prices for a type of merchandise, it creates a price line. Price lining is offering a product line with several items placed in the line at specific price points. Examples include Hon offering file cabinets at $125, $250, and $400, and The Limited offering dresses at $40, $70, and $100. Advantages include (1) reduction of confusion for salespeople and consumers, (2) a wider variety of merchandise offered to the buyer at each price, (3) the ability of the seller to reach several market segments, and (4) smaller total inventories for the seller. Disadvantages include (1) rising costs that force confusing changes in price line prices and (2) difficulty in determining where to place the prices within a line.

Leader pricing: This is an attempt by the marketing manager to induce store patronage through selling a product near or below cost. This type of pricing is common in supermarkets and is also used at department and specialty stores. Advantages include (1) increase in store patronage, (2) potential higher volume of sales per customer, and (3) inducement of store switching. Disadvantages include (1) potential of consumers to stock up on only the leader items and (2) lack of response because of competition with other stores offering similar bargains.

Bait pricing: This is a deceptive tactic that tries to get consumers into a store though false or misleading advertising. Once in the store, high-pressure sales tactics are used to persuade the consumer to buy more expensive merchandise. Advantages may include (1) increase in store patronage, (2) potential higher volume of sales per customer, and (3) inducement of store switching. The main disadvantage is that the practice is illegal.

Odd-even pricing: This tactic establishes prices ending in odd or even numbers. Odd-numbered prices are intended to denote bargains, while even-numbered prices are used to imply quality. Retail food stores often use odd-numbered pricing, while prestige products such as perfumes, fur coats, or luxury watches are frequently sold at even-numbered prices. Advantages include (1) implied bargains (odd) or quality (even) and (2) stimulation of demand for some products. Disadvantages include (1) creation of a saw-toothed demand curve and (2) changes in the price elasticity of demand.

Price bundling: In this case, two or more goods and/or services are combined into a single package for a special price. Examples include the sale of maintenance contracts with appliances or office equipment, vacation packages, complete stereo systems, and options on automobiles. Service industries often use bundling. Advantages include (1) stimulation of demand for the bundled items if the consumers perceive the price as a good value, (2) better coverage of constant fixed costs (especially in service industries), and (3) assistance in selling the maximum number of options (on a car, for example). Disadvantages include (1) customers' resistance if one of the bundled items is not wanted and (2) consumers' incorrect value perceptions.

Unbundling: With unbundling, services are split off and charged for. For example, a hotel may charge for parking, or department stores may charge for gift wrapping. Advantages include keeping costs down. A possible disadvantage is that customers may not want to pay "extra" for items that have typically been bundled.

Two-part pricing: This involves two separate charges to consume a single product or service. There is usually some type of base fee, plus a charge per use. Examples include health clubs, amusement parks, and telephone companies. Advantages include (1) consumers' preference of two-part pricing when they are unsure of utilization, (2) high-use consumers paying a higher total price, and (3) possible increase in revenue for the seller by attracting low-use consumers. Disadvantages include (1) difficulty in establishing pricing levels from usage estimates, and (2) resistance by high-use consumers.
(text, pp. 515-518)

5. Product price lining is used when the following conditions exist:
   - Items in the product line are complementary; that is, demand for one may impact demand for the other. An example is that demand for coffee affects the demand for coffee filters.
   - Two products in a line can be substitutes for each other. For example, liquid laundry detergent is a substitute for powdered laundry detergent.
   - A neutral relationship can exist between two products. For example, dog food has no impact on the sale of cereal to adults.
   (text, pp. 519-520)

6. During a recession, you could use:
   Value Pricing: You could stress the long life of the car as a value to the consumer.
   Bundling: You could offer greater service with the purchase of the car (longer warranty, special services such as a special valet service for cars that have problems or free car washes at the dealer on weekends).
   (text, pp. 520-522)

APPLICATION SOLUTION

The FabLam Corporation should continue to manufacture and sell all three types of machines. An investigation of overall figures shows that a $60,000 profit was earned on the three items in the line:

	Portable	Vending	Desktop	Total
Sales	$40,000	$80,000	$90,000	$210,000
Less: Cost of goods sold	50,000	50,000	50,000	150,000
Gross margin	($10,000)	$30,000	$40,000	$ 60,000

The portable line should not be dropped just because it is currently showing a loss; the joint costs would have to be allocated to the remaining two lines:

	Vending	Desktop	Total
Sales	$80,000	$90,000	$170,000
Less: Cost of goods sold	75,000	75,000	150,000
Gross margin	$ 5,000	$15,000	$ 20,000

Equal allocation of joint costs may not be the right way to distribute the costs. Other allocation bases that may be used include weighting, market value, or quantity sold. Other allocation methods would change the figures for each machine type, but not overall figures.

CHAPTER 17: ONE-TO-ONE AND INTERNET MARKETING

PRETEST SOLUTIONS

1. Six forces are:
    - A more diverse society
    - More demanding and time-poor consumers
    - A decline in brand loyalty
    - The explosion of new media alternatives
    - Changing channels of distribution
    - Demand for marketing accountability

    (text pp. 538-540)

2. In one-to-one marketing, the communications process differs in that there is less "noise" in the process of sending a traditional message; messages are personalized to the customer; and feedback from the customers is more direct (and often less costly to obtain).
    (text pp. 541-542)

3. Eight common applications are:
    - Identifying the best customers
    - Retaining loyal customers
    - Cross-selling other products or services
    - Designing targeted marketing communications
    - Reinforcing consumer purchase decisions
    - Inducing product trial by new customers
    - Increasing the effectiveness of distribution channel marketing
    - Maintaining control over brand equity

    (text p. 543)

4. The ways that the Internet affects business practices are:
    - **New channel:** The Internet has opened a new electronic channel through which to conduct all sorts of marketing activities.
    - **Financially:** Companies using the Internet can often reduce costs and inventory. In addition, the Internet has created new business models and opportunities that did not exist before.
    - **Marketing research:** The speed and expense of marketing research has been greatly affected by the Internet (speed and responsiveness have increased, costs have decreased).
    - **Strategic synergies:** Companies that integrate their Internet strategy into their conventional marketing strategy can realize cross-channel synergies that improve overall marketing performance.

    (text pp. 555-558)

5. Ways to conduct marketing research on-line include: accessing secondary data (like on-line information search engines, trade magazine and journal archives, and electronic news services), gathering primary data (through electronic surveys, industry newsgroups and discussion lists, and cyber focus groups), and gathering competitive intelligence.
    (text pp. 557-558)

6.   The three main types of on-line promotions are:
- **Banner, button, or pop-up advertisements**: interactive ads that are either part of the Web page design or appear while you are waiting for the main page to load
- **E-mail marketing**: either targeted to qualified recipients, or untargeted mass e-mail marketing (spamming)
- **E-zines**: electronic magazines are similar to paper newsletters, focused on a particular subject, and circulated electronically

(text pp. 569-571)

VOCABULARY PRACTICE SOLUTIONS

1.   one-to-one marketing
2.   one-to-one marketing communications process
3.   data-driven marketing, database, marketing database
4.   response list, compiled list
5.   database enhancement, modeled data, custom data
6.   recency, frequency, and monetary (RFM) analysis; lifetime value (LTV) analysis; predictive modeling; data mining
7.   business-to-business e-commerce (B2C), business-to-business e-commerce (B2B)
8.   virtual community, e-zine
9.   corporate Web site, interactive/transactional Web site
10.   e-tailing, e-marketplace
11.   clickstream
12.   banner advertisements, button advertisements
13.   interstitial advertisements
14.   untargeted e-mail marketing, targeted e-mail marketing
15.   hit, page view, cookie

TRUE/FALSE SOLUTIONS

(question number / correct answer / text page reference / answer rationale)

1. T   536
2. F   539   *Declining* brand loyalty is an influence on the emergence of one-to-one marketing.
3. T   538
4. T   542
5. T   542
6. F   543   This is an example of cross selling other products.
7. T   543
8. T   549
9. F   552   The business in conducting lifetime value analysis (LTV).
10. F   555   The Internet represents a completely new marketing channel that plays a role in product, place, and   price decisions – not just promotions
11. F   555   The Internet can be extremely valuable to small as well as large businesses.
12. T   557
13. F   560   The digital divide typically refers to a socioeconomic divide between Internet users (generally more affluent and more educated) and Internet non-users (generally lower income, less education)
14. T   560
15. F   561   Universal language translators have facilitated communication, but they have not eliminated the problems associated with language barriers.
16. F   561   The Internet can enhance and broaden access to developing nations, but it cannot eliminate the disadvantages of doing business in those locations.
17. F   561   The winners in the Internet technology adoption process have been distribution and transportation firms, like UPS and FedEx.
18. T   563
19. F   564   It is insufficient to build a site and expect people to find it. Marketers must drive traffic to their sites.
20. F   566   The advantage of a corporate Web site is that you can pass along information efficiently. Not being able to interact with consumers can be considered a disadvantage.
21. T   564
22. T   565

23. F 566 E-tailing is using the Internet to retail products and services.

24. T 567

25. F 568 The Internet is a good selling channel for many near-commodity items because they are small and relatively inexpensive, as well as for customized products (like Dell, Reflect, and others)

26. F 568 Branding is a powerful Internet marketing tool that helps companies reassure reluctant consumers.

27. T 568 Internet shortens distribution channels by cutting out intermediaries.

28. T 569

29. F 570 Banner ads are larger than button ads.

30. T 570

31. F 571 Marketers should determine a pricing strategy that makes sense for their offerings. This may mean having different prices in different channels, or having the same price in all channels.

32. F 572 A page view is a better measurement than a hit because it indicates which pages (not which areas of a page) have been requested from a Web site.

33. F 572 A clickstream tracks the order in which a visitor to a site views the pages of the site. It is a road map of page views.

34. F 573 Privacy is a major concern to most customers.

AGREE/DISAGREE SOLUTIONS
(question number / sample answers)

1. Reason(s) to agree: Database technology is making is easier for marketers to personalize and individualize products and services to customers. Once one-to-one marketing becomes more common, no consumer would want to be part of a mass marketing effort.
   Reason(s) to disagree: Some products and industries still lend themselves better to mass marketing. Though products such as Coca-Cola can target special promotions on a one-to-one basis, its product offerings would still be better to market on a mass level.

2. Reason(s) to agree: Business marketing involves larger and more concentrated customers. Business marketing has always included aspects of one-to-one marketing because of the importance of each customer to a firm's sales a nd profits.
   Reason(s) to disagree: One-to-one marketing can be as effective on consumer markets as on business markets. Because consumer markets are more fragmented and more difficult to reach, one-to-one marketing may be more difficult. However, database technology has allowed marketers to overcome these issues and to personalize messages to an otherwise anonymous audience.

3. Reason(s) to agree: One-to-one marketing requires a database full of personal information about consumers—such as demographic information, their purchasing patterns, and their interests. Without these vital data, one-to-one marketing would not be feasible.
   Reason(s) to disagree: Marketers with "lower tech" methods can still use one-to-one marketing. They can still create lists by collecting information by mail or through response cards (such as product registration). The process may be cumbersome but is quite feasible.

4. Reason(s) to agree: Consumers are being inundated with personalized messages from marketers. Eventually, consumer lobby groups will force more legislation to protect the privacy of all consumers.
   Reason(s) to disagree: Even if legislation stifles the effort of some one-to-one marketers, companies may use the legislation to their benefit. By honouring privacy and sending messages only to those who are interested, marketers can better identify which customers are most likely to purchase their products.

5. Reason(s) to agree: The Internet has increased the number of ways in which a company can reach its customers. By using e-mail, home pages, newsgroups and other Internet-based communication vehicles, companies can now reach their customers 24 hours a day.
   Reason(s) to disagree: The Internet has made marketing much more complex. In order to keep up with competition, a company must now use all Internet vehicles to reach its target markets. Communication technology has made it easier to communicate, but now communication is more frequent. Staff must be trained to handle customer communication on-line.

6. Reason(s) to agree: Though Internet usage has become mainstream, samples of people responding to surveys over the Internet may still be biased. For instance, if a marketer is trying to conduct a survey to people aged sixty or above, the sample responding to the survey may be biased (more active, more technologically driven than the typical sixty-year-old).
   Reason(s) to disagree: Whether a marketing research sample is biased depends on the target market it is supposed to represent. Some target markets are well represented through the Internet, which can be an inexpensive and quick way to get information. There are techniques that can be used to take the bias out of the sample.

7.   Reason(s) to agree: The Internet has changed all four Ps: product (by the type of service offered on a home page); price (firms can offer either offer lower prices because of lowered costs or higher prices because of offering more convenient shopping); promotion (the Internet has increased the variety of ways in which companies can communicate with their markets); and distribution (certain types of services can actually even be distributed on-line).

Reason(s) to disagree: The four Ps still hold true for the Internet. Technology has just provided another means of reaching target markets.

MULTIPLE-CHOICE SOLUTIONS
(question number / correct answer / text page reference / answer rationale)

1. b   536   One-to-one marketing does not focus on share of market.
2. a   538   Lower production costs have not affected the emergence of one-to-one marketing.
3. c   539   Sales promotions, increased power of retailers, and brand proliferation have all contributed to decreased loyalty.
4. b   542   Because the communication occurs directly from the marketer to the customer, there is less distraction from competing products.
5. c   541   Reading and interpreting a message is considered decoding.
6. d   543   Providing sales leads is not a common application of one-to-one marketing.
7. a   544   Providing points to encourage customers to continue choosing the hotel is an example of retaining loyal customers.
8. b   545   Sending a team to congratulate the customer is an example of reinforcing a purchase decision.
9. c   545   Suggesting other titles is an example of cross-selling other products.
10. b   548   The compilation of names, addresses, and other information about customers is a marketing database.
11. e   549   A response list is created from people who have responded to an offer, such as a rebate.
12. c   550   A compiled list is created from names and addresses gleaned from directories or membership rosters.
13. d   551   Modelled data are information that has already been sorted into distinct groups or clusters or customers.
14. b   551   Custom data are enhancement information acquired by the marketer through customer surveys, customer participation programs, product registration, warranty cards, or loyalty marketing programs.
15. e   552   Recency-frequency-monetary analysis identifies those customers who bought most recently, bought most frequently, or spent a specified amount of money.
16. c   553   Lifetime value analysis projects the future value of the customer over a period of years.
17. d   555   Though Internet use is still on the rise, not everybody has a computer with Internet connection.
18. e   555   It is not illegal for these organizations to sell information about their customers and students to others.
19. a   556   No federal regulation exists involving privacy issues on the Internet.
20. e   557   The Internet has many marketing uses.
21. a   560   Technology provided information that can be used to improve customer relationships.
22. b   560   Low barriers increase competition.
23. c   561   Web-based services allow use of graphics and multi-media.
24. e   560   The digital divide is narrowing.
25. e   560   Many factors influence on-line purchasing.
26. d   563   Mortality rates are not affecting Internet expansion.
27. e   563   The Internet does not overcome language barriers, even though translation software exists.
28. c   565   Atoms to bits refers to the growing importance and value of information.
29. e   567   Successful Internet marketing requires many efforts.
30. d   568   Fred could improve customer service by having a FAQ and answering questions by e-mail.
31. a   571   Digital products are best suited for Internet sales.
32. b   572   Hits record the number of files requested.
14. c   574   Brands increase consumer trust facilitating sales.
15. b   575   On-line buyers are probably a more price sensitive segment of the market.

SCENARIO #1 SOLUTIONS

1. False   E-College uses a one-to-one marketing approach.
2. True
3. False   E-College is the wave of the future in higher education.
4. b   Though all the forces could have had an impact on the college being established, more demanding and time-poor consumers was probably the greatest force, according to the scenario.
5. a   Customer segmentation analysis is used to develop a picture of the current customer by using demographic, geographic, psychographic or behavioural variables.
6. d   Predictive modeling can determine a number of predictable things, such as the impact that current students have on future enrolment.
7. c   "Product trial" is not mentioned in the scenario; all others are (using different terms).
8.   A variety of applications of one-to-one marketing are not mentioned in the scenario. The college could use its database for an aggressive direct marketing effort through the Internet, mass media, or other media. It could also "cross sell" customers on other products or services. It could reinforce customer purchase decisions.

SCENARIO #2 SOLUTIONS

1. False   Small businesses also benefit from Internet technology.
2. True
3. False   Although E-point is a service that will be used by consumers, Jeff is marketing the product to businesses, hence is engaging in business-to-business e-commerce.
4. e   The demographics of Internet users will affect the numbers of people comfortable with using the Internet as an on-line scheduling tool.
5. b   Virtual communities can be organized around people with a common interest.
6. a   By using an opt-in feature, E-point would only send healthcare product announcements to those people who requested them.
7. a   Only product (the software is an Internet-only offering), place (the service is delivered only over the Internet), and promotion (affiliate marketing is used to promote the product) are affected by the Internet. The Internet does not affect the price of the service.
8.   Jeff could incorporate more promotional tools into his marketing plan by: adding more types of Internet advertising; adding off-line advertising on television, radio, outdoor, and other media; offering discounts to service providers such as a free trial period, cumulative discounts on quantities of appointments booked, or promotional allowances for such things as point-of-purchase advertisements, flyers; and so forth.

ESSAY QUESTION SOLUTIONS

1.   Five advantages of one-to-one marketing are:
   - **The ability to identify the most profitable and least profitable customers**: The retailers can identify which customers bought the most merchandise most recently so that it can target special promotions and loyalty programs to these customers.
   - **The ability to create long-term relationships with customers**: The retailer likely has customers who visit the store frequently and should try to hold onto them. By conducting one-to-one marketing, the retailer can make their customers even more loyal.
   - **The ability to target marketing efforts only to those people most likely to be interested**: The retailer can save time and money by focusing its efforts on people who enjoy the outdoors and therefore more likely to purchase their merchandise.
   - **The ability to offer varied messages to different consumers**: The retailer may find through its marketing efforts that certain customers buy certain merchandise, based on their sports interests. For example, if a customer has purchased merchandise for camping, the retailer can target promotional messages to this customer based on camping merchandise.
   - **Increased knowledge about customers and prospects**: The more the retailer understands its customers, the more it can target special marketing programs to them. The customer can also become a valuable marketing tool by referring the store to other prospects.

   (text pp. 538-540)

2.	Eight applications for this database are:
- **Identify the best customers**: The resort can identify which customers have enough income, the correct demographic profile, and the lifestyle and interests that would be suited to the service that it offers.
- **Retain loyal customers**: The resort can use its list of past customers to target loyalty programs, such as awarding points that can be redeemed toward free stays or upgrades in rooms.
- **Cross-sell other products**: The resort can use the database to sell other services, such as vacation or tour packages.
- **Design targeted marketing communications**: The resort can identify which features certain customers enjoyed the most and provide promotional offers regarding these features (such as a free dinner to customers who enjoyed one of the resort's resta urants).
- **Reinforce consumer purchase decisions**: The resort can use the database to send warm greetings to new customers who have just made a decision about coming to the resort but who have not yet arrived. This will give the new customer a better feeling about the purchase decision.
- **Induce product trial by new customers**: The database can contain names and addresses of people who dined at one of the restaurants at the resort but who did not stay at the resort. The resort can then send special messages or promotional offers to these customers to encourage them to stay at the resort.
- **Increase the effectiveness of distribution channel marketing**: The database can also contain the names and addresses of key travel agencies that recommend the resort most often. Special offers can then be provided these agencies to further encourage these recommendations. In addition, information about customers can be given to travel agents so that they understand the kind of people who enjoy the resort the most.
- **Maintain control over brand equity**: The resort can also protect the brand name "Isl and Breeze" and to provide consumers with a good overall feeling about the resort.

(text pp. 543-547)

3.	Five data manipulation techniques are:
- **Customer segmentation:** You can take the data and divide it into different customer segments using demographic, geographic, psychographic, or buying behavior information. For example, you can develop customer profiles for each of the models of cars you sell.
- **Recency-frequency-monetary analysis (RFM):** You can determine which customers have bought recently and most frequently and how much they have spent to date. This information can be used to build loyalty programs and to target specific messages about new car models that are coming out.
- **Lifetime value analysis (LTV):** You can conduct an LTV to determine how much your most loyal customer is worth in actual dollars. You can then select the most loyal and create long-term relationships with them.
- **Predictive modeling:** You can develop certain criteria, such as demographic or lifestyle profiles, and determine how likely it is that certain customers will buy another vehicle from you.
- **Data mining:** You can discover other independent and nonobvious variables that lead to purchase, such as occupation or personality, so that you can better understand how to target future marketing efforts.

(text pp. 552-554)

4.	Elements of the Web site strategic plan could include:
- Including the Web address in print advertisements and stationery. Make sure your company's phone number is also available.
- Registering with on-line search engines such as Infoseek, Yahoo, and Lycos along with key words so that visitors can get to your home page instantly.
- Advertising through an offline subscription service. Several companies can automatically load changing Web site content, including advertising, onto subscribers' computers.
- Frequently changing the Web site's content. This way, retrieval services and people have a reason to frequent the site.
- Paying consumers to visit the site.

Other options could be to:

Send e-mail. Sending and retrieving electronic messages is the most frequently performed Internet activity. The method is quick, inexpensive, and selective. However, marketers should be careful to avoid spamming.

Create a newsgroup or discussion list. These Internet services allow people to participate in on-line discussions about specific topics of interest.

Sponsor an established group, list, or site. Sponsoring established Internet communication groups, discussion lists, or Web sites instantly gives businesses a targeted audience.

(text pp. 564-567)

5.   You should cover these topics regarding the marketing mix:
       Product. The focus is on branded commodities: the lowest worldwide price for well-known goods. Pre-technology focuses were on availability of delivered goods, and on manufacturer's image, reputation, and product quality.
       Place. The focus is on shipping from the home or office via desktop computer. Previously, products had to be bought from local vendors, or transportation could be used to broaden the geographic availability of products.
       Promotion. Modern promotion is via Internet-based Web sites. Ads can be interactive, targeted, and personalized.
       Price. Today, intelligent software agents located the lowest worldwide price. In the past, price could be set by local sellers until some price competition generated lower prices.
       (text pp. 568-571)

APPLICATION SOLUTIONS

There are many different experiences that a shopper can have, depending on the Web site being used. Amazon.com is one of the largest Web sites used for shopping for a variety of items. Here is an example:

1) Once you've l ogged in, Amazon.com personally greets you by name.

2) On the same page of the greeting, the company may suggest some books that you would like, based on your purchase history. (This assumes, of course, that you like to read a certain genre of book.) The Web site does the same for music or other types of products you've purchased in the past.

3) Amazon asks for basic information, such as your first and last name, your address (or where the purchased products should be shipped), your phone number, your email address to send a confirmation, and your credit card number. Other Web sites may ask for other information, such as your interests, your age, and the number of people in your family. Many indicate that this information is optional.

4) Amazon's intent is to make you feel "special;" that your information is stored and retrieved once you log into the Web site. It is a type of one-to-one customer service that you might expect from a small mom-and-pop store where the owners know you personally. However, most people might be cynical about the attempt of such large on-line retailers to make it seem as though the company knows them personally when, in fact, no one from the company really knows the shoppers.

CHAPTER 18: CUSTOMER RELATIONSHIP MANAGEMENT

PRETEST SOLUTIONS

1.   Customer relationship management is a company-wide business strategy designed to optimize profitability, revenue, and customer satisfaction by focusing on highly defined and precise customer groups.
       (text p. 590)

2.   Three important concepts in establishing a customer-centric organization are: learning (an informal process of collecting customer data through customer comments and feedback on products or service performance); knowledge management (process by which learned information is centralized and shared in order to enhance the relationship between customers and the organization); and empowerment (delegation of authority to solve customers' proble ms quickly).
       (text pp. 593-594)

3.   Following is a brief summary of the process of acquiring and capturing customer data:
       - The customer is approached through a CHANNEL, or a medium of communication, such as a store, through a salesperson, or a personal computer.
       - Then there is a TRANSACTION, which is an interaction between the company and the customer involving an exchange of information as well as an exchange of products or services.
       - Finally, the physical consumption of the PRODUCT OR SERVICE occurs and constitutes another touch point between the customer and the company.
       (text pp. 599-598)

4.   A data warehouse is a central repository for data from various functional areas of the organization that are stored and inventoried on a centralized computer system so that the information can be shared across all functional departments of the business.
       (text p. 601)

5.   Data mining is a data analysis procedure that identifies significant patterns of variables and characteristics that pertain to particular customers or customer groups.
       (text p. 602)

VOCABULARY PRACTICE SOLUTIONS

1. customer relationship management
2. customer-centric, learning, knowledge management
3. empowerment, interaction
4. touch point, knowledge centre
5. Web-based interactions, point-of-sale interactions, transaction-based interactions
6. channel, transaction
7. data warehouse
8. data mining, modelling, score
9. campaign management

TRUE/FALSE SOLUTIONS
(question number / correct answer / text page reference / answer rationale)

1. F 590 Customer relationship management focuses first on establishing customer relationships *within* the organization.
2. T 593
3. T 594
4. F 595 Touch points can occur in many different forms: face-to-face, on the telephone, in written form, on-line, and so forth. They include all areas where customers communicate with the business.
5. T 599
6. F 601 A data warehouse involves some kind of computer system.
7. T 602
8. T 602
9. T 605
10. F 607 In general, European companies have been slow to use customer relationship management.

AGREE/DISAGREE SOLUTIONS
(question number / sample answers)

1. Reason(s) to agree: Both customer relationship management and the marketing concepts put the customer at the centre of organizational activities. In both concepts, the customer is the most important person to the organization, and all activities are related directly and indirectly to the customer.

   Reason(s) to disagree: Customer relationship management requires much more sophisticated technology that is not necessarily used by all marketers.

2. Reason(s) to agree: Knowledge about the customer works hand-in-hand with empowerment. When company representatives – including customer services reps, delivery people, or salespeople – work with a customer, they must share customer knowledge and be empowered to make decisions on the spot.

   Reason(s) to disagree: Knowledge is not the same as empowerment. A company representative can acquire knowledge about customers, but he or she may not be empowered to do anything about it. This causes delays in solving customer problems.

3. Reason(s) to agree: Customer relationship management requires a database full of personal information about consumers—such as demographic information, their purchasing patterns, and their interests. Without these vital data, one-to-one marketing would not be feasible.

   Reason(s) to disagree: Savvy marketers can still build customer relationships without sophisticated technology. A good example is an effective but old-fashioned salesman who keeps a Rolodex of customers and records all kind of information about the customer on the cards, including the names of the customers' kids, their birthdays, and their favourite restaurants.

4. Reason(s) to agree: On-line businesses have developed their systems to capture all kinds of customer data from the beginning. Every transaction that the customer makes through the Web site can be captured and stored for future use, and the businesses can greet the customer in person when he/she comes back to the Web site.

   Reason(s) to disagree: Even businesses that don't operate on-line can have an effective customer relationship management system. Every phone call or in-person inquiry can be recorded and used for future interactions.

MULTIPLE-CHOICE SOLUTIONS

(question number / correct answer / text page reference / answer rationale)

1. e   590   Organizations must first establish customer relationships within the organization before it builds the relationships externally.
2. d   592   By managing the database and making the information available, Loretta is disseminating information.
3. b   593   Learning is an informal process of collecting customer data through customer comments and feedback on product or service performance.
4. c   594   Empowerment is the delegation of authority to solve customers' problems quickly. In this case, Gloria was able to make a decision without consulting with a resort manager.
5. d   595   Definition of touch points.
6. a   596   Text definition.
7. d   599   Television does not allow for interaction to occur since it is one-sided.
8. c   600   A transaction is an interaction between a customer and a company involving an exchange of information or an exchange of products or services.
9. b   600   An ethical CRM system does not sell customer data to outside sources.
10. b   601   A data warehouse stores and inventories customer data on a centralized computer system that can be accessed and shared by various functional areas in an organization.
11. e   601   Creating superior customer service is based on management issues, not what a data warehouse can provide.
12. a   602   Data mining involves analyzing significant patterns of variables and characteristics that pertain to particular customers customer groups.
13. d   603   Definition of modelling.
14. c   605   Campaign management has the goal of developing products or services for particular customer segments and pricing and communicating these offerings for the purpose of enhancing customer relationships.
15. e   605   Campaign management includes all these things.

SCENARIO SOLUTIONS

1. True
2. True
3. False   Tronica appears to follow a marketing orientation, which would be consistent with its customer-centric philosophy.
4. a   A data warehouse is a central repository for data from various functional areas of the organization.
5. c   Data mining is a data analysis procedure that identifies significant patterns of variables and characteristics that pertain to particular customers or customer groups.
6. d   Customer information being passed onto another department that didn't have direct contact with the customer is an example of an internal touch point, not an external one.
7. b   Leveraging and disseminating customer information throughout the organization requires that the organization has gone through all the other steps of customer relationship management.
8.   To engage in campaign management, all functional areas of the organization must be involved in the development of programs targeted to its customers.

ESSAY QUESTION SOLUTIONS

1.   Phases of the customer relationship cycle:
   *   **Establish customer relationships within the organization**: All college employees should view the students as a type of customer. This can be very difficult as many professors prefer not to think of students as customers for fear that students will demand what they don't deserve (such as a passing grade for the simple act of paying tuition). However, unless the college takes the view that students are a type of customer, it may lose enrolment during rough times. The student as "customer" is especially important in areas such as the Bursar's Office, Admissions and Records, Academic Advisement, and other student services. Enrolled students deserve a certain type of "customer service" from these departments.
   *   **Determine the level of interaction each customer has with the company**: Students normally have a lot of interaction with the college, though this could vary greatly by student. Students will have a lot of interaction at least with their instructors or in their classes.

- **Acquire and capture all relevant information about the customer**: Colleges ask for lots of information about college students, including addresses, phone numbers, email addresses, majors, etc. Generally, students have filled out forms either in print or by email when they registered at the college for the first time.
- **Use technology to store and integrate customer data**: Most colleges have sophisticated databases that contain all kinds of student information, including academic plans, transcripts, financial aid information, etc. Colleges do not normally survey students about "purc hase preferences" like a business might, but the information they do have could help them develop a good relationship with the student.
- **Analyze data for profitable/unprofitable segments**: Colleges don't usually refer to their students as being "p rofitable" or "u nprofitable," but they may use the databases to analyze who is likely to finish college and need further services, who is "at risk" and needs counselling or other help, and who owes money.
- **Leverage and disseminate customer information throughout the enterprise**: Most support staff at colleges have access to some student information so that they can provide services that students need. For instance, the academic advising department probably has access to student computer records such as transcripts so that it can provide assistance to students who need to determine what courses to take next.

(text pp. 590-592)

2. One of the premises of an effective customer relationship management system is the acquisition, capture, sharing, and retrieval of customer data used to build customer relationships. Technology provides the most practical and efficient means of collecting data and making it available to all important parties.
(text pp. 595-596)

3. A data warehouse is a central repository for data from various functional areas of the organization that are stored and inventoried on a centralized computer system so that the information can be shared across all functional departments of the business. Data mining is an analysis procedure that identifies significant patterns of variables and characteristics that pertain to particular customers or customer groups. Data mining can only be accomplished when a data warehouse exists, since the data needs to be stored somewhere. The "ware house" is where the data is kept, and the "mini ng" occurs within the warehouse.
(text pp. 601- 603)

APPLICATION SOLUTIONS

Answers will vary widely, depending on your own personal experience and the product or service that you purchased. Here is a sample answer for the purchase of a car from a Toyota dealership:

1) The Toyota dealership is somewhat customer-centric in that it offered a fairly broad range of vehicles in a large range of prices to appeal to many different market segments. However, the dealership was much more driven by a "sales" mentality than a customer-centric philosophy, with the salesman trying to push the vehicle onto the customer. The negotiation process is seldom customer-centric; it is a process that annoys even the most patient customers who don't want to spend hours haggling on price. Some other dealerships have gone to a "fixe d price" system where customers don't have t o haggle on price.
2) Typical touch points in a car dealership include the showroom floor, the parking lot, the sales office, the financing office, and the auto repair garage. Other touch points are through the mail (if, for instance, the dealership sends a personal direct mail piece to the potential customer), the phone, and email.
3) Dealerships collect all kinds of information about you as a customer, including the basic information of your name and address, your preferences for vehicle models and features, your income and other finance-related information, whether you prefer to lease or purchase vehicles, and your occupation.
4) If the dealership is smart, it will use this information to continue building a relationship with you after you purchase a vehicle. The dealership knows, for instance, when your lease is up and can start suggesting new car models or providing promotional deals to get you back into the dealership.